NLT STUDY SERIES
GENESIS

GENESIS

See Our Story Begin

Andrew Schmutzer, Allen P. Ross
Tremper Longman III
Sean A. Harrison, General Editor

Tyndale House Publishers, Inc.
Carol Stream, Illinois

Visit Tyndale's exciting Web sites at www.nltstudybible.com, www.newlivingtranslation.com, and www.tyndale.com

NLT Study Series: Genesis

Copyright © 2009 by Tyndale House Publishers, Inc. All rights reserved.

Cover photograph copyright © by Amanda Rohde/iStockphoto. All rights reserved.

The text of Genesis is taken from the *Holy Bible,* New Living Translation, copyright © 1996, 2004, 2007 by Tyndale House Foundation. All rights reserved.

Designed by Timothy R. Botts and Dean Renninger

Edited by Sean A. Harrison

This Bible portion is typeset in the typeface *Lucerna,* designed by Brian Sooy & Co. exclusively for Tyndale House Publishers, Inc. All rights reserved.

TYNDALE, New Living Translation, NLT, the New Living Translation logo, and Tyndale's quill logo are registered trademarks of Tyndale House Publishers, Inc.

NLT Study Bible is a trademark of Tyndale House Publishers, Inc.

ISBN 978-1-4143-2199-8 Softcover

Printed in the United States of America

15 14 13 12 11 10 09
7   6   5   4   3   2   1

SERIES FOREWORD

The purpose of the *NLT Study Series* is to call individuals and groups into
serious conversation with God and engagement with his word.

We have designed these studies to provide you and your group with a complete, new Bible study
experience. Our aim has been to help you engage seriously with the Bible's content, interacting
with it in a meaningful and deeply personal way, not just regurgitating rote answers to fill-in-
the-blank questions or producing purely subjective opinions. We also hope to encourage true
community study, with the honest sharing of different perspectives and experiences. Most of all,
we want to help foster your direct communication with God, encouraging you to tell God what is
on your mind and heart. We want to help you understand what God is teaching you and apply it to
the realities of personal and community life.

To this end, each study in the *NLT Study Series* includes twelve weeks of individual and group
studies focusing on understanding the meaning of the text of Scripture, reflecting on it personally and with others, and responding actively to what God is saying to you through it.

Each volume of the *NLT Study Series* can be used by itself, with no other resources, but you
can also use it with your Bible of choice. Each volume of the *NLT Study Series* includes, along with
the twelve-week study, one book of the *NLT Study Bible*, with both the text of Scripture and all of
the study aids alongside it. The *NLT Study Bible* was designed to open up the world of the Bible
and to make the meaning and significance of Scripture clear, so it makes a great personal and
small-group study resource.

It is our hope and prayer that these studies will help you and those in your group to understand God's word more clearly, to walk with God more fully, and to grow with one another in relationship with our God.

Open my eyes to see
   the wonderful truths in your instructions.   PSALM 119:18
Come . . . let us walk in the light of the LORD!   ISAIAH 2:5

Sean A. Harrison
General Editor

CONTENTS

Series Foreword A5

Introduction to the Genesis Study A9

How to Use This Study A11

Introductory Session. Orientation to Genesis A13

WEEK 1 **Creation** (Genesis 1:1–2:25) A15

WEEK 2 **The Fall and Its Aftermath** (Genesis 3:1–5:32) A23

WEEK 3 **The Flood and the Tower of Babel** (Genesis 6:1–11:26) A31

WEEK 4 **God's Promise to Abram and His Struggle with Faith**
(Genesis 11:27–13:18) A39

WEEK 5 **Abram and Melchizedek and God's Reassurances** (Genesis 14:1–17:27) A47

WEEK 6 **Abraham's Mature Faith** (Genesis 18:1–23:20) A55

WEEK 7 **Isaac: From Abraham to Jacob and Esau** (Genesis 24:1–28:9) A63

WEEK 8 **Jacob in Paddan-aram** (Genesis 28:10–31:55) A71

WEEK 9 **Jacob Back in the Promised Land** (Genesis 32:1–37:1) A79

WEEK 10 **Joseph Goes Down to Egypt, from Slave to Prince** (Genesis 37:2–41:57) A87

WEEK 11 **Joseph and His Brothers** (Genesis 42:1–45:28) A95

WEEK 12 **You Meant It for Evil; God Meant It for Good** (Genesis 46:1–50:26) A103

The Book of GENESIS from the *NLT Study Bible* 14

Introduction to the New Living Translation B1

Bible Translation Team B5

NLT Study Bible Contributors B7

INTRODUCTION TO THE
Genesis Study

GENESIS IS THE FOUNDATION of the Torah, the first five books of the Bible. Thus, it is also the foundation of the whole Old Testament. Indeed, we will see that it is pivotal to understanding the New Testament as well.

The following study, used along with the *NLT Study Bible*, will guide the reader into a deeper understanding of the book of Genesis and its marvelous and life-changing themes. This study intends to help you uncover the important themes of Genesis and to consider how the teaching of Genesis helps us understand ourselves better today.

The study is divided into twelve parts. The study in week 1 covers the creation (Gen 1–2), while weeks 2-3 focus on the Fall and other stories of sin, judgment, and grace that follow it (Gen 3–11). Weeks 4-6 then follow Abraham's journey of faith and invite the readers to reflect on their own journeys of faith. In week 7, attention turns to Abraham's promised son, Isaac, whose story really serves as a bridge between his father and his son, Jacob. Weeks 8-9 then follow Jacob's life, and we observe how the deceiver himself gets deceived and grows in maturity through the process. Finally, weeks 10-12 are devoted to the story of Joseph and how God providentially guides his life through suffering for the salvation of the family of God.

As you read through Genesis using this study guide, keep an eye on the central theme of blessing. God created Adam and Eve and blessed them greatly in the Garden. When they forfeited that blessing through their rebellion, God immediately pursued them with the desire to restore his relationship with them and bless them once again. He chooses Abraham in order to bless him along with the whole world. The blessing theme reverberates through the rest of Genesis.

May God bring blessing into your life as you seek to know him better through the study of his word.

Tremper Longman III
Santa Barbara, California
March 2009

How to Use This Study

THE PRIMARY WAY we recommend using this Bible study guide is for personal daily meditation and study, along with weekly fellowship and discussion.

The introductory session (p. A13) is designed to launch the group study. Group participants need not prepare for this session, but the leader is encouraged to work through it in advance in order to be able to guide the group effectively. The introductory session provides orientation to the book of Genesis, and gives a taste of what the daily and weekly study will be like for the following twelve weeks.

Each week there are five personal daily studies plus a group session. You can use the daily study guide for your personal daily conversation with God, or you can use it around the table with your family.

You don't need to participate in a weekly group meeting in order to use this study guide. For instance, you can just do the study individually, working through the daily studies and then using the weekly group session as a time of reflection.

Similarly, you don't have to use the study on a daily basis in order to benefit from using it in a group setting. You can just do the study with the group each week by reading the passages, thinking about the discussion questions, and participating in the group discussion.

Ultimately, it's between you and God how you use this study. The more you put into it, the more you will get out of it. If you are meeting with a group, we encourage you to decide together what your level of commitment will be, and then encourage each other to stick with it. Then keep up your part of your commitment to the group.

RECOMMENDATIONS FOR DAILY STUDY

Each daily study is designed to be completed within 15 minutes, but optional "Further Study" is usually provided for those who want to go into greater depth.

Start the daily study by reading the passage recommended for each day. Reflect on what it means, and write down your questions and thoughts about it.

You can use the space provided in the book to write thoughts and answers to questions. If you find that you need more space, we recommend purchasing a small blank book with lined paper to use as a Bible study journal. Use the journal to write your answers to the reflection questions, your own thoughts about the passage, what you think God is saying to you, and your prayers to God about what you have studied.

The NLT Study Series is designed to be used with the *NLT Study Bible*. The book of Genesis from the *NLT Study Bible* is included for your reading and study. You can also use the *NLT Study Bible* itself, either the print edition or the online version at www.nltstudybible.com. Please note that the included section of the *NLT Study Bible* retains its page numbering, so the study guide can be used to refer to either the included section or the *NLT Study Bible* itself.

It can be helpful to highlight or mark the Bible text and study materials where they answer your questions or speak to you in some way. You can:

- underline, circle, or highlight significant words and phrases,
- put brackets around sections of text,
- write keywords in the margin to indicate a topic,
- write page numbers cross-referencing the study guide,
- write dates cross-referencing your journal entries.

Finally, talk with God about what you are learning and how you are responding to it, but also take time to listen to him and hear what he might be saying to you through it. Cultivate your relationship with God day by day.

RECOMMENDATIONS FOR GROUP STUDY

When the group comes together, read the entire passage for the week together, then spend some time letting each person share their own dialogue with God and the Bible that week: insights they've gained, questions they have, and so on.

Then use the discussion questions to stimulate the discussion for that week. You don't have to do all of the questions—you can pick just one.

When the discussion is winding down, spend some time reflecting on what God is saying to you as a group, and how you are going to respond to what God is saying. Spend some time praying together about these things.

Finally, take a look at the passage for the coming week, and make sure everyone understands what they will be doing in preparation for the next meeting of the group.

Orientation to Genesis

SESSION GOALS
- Get oriented to the book of Genesis.
- Discuss what members hope to learn and how they hope to grow in this study.
- Introduce how we are going to be studying together.
- Answer any questions about how to begin.
- Commit ourselves to the Lord and to each other, to participate to the best of our ability.

GETTING ORIENTED TO GENESIS
Answer the following questions, either individually, or in discussion together with your group.

What do you know about the book of Genesis?

What interests you about the book of Genesis? What do you hope to learn?

What questions do you have about Genesis and its meaning that you would like to answer during this study?

How do you hope to grow—spiritually, personally, in relationship to God and others— through this study?

GENESIS INTRODUCTION
Look at the Genesis Introduction, pp. 14-19.

Read the first paragraph on p. 14, which gives a brief overview of what Genesis is all about. What strikes you as significant about Genesis?

Does the quotation in the margin on p. 17 surprise you? How does it affect your perceptions of Genesis and the people in it?

READING: **GENESIS 1:1–2:3**

Read this passage aloud; if you're in a group, choose one reader. Read slowly, clearly, thoughtfully. What questions or observations do you have after reading this passage? Write them down.

STUDY: **GENESIS 1:1-2**

What does it mean that God *created* (Gen 1:1)?

In Gen 1:1, the Hebrew word *bara'* is translated "created." Read the other verses where this word is used (Gen 1:27; 2:3; 6:7; Ps 51:10; 148:5; Eccl 12:1; Isa 40:28; 43:15; 65:17; Mal 2:10). What similarities in usage do you see? How would you summarize the meaning of the word *bara'*?

Read the study note on Gen 1:1. What is the significance of the word *bara'* in Gen 1:1?

Read the first section of the study note on Gen 1:1. What is the message of Gen 1:1?

What is the significance of the background state being "formless and empty," and as the study note on 1:2 describes it, "inhospitable chaos"?

REFLECTION

What is Gen 1:1-2 saying to you? What might God be saying to you through this passage?

QUESTIONS

Do you have questions about doing the daily study or preparing for the next meeting?

PRAYER

Take turns praying about this Bible study and the next twelve weeks. You can tell God what your thoughts and questions are, and ask him for his help, strength, and insight. You can thank him for this Bible study and for the Bible itself. You can ask him to speak to you and to the others in the group. The leader, in closing, can also commit this study to God.

OUTLINE

DAY 1 ... Genesis Introduction

DAY 2 ... Genesis 1:1-23

DAY 3 ... Genesis 1:24–2:3

DAY 4 ... Genesis 2:4-17

DAY 5 ... Genesis 2:18-25

Group Session

DAY **1** ◆ Genesis Introduction

READING: **GENESIS INTRODUCTION** (pp. 14-19)

Begin with prayer, asking God to give you insight, understanding, and an open heart to listen to and follow his word.

Read the Genesis Introduction. You can shorten the reading by reading only the Overview (the first paragraph on p. 14), "Setting," "Summary," and "Meaning and Message."

STUDY

Read the "Setting," p. 14. What similarities, if any, are there between your situation and the situation of the children of Israel when Genesis was written? What similarities are there between your needs and theirs?

Hopeless w/o GOD   TOO STUBBORN TO REALIZE it need to understand Him + my relationship to Him

Read the "Summary," pp. 15-16. How would you summarize the structure of Genesis?

Stories + accounts arranged to show God's work of redemption

Read the "Meaning and Message," pp. 18-19. What is the message of Genesis for ancient Israel? *you are MINE*

FURTHER STUDY (Optional)

Read "Authorship," p. 16. According to the *NLT Study Bible*, who was the human author of Genesis? What do you think?

Read "Composition," pp. 16-17. How does the *NLT Study Bible* account for information in Genesis that was known only later in history? Does this explanation make sense to you? Why or why not?

REFLECTION

What questions does the Genesis Introduction answer for you? What questions does it raise?

Talk to God about what you have read, any questions or concerns you might have, and what you think he might be saying to you today. You can write your prayer here if you wish.

DAY 2 ◆ Genesis 1:1-23

READING: GENESIS 1:1-23

Begin with prayer, asking God to give you insight, understanding, and an open heart to listen to and follow his word.

Gen 1 presents a beautiful picture of God's creation of the whole universe. God first creates the "formless and empty" earth and then over the next six days he shaped and filled it and made it ready for human habitation.

STUDY

Read the study note on 1:1–2:3, then look at "The Structure of the Creation Account" on p. 21, and read the caption. Also read the study notes on 1:3-13, 1:6-8, and 1:14-31. Describe the structure of Gen 1:1–2:3 in your own words.

God speaks the cosmos into existence, pulls order out of chaos and populates and blesses it.

Read the study notes on 1:4, 1:5, 1:9-10, 1:16, and 1:21. According to Gen 1, what is God's relationship to the created order? How does this perspective contrast with perspectives in our world today?

His idea + design   He reigns over it

FURTHER STUDY (Optional)

Read "The Creation" on p. 20. How does this article impact your understanding of the creation account? *explains the fundamentals of life and our relationship w/ God.*

REFLECTION

What questions does Gen 1:1-23 answer for you? What questions does it raise?

Ans. - Who's the Boss?

Raise - Eternal? Eternity? 6 days?

What do you think God is saying to you through your study of Gen 1:1-23?

I AM HOLY   BE REVERANT

PRAYER

Talk to God about what you have read, any questions or concerns you might have, and what you think he might be saying to you today. You can write your prayer here if you wish.

Thank you for your creation. You are perfect. Have mercy on me a sinner

DAY 3 ◆ Genesis 1:24–2:3

READING: **GENESIS 1:24–2:3**

Begin with prayer, asking God to give you insight, understanding, and an open heart to listen to and follow his word.

After the stage is set in the first five days, God creates the animals and also creates finally human beings in his own image. On the seventh day God rests, introducing the Sabbath as a fundamental principle of life in his creation.

STUDY

Read the study note on 1:27. Why does the NLT translate the Hebrew term *'adam* as "human beings"?

Read the first part of the study note on 1:28. In what ways has God blessed humankind? What does that blessing mean to you?

Read the rest of the study note on 1:28. What are the implications of God giving human beings the job of governing creation?

FURTHER STUDY (Optional)

Read "Human Sexuality" on p. 23. The article mentions "those who commit their sexuality to Christ." What are the practical outworkings of doing this?

What questions does Gen 1:24–2:3 answer for you? What questions does it raise?

What do you think God is saying to you through your study of Gen 1:24–2:3?

PRAYER

Talk to God about what you have read, any questions or concerns you might have, and what you think he might be saying to you today. You can write your prayer here if you wish.

DAY **4** ◆ Genesis 2:4-17

READING: **GENESIS 2:4-17**

Begin with prayer, asking God to give you insight, understanding, and an open heart to listen to and follow his word.

Gen 2 is a further expansion on the creation story, this time with a focus on the creation of the first man and woman. Gen 2:4-17 describes the creation of Adam and his first days in the Garden of Eden.

STUDY

Read the study notes on 2:5 and 2:15. What are the implications for work today?

Read the study note on 2:7. What is the significance of the fact that humans were created from the "dust of the ground" and the "breath" of God?

Read the study note on 2:9. What do the tree of life and the tree of the knowledge of good and evil represent? Why does God prohibit Adam from eating from the tree of the knowledge of good and evil?

Read the study notes on 2:8 and 2:13 and "The Location of Eden" on p. 25. Where was Eden located? Do you think it was a real place, or does it describe an earlier state of innocence, or both? Why do you think so?

Read the study note on 2:17. Was there law in the Garden of Eden? Does this surprise you? Why or why not?

REFLECTION

What do you think was the message of Gen 2:4-17 for the people of Israel? What do you think the message of Gen 2:4-17 is for you?

PRAYER

Talk to God about what you have read, any questions or concerns you might have, and what you think he might be saying to you today. You can write your prayer here if you wish.

DAY 5 ◆ Genesis 2:18-25

READING: **GENESIS 2:18-25**

Begin with prayer, asking God to give you insight, understanding, and an open heart to listen to and follow his word.

In response to Adam's loneliness, God creates Eve and institutes marriage.

STUDY

Read the study note on 2:19-20. What does the naming of the animals tell us about human beings' relationship with the animals? How then should we treat them?

Read the study notes on 2:21 and 2:23. What do we learn about women from the way Eve's creation is described?

FURTHER STUDY (Optional)

Read "Biblical Marriage" on p. 24 and the study note on 2:24. If you are married, think about the ways your marriage reflects the description in Gen 2:18-25. If you are single, read the study note on 2:18-23 and think about legitimate ways you can fulfill the divinely instilled desire for human intimacy.

What does Gen 2:18-25 teach about the relationship between men and women today?

REFLECTION

What does God seem to be saying to you through what you have studied today?

PRAYER

Talk to God about what you have read, any questions or concerns you might have, and what you think he might be saying to you today. You can write your prayer here if you wish.

GROUP SESSION

READING: **GENESIS 1:1–2:25**

Read the passage together as a group.

DISCUSSION

You can use the following questions to guide what you share in the discussion. Give each person at least one opportunity to share with the others.

What did you learn from Gen 1:1–2:25? What was one thing that stood out to you as you studied this passage? How did Gen 1:1–2:25 surprise you? Do you have questions about this passage or the study materials that haven't been answered? What does God seem to be saying to you through what you have studied?

TOPICS FOR DISCUSSION

You can choose from among these topics to generate a discussion among the members of your group, or you can write your thoughts about one or more of these topics if you're studying solo.

1. Gen 1 teaches that God alone is the only Creator and sovereign King of the universe. What are the implications today? What questions does it raise? What changes of worldview or lifestyle does it imply?

2. Gen 1:26-28 and 2:15-20 teach that God gave humankind the role of governing creation. Is this government still effective, or was it broken by the Fall? What are the implications today?

3. Gen 2:18-25 tells of the creation of woman and the beginning of the first human family. What was the original purpose of the marriage relationship? Is that purpose being fulfilled by most marriages? Is it being fulfilled among those in your family? How can marriages that are not fulfilling God's original purpose be restored?

GROUP REFLECTION

What is God saying to us as a group through Gen 1:1–2:25?

ACTION

What are we going to do, individually or as a group, in response to what God is saying to us?

PRAYER

How should we pray for each other in response to God's message to us in this passage?

Take turns talking to God about this passage and about what he is saying.

NEXT: **GENESIS 3:1–5:32 (The Fall and Its Aftermath)**

*The Fall
and
Its Aftermath*

GENESIS
3:1–5:32

OUTLINE

DAY 1 ... Genesis 3:1-13

DAY 2 ... Genesis 3:14-24

DAY 3 ... Genesis 4:1-16

DAY 4 ... Genesis 4:17-26

DAY 5 ... Genesis 5:1-32

Group Session

DAY **1** ◆ Genesis 3:1-13

READING: **GENESIS 3:1-13**

Begin with prayer, asking God to give you insight, understanding, and an open heart to listen to and follow his word.

Gen 3:1-8 records a horrible shift that begins with a dialogue between the serpent and Eve and a tragic act on the part of both Adam and Eve.

STUDY

Read the study note on 3:1. Who is the serpent? How would you describe his tactics in his interaction with Eve? *SATAN, enemy, most cunning*

Read the study note on 3:2-3. Though Eve was trying to defend God in her response to the serpent, how or where did her response go wrong? *focused on the negative rather than the positive. "freely eat" was left out & she added to God's words.*

Read the study note on 3:4-5. What is so wrong with wanting to "be like God, knowing both good and evil"? *Pride and usurping God is the cause of Satan's fall.*

FURTHER STUDY (Optional)

Read the study note on 3:6. What did Eve do wrong, and what did Adam do wrong? Can you identify with their sin? *assumed the right to divide good & evil, coveted God's wisdom adam did not lead or intervene*

According to the study notes on 3:7 and 3:9-10, what was Adam and Eve's immediate reaction to their sin? How was their reaction manifested? *fear & shame   sewed fig leaves*

REFLECTION

What does God seem to be saying to you through what you have studied today?

PRAYER

Talk to God about what you have read, any questions or concerns you might have, and what you think he might be saying to you today. You can write your prayer here if you wish.

DAY 2 ◆ Genesis 3:14-24

READING: **GENESIS 3:14-24**

Begin with prayer, asking God to give you insight, understanding, and an open heart to listen to and follow his word.

STUDY

Read the study notes on 3:14 and 3:15. What is the punishment that comes on the serpent? Is it appropriate to him? Why or why not? *crawl in dirt yes - posture of defeat*

Read the study note on 3:16. What is the punishment that comes on Eve? Is it appropriate to her and to women in general? Why or why not?. *pain in childbirth + conflict in marriage*

Read the study note on 3:17-19. What is the punishment that comes on Adam? Is it appropriate to him and to men in general? Why or why not? *a ordering in toil + sweat for survival (food) eating will be difficult due to sin of eating fruit.*

Read the study notes on 3:22 and 3:23. In what way was Adam and Eve's expulsion from the Garden of Eden both a curse and a blessing? *keep them from living forever in a fallen state*

FURTHER STUDY (Optional)

Read "Adam" on p. 27. Compare and contrast the "first Adam" of Gen 2:4–3:24 with the "last Adam" of the New Testament. *Adams sinned brought death to all, Christs death brought life to all*

Read the study note on 3:21. How did God demonstrate his continuing grace to Adam and Eve? *provided more substantial clothing*

REFLECTION

What does God seem to be saying to you through what you have studied today?

He loves us inspite of our Sin all sin

PRAYER

Talk to God about what you have read, any questions or concerns you might have, and what you think he might be saying to you today. You can write your prayer here if you wish.

DAY 3 ◆ Genesis 4:1-16

READING: GENESIS 4:1-16

Begin with prayer, asking God to give you insight, understanding, and an open heart to listen to and follow his word.

The story of Cain and Abel shows that human beings continue to sin. God judges—but he also extends his grace to sinners.

STUDY

Read the study notes on 4:3 and 4:4-5. Why did God accept Abel's sacrifice but reject Cain's? What do we learn about true worship from Abel's sacrifice?

1st born / some   The best he had to offer - True worshp

Read the study note on 4:7. What does the image of sin crouching at the door tell us about sin?

an ever present threat - Predator

How does the "mark" mentioned in the study note on 4:15 indicate God's grace to Cain?

mercy - not getting the penalty he deserved

FURTHER STUDY (Optional)

What does the study note on 4:9 tell us about how Cain responded to God's exposure of his sin?

defiant, prideful attitude

Read the study notes on 4:13-14 and 4:16. What exactly was the punishment that God placed on Cain?

Banishment, homelessness

REFLECTION

What does God seem to be saying to you through what you have studied today?

God is Holy   worship is serious

PRAYER

Talk to God about what you have read, any questions or concerns you might have, and what you think he might be saying to you today. You can write your prayer here if you wish.

DAY 4 ◆ Genesis 4:17-26

READING: GENESIS 4:17-26

Begin with prayer, asking God to give you insight, understanding, and an open heart to listen to and follow his word.

The genealogy of Cain attests that the serpent continues to have human followers who rebel against God. The passage also has a note of hope with the birth of Seth.

STUDY

Read the study note on 4:17. What, if anything, does this note tell us about cities today?

Read the study note on 4:18. How legitimate is it to use the numbers in this genealogy to try to determine how old the earth is?

Read the study notes on 4:25 and 4:26. How does the birth of Seth provide a note of hope following the genealogy of Cain?

Read the study note on 4:20-22. What does this genealogy tell us about technological advancements? Does it imply that it is always a good thing? Always a bad thing?

Read the study note on 4:23-24 and compare Lamech with Cain. What do we learn about sin?

REFLECTION

What does God seem to be saying to you through what you have studied today?

PRAYER

Talk to God about what you have read, any questions or concerns you might have, and what you think he might be saying to you today. You can write your prayer here if you wish.

DAY 5 ◆ Genesis 5:1-32

READING: **GENESIS 5:1-32**

Begin with prayer, asking God to give you insight, understanding, and an open heart to listen to and follow his word.

In contrast to Gen 4:17-24, Gen 5 gives us the genealogy of those who follow God, beginning with Adam through his son Seth.

STUDY

Read the study note on 5:1-32. How does this note change or enrich your understanding of biblical genealogies?

Read the study note on 5:5. What does the refrain "and he died" teach us in this chapter?

Read the study note on 5:22. Compare and contrast Lamech and Enoch.

FURTHER STUDY (Optional)

Go back and review the study note on 1:26 and read the study note on 5:3. What does it mean to be created in God's image? What does 5:3 add to our understanding from 1:26?

Read the study note on 5:24. What is the significance of the fact that Enoch "disappeared" rather than "died"?

REFLECTION

What does God seem to be saying to you through what you have studied today?

PRAYER

Talk to God about what you have read, any questions or concerns you might have, and what you think he might be saying to you today. You can write your prayer here if you wish.

GROUP SESSION

READING: **GENESIS 3:1–5:32**

Read the passage together as a group.

DISCUSSION

You can use the following questions to guide what you share in the discussion. Give each person at least one opportunity to share with the others.

What did you learn from Gen 3:1–5:32? What was one thing that stood out to you as you studied this passage? How did Gen 3:1–5:32 surprise you? Do you have questions about this passage or the study materials that haven't been answered? What does God seem to be saying to you through what you have studied?

Where did Cain's wife come from?

BODY, SOUL SPIRIT ? HEBREWS

TOPICS FOR DISCUSSION

You can choose from among these topics to generate a discussion among the members of your group, or you can write your thoughts about one or more of these topics if you're studying solo.

1. Gen 4:1-16 has a similar structure to Gen 3:1-24. They both narrate a sin, followed by a judgment speech from God, then some sign of God's continuing grace before the judgment is executed. Identify the sin, the judgment speech, the token of grace, and the act of judgment in each story.

   Gen 3:1-24.

   Gen 4:1-16.

2. In the Bible, genealogies do more than simply record the passing of generations. What does the genealogy of Cain (Gen 4:17-24) teach us about human beings? How about the genealogy of Seth (Gen 5:1-32)?

3. Both the narratives and the genealogies of this section of Scripture teach us that human beings are sinners and that God judges sin. Does this ring true to reality?

GROUP REFLECTION

What is God saying to us as a group through Gen 3:1–5:32?

ACTION

What are we going to do, individually or as a group, in response to what God is saying to us?

PRAYER

How should we pray for each other in response to God's message to us in this passage?

Take turns talking to God about this passage and about what he is saying.

NEXT: GENESIS 6:1–11:26 (The Flood and the Tower of Babel)

WEEK
THREE

*The Flood
and the
Tower of Babel*

GENESIS
6:1–11:26

OUTLINE

DAY 1 ... Genesis 6:1-22

DAY 2 ... Genesis 7:1–8:22

DAY 3 ... Genesis 9:1-29

DAY 4 ... Genesis 10:1-32

DAY 5 ... Genesis 11:1-26

Group Session

DAY **1** ◆ Genesis 6:1-22

READING: **GENESIS 6:1-22**

Begin with prayer, asking God to give you insight, understanding, and an open heart to listen to and follow his word.

Sin pervades the world, and here we learn of one particularly horrible example, the marriage of the "sons of God" with beautiful women. God responds with judgment, but shows his grace though his warning to Noah.

STUDY

Read the study note on 6:1-2. Which of the different interpretations given for these verses do you think makes most sense?

Read the study note on 6:3. How did God punish people for the sin described in 6:1-2?

Read the study note on 6:6. How does God respond to human sin? Is this how you typically think of God responding to sin? Why or why not?

Read the caption to "Noah's Ark" on p. 33 and the study notes on 6:14, 6:15, and 6:16. How would you describe the ark to someone unfamiliar with the story? Does it seem reasonable to think that all the land animals could get on board? Why or why not?

FURTHER STUDY (Optional)

Read "Noah" on p. 32. How did God use Noah? How does he compare to Adam?

Read the study note on 6:4. Who were the Nephilites?

Read the study note on 6:17. How large was the flood? What was its purpose?

What does God seem to be saying to you through what you have studied today?

Sin grieves God
judgement, I off love

PRAYER
Talk to God about what you have read, any questions or concerns you might have, and what you think he might be saying to you today. You can write your prayer here if you wish.

DAY 2 ◆ Genesis 7:1–8:22

READING: GENESIS 7:1–8:22
Begin with prayer, asking God to give you insight, understanding, and an open heart to listen to and follow his word.

God sends the floodwaters to punish humans for their sin, but God spares Noah and his immediate family from death.

STUDY
Read the study note on 8:1. What is the significance of fact that God remembered Noah?

Read the study notes on 8:7 and 8:11. What was the significance of Noah sending out ravens and doves from the ark?

According to 8:20-21 and the study notes, what was the first thing Noah did after leaving the ark? What is the significance of this act?

FURTHER STUDY (Optional)
Read "Retribution" on p. 35. What is retribution? Does it seem fair? How does retribution affect God's people?

Read the study note on 8:21. What was the purpose of the flood?

Read the study note on 8:22. The flood turned the world back to its formless state (Gen 1:2: "formless and empty"). What did God do after the flood to change this?

REFLECTION

What does God seem to be saying to you through what you have studied today?

PRAYER

Talk to God about what you have read, any questions or concerns you might have, and what you think he might be saying to you today. You can write your prayer here if you wish.

DAY 3 ◆ Genesis 9:1-29

READING: **GENESIS 9:1-29**

Begin with prayer, asking God to give you insight, understanding, and an open heart to listen to and follow his word.

In the aftermath of the flood, God enters into a covenant with Noah and reestablishes the rhythms of life. Soon, however, human sin again rears its ugly head.

STUDY

Read the study note on 9:9-10 and "God's Covenant with Noah" on p. 37. What does God's covenant with Noah tell us about God and his relationship with humanity after the flood?

Read the study notes on 9:1-7, 9:1, and 9:2-3. How does the post-flood world compare and contrast with the world as described right after its creation in Gen 1–2?

What is the purpose of the rainbow (see the study notes on 9:12 and 9:13-16)?

Read the study note on 9:6. How do you think this should verse shape our thinking about murder and the death penalty?

Read the study note on 9:5-6. How does law function in the post-flood world? What are the implications for society today?

Read the study notes on 9:18 and 9:22. How does the story of Ham and Noah connect to Israel's later relationship with Egypt and Canaan?

REFLECTION

What does God seem to be saying to you through what you have studied today?

PRAYER

Talk to God about what you have read, any questions or concerns you might have, and what you think he might be saying to you today. You can write your prayer here if you wish.

DAY 4 ◆ Genesis 10:1-32

READING: **GENESIS 10:1-32**

Begin with prayer, asking God to give you insight, understanding, and an open heart to listen to and follow his word.

This chapter describes how the descendants of Noah's sons (Shem, Ham, and Japheth) multiplied and scattered through the land, forming nations and speaking different languages.

STUDY

Read "Nations of the Ancient World" (p. 39) and study the map. How widely did the descendants of Noah scatter throughout the world?

Read the study notes on 10:8-12 and 10:10-12. Why is special attention given to Babylonia and Assyria, and what do we learn about them?

Read the study note on 10:21. How do Abram and the later Israelites relate to Shem?

REFLECTION

What does God seem to be saying to you through what you have studied today?

PRAYER

Talk to God about what you have read, any questions or concerns you might have, and what you think he might be saying to you today. You can write your prayer here if you wish.

DAY 5 ◆ Genesis 11:1-26

READING: **GENESIS 11:1-26**

Begin with prayer, asking God to give you insight, understanding, and an open heart to listen to and follow his word.

The Tower of Babel story (11:1-9) informs us why there are so many languages in the world (as reflected in Gen 10). The rest of the chapter is a transition to the important story of Abram that follows.

STUDY

Read the study note on 11:1-9. How did the attitude of the builders of the Tower resemble that of Adam and Eve?

Read the study note on 11:4. In the light of ancient Near Eastern culture, what was the Tower? What did it represent?

Read the study note on 11:6. What did God's destruction of the Tower prevent?

FURTHER STUDY (Optional)
Read the study note on 11:10. How does transition to Shem and his descendants in 11:20-26 shift the focus to Abram and the next section of the book of Genesis?

REFLECTION
What does God seem to be saying to you through what you have studied today?

PRAYER
Talk to God about what you have read, any questions or concerns you might have, and what you think he might be saying to you today. You can write your prayer here if you wish.

GROUP SESSION

READING: **GENESIS 6:1–11:26**
Read the passage together as a group.

DISCUSSION
You can use the following questions to guide what you share in the discussion. Give each person at least one opportunity to share with the others.

What did you learn from Gen 6:1–11:26? What was one thing that stood out to you as you studied this passage? How did Gen 6:1–11:26 surprise you? Do you have questions about this passage or the study materials that haven't been answered? What does God seem to be saying to you through what you have studied?

TOPICS FOR DISCUSSION

You can choose from among these topics to generate a discussion among the members of your group, or you can write your thoughts about one or more of these topics if you're studying solo.

1. It has been said that, with the flood, "God reversed creation." What do you think is meant by this phrase? Why did God do it?

2. What do we learn about human beings and God in the flood story and the account of the Tower of Babel? What are the implications for us today?

3. How does the list of nations and their languages in Gen 10 show God's judgment and his mercy to humanity in the aftermath of the "confusion of languages" in the Tower of Babel story?

GROUP REFLECTION

What is God saying to us as a group through Gen 6:1–11:26?

ACTION

What are we going to do, individually or as a group, in response to what God is saying to us?

PRAYER

How should we pray for each other in response to God's message to us in this passage?

Take turns talking to God about this passage and about what he is saying.

NEXT: GENESIS 11:27–13:18 (God's Promise to Abram and His Struggle with Faith)

WEEK
FOUR

God's Promise to Abram and His Struggle with Faith

GENESIS
11:27–13:18

OUTLINE

DAY 1 . . . Genesis 11:27-32

DAY 2 . . . Genesis 12:1-3

DAY 3 . . . Genesis 12:4-9

DAY 4 . . . Genesis 12:10-20

DAY 5 . . . Genesis 13:1-18

Group Session

DAY 1 ◆ Genesis 11:27-32

READING: **GENESIS 11:27-32**

Begin with prayer, asking God to give you insight, understanding, and an open heart to listen to and follow his word.

Here we read the genealogy of Terah, the father of Abram, whom God chooses as the father of a people through whom he will reach the world with his salvation.

STUDY

Read the study note on 11:27-32. How does this section of Scripture make the transition to the story of Abram? *Shows that his family lived in idolatrous culture & GOD wanted them out*

Read the study note on 11:31. What is the significance of Haran to the story and to Terah's family? *Patriarchal lineage + moon WORSHIP*

Read the study notes on 11:27-32 and 11:29. How does knowledge of Abram's family's idolatrous past change your perspective on him? How does it make you think of the spiritual heritage of your family? *SPIRITUAL WARFARE WAS & IS 'ON' all the time. How important it is TO walk w/ GOD — TRUST & OBEY*

FURTHER STUDY (Optional)

Use the map on p. 45 to find Ur, Haran, and the land of Canaan.

Read the study note on 11:28. Ur was the most developed city of the day, equivalent to New York City or London. What would it be like to move from there (via Haran) to the unsophisticated land of Canaan?

Read the study note on 11:30. How is Sarai's barrenness significant to her role in the story to come? What does it show you about God? *Shows off GOD'S sovereignty over the womb*

REFLECTION

What does God seem to be saying to you through what you have studied today? *Satan wants to kill me — us*

Talk to God about what you have read, any questions or concerns you might have, and what you think he might be saying to you today. You can write your prayer here if you wish.

DAY 2 ♦ Genesis 12:1-3

READING: GENESIS 12:1-3

Begin with prayer, asking God to give you insight, understanding, and an open heart to listen to and follow his word.

This short passage is of immense importance. Here God initiates a special relationship with Abram and his future descendants.

STUDY

Read the study note on 12:1. Why did Abram need to have faith to leave his "native country"? How does this relate to your journey of faith? *THE UNKNOWN ELEMENTS - UNSEEN DESTINATION Following blindly - loss of control - surrender*

Read the study note on 12:2. How was Abram's fame so different from that sought by the builders of the Tower of Babel? What does that tell us about our own ambitions? *Abram was interested in God's fame before his own.*

Read "God's Covenant Relationships" on p. 44. How would you describe to someone else what a covenant is? *A BINDING AGREEMENT, GUARANTEE, PROMISE*

FURTHER STUDY (Optional)

Read the study note on 12:3. How is the world today blessed through the promise to Abram? *Thru faith, all the covenants are wrapped up for all of us in Christ*

Read "God's Covenant Relationships" on p. 44. Are you in a covenant relationship with God? If so, describe the nature of that covenant. *It is by Grace I am saved thru faith.... the gift of GOD Eph. 2:8&9 NOT BY WORKS*

Read the study notes on 12:1-3 and 12:2. What is a blessing? And how will Abram and his descendants be a blessing to others? *Benefitting, showing favor, saving*

REFLECTION

What does God seem to be saying to you through what you have studied today?

"I have Totally paid for your existance before you ever existed."

PRAYER

Talk to God about what you have read, any questions or concerns you might have, and what you think he might be saying to you today. You can write your prayer here if you wish.

DAY 3 ◆ Genesis 12:4-9

READING: GENESIS 12:4-9

Begin with prayer, asking God to give you insight, understanding, and an open heart to listen to and follow his word.

Abram obeys God's call to leave his "native country" and begins his life in the land to which God sent him.

STUDY

Read the study note on 12:4. What was Abram like when God spoke to him? What were you like when you became a Christian?

Grown, Established, Pagan

Read the study note on 12:5. What does this verse say about Abram's blessing on others? Does it tell us how we might also be a blessing to those around us?

lead others to GOD

Read the study note on 12:7. What part does faith play in receiving the promises of God? Does faith play a role in your life?

knowing He will keep His word

FURTHER STUDY (Optional)

Read the study note on 12:6-7. What is the significance of Abram's association with the "oak of Moreh"? What would be the modern equivalent today?

worshipped, testified, preached made converts

A42

Read the study note on 12:6-7. Why do you think Abram set up an altar wherever he settled in the Promised Land?

To Bless

What does 12:8 (read the study note) tell you about worship today?

proclaim the LIVING GOD

REFLECTION

What does God seem to be saying to you through what you have studied today?

PRAYER

Talk to God about what you have read, any questions or concerns you might have, and what you think he might be saying to you today. You can write your prayer here if you wish.

DAY 4 ◆ Genesis 12:10-20

READING: **GENESIS 12:10-20**

Begin with prayer, asking God to give you insight, understanding, and an open heart to listen to and follow his word.

God gave Abram a promise that his descendants would be a great nation that would bless the world. When Abram arrives at his new home, though, there is a famine and he has to leave. How will he respond to this threat to the fulfillment of the promise?

STUDY

Read the study notes on 12:10-20 and 12:10-13. Why and how did Abram jeopardize the promise? Think about your life journey. How have you jeopardized God's promises to you? *stopped relying on God, took control stopped worshipping + leading*

Read the study note on 12:13. Why did Abram say Sarai was his sister? *afraid they would kill Him + thought that he could control situation*

How did God protect Abram from his foolhardy behavior? Can you think of times in your life when God intervened to keep you from doing something foolish?

FURTHER STUDY (Optional)

Read the study note on 12:14-16. While Abram benefited from his deception, how did he also suffer? What successes in your life have brought pain?

had to separate from Lot

Read the study note on 12:20, which notes the similarity between Pharaoh's command to Abram in 12:20 and God's command in 12:1. What is the difference in Abram's response? What does this teach us about acting in fear? *Had to leave w/o his integrity. Puts our integrity on the table a in play.*

REFLECTION

What does God seem to be saying to you through what you have studied today?

Trust my strength, not yours

PRAYER

Talk to God about what you have read, any questions or concerns you might have, and what you think he might be saying to you today. You can write your prayer here if you wish.

DAY 5 ◆ Genesis 13:1-8

READING: **GENESIS 13:1-18**

Begin with prayer, asking God to give you insight, understanding, and an open heart to listen to and follow his word.

God has blessed both Abram and Lot with so much prosperity that they need to split their herds. One man grasps at the best land, while the other waits for God to bring him into possession of the land.

STUDY

The study note on 13:1-7 refers to "conflict amidst God's blessings." Read the verses. What are the blessings and what is the conflict? *material wealth — herds + livestock*

Read the study note on 13:8-13. What does Abram's attitude as displayed in this story tell us about the quality of his faith at this time? Are you more like Lot or Abram?

FURTHER STUDY (Optional)

Read the study notes on 13:10 and 13:11. Turn to the map on p. 48 and find Sodom, Gomorrah, and the cities of the plain (Bela, Admah, Zeboiim). How would you describe their location? How is Lot's choice similar to Adam and Eve's? *Pleasing to the eye, desire, selfishness*

Read the study notes on 13:11-18, 13:11, 13:13, and 13:14-17. List the contrasts between Lot and Abram. *Lot trusted himself, Abram trusted God*

REFLECTION

What does God seem to be saying to you through what you have studied today? *Trust in the Lord... lean not on my understanding*

PRAYER

Talk to God about what you have read, any questions or concerns you might have, and what you think he might be saying to you today. You can write your prayer here if you wish.

GROUP SESSION

READING: GENESIS 11:27–13:18

Read the passage together as a group.

DISCUSSION

You can use the following questions to guide what you share in the discussion. Give each person at least one opportunity to share with the others.

What did you learn from Gen 11:27–13:18? What was one thing that stood out to you as you studied this passage? How did Gen 11:27–13:18 surprise you? Do you have questions about this passage or the study materials that haven't been answered? What does God seem to be saying to you through what you have studied?

TOPICS FOR DISCUSSION

You can choose from among these topics to generate a discussion among the members of your group, or you can write your thoughts about one or more of these topics if you're studying solo.

1. God promised Abram that he would bless him and that Abram would be a blessing to "all the families of the earth." How has God blessed you and others through Abram?

2. When Abram arrived in the Promised Land, he began a practice of building altars everywhere he went. What does this tell us about Abram? Is there a lesson here for us today?

3. Abram received promises from God including the gift of land. When he arrived, he encountered threats to the fulfillment of the promises. How did he respond to the famine (12:10-20)? How did he respond to the need to separate from Lot (13:1-18)? Do these stories tell us anything about our own journey of faith?

GROUP REFLECTION

What is God saying to us as a group through Gen 11:27–13:18?

ACTION

What are we going to do, individually or as a group, in response to what God is saying to us?

PRAYER

How should we pray for each other in response to God's message to us in this passage?

Take turns talking to God about this passage and about what he is saying.

NEXT: **GENESIS 14:1–17:27 (Abram and Melchizedek and God's Reassurances)**

Abram and Melchizedek and God's Reassurances

GENESIS
14:1–17:27

OUTLINE

DAY 1 ... Genesis 14:1-16

DAY 2 ... Genesis 14:17-24

DAY 3 ... Genesis 15:1-21

DAY 4 ... Genesis 16:1-16

DAY 5 ... Genesis 17:1-27

Group Session

DAY **1** ◆ Genesis 14:1-16

READING: **GENESIS 14:1-16**

Begin with prayer, asking God to give you insight, understanding, and an open heart to listen to and follow his word.

God enables Abram to defeat four Near Eastern kings who have raided Canaan and kidnapped Lot. As you read, trace the movements of the eastern kings and Abram's pursuit on the map on p. 48 ("The Battle at Siddim Valley").

STUDY

Read the study notes on 14:1-16, 14:1-2, 14:4-5, and 14:4. What were the politics behind and the goals of these battles? Are there similarities and differences from battles today?

Read the study note on 14:8-12. What role did Lot play in this story? How does his decision to move to Sodom look now?

FURTHER STUDY (Optional)

Read the study note on 14:14-16. What role did God play in the battle? Is this typical of other Old Testament battles? What does this tell us about our spiritual battles today?

Read the study note on 14:14. How does Abram's role in this story relate to God's promise to him in 12:1-3?

REFLECTION

What does God seem to be saying to you through what you have studied today?

PRAYER

Talk to God about what you have read, any questions or concerns you might have, and what you think he might be saying to you today. You can write your prayer here if you wish.

DAY 2 ◆ Genesis 14:17-24

READING: **GENESIS 14:17-24**

Begin with prayer, asking God to give you insight, understanding, and an open heart to listen to and follow his word.

After his victory over the foreign kings, Abram meets Melchizedek, the mysterious priest-king of Salem (Jerusalem) and gives him a tithe of the plunder.

STUDY

Read the study note on 14:18 about Melchizedek, and read the passages cited there (Ps 110:4; Heb 7:1-19). Who is Melchizedek? How do you think he relates to Christ?

Read the study note on 14:19-20. What does the tithe represent about the relationship between God and Abram? What significance does this have for the meaning of our offerings to God today?

Read the study note on 14:21-24. Why did Abram reject the king of Sodom's reward? Are there times today when Christians have to turn down offers? Why? What are some examples of this?

FURTHER STUDY (Optional)

Read the study note on 14:18. What does the meaning of Melchizedek's name tell you about his character?

Read "Melchizedek" on p. 50. What is the author of Hebrews saying about the priesthood of Christ by comparing him to Melchizedek?

REFLECTION

What does God seem to be saying to you through what you have studied today?

A49

Talk to God about what you have read, any questions or concerns you might have, and what you think he might be saying to you today. You can write your prayer here if you wish.

DAY 3 ◆ Genesis 15:1-21

READING: GENESIS 15:1-21

Begin with prayer, asking God to give you insight, understanding, and an open heart to listen to and follow his word.

God comes to a doubting Abram and reconfirms his covenant promises, particularly that he will have a son.

STUDY

Read the study note on 15:1. Why did God encourage Abram not to fear? When in your life have you needed this kind of assurance?

Read the study note on 15:2-3. What role does Eliezer play in this story? What does Abram's comment to God reveal about his faith?

Read the study note on 15:6. What does God's statement to Abram say about Abram's faith at this point? Why do you think this verse is quoted so often in the New Testament?

Read "God's Covenant with Abraham" on p. 51. At what points of history did the blessing of this covenant come into realization? In what way? How do people benefit today?

FURTHER STUDY (Optional)

Read the study note on 15:18-19. What does God's oath to Abram tell us about God's determination to fulfill his promises? How does that speak to us today?

Read the study notes on 15:10, 15:11, and 15:17-18, regarding the ritual of dividing the animals in half. How does this illumine your understanding of the passage?

What does God seem to be saying to you through what you have studied today?

PRAYER

Talk to God about what you have read, any questions or concerns you might have, and what you think he might be saying to you today. You can write your prayer here if you wish.

DAY 4 ◆ Genesis 16:1-16

READING: **GENESIS 16:1-16**

Begin with prayer, asking God to give you insight, understanding, and an open heart to listen to and follow his word.

In spite of God's assurances that he will give Abram and Sarai a child, they try to manufacture their own heir through a second wife, Hagar.

STUDY

Read the study notes on 16:1-16 and 16:1-3. How does taking Hagar as a wife show Abram and Sarai's lack of faith? Are there similar ways by which Christians demonstrate their lack of faith today?

Read the study note on 16:7. Who is the angel of the Lord?

Read the study note on 16:14-15. What does the name Beer-lahai-roi tell us about God's attitude toward the afflicted even today?

Read the study note on 16:8-12. Why do you think God would make Hagar return to a hard situation? Does God ever want us to persist in a difficult situation? Why?

FURTHER STUDY (Optional)

Read "Hagar" on p. 52. What is the significance, in Gal 4:22-31, of the fact that Sarah represents "the heavenly Jerusalem" and Hagar represents "Mount Sinai"?

Read the study notes on 16:8-12, 16:11, and 16:13. Describe the relationship between Hagar and God.

REFLECTION

What does God seem to be saying to you through what you have studied today?

PRAYER

Talk to God about what you have read, any questions or concerns you might have, and what you think he might be saying to you today. You can write your prayer here if you wish.

DAY 5 ◆ Genesis 17:1-27

READING: **GENESIS 17:1-27**

Begin with prayer, asking God to give you insight, understanding, and an open heart to listen to and follow his word.

God appears to Abram one more time to assure him that he will fulfill his promises to him. In the process, he introduces the ritual of circumcision as a sign of the covenant.

STUDY

Read the study notes on 17:4-5 and 17:15-16. What is the meaning and significance of the name changes?

Read the study notes on 17:17-18 and 17:23-27. What does Abraham's obedience signify about his faith? What does this story tell us about the relationship of faith and obedience?

Read the study note on 17:14. What is the consequence of not being circumcised? Why?

FURTHER STUDY (Optional)

Read "Circumcision" on p. 54. What is circumcision? What does it represent? What is "circumcision of the heart"?

How does this Old Testament practice inform our understanding of baptism today?

REFLECTION

What does God seem to be saying to you through what you have studied today?

PRAYER

Talk to God about what you have read, any questions or concerns you might have, and what you think he might be saying to you today. You can write your prayer here if you wish.

GROUP SESSION

READING: **GENESIS 14:1–17:27**

Read the passage together as a group.

DISCUSSION

You can use the following questions to guide what you share in the discussion. Give each person at least one opportunity to share with the others.

What did you learn from Gen 14:1–17:27? What was one thing that stood out to you as you studied this passage? How did Gen 14:1–17:27 surprise you? Do you have questions about this passage or the study materials that haven't been answered? What does God seem to be saying to you through what you have studied?

TOPICS FOR DISCUSSION

You can choose from among these topics to generate a discussion among the members of your group, or you can write your thoughts about one or more of these topics if you're studying solo.

1. How do Abram's actions and statements in Gen 14–17 reflect on the quality of his faith? How does his behavior mirror our own faith journey?

2. In Gen 15, God undertakes a ritual to make an oath, and in Gen 17 he insists that his people perform an oath through the ritual of circumcision. What is the significance of these obligations?

3. Gentiles (Melchizedek and Hagar) play important roles in Gen 14–17. How do they relate to God's promises to Abram in Gen 12:1-3?

GROUP REFLECTION

What is God saying to us as a group through Gen 14:1–17:27?

ACTION

What are we going to do, individually or as a group, in response to what God is saying to us?

PRAYER

How should we pray for each other in response to God's message to us in this passage?

Take turns talking to God about this passage and about what he is saying.

NEXT: **GENESIS 18:1–23:20 (Abraham's Mature Faith)**

*Abraham's
Mature Faith*

GENESIS
18:1–23:20

OUTLINE

DAY 1 ... Genesis 18:1-33

DAY 2 ... Genesis 19:1-38

DAY 3 ... Genesis 20:1–21:34

DAY 4 ... Genesis 22:1-19

DAY 5 ... Genesis 22:20–23:20

Group Session

DAY **1** ◆ Genesis 18:1-33

READING: GENESIS 18:1-33

Begin with prayer, asking God to give you insight, understanding, and an open heart to listen to and follow his word.

God again assures the doubting and aging couple that they really will have a child. In the process, Abraham learns that sinful Sodom and Gomorrah are about to be judged, so he intercedes for the righteous people who live there.

STUDY

Read the study notes on 18:1-15 and 18:2-8. What was the significance of Abraham's generous hospitality? Is there any application to how we show hospitality to others?

respected them as sent from God himself

Read the study note on 18:14 and reflect on your own life. Are there any issues or situations that you think are beyond God's reach? *mentally, I know He can handle anything (do anything —.) in my heart I still hold on to some things. — POLITICS - WORK - SIN*

Read the study note on 18:16-33. Do you think we can emulate Abraham's prophetic intercession for others? *we are prophets as abrahams descendents,*

Read the study note on 18:20-21. What does God's attitude toward Sodom and Gomorrah tell us about his judgments?

FURTHER STUDY (Optional)

Study the study note on 18:22-33 and how Abraham prayed. What do we learn about prayer from his example?

Read the study note on 18:3. How does God make his presence known to us today?

His word, His people, nature, miracles

REFLECTION

What does God seem to be saying to you through what you have studied today?

Talk to God about what you have read, any questions or concerns you might have, and what you think he might be saying to you today. You can write your prayer here if you wish.

DAY 2 ◆ Genesis 19:1-38

READING: **GENESIS 19:1-38**

Begin with prayer, asking God to give you insight, understanding, and an open heart to listen to and follow his word.

While Sodom and Gomorrah are destroyed, God allows Lot and his family to flee.

STUDY

Read the study note on 19:1-38. Lot lived in a corrupt culture. How did it affect him? How does our culture affect us? *Infiltrates our life and causes separation from God*

Read the study note on 19:1. What is the significance of the fact that Lot was sitting at the gate of Sodom? Should Christians take positions of influence in their societies? Why or why not? *Leadership, business success yes, to influence culture for good*

Read the study notes on 19:6-9 and 19:9. What was the relationship between Lot and the townspeople? What does this reveal about them?

Read the study note on 19:26. Why was Lot's wife turned into a "pillar of salt"? Do you think she was treated fairly? Why or why not?

FURTHER STUDY (Optional)

Read the study note on 19:15-23. How do Christians today live a "conflicted lifestyle"?

Read the study notes on 19:30-35 and 19:36-38. What is the significance of this story for the later history of Israel?

Read "Lot" on p. 58. How do Lot's actions reveal his character?

Read "Lot" on p. 58.

REFLECTION

What does God seem to be saying to you through what you have studied today?

PRAYER

Talk to God about what you have read, any questions or concerns you might have, and what you think he might be saying to you today. You can write your prayer here if you wish.

DAY 3 ◆ Genesis 20:1–21:34

READING: **GENESIS 20:1–21:34**

Begin with prayer, asking God to give you insight, understanding, and an open heart to listen to and follow his word.

God's promise finds fulfillment when Isaac is born. Hagar and Ishmael are sent away, and Abraham enters into a treaty with a powerful neighbor.

STUDY

Read the study notes on 20:1-18, 20:2, and 20:11-13 about the second "sister story." What does Abraham's having lied twice tell us about him? What is God's role in the story?

Read the study note on 20:6. How did God deal with Abimelech? What does this tell us about God?

Read the study note on 21:6. What does Isaac's name mean and how does its meaning relate to the events of this story?

FURTHER STUDY (Optional)

Read the study note on 21:14-21. What does this story tell us about God's attitude toward Gentiles?

Read the study note on 21:22-23. Why does Abimelech feel it necessary to have a treaty with Abraham? What does this situation tell us about how important it is for Christians today to deal honestly with nonbelievers?

REFLECTION
What does God seem to be saying to you through what you have studied today?

PRAYER
Talk to God about what you have read, any questions or concerns you might have, and what you think he might be saying to you today. You can write your prayer here if you wish.

DAY 4 ◆ Genesis 22:1-19

READING: **GENESIS 22:1-19**

Begin with prayer, asking God to give you insight, understanding, and an open heart to listen to and follow his word.

Abraham's faith is tested once more when God tells him to take his son Isaac to Mount Moriah to sacrifice him there.

STUDY

Read the study note on 22:1. Why would God ask such a sacrifice of Abraham?

Read the study note on 22:2. What is the connection between this verse and Gen 12:1?

Read the study note on 22:9-19. What did this account teach Abraham (and Israel after him) about sacrifice? What does it teach us today?

FURTHER STUDY (Optional)

Read the study note on 22:13. What parallels are there between the event on Mount Moriah and the Gospel?

Read the study note on 22:17. What do you make of the statement in the note that the church will be the ultimate fulfillment of God's blessing here?

REFLECTION

What does God seem to be saying to you through what you have studied today?

PRAYER

Talk to God about what you have read, any questions or concerns you might have, and what you think he might be saying to you today. You can write your prayer here if you wish.

DAY **5** ◆ Genesis 22:20–23:20

READING: **GENESIS 22:20–23:20**

Begin with prayer, asking God to give you insight, understanding, and an open heart to listen to and follow his word.

At the death of Sarah, Abraham for the first time comes into possession of land when he purchases a cave for her burial.

STUDY

Read the study note on 23:3-4. In relationship to Gen 12:1-3, what is the significance of the statement that Abraham is a "stranger and foreigner"?

Read the study notes on 23:9 and 23:16-20. What is the significance of the fact that Abraham now would actually own a small piece of the land?

Read the study notes on 23:11, 23:12-13, 23:15, and 23:16-20. What do these verses tell us about the nature of the transaction between Abraham and Ephron?

FURTHER STUDY (Optional)

Read the study note on 23:5-6 and "Abraham" on p. 46. How did Abraham live in the land? How was he viewed by others?

REFLECTION

What does God seem to be saying to you through what you have studied today?

PRAYER

Talk to God about what you have read, any questions or concerns you might have, and what you think he might be saying to you today. You can write your prayer here if you wish.

GROUP SESSION

READING: **GENESIS 18:1–23:20**

Read the passage together as a group.

DISCUSSION

You can use the following questions to guide what you share in the discussion. Give each person at least one opportunity to share with the others.

What did you learn from Gen 18:1–23:20? What was one thing that stood out to you as you studied this passage? How did Gen 18:1–23:20 surprise you? Do you have questions about this passage or the study materials that haven't been answered? What does God seem to be saying to you through what you have studied?

TOPICS FOR DISCUSSION

You can choose from among these topics to generate a discussion among the members of your group, or you can write your thoughts about one or more of these topics if you're studying solo.

1. In what ways is our own culture like that of Sodom and Gomorrah, and in what ways is it different? Are there lessons in this story about how we as Christians should engage our culture?

2. In Gen 22 (and earlier in Gen 12:1) Abraham is called to obey God. In what ways are we called to obey God today?

3. In Gen 12:1-3, God promised Abram that he would be a great nation and a blessing to other nations. In Gen 18:1–23:20, how do we see the beginning of the fulfillment of these promises? Has God made the church promises? Are there ways in which we can see these coming to fulfillment even now?

GROUP REFLECTION

What is God saying to us as a group through Gen 18:1–23:20?

ACTION

What are we going to do, individually or as a group, in response to what God is saying to us?

PRAYER

How should we pray for each other in response to God's message to us in this passage?

Take turns talking to God about this passage and about what he is saying.

NEXT: GENESIS 24:1–28:9 (Isaac: From Abraham to Jacob and Esau)

*Isaac:
From Abraham
to
Jacob and Esau*

GENESIS
24:1–28:9

OUTLINE

DAY 1 ... Genesis 24:1-67

DAY 2 ... Genesis 25:1-26

DAY 3 ... Genesis 25:27-34

DAY 4 ... Genesis 26:1-35

DAY 5 ... Genesis 27:1–28:9

Group Session

DAY **1** ◆ Genesis 24:1-67

READING: **GENESIS 24:1-67**

Begin with prayer, asking God to give you insight, understanding, and an open heart to listen to and follow his word.

God had promised Abraham that his descendants would become a great nation. Then came Isaac, who would continue the line of promise. Here we read of Isaac's marriage to Rebekah. Together they would produce the next generation of the people of God.

STUDY

Read the study notes on 24:1-9, 24:2, 24:3, and 24:6-8. Why did Abraham send his servant so far away to find a bride for Isaac? Are any of these reasons still applicable?

Read the study note on 24:14. How does Rebekah show hospitality toward Abraham's servant? What does that tell us about her character?

Read the study note on 24:27. What does this story tell us about the relationship between God and Abraham?

Read the study note on 24:48. How does God work behind the scenes in your life?

FURTHER STUDY (Optional)

Read the study notes on 24:10-60 and 24:26. How does the servant respond to God's guidance on his mission? Have you ever experienced God's guidance in your life?

Read the study note on 24:33-48. Do you think modern Christians are as sensitive to God's leading as Abraham's servant in this story? Why or why not?

REFLECTION

What does God seem to be saying to you through what you have studied today?

PRAYER

Talk to God about what you have read, any questions or concerns you might have, and what you think he might be saying to you today. You can write your prayer here if you wish.

DAY 2 ◆ Genesis 25:1-26

READING: **GENESIS 25:1-26**

Begin with prayer, asking God to give you insight, understanding, and an open heart to listen to and follow his word.

Abraham lived to a ripe old age and then died and was given a proper burial. We also hear of both Ishmael's and Isaac's descendants, in particular the birth of Jacob and Esau.

STUDY

Read the study notes on 25:1-11 and 25:2-4. Why is the narrator interested in the other descendants of Abraham? Why is the narrator especially interested in the story of Isaac?

Read the study notes on 25:25 and 25:26. What is the significance of Esau's and Jacob's names? How does this fit into the story of their lives?

Read the study note on 25:21. Compare and contrast Abraham's and Isaac's responses to their wives' barrenness.

FURTHER STUDY (Optional)

Read "Infertility" on p. 70. Why was infertility so frightening in ancient Israel? Why do you think there were so many infertile women in the story of the patriarchs (including here with Rebekah)? Do these stories of infertility say anything to couples today who have trouble having a child? Why or why not?

Read the study note on 25:7-8. What does this note tell you about how Scripture is sometimes organized?

REFLECTION

What does God seem to be saying to you through what you have studied today?

PRAYER

Talk to God about what you have read, any questions or concerns you might have, and what you think he might be saying to you today. You can write your prayer here if you wish.

DAY 3 ◆ Genesis 25:27-34

READING: **GENESIS 25:27-34**

Begin with prayer, asking God to give you insight, understanding, and an open heart to listen to and follow his word.

Though short, the story of Esau selling his birthright to Jacob is important for our understanding of these men and of the story that follows.

STUDY

Read the study note on 25:27-34. How does this story illustrate Esau's and Jacob's character?

Read the study note on 25:30. Esau's appetite for food harmed his spiritual values. Are there other similar appetites that can hurt our relationship with God?

Read the study note on 25:31-33. What was wrong with Jacob's behavior here? How can we avoid Jacob's error?

FURTHER STUDY (Optional)

Read the study notes on 25:29 and 25:30. What do Jacob and Esau's actions here tell us about each of their spiritual condition? Are there times in your life where you find yourself acting like both or either of them?

Read "Esau" on p. 71. How does the New Testament view Esau?

Read the study note on 25:33-34. How did Esau show contempt for his birthright? What birthright or blessings do we have as Christians? How can we show contempt for them?

REFLECTION

What does God seem to be saying to you through what you have studied today?

PRAYER

Talk to God about what you have read, any questions or concerns you might have, and what you think he might be saying to you today. You can write your prayer here if you wish.

DAY 4 ◆ Genesis 26:1-35

READING: **GENESIS 26:1-35**

Begin with prayer, asking God to give you insight, understanding, and an open heart to listen to and follow his word.

Despite his sin, God protects Isaac, as he did his father Abraham. Isaac's dealings with the Philistine king demonstrate God's blessing on him.

STUDY

Read the study note on 26:2-5. How did Abraham's obedience relate to the continuation of God's covenant promises to Isaac? What role does obedience play in the Christian life?

Read the study note on 26:6-11. Isaac's sin is similar to that of his father Abraham. Is it typical for children to repeat the sins of their parents? Does this mean sin is inevitable?

Read the study note on 26:10-11. What does this story tell us about marital purity? Why is it so important even today?

Read the study note on 26:17-22. How does God's blessing overcome the Philistines' attempts to undermine Isaac? Can you think of any parallel situations in your own life?

Read the study note on 26:26-33. The Philistines came to recognize the blessing of God on Isaac's life. Where would nonbelievers recognize God's blessings in your life?

REFLECTION

What does God seem to be saying to you through what you have studied today?

PRAYER

Talk to God about what you have read, any questions or concerns you might have, and what you think he might be saying to you today. You can write your prayer here if you wish.

DAY 5 ◆ Genesis 27:1–28:9

READING: **GENESIS 27:1–28:9**

Begin with prayer, asking God to give you insight, understanding, and an open heart to listen to and follow his word.

Earlier Jacob took Esau's birthright as firstborn son; now he steals his blessing, with implications for the future of God's people.

STUDY

Read the study note on 27:1-4. Isaac knew God's intent toward Jacob. Does this change your view of the story? What happens when we try to work against God's plans?

Read the study notes on 27:3-4 and 27:5-17. What does the story reveal about the attitudes of Rebekah, Jacob, and Esau?

Read the study note on 27:41-45. Can you think of any examples in your own life where your sin brought suffering?

FURTHER STUDY (Optional)

Read the study notes on 28:1-2 and 28:6-9. Contrast Jacob and Esau's choice of wives. What does this tell us about them?

Why is it so important to marry someone who shares our faith and values?

REFLECTION

What does God seem to be saying to you through what you have studied today?

PRAYER

Talk to God about what you have read, any questions or concerns you might have, and what you think he might be saying to you today. You can write your prayer here if you wish.

GROUP SESSION

READING: **GENESIS 24:1–28:9**

Read the passage together as a group.

DISCUSSION

You can use the following questions to guide what you share in the discussion. Give each person at least one opportunity to share with the others.

What did you learn from Gen 24:1–28:9? What was one thing that stood out to you as you studied this passage? How did Gen 24:1–28:9 surprise you? Do you have questions about this passage or the study materials that haven't been answered? What does God seem to be saying to you through what you have studied?

TOPICS FOR DISCUSSION

You can choose from among these topics to generate a discussion among the members of your group, or you can write your thoughts about one or more of these topics if you're studying solo.

1. Marriages play a big role in Gen 24:1–28:9. Name all the marriages mentioned in these chapters. In light of these stories, what makes a good marriage? What makes a bad marriage? What lessons can we learn about marriage today?

2. How would you describe the character and spiritual condition of Isaac, Rebekah, Esau, and Jacob in these stories? How do their characters relate to the quality of their lives individually and together?

3. Why do you think God works with such less-than-perfect human beings? What implications does that have for us?

GROUP REFLECTION

What is God saying to us as a group through Gen 24:1–28:9?

ACTION

What are we going to do, individually or as a group, in response to what God is saying to us?

PRAYER

How should we pray for each other in response to God's message to us in this passage?

Take turns talking to God about this passage and about what he is saying.

NEXT: GENESIS 28:10–31:55 (Jacob in Paddan-aram)

*Jacob in
Paddan-aram*

GENESIS
28:10–31:55

OUTLINE

DAY 1 ... Genesis 28:10-22

DAY 2 ... Genesis 29:1-30

DAY 3 ... Genesis 29:31–30:24

DAY 4 ... Genesis 30:25-43

DAY 5 ... Genesis 31:1-55

Group Session

DAY **1** ◆ Genesis 28:10-22

READING: **GENESIS 28:10-22**

Begin with prayer, asking God to give you insight, understanding, and an open heart to listen to and follow his word.

Before Jacob leaves the Promised Land to begin his sojourn in Paddan-aram, God reveals himself in a dream and affirms that his promises to Abraham will continue through Jacob.

STUDY

Read the study note on 28:10-22. What is the major message that God is sending to Jacob through this dream?

Read the study note on 28:12-15. How does God make known his provision and protection to us today?

How does the study note on 28:12-13 enrich your understanding of the passage? (You might also read the study note on 11:4 to learn more about ziggurats.)

Read the study note on 28:15. What is the significance of the phrase "I am with you"? How do you experience the presence of God in your life?

FURTHER STUDY (Optional)

What is the connection between John 1:51 and Jacob's vision of the stairway?

Read the study note on 28:16-22. How does Jacob respond to God's presence? Can you give other examples from the Bible of similar responses to the presence of God? How is our response similar or different today?

Read the study note on 28:19 and the Scripture passages cited there. What is the significance of Bethel in the history of Israel?

Read the study notes on 28:20-22 and 28:22. Should Christians take vows today? Should they offer tithes? Why or why not?

REFLECTION

What does God seem to be saying to you through what you have studied today?

PRAYER

Talk to God about what you have read, any questions or concerns you might have, and what you think he might be saying to you today. You can write your prayer here if you wish.

DAY 2 ◆ Genesis 29:1-30

READING: **GENESIS 29:1-30**

Begin with prayer, asking God to give you insight, understanding, and an open heart to listen to and follow his word.

Jacob arrives in Paddan-aram where he meets his future wife Rachel by the well. However, her father, Laban, tricks Jacob the trickster into marrying her sister, Leah, first.

STUDY

Read the study notes on 29:1–31:55 and 29:14b-30. What is the role of Laban's deception in this story?

Read the study note on 29:1. How did Jacob's experience at Bethel (28:10-22) affect his attitude? Can you give examples from your own life where an experience of God's presence caused you to "pick up your feet"?

Read the study note on 29:2-12. What similarities are there with the story of Rebekah in Gen 24:12-20? What significance do these similarities have?

FURTHER STUDY (Optional)
Read "Rachel" on p. 78 and "Leah" on p. 79. What contrasts do you see between these two women? What roles do they play in the story of Jacob's life?

Read the study note on 29:23-26. How was Laban's deception of Jacob similar to Jacob's deception of Isaac? Have you ever seen someone's sin come back to hurt him or her in a similar way?

Read the study note on 29:30. Why do you think people show favoritism in a family even when there is the possibility of horrible consequences?

REFLECTION
What does God seem to be saying to you through what you have studied today?

PRAYER
Talk to God about what you have read, any questions or concerns you might have, and what you think he might be saying to you today. You can write your prayer here if you wish.

DAY 3 ◆ Genesis 29:31–30:24

READING: **GENESIS 29:31–30:24**
Begin with prayer, asking God to give you insight, understanding, and an open heart to listen to and follow his word.

Jacob's wives are Rachel and her sister, Leah. They are jealous of each other and begin to compete in the area of providing Jacob with children. These children are the ancestors of the various tribes of Israel and the story of their lives has implications for the later relationship among the tribes.

Read the study note on 29:31–30:24. How does God's treatment of Leah show how he helps the despised and oppressed?

Read the study note on 30:1-8. What does Rachel's naming of her sons through her concubine Bilhah tell us about her emotional and spiritual state?

Read the study note on 30:14-17. How do you assess Rachel's values in her use of the mandrakes?

Read the study note on 30:22-24. Why do you think God waited so long before allowing Rachel to have her own child?

FURTHER STUDY (Optional)

Read the study notes on 29:32, 29:33, 29:34, 29:35, 30:5-6, 30:7-8, 30:10-13, 30:18, 30:19-20, 30:22-24. What is the significance of the names of Jacob's children?

REFLECTION

What does God seem to be saying to you through what you have studied today?

PRAYER

Talk to God about what you have read, any questions or concerns you might have, and what you think he might be saying to you today. You can write your prayer here if you wish.

DAY 4 ◆ Genesis 30:25-43

READING: **GENESIS 30:25-43**

Begin with prayer, asking God to give you insight, understanding, and an open heart to listen to and follow his word.

The two tricksters, Jacob and Laban, go at it again. Jacob feels it is time to return to the Promised Land. Laban acts like he wants to pay him for his work, but then tries to keep him from any substantial gain. So Jacob devises a plan to foil Laban's attempts.

Read the study notes on 30:25-34, 30:27, and 30:30-33. Why do Jacob and Laban agree to these terms of payment?

Read the study note on 30:25-34. What does this story tell us about Jacob's and Laban's character and spiritual condition?

Read the study notes on 30:37-43. Why do you think Jacob's plan worked?

REFLECTION

What does God seem to be saying to you through what you have studied today?

PRAYER

Talk to God about what you have read, any questions or concerns you might have, and what you think he might be saying to you today. You can write your prayer here if you wish.

DAY 5 ◆ Genesis 31:1-55

READING: **GENESIS 31:1-55**

Begin with prayer, asking God to give you insight, understanding, and an open heart to listen to and follow his word.

Having increased his wealth at Laban's expense, Jacob and his wives and family steal away to return to the Promised Land. Laban catches up with them and accuses them of theft. God allows Jacob to get away and continue their journey home.

STUDY

Read the study note on 31:3. What are the similarities between Jacob's return from Paddan-aram and the later exodus from Egypt?

Read the study notes on 31:4-13 and 31:14-16. Were Leah and Rachel right to listen to their husband Jacob rather than their father Laban? How does marriage change people's relationships to their parents (see Gen 2:24)?

Read the study note on 31:24. Why is it so tempting for us to take justice into our own hands despite God's sovereignty and justice?

FURTHER STUDY (Optional)

Read the study notes on 31:19-20 and 31:22-23. What is the significance of Rachel's theft of Laban's idols?

Read the study note on 31:45-48. What was the purpose of the monument? Is there any equivalent today?

REFLECTION

What does God seem to be saying to you through what you have studied today?

PRAYER

Talk to God about what you have read, any questions or concerns you might have, and what you think he might be saying to you today. You can write your prayer here if you wish.

GROUP SESSION

READING: **GENESIS 28:10–31:55**

Read the passage together as a group.

DISCUSSION

You can use the following questions to guide what you share in the discussion. Give each person at least one opportunity to share with the others.

What did you learn from Gen 28:10–31:55? What was one thing that stood out to you as you studied this passage? How did Gen 28:10–31:55 surprise you? Do you have questions about this passage or the study materials that haven't been answered? What does God seem to be saying to you through what you have studied?

TOPICS FOR DISCUSSION

You can choose from among these topics to generate a discussion among the members of your group, or you can write your thoughts about one or more of these topics if you're studying solo.

1. How do you think God used Jacob's sojourn in Paddan-aram, outside of the Promised Land, to develop his character? Can you think of a period of time in your life when God used difficulties to form your character?

2. Both Jacob and Laban use deception as a strategy of living. Is deception always wrong? Can you describe situations in the story or in your life where deception was right?

3. What can we learn positively and/or negatively about marriage and family from Jacob's interactions with Leah and Rachel?

GROUP REFLECTION

What is God saying to us as a group through Gen 28:10–31:55?

ACTION

What are we going to do, individually or as a group, in response to what God is saying to us?

PRAYER

How should we pray for each other in response to God's message to us in this passage?

Take turns talking to God about this passage and about what he is saying.

NEXT: **GENESIS 32:1–37:1 (Jacob Back in the Promised Land)**

Jacob Back in the Promised Land

GENESIS
32:1–37:1

OUTLINE

DAY 1 ... Genesis 32:1-32

DAY 2 ... Genesis 33:1-20

DAY 3 ... Genesis 34:1-31

DAY 4 ... Genesis 35:1-20

DAY 5 ... Genesis 35:21–37:1

Group Session

READING: **GENESIS 32:1-32**

Begin with prayer, asking God to give you insight, understanding, and an open heart to listen to and follow his word.

Jacob's return to the Promised Land brings him in contact with Esau, who believes Jacob wronged him. Jacob makes his preparations to meet his brother and God uses the occasion to deepen his relationship with him.

STUDY

Read the study note on 32:9-12. From Jacob's prayer, what can we learn about how to pray?

BASED APPEAL ON GOD'S WILL, COMMANDS + PROMISES

Read the study notes on 32:27 and 32:28. What was the significance of the change of Jacob's name to Israel? *Transformation - from self reliance to faith*

Read the study note on 32:29. Why wouldn't the man reveal his name?

on demand

FURTHER STUDY (Optional)

Read the study notes on 32:25 and 32:31. What is the significance of Jacob's crippling?

made him dependent on God

REFLECTION

What does God seem to be saying to you through what you have studied today?

Trust + obey

PRAYER

Talk to God about what you have read, any questions or concerns you might have, and what you think he might be saying to you today. You can write your prayer here if you wish.

DAY 2 ◆ Genesis 33:1-20

READING: **GENESIS 33:1-20**

Begin with prayer, asking God to give you insight, understanding, and an open heart to listen to and follow his word.

STUDY

Read the study notes on 33:1-17 and 33:4. What is surprising about Jacob's encounter with Esau? What do you think changed Esau's mind?

it was cordial, not vengeful or hateful   God had changed it!

Read the study notes on 33:1-2 and 33:3-13. What do Jacob's actions tell us about his character? Why doesn't he act differently in light of his encounter with God in chapter 32?

still a control freak   immature faith

Read the study note on 33:11. What was the purpose of the gift to Esau?

appeasement

FURTHER STUDY (Optional)

Read the study note on 33:18-20. How do Jacob's actions relate to Abraham's life? What is the significance of these actions?

repetition of ABE's story + the Promise

Read the study note on 33:20. What is the significance of the name of Jacob's altar?

he had a new relationship w/ God

REFLECTION

What does God seem to be saying to you through what you have studied today?

PRAYER

Talk to God about what you have read, any questions or concerns you might have, and what you think he might be saying to you today. You can write your prayer here if you wish.

DAY **3** ◆ Genesis 34:1-31

READING: **GENESIS 34:1-31**

Begin with prayer, asking God to give you insight, understanding, and an open heart to listen to and follow his word.

Jacob's daughter Dinah is raped by the local Canaanite prince, who then wants to marry her. Her brothers Levi and Simeon then execute a bloody revenge.

STUDY

Read the study notes on 34:1-2 and 34:3-4. What does this story tell us about the character of the Canaanites?

Read the study note on 34:1-31. What does this story say to later Israelites about their relationship with the Canaanites? Does this story have any implications for how Christians live in the world today?

Read the study note on 34:5-7. How would you evaluate Jacob's actions in response to the rape of his daughter? How should he have acted?

Read the study note on 34:13-17. How does deception again play a role in the life of Jacob and his family? Is this a legitimate or illegitimate strategy? Why or why not?

FURTHER STUDY (Optional)

Read the study note on 34:8-10. Why would Hamor want an alliance with Jacob?

Read the study note on 34:30. Why does Jacob respond with fear? Is it justified?

REFLECTION

What does God seem to be saying to you through what you have studied today?

Talk to God about what you have read, any questions or concerns you might have, and what you think he might be saying to you today. You can write your prayer here if you wish.

DAY 4 ♦ Genesis 35:1-20

READING: **GENESIS 35:1-20**
Begin with prayer, asking God to give you insight, understanding, and an open heart to listen to and follow his word.

Jacob and his family make a clean break with the paganism of Paddan-aram, and God reaffirms his covenant with Abraham through his grandson Jacob.

STUDY
Read the study note on 35:1-7 and Gen 28:20-22. Why did Jacob return to Bethel now?

Read the study note on 35:2-4. Why was it appropriate that Jacob's family destroyed all their idols at this moment? What constitutes an idol in our world today?

Read the study notes on 35:5 and 35:11-12. How does God's name "El Shaddai" ("God Almighty") help explain the terror on the part of the surrounding people and the confidence of Jacob and his family?

Read the study note on 35:20. What does this comment tell us about the composition of Genesis and about the factuality of the event?

FURTHER STUDY (Optional)
Read the study note on 35:6-7 and "Altars" on p. 91. What is the significance behind Jacob's construction of altars in the places where he lived?

Read the study note on 35:10 and go back and read 32:22-32. Why do you think Jacob's name change is reaffirmed here?

Read the study note on 35:3. Where has God made his presence known to Jacob so far in his life story?

REFLECTION
What does God seem to be saying to you through what you have studied today?

PRAYER
Talk to God about what you have read, any questions or concerns you might have, and what you think he might be saying to you today. You can write your prayer here if you wish.

DAY 5 ◆ Genesis 35:21–37:1

READING: **GENESIS 35:21–37:1**
Begin with prayer, asking God to give you insight, understanding, and an open heart to listen to and follow his word.

With Isaac's death, one era closes and another one begins. Attention now turns to the children of Esau, the unchosen line, and then to the children of Jacob, the chosen line.

STUDY
Read the study note on 36:1-43. Why did the narrator of Genesis deal with Esau before Jacob (similarly, Ishmael's descendants are treated in 25:12-26 before Isaac's)?

Read the study note on 36:1-8. What is the significance of the contrast between the birth places and ultimate locations of Esau's and Jacob's children?

Read the study notes on 36:15-19 and 36:40-43. What do these verses tell us about Esau and the nation (Edom) that descended from him?

FURTHER STUDY (Optional)

Read the study note on 35:22. What was Reuben's intent in this act and what were the consequences that resulted?

Read the study note on 37:1. Do you find it true that worldly success comes more quickly than spiritual blessing? Explain.

REFLECTION

What does God seem to be saying to you through what you have studied today?

PRAYER

Talk to God about what you have read, any questions or concerns you might have, and what you think he might be saying to you today. You can write your prayer here if you wish.

GROUP SESSION

READING: **GENESIS 32:1–37:1**

Read the passage together as a group.

DISCUSSION

You can use the following questions to guide what you share in the discussion. Give each person at least one opportunity to share with the others.

What did you learn from Gen 32:1–37:1? What was one thing that stood out to you as you studied this passage? How did Gen 32:1–37:1 surprise you? Do you have questions about this passage or the study materials that haven't been answered? What does God seem to be saying to you through what you have studied?

You can choose from among these topics to generate a discussion among the members of your group, or you can write your thoughts about one or more of these topics if you're studying solo.

1. How does Jacob's character change as he moves into the Promised Land?

2. How does God work in Jacob's life to make him more spiritually mature? Has God worked in similar or comparable ways in your life or in the lives of people you know?

3. What do we learn from the relationship between Jacob and Esau in these chapters? What does it tell us about them and about later Israel and Edom? Can we learn anything about ourselves and our relationships from these stories?

GROUP REFLECTION

What is God saying to us as a group through Gen 32:1–37:1?

ACTION

What are we going to do, individually or as a group, in response to what God is saying to us?

PRAYER

How should we pray for each other in response to God's message to us in this passage?

Take turns talking to God about this passage and about what he is saying.

NEXT: **GENESIS 37:2–41:57 (Joseph Goes Down to Egypt, from Slave to Prince)**

*Joseph Goes
Down to Egypt,
from Slave
to Prince*

GENESIS
37:2–41:57

OUTLINE

DAY 1 ... Genesis 37:2-36

DAY 2 ... Genesis 38:1-30

DAY 3 ... Genesis 39:1-23

DAY 4 ... Genesis 40:1-23

DAY 5 ... Genesis 41:1-57

Group Session

READING: GENESIS 37:2-36

Begin with prayer, asking God to give you insight, understanding, and an open heart to listen to and follow his word.

Jacob's favoritism leads to sibling rivalry that ends with Joseph being sold to traders who take him to Egypt.

STUDY

Read the study note on 37:3. How does Jacob show his favoritism toward Joseph? Why does Jacob favor Joseph over his other sons? *Coat - inheritance Rachel, old age*

Read the study note on 37:8. What differences do you see between Joseph and his brothers? Can you give examples from your own life where you have seen envy destroy a person's ability to lead? *jealousy, bitterness*

Read the study notes on 37:21-24, 37:26, and 37:29-30. Compare and contrast the roles of Reuben and Judah in this passage. *R - deception   J - concern for Joseph*

FURTHER STUDY (Optional)

Read the study note on 37:28. Why would the text refer to the caravan as both Ishmaelite as well as Midianite? *also decendents of A B.*

Read the study note on 37:31-35. How does deception continue to play a role in Jacob's life? *now he is being lied too*

REFLECTION

What does God seem to be saying to you through what you have studied today? *O what a tangled web   what man intends for evil God can use for good*

A88

PRAYER

Talk to God about what you have read, any questions or concerns you might have, and what you think he might be saying to you today. You can write your prayer here if you wish.

DAY 2 ◆ Genesis 38:1-30

READING: **GENESIS 38:1-30**

Begin with prayer, asking God to give you insight, understanding, and an open heart to listen to and follow his word.

The focus turns to Judah. His two older sons act wickedly and are killed, and then Judah himself wrongs his daughter-in-law, Tamar.

STUDY

Read the study note on 38:1-30. Why is there an interruption of the story of Joseph and his brothers with this story that focuses on Judah and his family? *accents the problem of assimilation IDOLITRY*

Read the study note on 38:8. What is levirate marriage and how does it play out in this story? *Continue ones lineage · family name*

Read the study notes on 38:24-26 and 38:26. In what way is Tamar more righteous than Judah? *honesty*

FURTHER STUDY (Optional)

Read "Judah" on p. 107. How does the episode with Tamar fit into the context of Judah's whole life? *He is humbled + man's up, helps him become prepared - "transform".*

Read the study notes on 38:17 and 38:18. What would be the modern equivalent to Judah leaving his seal? *Collateral*

REFLECTION

What does God seem to be saying to you through what you have studied today? *God is in control*

A89

Talk to God about what you have read, any questions or concerns you might have, and what you think he might be saying to you today. You can write your prayer here if you wish.

DAY 3 ◆ Genesis 39:1-23

READING: **GENESIS 39:1-23**

Begin with prayer, asking God to give you insight, understanding, and an open heart to listen to and follow his word.

Joseph's presence as a servant in the Egyptian Potiphar's house results in divine blessing and prosperity. However, Joseph is falsely accused by his owner's wife and ends up in an Egyptian jail.

STUDY

Read the study note on 39:1-23. How does Joseph contrast with Judah as in the previous chapter? Why did Potiphar's house prosper?

Integrity , God's blessing

Read the study note on 39:6-10. How do Joseph's decisions in this chapter reflect the teaching of Proverbs?

J. was guided by the fear of the Lord - the Beginning of wisdom

Read the study note on 39:21-23. Why did the prison prosper? What does this tell us about Joseph?

God was with him + kept giving him responsibility. faithful in a little ...

FURTHER STUDY (Optional)

Read the study note on 39:19-20. Why do you think God would let Joseph be treated so unfairly?

Joseph is a TYPE of Christ. a life given away to save the people

REFLECTION

What does God seem to be saying to you through what you have studied today?

God is strong and loving and in control

A90

DAY 4 ◆ Genesis 40:1-23

READING: **GENESIS 40:1-23**

Begin with prayer, asking God to give you insight, understanding, and an open heart to listen to and follow his word.

In jail, Joseph interprets the dreams of two of Pharaoh's officers, the chief cup-bearer and the chief baker.

STUDY

Read the study note on 40:1-23. What do Joseph's actions in this chapter tell us about his relationship with God?

Read the study note on 40:5-8. Why do the dreams bother the two Egyptian officials?

Do you think God still communicates to us through dreams? Why or why not?

FURTHER STUDY (Optional)

Read the study note on 40:1-4. Why is Joseph given more and more responsibility in the prison? Are there any lessons for your life in this?

Read the study notes on 40:14-15 and 40:23. What did Joseph hope for from the chief cup-bearer? Were his hopes eventually realized?

REFLECTION

What does God seem to be saying to you through what you have studied today?

Talk to God about what you have read, any questions or concerns you might have, and what you think he might be saying to you today. You can write your prayer here if you wish.

DAY 5 ◆ Genesis 41:1-57

READING: GENESIS 41:1-57

Begin with prayer, asking God to give you insight, understanding, and an open heart to listen to and follow his word.

Pharaoh has had disturbing dreams, and Joseph's ability to interpret dreams comes to his attention. Joseph interprets the dreams as warning about a coming famine and is promoted to a position of importance, in which he helps Egypt prepare for the famine.

STUDY

Read the study notes on 41:8 and 41:16. What does the contrast between Joseph and the Egyptian wise men tell us about God?

Read "Famine" on p. 103. What is the role of the famine in the story about Joseph?

Read the study note on 41:45. What do these gifts from Pharaoh signify?

FURTHER STUDY (Optional)

Read the study note on 41:33-36. How do Joseph's actions illustrate Proverbs' teaching about planning?

Read the study note on 41:37-40. Exactly how would this story about Joseph encourage later Israelites?

Read the study note on 41:50-52. At the end of this chapter, what can we say about Joseph's character?

REFLECTION

What does God seem to be saying to you through what you have studied today?

PRAYER

Talk to God about what you have read, any questions or concerns you might have, and what you think he might be saying to you today. You can write your prayer here if you wish.

GROUP SESSION

READING: **GENESIS 37:2–41:57**

Read the passage together as a group.

DISCUSSION

You can use the following questions to guide what you share in the discussion. Give each person at least one opportunity to share with the others.

What did you learn from Gen 37:2–41:57? What was one thing that stood out to you as you studied this passage? How did Gen 37:2–41:57 surprise you? Do you have questions about this passage or the study materials that haven't been answered? What does God seem to be saying to you through what you have studied?

TOPICS FOR DISCUSSION

You can choose from among these topics to generate a discussion among the members of your group, or you can write your thoughts about one or more of these topics if you're studying solo.

1. In Gen 50:20 Joseph looks over his life and says, "You intended to harm me, but God intended it all for good. He brought me to this position so I could save the lives of many people." Reviewing Gen 37:2–41:57, describe how God has used harmful things to bring about good things so far in the story.

2. How is Joseph a role model for our character, attitudes, and actions today?

3. Summarize the roles that Reuben and Judah play in Gen 37:2–41:57.

GROUP REFLECTION

What is God saying to us as a group through Gen 37:2–41:57?

ACTION

What are we going to do, individually or as a group, in response to what God is saying to us?

PRAYER

How should we pray for each other in response to God's message to us in this passage?

Take turns talking to God about this passage and about what he is saying.

NEXT: **GENESIS 42:1–45:28 (Joseph and His Brothers)**

*Joseph and
His Brothers*

GENESIS
42:1–45:28

OUTLINE

DAY 1 ... Genesis 42:1-28

DAY 2 ... Genesis 42:29–43:18

DAY 3 ... Genesis 43:19–44:13

DAY 4 ... Genesis 44:14-34

DAY 5 ... Genesis 45:1-28

Group Session

DAY **1** ◆ Genesis 42:1-28

READING: **GENESIS 42:1-28**

Begin with prayer, asking God to give you insight, understanding, and an open heart to listen to and follow his word.

The famine hits Canaan, and Joseph's brothers come to Egypt to ask for food. Joseph treats them with suspicion and demands that they bring their youngest brother, Benjamin, to prove that they are not spies.

STUDY

Read the study notes on 42:1–44:34 and 42:8. What was Joseph's purpose behind hiding his identity from his brothers? Why did the brothers not recognize Joseph?

Read the study notes on 42:9 and 42:15-17. Why did Joseph treat his brothers as he did?

Read the study note on 42:21-23. In light of the brother's reaction, how had they changed?

FURTHER STUDY (Optional)

Read the study note on 42:6-7. Exactly how was Joseph's first dream (37:5-11) fulfilled?

Read the study notes on 42:24, 42:25-28, and 42:25. If Joseph had already forgiven his brothers, why does he continue to test them?

REFLECTION

What does God seem to be saying to you through what you have studied today?

PRAYER

Talk to God about what you have read, any questions or concerns you might have, and what you think he might be saying to you today. You can write your prayer here if you wish.

DAY 2 ◆ Genesis 42:29–43:18

READING: **GENESIS 42:29–43:18**

Begin with prayer, asking God to give you insight, understanding, and an open heart to listen to and follow his word.

The brothers return to Jacob and report that the Egyptian official wants them to bring Benjamin. Jacob refuses, but after the famine grows more severe, he reluctantly relents.

STUDY

Read the study note on 42:29-34. Why do you think the brothers did not talk with Jacob about their sense of divine retribution for their wrong against Joseph? What does this tell you about the nature of guilt?

Read the study note on 42:37. What do you think of Reuben's attempt to get his father to allow Benjamin to go with them to Egypt?

Read the study note on 43:8-10. What do you think of Judah's attempt to get his father to allow Benjamin to go with them to Egypt? How does it compare and contrast with Reuben's attempt?

FURTHER STUDY (Optional)

Read the study note on 43:13-14. What do Jacob's words reveal about his character and attitude? Is he a good role model for us?

Read the study note on 43:16. In what way was the feast a test? In what way was it a celebration?

REFLECTION
What does God seem to be saying to you through what you have studied today?

PRAYER
Talk to God about what you have read, any questions or concerns you might have, and what you think he might be saying to you today. You can write your prayer here if you wish.

DAY **3** ◆ Genesis 43:19–44:13

READING: **GENESIS 43:19–44:13**
Begin with prayer, asking God to give you insight, understanding, and an open heart to listen to and follow his word.

Joseph (still unrecognized) gives his brothers grain. Unknown to them, however, he also puts his silver cup in Benjamin's sack. Joseph's men arrest Benjamin, setting off a crisis.

STUDY
Read the study note on 43:30. Why was Joseph still unwilling to reveal his identity to his brothers even though they brought Benjamin safe and sound?

Read the study note on 44:1-34. How had the brothers showed they had changed?

Read the study note on 44:2. Do you think Joseph was going overboard in his testing of his brothers? When is enough, enough?

FURTHER STUDY (Optional)
Read the study note on 44:9-10. Why would the brothers propose such a harsh penalty for themselves?

Read the study note on 44:5. What was Joseph doing with a diviner's cup?

Read the study note on 44:13. What do you imagine was going through the brothers' minds when the attendant discovered Joseph's diviner's cup in Benjamin's sack?

REFLECTION
What does God seem to be saying to you through what you have studied today?

PRAYER
Talk to God about what you have read, any questions or concerns you might have, and what you think he might be saying to you today. You can write your prayer here if you wish.

DAY 4 ◆ Genesis 44:14-34

READING: **GENESIS 44:14-34**
Begin with prayer, asking God to give you insight, understanding, and an open heart to listen to and follow his word.

When confronted with the possibility of having to leave Benjamin in Egypt, Judah steps forward to offer himself as a slave in Benjamin's place.

STUDY
Read the study note on 44:14. Why were the brothers so fearful? How did the event fulfill the dream in Gen 37:10?

Read the study note on 44:16. How does Judah's statement show his growing maturity?

Read the study note on 44:18-34. What do Judah's actions and statements teach us about the nature of intercession?

FURTHER STUDY (Optional)
Read the study note on 44:32-34. Compare and contrast Judah's willingness to sacrifice himself with the sacrifice of Christ.

Read "Judah" on p. 107. Summarize how Judah's character developed through the story of Joseph.

How has God used Judah and his descendants in redeeming the world (see especially Gen 49:10)? Do you see a connection between his character and the way God used him?

REFLECTION

What does God seem to be saying to you through what you have studied today?

PRAYER

Talk to God about what you have read, any questions or concerns you might have, and what you think he might be saying to you today. You can write your prayer here if you wish.

DAY 5 ◆ Genesis 45:1-28

READING: **GENESIS 45:1-28**

Begin with prayer, asking God to give you insight, understanding, and an open heart to listen to and follow his word.

In response to Judah's intercession, Joseph reveals his true identity to his brothers. They reconcile, and Pharaoh invites them to go get their father and move to Egypt.

STUDY

Read the study note on 45:5-8. How did God bring Joseph to Egypt for the purpose of keeping the people of God alive during the famine?

Read the study note on 45:9-13. Why did Jacob and his family have to move to Egypt?

Read the study note on 45:14-15. What can we learn about reconciliation from this story?

FURTHER STUDY (Optional)

Read the study note on 45:24. From what we know about the brothers, why do you think

Joseph had to warn them not to argue with each other? If they did argue with each other, what do you think they would say?

Read the study note on 45:27. How did Jacob react to the news about and from Joseph? How is this a fulfillment of Gen 15:13-16?

Read the study note on 45:10. Then look at the map on p. 109 ("Egypt, about 1700 BC") and read the accompanying caption. Why was Goshen a good place to settle?

REFLECTION

What does God seem to be saying to you through what you have studied today?

PRAYER

Talk to God about what you have read, any questions or concerns you might have, and what you think he might be saying to you today. You can write your prayer here if you wish.

GROUP SESSION

READING: GENESIS 42:1–45:28

Read the passage together as a group.

DISCUSSION

You can use the following questions to guide what you share in the discussion. Give each person at least one opportunity to share with the others.

What did you learn from Gen 42:1–45:28? What was one thing that stood out to you as you studied this passage? How did Gen 42:1–45:28 surprise you? Do you have questions about this passage or the study materials that haven't been answered? What does God seem to be saying to you through what you have studied?

TOPICS FOR DISCUSSION

You can choose from among these topics to generate a discussion among the members of your group, or you can write your thoughts about one or more of these topics if you're studying solo.

1. In these chapters, Joseph puts his brothers through an elaborate test to see if they had changed before he revealed his identity to them. Can you imagine similar situations today where someone might put others through a test like this?

2. Study the roles of Reuben, Judah, Simeon, and Benjamin in these chapters. How would you describe their characters?

3. In Gen 50:20 Joseph looks over his life and says, "You intended to harm me, but God intended it all for good. He brought me to this position so I could save the lives of many people." Review Gen 42:1–45:28 and describe how God has used harmful things to bring about good things so far in the story. Have there been similar situations in your life or the lives of those you know?

GROUP REFLECTION

What is God saying to us as a group through Gen 42:1–45:28?

ACTION

What are we going to do, individually or as a group, in response to what God is saying to us?

PRAYER

How should we pray for each other in response to God's message to us in this passage?

Take turns talking to God about this passage and about what he is saying.

NEXT: **GENESIS 46:1–50:26 (You Meant It for Evil; God Meant It for Good)**

You Meant It for Evil; God Meant It for Good

GENESIS
46:1–50:26

OUTLINE

DAY 1 ... Genesis 46:1-34

DAY 2 ... Genesis 47:1-31

DAY 3 ... Genesis 48:1-22

DAY 4 ... Genesis 49:1-33

DAY 5 ... Genesis 50:1-26

Group Session

DAY **1** ◆ Genesis 46:1-34

READING: **GENESIS 46:1-34**

Begin with prayer, asking God to give you insight, understanding, and an open heart to listen to and follow his word.

In response to Pharaoh's invitation, Jacob and his family move to Egypt and arrive in the land of Goshen.

STUDY

Read the study note on 46:1. Turn to the map on p. 49 ("Abram in Canaan") and locate Beersheba. What historical echoes come to mind when thinking of Jacob's (Israel's) journey to Egypt?

Read the study note on 46:8-27. What is the significance of this genealogy?

FURTHER STUDY (Optional)

Read the study note on 46:27. What is the significance of the number seventy?

Read the study note on 46:30. What is the significance of this reunion?

REFLECTION

What does God seem to be saying to you through what you have studied today?

PRAYER

Talk to God about what you have read, any questions or concerns you might have, and what you think he might be saying to you today. You can write your prayer here if you wish.

DAY 2 ◆ Genesis 47:1-31

READING: **GENESIS 47:1-31**

Begin with prayer, asking God to give you insight, understanding, and an open heart to listen to and follow his word.

As Jacob's family settles in Goshen, Jacob meets and blesses Pharaoh. Joseph's management during the famine allows Pharaoh to amass great wealth and allows both Egypt and the people of God to survive.

STUDY

Read the study note on 47:7-10. How does Jacob's blessing of Pharaoh relate to the promise to Abraham in Gen 12:1-3?

Read the study note on 47:27. How does the fact that Israel's population grew in Egypt relate to the Abrahamic promise in Gen 12:1-3?

Read the study note on 47:29-31. Why would Jacob care whether or not he was buried with his ancestors?

FURTHER STUDY (Optional)

Read the study note on 47:21. How did Pharaoh make all the people slaves? What role did Joseph play in the strengthening of the house of Pharaoh?

Read the study note on 47:31. What do Jacob's actions and words tell us about his character?

REFLECTION

What does God seem to be saying to you through what you have studied today?

Talk to God about what you have read, any questions or concerns you might have, and what you think he might be saying to you today. You can write your prayer here if you wish.

DAY 3 ◆ Genesis 48:1-22

READING: **GENESIS 48:1-22**

Begin with prayer, asking God to give you insight, understanding, and an open heart to listen to and follow his word.

Jacob blesses Joseph's sons, Manasseh and Ephraim.

STUDY

Read the study note on 48:1-22. What role does faith play in Jacob's blessing of Ephraim and Manasseh?

Read the study note on 48:5-7. Why did Jacob bless Ephraim and Manasseh?

Read the study note on 48:14. Why did God often choose the second rather than the firstborn?

FURTHER STUDY (Optional)

Read "Blessing" on p. 113. What are the similarities and differences of blessing as described in the Old Testament and the New Testament?

Read the study note on 48:15-16. What do we learn about God from Jacob's threefold invocation?

REFLECTION

What does God seem to be saying to you through what you have studied today?

PRAYER

Talk to God about what you have read, any questions or concerns you might have, and what you think he might be saying to you today. You can write your prayer here if you wish.

DAY 4 ◆ Genesis 49:1-33

READING: **GENESIS 49:1-33**

Begin with prayer, asking God to give you insight, understanding, and an open heart to listen to and follow his word.

Jacob delivers his last blessings and curses on his children in a way that will impact their descendants.

STUDY

Read the study note on 49:1-28. What do you make of the fact that each son's character and behavior affects the lives of his descendants?

Read the study note on 49:5-7. Why were Levi and Simeon not blessed with land? Why did Levi become more important than Simeon?

Read the study note on 49:10. What role was Judah to play in the future?

FURTHER STUDY (Optional)

Read "Death" on p. 115. What surprises you about the biblical view of death? Does death bring you comfort or fear?

Read the study note on 49:8-12. What do these metaphorical descriptions of Judah mean in relationship to the Messiah?

Read the study note on 49:33. Reflect on Jacob's long life. In what ways did he change from the time he was born till the time of his death?

REFLECTION

What does God seem to be saying to you through what you have studied today?

PRAYER

Talk to God about what you have read, any questions or concerns you might have, and what you think he might be saying to you today. You can write your prayer here if you wish.

DAY 5 ◆ Genesis 50:1-26

READING: **GENESIS 50:1-26**

Begin with prayer, asking God to give you insight, understanding, and an open heart to listen to and follow his word.

Jacob dies and the brothers fear for their lives, thinking that Joseph will now punish them. In his reply Joseph expresses his clear sense of God's hand behind all of his life's events. The book closes with the notice of Joseph's death.

STUDY

Read the study note on 50:3. Why would the Egyptians mourn for Jacob?

Read the study note on 50:15-18. Why did the brothers fear reprisal? Why did Joseph weep?

Read the study note on 50:19-21. Why didn't Joseph seek revenge against his brothers?

FURTHER STUDY (Optional)

Read the study note on 50:7-9. What emotions do you think Joseph felt after returning (even temporarily) to the Promised Land after such a long time away?

Read the study note on 50:24-25. Why did Joseph want his bones taken back to the Promised Land?

Read the study note on 50:26. Why do you think Genesis ends with a comment about Joseph's death? What does this section anticipate in the future?

REFLECTION

What does God seem to be saying to you through what you have studied today?

PRAYER

Talk to God about what you have read, any questions or concerns you might have, and what you think he might be saying to you today. You can write your prayer here if you wish.

GROUP SESSION

READING: **GENESIS 46:1–50:26**

Read the passage together as a group.

DISCUSSION

You can use the following questions to guide what you share in the discussion. Give each person at least one opportunity to share with the others.

What did you learn from Gen 46:1–50:26? What was one thing that stood out to you as you studied this passage? How did Gen 46:1–50:26 surprise you? Do you have questions about this passage or the study materials that haven't been answered? What does God seem to be saying to you through what you have studied?

TOPICS FOR DISCUSSION

You can choose from among these topics to generate a discussion among the members of your group, or you can write your thoughts about one or more of these topics if you're studying solo.

1. Why did God bring his people to Egypt?

2. God made a promise to Abraham in Gen 12:1-3. How does the story of Joseph show that God continued to be faithful to his promises?

3. How does Joseph's life illustrate that God can use even evil actions to bring about his good blessings (see Gen 50:19-20)? How does Jesus' death and resurrection illustrate this principle (Acts 2:22-24; 3:14-21)? How does this relate to Paul's words that all things work for the good of those who love God (Rom 8:26-28)?

GROUP REFLECTION

What is God saying to us as a group through Gen 46:1–50:26?

ACTION

What are we going to do, individually or as a group, in response to what God is saying to us?

PRAYER

How should we pray for each other in response to God's message to us in this passage?

Take turns talking to God about this passage and about what he is saying.

THE BOOK OF GENESIS

THE BOOK OF

GENESIS

Genesis is the book of beginnings—of the universe and of humanity, of sin and its catastrophic effects, and of God's plan to restore blessing to the world through his chosen people. God began his plan when he called Abraham and made a covenant with him. Genesis traces God's promised blessings from generation to generation, to the time of bondage and the need for redemption from Egypt. It lays the foundation for God's subsequent revelation, and most other books of the Bible draw on its contents. Genesis is a source of instruction, comfort, and edification.

SETTING

When Genesis was written, the children of Israel had been slaves in Egypt for 400 years. They had recently been released from bondage and guided through the desert to meet the Lord at Mount Sinai, where he had established his covenant relationship with them and had given them his law through Moses. Israel was now poised to enter the Promised Land and receive the inheritance that God had promised Abraham.

While enslaved in Egypt, the Israelites had adopted many pagan ideas and customs from their Egyptian masters (e.g., Exod 32:1-4). They were influenced by false concepts of God, the world, and human nature (e.g., Exod 32), and were reduced to being slaves rather than owners and managers of the land. Perhaps they had forgotten the great promises that God had made to Abraham, Isaac, and Jacob, or perhaps they had concluded that the promises would never be fulfilled.

Before entering the Promised Land, the Israelites needed to understand the nature of God, his world, and their place in it more clearly. They needed to embrace their identity as descendants of Abraham, Isaac, and Jacob. Genesis provided the needed understanding.

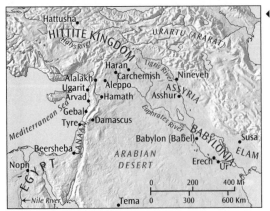

◀ **The Ancient Near East, about 2100 BC.** Humanity spread out from the mountains of URARTU (ARARAT) and populated the early centers of civilization. By the time of the patriarchs (Abraham, Isaac, and Jacob), many of the cities were ancient.
ASSHUR 2:14; 10:22; 25:3; 25:18
ASSYRIA 10:11
BABYLON (BABEL), BABYLONIA 10:9-10; 11:1-9; 14:1, 9
CANAAN 9:18-27; 10:18-19; 12:5-10
DAMASCUS 14:15; 15:2
EGYPT 12:10–13:1; 15:18; 37:28-36; 39:1–50:26
ELAM 10:22; 14:1, 9
ERECH 10:10; Ezra 4:9
HAMATH 10:18; 2 Sam 8:9-10; 2 Kgs 14:28; 23:33
HARAN 11:26-32; 12:4-5; 27:43; 28:10; 29:4; Acts 7:2-4
SUSA Ezra 4:9; Neh 1:1; Esth 1:2; Dan 8:2
UR 11:28, 31; 15:7; Neh 9:7
URARTU (ARARAT) 8:4

SUMMARY

Genesis traces God's work to overcome with blessing the curse that came on humankind because of sin. The book arranges family traditions, genealogies, historical events, and editorial comments into a single, sustained argument.

Every section but the first has the heading, "This is the account" (or *These are the generations;* Hebrew *toledoth*); each of the *toledoth* sections explains the history of a line of descent. In each case, a deterioration of well-being is followed by an increasing focus on God's plan to bless the world. This plan is the basis for God's covenant with his people; as the blessing develops, the covenant is clarified. By the end of the book, the reader is ready for the fulfillment of the promises in Israel's redemption from bondage (see Exodus).

The first section (1:1–2:3) does not have the *toledoth* heading, and logically so—it is the account of creation "in the beginning" (1:1). The work of creation is wrapped in God's approval and blessing as he fulfills his plan.

The next section (2:4–4:26) focuses on the creation of human life (2:4-25) and traces what became of God's creation because of Adam's and Eve's sin (3:1-13), the curse on their sin (3:14-24), and the extension of sin to their descendants (4:1-24). Humanity no longer enjoyed God's rest; instead, they experienced guilt and fear. So they fled from God and developed a proud civilization.

Independence from God resulted in the downward drift of human life (5:1–6:8). The genealogy of 5:1-32 begins by recalling that human beings were made in God's image and were blessed by him (5:1-2). As the genealogy is traced, the death of each generation reminds the reader of the curse, with Enoch providing a ray of hope that the curse is not final. In 6:1-8, we learn that God regretted having made humans and decided to judge the earth. Noah, however, received God's favor and provided a source of hope (5:29; 6:8).

The next section (6:9–9:29) brings the curse of judgment through the flood followed by blessing in a new beginning. A renewed creation began, purged of the abominable evil that had invaded and ruined the human race.

The world's population expanded into various nations (10:1–11:9) whose people were bent on disobedience. The population of the earth by Shem,

OUTLINE

1:1–2:3
Creation

2:4–4:26
What Happened to the Creation

5:1–6:8
The Account of Adam's Descendants

6:9–9:29
The Account of Noah's Family

10:1–11:9
The Account of Noah's Sons

11:10-26
The Account of Shem's Descendants

11:27–25:11
The Account of Terah's Descendants

25:12-18
The Account of Ishmael's Descendants

25:19–35:29
The Account of Isaac's Descendants

36:1–37:1
The Account of Esau's Descendants

37:2–50:26
The Account of Jacob's Descendants

TIMELINE

2166 / 1990 BC*
Abraham is born

2091 / 1915 BC
Abraham moves to Canaan

2080 / 1904 BC
Ishmael is born

2066 / 1890 BC
Sodom and Gomorrah are destroyed, Isaac is born

2006 / 1830 BC
Jacob and Esau are born

1898 / 1722 BC
Joseph is sold into slavery

1885 / 1709 BC
Joseph begins governing Egypt

1876 / 1661 BC
Jacob moves to Egypt

1446 / 1270 BC
Israel leaves Egypt (the Exodus), moves to Mount Sinai

1406 / 1230 BC
Israel enters Canaan

* The two dates harmonize with the traditional "early" chronology and a more recent "late" chronology of the Exodus. All dates are approximate. Please see "Chronology: Abraham to Joshua," p. 118.

Ham, and Japheth seemed fruitful (10:1-32), but the nations were divided by languages and boundaries (10:5, 20, 31). Because of their rebellion, God dispersed them to prevent greater wickedness (11:1-9).

After the chaos of the scattered nations, 11:10-26 brings the focus to Abram, through whom God chose to bring blessing to all. The rest of the book (11:27–50:26) tells of God's blessing Abram and his descendants. God first made a covenant with Abram (11:27–25:11), promising him a great nation, land, and name. As time went on, God made the specific terms of the covenant clearer, and Abram's faith grew deeper.

In each generation, Genesis gives a brief account of the families that are not Israel's ancestors before turning to the line of Israel. After briefly reporting what became of Ishmael (25:12-18), Genesis traces in detail what happened to Isaac and his family (25:19–35:29).

True to the pattern of the book, Esau's line (Edom) is dealt with briefly (36:1–37:1) before the chosen line of Jacob the heir. The final section (37:2–50:26) concerns Jacob's family, centering on the life of Joseph. In the land of Canaan, the family became corrupt under Canaanite influence to the point of beginning to merge with them (ch 38). To preserve the line of blessing, God sent the family into Egypt where they could flourish, remain separate (43:32; 46:34), and become a great nation. The book closes with the promise of the Lord's coming to rescue his people from Egypt (50:24-26).

"God rested on the seventh day from all his work that he had done. And he blessed the seventh day. . . ." And we ourselves will be a "seventh day" when we shall be filled with his blessing and remade by his sanctification. . . . Only when we are remade by God and perfected by a greater grace shall we have the eternal stillness of that rest in which we shall see that he is God.

ST. AUGUSTINE
City of God, sec. 22.30

AUTHORSHIP

Both Scripture and tradition attribute the Pentateuch (Genesis—Deuteronomy) to Moses. No one was better qualified than Moses to have written this book. Since he was educated in all the wisdom of the Egyptians (Acts 7:22), he had the literary skills to collect and edit Israel's traditions and records and to compose this theological treatise. His unique communion with God gave him the spiritual illumination, understanding, and inspiration needed to guide him. He had good reason to write this work—to provide Israel with the theological and historical foundation for the Exodus and the covenant at Sinai, and to establish the new nation in accord with the promises made to their ancestors.

Most scholars, however, do not accept that Moses wrote Genesis. The prevailing critical view, called the *Documentary Hypothesis*, is that Genesis was compiled from various sources by different groups of people. In such approaches, there is seldom a word about divine revelation or inspiration. For those who understand the Bible as God's inspired word, such theories often seem unnecessarily complicated and conjectural. Genesis can be understood much more straightforwardly as the product of Moses' genius under God's inspiration with later editorial adjustments. (See further "Introduction to the Pentateuch: Authorship," p. 12).

COMPOSITION

Biblical scholars of all stripes have always acknowledged that various sources were used in writing Genesis and other historical texts in the Bible (such as Kings and Luke). Moses used collections of family records, oral traditions, ancient accounts of primeval events, and genealogies to write Genesis. Those sources could have been incorporated as received, or the author may have changed their style and wording, stitching them together with additional material for the particular purpose of tracing the foundations of Israelite faith.

Genesis also includes passages and expressions that are obviously later editorial glosses. Some sections (such as the list of Edomite kings, 36:31-43) could have been added during the early days of the monarchy. There is no conflict in saying that Genesis was authored by Moses and augmented by subsequent editors whose work was guided by the Holy Spirit. Given these considerations, conservative scholars find it plausible that the biblical material accurately records actual events.

LITERARY CHARACTER

Genesis includes various types of literature. Several suggestions have been made as to the nature of the materials.

Myth. Mythological literature explains the origins of things symbolically through the deeds of gods and supernatural creatures. For ancient peoples, myths were beliefs that explained life and reality. Whole systems of ritual activities were developed to ensure that the forces of fertility, life, and death would continue year by year. Some of these rituals gave rise to cult prostitution (see 38:15, 21-22).

It would be very difficult to classify the material in Genesis as myth. Israel had one God, not a multitude. The nation of Israel had a beginning, a history, and a future hope. They saw God, rather than gods and other supernatural creatures, as the primary actor in the world. Their worship was not cosmic, magical, or superstitious, but a reenactment of their own rescue from Egypt and a celebration of God's factual intervention in history and their hope in his promises.

If Genesis uses elements of mythological language, it is to display a deliberate contrast with pagan concepts and to show that the Lord God is sovereign over such ideas. For example, the ancients worshiped the sun as a god, but in Genesis the sun serves the Creator's wishes (1:14-18). The book of Genesis is a cemetery for lifeless myths and dead gods. Genesis is not myth.

Etiology. A number of scholars describe the Genesis narratives as *etiologies,* stories that explain the causes of factual reality or traditional beliefs. The implication is that such stories were made up for explanatory purposes and do not describe historical events. For example, if one says that the story of Cain and Abel was made up to explain why shepherds and farmers do not get along, the account loses its integrity as factual history.

Etiological elements certainly occur in Genesis, because the book gives the foundation and rationale for almost everything that Israel would later do. For example, the creation account of Gen 2 ends with the explanation, "This explains why a man leaves his father and mother. . . ." The event as it happened explains why marriage was conducted the way it was, but to say that a story explains something is quite different from saying that the story was fabricated to explain it. The stories of Genesis are not fictional tales invented to explain later customs and beliefs.

History. Many scholars object to regarding Genesis as history, for two basic reasons: (1) Genesis explains events as caused by God, and the inclusion of the supernatural is regarded as proof that the material is theological reflection and thus not historically reliable; and (2) the events in Genesis cannot be validated from outside sources; no other records have demonstrated that Abraham existed or that any of his family history occurred.

> *Genesis is not interested in parading Abraham, Isaac, and Jacob as examples of morality. Therefore, it does not moralize on them. [Genesis] is bringing together the promises of God to the patriarchs and the faithfulness of God in keeping those promises.*
>
> VICTOR P. HAMILTON
> *The Book of Genesis: Chapters 1–17,* p. 46

Modern philosophies of history exclude the supernatural as an explanation of historical events, but there is no reason to do so arbitrarily. If God exists and is able to act, then he might very well be the ultimate cause of all historical events and the immediate cause of specific historical events. The Israelites were not as distrustful of supernatural events as are modern critics; they experienced such events frequently as God acted among them to fulfill the promises recorded in Genesis.

It is true that no direct evidence of the patriarchs or the events in Genesis has been found, but archaeology confirms the plausibility of Genesis by showing that the historical situation in that era (Middle Bronze I, 2000–1800 BC) corresponds closely to what Genesis portrays. It is unlikely that this would be so if Genesis were not an accurate record of the facts. When all the archaeological and historical data are assembled around the events, they fit perfectly within the setting, and the details of the narratives make perfectly good sense.

Theological Interpretation.   Genesis was not intended as a chronicle of the lives of the patriarchs, a history for history's sake, or a complete biography. It is clearly a theological interpretation of selected records of the nation's ancestors, but this does not destroy its historicity. Interpretations of an event can differ, but the offering of interpretations is a good witness to the actuality of the events. The author retold the events in his own way, but he did not invent them.

Tradition.   What was thus committed to writing is tradition in the reverent care of literary genius. Scholars prefer words such as "traditions" or even "sagas" to describe these narratives. Doing so only makes the claim that the stories preserve the memory of the people of Israel; it makes no claim that the events themselves are historical. The biblical understanding, however, is that these stories were recorded under divine inspiration and are therefore historically true and reliable.

In all probability, Abram brought the primeval accounts and the family genealogies from Mesopotamia, and stories about the family were added to these collections. Joseph could easily have preserved all the traditions, both written and oral, in Egypt with his own records. Moses could then have compiled the works substantially in their present form while adding his editorial comments. Since he worked under God's inspiration and guidance, the narratives record exactly what God wanted written and correspond precisely to reality.

Instructional Literature.   Since Genesis is the first book of the Pentateuch (the "Torah" or Law), it may be best to classify it as "Torah Literature" (Hebrew *torah,* "instruction, law"). Genesis is instructional literature that lays the foundation for the Law. It is theological interpretation of the historical traditions standing behind the covenant at Sinai. In the way it is written, one may discern that Moses was preparing his readers to receive God's law and the fulfillment of the promises made to their forefathers. Genesis is therefore a unique work. Theology, history, and tradition come together to instruct God's people and prepare them for blessing.

MEANING AND MESSAGE
Israel's most important questions were answered by the Genesis narratives. Life and death, the possession of the land of Canaan, and how Israel ended up in Egypt are explained as God's providential working in history. Israel was part of God's plan in this world. His plan had

a starting point at creation and will have an end point in the future when the promises are completely fulfilled.

Israel, the Chosen People.   The central theme of Genesis is that God made a covenant with Abraham and his descendants. He promised to make them his own people, heirs of the land of Canaan, and a blessing to the world. Genesis gave Israel the theological and historical basis for its existence as God's chosen people.

Israel could trace its ancestry to the patriarch Abraham and its destiny to God's promises (12:1-3; 15:1-21; 17:1-8). Because the promise of a great nation was crucial, much of Genesis is devoted to family concerns of the patriarchs and their wives, their sons and heirs, and their birthrights and blessings. The record shows how God preserved and protected the chosen line through the patriarchs. Israel thus knew that they had become the great nation promised to Abraham. Their future was certainly not in slavery to the Egyptians, but in Canaan, where they would live as a free nation and as the people of the living God, and where they could mediate God's blessings to the people of the world.

Blessing and Curse.   The entire message of Genesis turns on the motifs of blessing and cursing. The promised blessing would give the patriarchs innumerable descendants and give the descendants the land of promise; the blessing would make them famous in the earth, enable them to flourish and prosper, and appoint them to bring others into the covenant blessings. The curse, meanwhile, would alienate, deprive, and disinherit people from the blessings. The effects of the curse are felt by the whole race as death and pain and as God's judgment on the world.

These motifs continue throughout the Bible. Prophets and priests spoke of even greater blessings in the future and an even greater curse for those who refuse God's gift of salvation and its blessings. The Bible reminds God's people not to fear human beings, but to fear God, who has the power to bless and to curse.

Good and Evil.   In Genesis, that which is good is blessed by God: It produces, enhances, preserves, and harmonizes with life. That which is evil is cursed: It causes pain, diverts from what is good, and impedes or destroys life. Genesis traces the perpetual struggle between good and evil that characterizes our fallen human race. God will bring about the greater good, build the faith of his people, and ultimately triumph over all evil (cp. Rom 8:28).

God's Plan.   Genesis begins with the presupposition that God exists and that he has revealed himself in word and deed to Israel's ancestors. It does not argue for the existence of God; it simply begins with God and shows how everything falls into place when the sovereign God works out his plan to establish Israel as the means of restoring blessing to the whole world.

God's Rule.   Genesis is the fitting introduction to the founding of theocracy, the rule of God over all creation that was to be established through his chosen people. Genesis lays down the initial revelation of God's sovereignty. He is the Lord of the universe who will move heaven and earth to bring about his plan. He desires to bless people, but he will not tolerate rebellion and unbelief. His promises are great, and he is fully able to bring them to fruition. To participate in his plan has always required faith, for without faith it is impossible to please him (Heb 11:6).

FURTHER READING

VICTOR P. HAMILTON
The Book of Genesis (1990)

DEREK KIDNER
Genesis (1967)

KENNETH A. MATHEWS
Genesis (1996)

ALLEN P. ROSS
Creation and Blessing (1988)
Genesis in *Cornerstone Biblical Commentary*, vol. 1 (2008)

GORDON WENHAM
Genesis 1–15 (1987)
Genesis 16–50 (1994)

1. CREATION (1:1–2:3)
In the Beginning (1:1-2)

1 In the beginning God ᵃcreated the ᵇheavens and the ᶜearth. ²The earth was formless and empty, and darkness covered the deep waters. And the ᵈSpirit of God was hovering over the surface of the waters.

Six Days of Creation (1:3-31)
Day One: Light, Darkness

³Then God said, "Let there be light," and there was light. ⁴And God saw that the light was good. Then he separated the light from the darkness. ⁵God called the light "day" and the darkness "night."

And evening passed and morning came, marking the first day.

Day Two: Sky, Waters

⁶Then God said, "Let there be a space between the waters, to separate the waters of the heavens from the waters of the earth." ⁷And that is what happened. God made this space to separate the waters of the earth from the waters of the heavens. ⁸God called the space "sky."

And evening passed and morning came, marking the second day.

Day Three: Land, Sea, Vegetation

⁹Then God said, "Let the waters beneath the sky flow together into one place, so dry ground may appear." And that is what happened. ¹⁰God called the dry ground "land" and the waters "seas."

1:1
Ps 89:11; 102:25
Isa 42:5; 48:13
John 1:1-2
ᵃ*bara'* (1254)
ᵇ*shamayim* (8064)
▸ Gen 1:27
▸ Exod 16:4
ᶜ*'erets* (0776)
▸ Gen 9:11

1:2
Isa 45:18
ᵈ*ruakh* (7307)
▸ Gen 45:27

1:3
Isa 45:7
2 Cor 4:6

1:6
Job 26:10
Ps 136:5-6

1:9
Ps 95:5
Prov 8:29
Jer 5:22
2 Pet 3:5

. . . .

The Creation (1:1–2:3)

Ps 33:6-9
Prov 3:19; 8:22-31
Isa 40:26-28; 45:11-12, 18-19
Jer 10:11-16
John 1:1-4
Rom 8:18-25
2 Cor 5:17
Col 1:15-20
Rev 4:11; 21:1-5

The creation account in Genesis is foundational to the message of the entire Bible, not just of Genesis or the Pentateuch. Understanding the early chapters of Genesis is thus crucial to forming a biblical worldview.

This part of Genesis deals with fundamental questions: Who created the world, and for what purpose? Why is the world in its present condition? Genesis answers these questions, dispelling the idolatry that Israel had acquired from their pagan masters in Egypt. In the Promised Land, they would also be surrounded by people who believed in many false gods and worshiped created things rather than the Creator. Genesis taught Israel that the one true God created and has absolute authority over all things; he alone is worthy of worship.

Every worldview attempts to explain where the world came from, what is wrong with the world, and how it can be set right again. The creation account in Genesis teaches that as God made the world, it was "very good" (1:31). Through creation, God turned disorder into restful order and emptiness into the fullness of abundant life. In this environment, humans enjoyed unbroken fellowship with their Creator until their rebellion severed that fellowship and implanted evil in human hearts (ch 3; see chs 4–6). The world's evil does not come from some defect in creation; God put the world under a curse because of human rebellion.

Since that first rebellion, humans have been alienated from the Creator and no longer recognize his presence and authority. This alienation results in shame, fractured relationships with God and other humans, estrangement from the rest of creation, and death (3:7-19). Since that time, God has been working purposefully in history to restore humans to fellowship with him, which he is doing through Jesus Christ. Restored humans are a new creation (Gal 6:15); through Jesus, eternal life is open to all and God will one day renew all things (see Isa 65:17-25; Rom 8:19-22). The whole cosmos will be made new (Rev 21:1).

. . . .

1:1–2:3 These verses introduce the Pentateuch (Genesis—Deuteronomy) and teach Israel that the world was created, ordered, and populated by the one true God and not by the gods of surrounding nations. • God blessed three specific things: animal life (1:22-25), human life (1:27), and the Sabbath day (2:3). This trilogy of blessings highlights the Creator's plan: Humankind was made in God's image to enjoy sovereign dominion over the creatures of the earth and to participate in God's Sabbath rest.

1:1 *In the beginning God created the heavens and the earth* (or *In the beginning when God created the heavens and the earth, . . .* or *When God began to cre-*

ate the heavens and the earth, . . .): This statement summarizes the entire creation account (1:3–2:3). Already a key question—Who created the world?—is answered (see also Prov 8:22-31; John 1:1-3). Although the modern naturalistic mindset rejects this question and that of creation's purpose, Genesis affirms God's role and purpose in creation. • The common name for *God* (Hebrew *'elohim*) emphasizes his grand supremacy. The word *'elohim* is plural, but the verbs used with it are usually singular, reflecting the consistent scriptural proclamation of a single, all-powerful God. • *created* (Hebrew *bara'*): In the OT, God is always the agent of creation

expressed by this verb. It describes the making of something fresh and new—notably the cosmos (1:1, 21; 2:3), humankind (1:27), the Israelite nation (Isa 43:1), and the future new creation (Isa 65:17). • *The heavens and the earth* are the entire ordered cosmos.

1:2 This verse gives the background for the summary in 1:1 and the detailed description in 1:3–2:3. God's creative utterances bring order to the chaotic state of the universe. • *formless . . . empty* (Hebrew *tohu . . . bohu*): This terse idiom means something like "wild and waste." It sets a stark contrast to the final ordered state of the heavens and the earth (1:1). • *deep waters*

1:10
Ps 33:7; 95:5

1:11
Gen 2:9
Ps 104:14
Matt 6:30

1:14
Ps 74:16; 104:19

1:15
Gen 1:5

1:16
Ps 8:3; 19:1-6;
136:8-9
1 Cor 15:41

1:18
Jer 33:20, 25

1:20
Gen 2:19
Ps 146:6
ᵉnepesh (5315)
▸ Gen 2:7

1:21
Ps 104:25-28

And God saw that it was good. ¹¹Then God said, "Let the land sprout with vegetation—every sort of seed-bearing plant, and trees that grow seed-bearing fruit. These seeds will then produce the kinds of plants and trees from which they came." And that is what happened. ¹²The land produced vegetation—all sorts of seed-bearing plants, and trees with seed-bearing fruit. Their seeds produced plants and trees of the same kind. And God saw that it was good.

¹³And evening passed and morning came, marking the third day.

Day Four: Sun, Moon, Stars
¹⁴Then God said, "Let lights appear in the sky to separate the day from the night. Let them be signs to mark the seasons, days, and years. ¹⁵Let these lights in the sky shine down on the earth." And that is what happened. ¹⁶God made two great lights—the larger one to govern the day, and the smaller one to govern the night. He also made the stars. ¹⁷God set these lights in the sky to light the earth, ¹⁸to govern the day and night, and to separate the light from the darkness. And God saw that it was good.

¹⁹And evening passed and morning came, marking the fourth day.

Day Five: Birds, Fish
²⁰Then God said, "Let the waters swarm with fish and other ᵉlife. Let the skies be filled with birds of every kind." ²¹So God created great sea creatures and every living thing that scurries and

. . . .

Formless	CHAOS	Empty
DAY 1 (1:3-5) Light, Dark	HEAVENS	DAY 4 (1:14-19) Sun, Moon, Stars
DAY 2 (1:6-8) Water, Sky	WATER & SKY	DAY 5 (1:20-23) Birds, Fish
DAY 3 (1:9-13) Sea, Land	EARTH	DAY 6 (1:24-31) Animals, Humans
Formed	COSMOS	Filled
	DAY 7 (2:2-3) Rest	

◄ **The Structure of the Creation Account** (1:1–2:3). God transformed chaos into the present cosmos. In the first three days, he transformed the formless void into the structured universe—the HEAVENS (outer space), the WATER and SKY, and the EARTH (cp. Exod 20:11; Ps 135:6). In the second three days, he populated each empty realm. The seventh day (2:1-3) stands apart: As God's day of rest, it provides the weekly pattern for human activity (Exod 20:8-11; 31:12-17) and speaks of the rest that God promised to those who live by faith in him (see Heb 3:7–4:11).

two collections of water (cp. Job 37:18; Ezek 1:22). In the ancient Near East, the cosmos was understood as a three-tier system, with rain originating from the outermost tier (see 7:11-12 and note).

1:9-10 *Let the waters . . . flow together:* Other ancient cultures viewed the sea as a hostile force. Genesis shows God as further restraining chaos (see note on 1:2) by prescribing specific boundaries for the sea. The flood—an act of God's judgment (6:7)—undid these boundaries and returned the earth to chaos (7:1-24).

1:14-31 On days 4–6, God filled the domains that had been formed during days 1–3 (1:3-13).

1:14 *Let them . . . mark the seasons, days, and years:* The movement of the heavenly bodies defined Israel's liturgical calendar, whose roots in creation gave a sacred timing to Israel's festivals and celebrations (see Exod 23:15; Lev 23:4).

1:16 In the surrounding pagan cultures, the *two great lights* were worshiped as deities, but in Genesis they serve God and humanity (see Ps 136:7-9; Jer 31:35). The sun and moon are not named; they are simply called *the larger one* and *the smaller one*. Not including their names may have reminded Israel that they were not gods. • *govern:* Cp. 1:26, 28; Ps 136:9. • *the stars:* The starry heavens testify to God's creative power as they proclaim his glory (Ps 19:1; 148:3). They do not predict the future, as Israel's neighbors believed (see Jer 10:2).

1:21 Contrary to the pagan idea that the *great sea creatures* were co-eternal with God, Genesis states that *God created* them and is sovereign over them. The Hebrew word *tanninim* ("*creatures*") elsewhere refers to crocodiles (Ezek 29:3), powerful monsters (Jer 51:34), or the sea creature, Leviathan (Isa 27:1; cp. Job 41:1-34).

(Hebrew *tehom*): Some scholars say this alludes to the Mesopotamian goddess Tiamat (representing chaos), but Genesis views *tehom* as inhospitable chaos, not as a deity or goddess that God engaged in cosmic battle. • *the Spirit of God:* God directly superintended the creation process.

1:3-13 In the first three days, God formed the chaos into a habitable world.

1:3 *Then God said:* Nothing in Gen 1 is created apart from God's powerful word (cp. Ps 33:6, 9). • *"Let there be . . . ,"* *and there was:* God's command enacted his will to create the world. God is not a part of creation or limited by it; he is the supreme ruler over everything (cp. Neh 9:6).

1:4 *Light* is antithetical to chaotic *darkness* (1:2); the light is declared *good* but the darkness is not (cp. John 1:5). God is the source of this light (cp. 1:14-19). God *separated* the light, as he did water

(cp. 1:6-8), by his creative word. Light is associated with life and blessing (Job 38:19-20; Ps 19:1-6; 97:11; 104:19-20; Isa 60:19-20) and sets a boundary on the darkness that would destroy cosmic order. Darkness often typifies terror, death, and evil (see 15:12; Job 18:6, 18; Ps 88:12; Eph 5:11-12; 1 Jn 1:5).

1:5 *God called* (or *named*): To name something is to exercise authority over it (see also 2:19-20). • *day:* The Hebrew *yom* can refer to daylight (1:5a), to a 24-hour period (1:5b), or to an unspecified time period (2:4b, "When," literally *in the day;* cp. Exod 20:8-11). • *evening . . . morning:* The Hebrew day began at sundown, just as the first day began with darkness and brought the first morning light.

1:6-8 The creation account describes the appearance of things from a human perspective. The *sky* is viewed as a shiny dome that is a buffer between

swarms in the water, and every sort of bird—each producing offspring of the same kind. And God saw that it was good. 22Then God blessed them, saying, "Be fruitful and multiply. Let the fish fill the seas, and let the birds multiply on the earth."

23And evening passed and morning came, marking the fifth day.

Day Six: Animals, Humankind
24Then God said, "Let the earth produce every sort of animal, each producing offspring of the same kind—livestock, small animals that scurry along the ground, and wild animals." And that is what happened. 25God made all sorts of wild animals, livestock, and small animals, each able to produce offspring of the same kind. And God saw that it was good.

26Then God said, "Let us make human beings in our image, to be like us. They will reign over the fish in the sea, the birds in the sky, the livestock, all the wild animals on the earth, and the small animals that scurry along the ground."

27 So God fcreated human beings in his own image.

In the image of God he fcreated them;
male and female he fcreated them.

28Then God blessed them and said, "Be fruitful and multiply. Fill the earth and govern it. Reign over the fish in the sea, the birds in the sky, and all the animals that scurry along the ground."

29Then God said, "Look! I have given you every seed-bearing plant throughout the earth and all the fruit trees for your food. 30And I have given every green plant as food for all the wild animals, the birds in the sky, and the small animals that scurry along the ground—everything that has life." And that is what happened.

31Then God looked over all he had made, and he saw that it was very good! And evening passed and morning came, marking the sixth day.

Sabbath Rest (2:1-3)
2 So the creation of the heavens and the earth and everything in them was completed. 2On the seventh day God had finished his work of creation, so he rested from all his work. 3And God gblessed the seventh day and declared it holy, because it was the day when he rested from all his work of hcreation.

1:24 Gen 2:19
1:26 Gen 5:1; 9:6 Ps 8:6-8 Acts 17:28-29
1:27 *Matt 19:4 *Mark 10:6 'bara' (1254) › Gen 2:3
1:29 Gen 9:3 Ps 104:13; 136:25
1:30 Ps 104:14; 145:15
1:31 Ps 104:24
2:1 Deut 4:19; 17:3 Ps 104:2 Isa 45:12
2:2 Exod 20:11; 31:17 *Heb 4:4
2:3 Isa 58:13 *barak* (1288) › Gen 12:2 *bara'* (1254) › Gen 6:7
2:4 Gen 1:3-31 Job 38:4-11

1:22 God blessed them: God's blessing commissions and enables the fulfillment of what God has spoken (see "Blessing" at 48:8-20, p. 113). • *Let the fish . . . let the birds:* These directives define the blessing. The fish and birds are fertile by God's command, not by pagan ritual, as some of Israel's neighbors thought.

1:26 Let us make is more personal than the remote "Let there be" (e.g., 1:3, 6). • The plural *us* has inspired several explanations: (1) the Trinity; (2) the plural to denote majesty; (3) a plural to show deliberation with the self; and (4) God speaking with his heavenly court of angels. The concept of the Trinity—one true God who exists eternally in three distinct persons—was revealed at a later stage in redemptive history, making it unlikely that the human author intended that here. Hebrew scholars generally dismiss the plural of majesty view because the grammar does not clearly support it (the plural of majesty has not been demonstrated to be communicated purely through a plural verb). The plural of self-deliberation also lacks evidence; the only clear examples refer to Israel as a corporate unity (e.g., 2 Sam 24:14). God's speaking to the heavenly court, however, is well-attested in the OT (see 3:22; 11:7; 1 Kgs 22:19-22; Job 1:6-12; 2:1-6; 38:7; Ps 89:5-6; Isa 6:1-8; Dan 10:12-13). • *human beings:* Or *man*; Hebrew reads *'adam*. • The descriptors *in our image* and *like us* are virtually synonymous in Hebrew. Humans enjoy a unique relationship with God. • *They will reign:* Humans represent the Creator as his ambassadors, vice-regents, and administrators on earth.

1:27 The first poetry of Genesis reflectively celebrates God's climactic feat in creating humankind. • *human beings* (Or *the man;* Hebrew reads *ha-'adam*): This term is often used to denote humanity collectively (see 6:1, 5-7; 9:5-6). Though traditionally translated "man," gender is not at issue here; both *male* and *female* are included.

1:28 God blessed them: See note on 1:22; see also 17:16; 48:16; Deut 7:13. • *said:* God's message to humankind is direct and intimate; we are stewards of his delegated authority. • *govern. . . . Reign:* As God's vice-regents, humans are entrusted with the care and management of the world God created (see also 9:2; Ps 8:5-8).

1:29-30 These verses highlight the extent (*throughout the earth*) and variety (*every seed-bearing plant . . . all the fruit trees*) of God's provision for humans, *animals*, and *birds*.

1:31 The Creator declares his work *good* seven times in ch 1; following the creation of human beings, God declares it all *very good*.

2:1-3 Humankind is the high point of God's creative acts (1:26-31), while day 7 is the climax of the creation week. When God *rested* (or *ceased*), he endorsed all of creation—there was nothing more to do! This seven-day framework structured Israel's week, with the *seventh day* as the precedent for their weekly Sabbath. The Sabbath was intended to celebrate God's finished work; the seventh day would be set apart as *holy* and dedicated to the Creator, who also rested (see Exod 20:8-11; 31:12-17; cp. Matt 12:1-8; Rom 14:5-6; Col 2:16-17; Heb 4:1-11).

2:3 The first six days of creation involved separation (light from darkness, day from night, water from dry land). The last act of creation separated what is ordinary from what is *holy*, thus laying the foundation for Israel's worship. It also anticipated a coming age of rest (Heb 4:1-11; 12:2; 13:14). • The absence of the usual "morning and evening" reflects the Creator's willingness to enter into unending fellowship with humankind.

2:5
Gen 1:11
2:7
Gen 3:19
Job 33:4
Ps 103:14
Ezek 37:5
Zech 12:1
John 20:22
*1 Cor 15:45
ʰnepesh (5315)
▸ Deut 12:23

2. WHAT HAPPENED TO THE CREATION (2:4–4:26)

Superscription (2:4a)

4This is the account of the creation of the heavens and the earth.

Creation of Man and Woman (2:4b-25)
Creation of the Man

When the LORD God made the earth and the heavens, 5neither wild plants nor grains were growing on the earth. For the LORD God had not yet sent rain to water the earth, and there were no people to cultivate the soil. 6Instead, springs came up from the ground and watered all the land. 7Then the LORD God formed the man from the dust of the ground. He breathed the breath of life into the man's nostrils, and the man became a living ⁱperson.

Human Sexuality (1:27-28)

Gen 2:18-25
Lev 18:1-30
Deut 22:13-29
Ruth 4:11-13
2 Sam 11:2-27
Ps 127:3-5
Eccl 2:8-11
Song 1–8
Mal 2:15-16
Matt 19:3-12
1 Cor 6:12–7:40
Eph 5:31-33
1 Thes 4:3-8

When God created the first human beings in his own image, he created them as sexual beings, male and female (1:27). Through their sexuality, they were to fill and govern the world (1:28) and provide intimate companionship for one another in marriage (2:18-25). Male and female sexuality is central to what it means to be human.

Sexual intimacy united the first man and woman as one being, an effect that sexual intimacy continues to have. Since biblical sexuality is not just physical but has the total person in view, it validates sexual relations only as part of the partners' mutual commitment to each other's ultimate good. The Bible speaks of engaging in sexual intercourse as literally "knowing" another person intimately (see note on 4:1). Since creation, the purpose of sexuality has been to join people in an intimate union of marriage—a permanent and loving heterosexual commitment—that God blesses and calls "very good" (1:27-28, 31). The sexual relationship cements the marriage bond in an intimacy that continues even when reproduction is no longer possible.

Although sexuality was created before sin, it did not emerge unscathed from human rebellion. Sexuality is a powerful force that is easily corrupted if not carefully channeled (see Lev 18; 1 Thes 4:3-8). Sexual intimacy apart from marital commitment perverts the order that God intended for creation. Incest, for example, violates sexual boundaries (see Lev 18:7-14), collapses family structures (see 19:30-38), and fragments the community. Whereas perverted sexuality tears the community down (see 38:1-30; 39:7-9; Judg 19:1–20:48) and exalts the individual (see 2 Sam 13:11-14), biblical sexuality builds up the sexual partners and the community.

Our sexual identity has been damaged through our fall into sin (ch 3), but God has redeemed it through the death and resurrection of Jesus Christ (see 1 Cor 6:12-20; Eph 5:31-33). He restores sexual wholeness in those who trust his work in their lives by the Holy Spirit (1 Cor 6:9-11, 15-20; 1 Thes 4:1-5). Those who commit their sexuality to Christ can testify to God's love for his people (Eph 5:25-33).

2:4–4:26 This account (see note on 2:4) of the heavens and the earth is not a second creation account; rather, it is a theological and historical expansion on 1:1–2:3. The focus is now on what the cosmos produced rather than on its creation. Special attention is given to the first man and woman. As the story progresses, it is colored by contrasts of good and evil, knowledge and ignorance, life and death, harmony and discord.

2:4 *This is the account* (literally *These are the generations*): This or a similar phrase is repeated throughout Genesis, creating an internal outline for the book. In other occurrences, it introduces the genealogy or story of a key personality (5:1; 6:9; 10:1; 11:10; 11:27; 25:12; 25:19; 36:1; 37:2). • Some have argued that the first half of 2:4 belongs with 1:1–2:3, but it is more likely the

introduction to the account that follows. • *LORD God* (Hebrew *Yahweh Elohim*) is the second name used for God in the early chapters of Genesis. *Elohim* (1:1–2:3) describes the all-powerful creator God. *Yahweh Elohim* speaks of the eternal God who formed a lasting covenant with Israel (Exod 3:6, 13-15). Accordingly, 2:4-25 focuses on God as provider more than as creator. The three themes of sexuality, dominion, and food in ch 1 are now addressed in reverse order (food, 2:8-17; dominion, 2:18-20; sexuality, 2:21-25).

2:5 *cultivate:* Work does not result from sin; it was part of the original structure of creation and is directly tied to human identity and purpose (1:28; 2:15).

2:6 *springs* (Or *mist,* as traditionally rendered): The word refers to subterranean springs that rose to the surface of the ground.

2:7 In 1:1–2:3, creation happens at a distance, by divine command ("Let there be . . . and that is what happened"). In this account, the creative act is much more intimate (see also 2:8-9, 21-22). • *from the dust of the ground:* In Hebrew, *'adamah* ("ground") forms a wordplay with *'adam* ("man"). The earth remains the definitive reference point for humans, who in death return to dust (3:17-19; 4:11; Job 4:19; 10:8-9; Isa 29:16). • *breathed . . . into the man's nostrils:* God's *breath* is not imparted to other animals; only humans are formed in God's image (1:27) and enjoy dialogue with their Creator (2:16-17; 3:8-13). They alone have spiritual awareness and moral conscience (see Job 32:8).

Creation of the Garden

⁸Then the LORD God planted a garden in Eden in the east, and there he placed the man he had made. ⁹The LORD God made all sorts of trees grow up from the ground—trees that were beautiful and that produced delicious fruit. In the middle of the garden he placed the tree of life and the tree of the knowledge of good and evil.

¹⁰A river flowed from the land of Eden, watering the garden and then dividing into four branches. ¹¹The first branch, called the Pishon, flowed around the entire land of Havilah, where gold is found. ¹²The gold of that land is exceptionally pure; aromatic resin and onyx stone are also found there. ¹³The second branch, called the Gihon, flowed around the entire land of Cush. ¹⁴The third branch, called the Tigris, flowed east of the land of Asshur. The fourth branch is called the Euphrates.

The First Command

¹⁵The LORD God placed the man in the Garden of Eden to tend and watch over it.

2:8
Gen 3:23; 13:10
Isa 51:3
Joel 2:3

2:9
Gen 3:22
Prov 3:18; 11:30
Rev 2:7; 22:2, 14

2:10
Rev 22:1, 17

2:14
Gen 15:18
Deut 1:7
Dan 10:4

2:15
Gen 2:8

Biblical Marriage (2:18-25)

Gen 24:65-67
Ps 45:8-15
Is 54:5
Hos 2:19-20
Mal 2:10-16
1 Cor 7:1-40
2 Cor 6:14-16
Eph 5:21-33
Heb 13:4
1 Pet 3:1-7

At the first wedding, God the Father gave the bride away to the groom and witnessed the couple's interaction in his sanctuary-garden (2:18-25). Married love is thus a binding covenant commitment before God. Breaching that covenant (e.g., through adultery) is a crime against persons and against God, who is a divine witness to and guarantor of the marriage covenant (see Mal 2:10-16; cp. Gen 39:6-9; Jer 3:1; 1 Cor 6:9-10; Heb 13:4). Although marriage is exclusive, it is not private. It is legally declared in public, with community recognition, witnesses, and accountability (see Lev 20:10-12; Deut 22:22; Jer 29:20-23).

Marriage is also a metaphor of the Lord's relationship with his people, first with Israel (see Exod 19:3-6; 20:2-6; 34:14; Isa 54:5; Ezek 16:1-63; Hos 2:19-20), and then with the church (see 2 Cor 11:2; Eph 5:21-33). A marriage points to something greater than itself—God's people (Christ's "bride") await the return of Christ (the "groom"). Married Christians are called to live in unity and dignity as they anticipate the wedding feast of the Lamb (Rev 19:6-9). Christ will live forever with his faithful people in glory (Rev 19:7; 21:2, 9).

2:8-14 Analogous to the sacred time marked out on the seventh day of creation (2:2-3), the sacred space of the **garden in Eden** was separate from the surrounding world. It functioned as a garden-temple or sanctuary because the Lord manifested his presence there in a special way.

2:8 *Eden* was the general location in which the **garden** was placed, not the garden itself. The term could mean "plain," "delight," or "fertility." The description that follows favors the idea of fertility. • *in the east:* The exact location of Eden is left to speculation, but it was east of Canaan, Israel's later home. • God *placed the man* in the garden for divine fellowship and physical blessing (see also 2:15 and note).

2:9 Beauty and bounty characterized humanity's original environment (cp. 13:10). • The *tree of life* represented God's presence and provision. The one who ate of it would have everlasting life (3:22), which made it a rich image for later Israelite and Christian reflection (Prov 3:18; 11:30; 13:12; Rev 2:7; 22:2, 14, 19). The candlestick in Israel's Tabernacle may have been a stylized representation of it (Exod 25:31-35). • Eating the fruit of the *tree of the knowledge of good and evil* enabled humanity's capacity for wisdom (3:6) and moral discernment (3:5, 22; cp.

Deut 1:39, "innocent"). Eating from it represented a human grasp for autonomy and wisdom that were God's alone (cp. Prov 30:1-4). Humans sidestepped God's revelation as the means of moral discernment, flaunting their independence rather than submitting to God's will (cp. Prov 1:7). Choosing human wisdom over God's instruction brings death and destruction (see Ps 19:7-9; Ezek 28:6, 15-17).

2:10-14 This detailed description portrays the eastern region around Eden as a mountain with rivers flowing out to the world. Eden's beauty and fertility enriched the whole earth.

2:10 The *river* that was *watering the garden* was a material blessing (bringing agricultural fertility) and a symbol of God's presence (cp. Ps 46:4; Ezek 47:1-12; Zech 14:8; Rev 22:1-2). • *dividing into four branches* (literally *heads*): The common understanding is that one river had its source in Eden, flowed down through the garden, and then split into the four rivers named.

2:11 The *Pishon* and the Gihon (2:13) cannot be identified with certainty. If *the land of Havilah* was in southeast Arabia or on the African coast, as some biblical data suggest (see 10:7; 25:18; 1 Sam 15:7), then the Pishon was possibly the Nile River. Josephus thought that Havilah and the Pishon were in India

(*Antiquities* 1.1.3). Two other proposals suggest: (1) rivers in the mountains of eastern Turkey where the Tigris and Euphrates (2:14) also flow, and (2) the marshy delta near the Persian Gulf. Current geographical conditions make any theory impossible to prove conclusively.

2:12 The magnificence and fertility of the garden are pictured as spreading to the surrounding regions through the rivers flowing out from it. The four rivers possibly imply that the garden's bounty flowed out to the four corners of the earth. • *Gold* and *onyx* were later used for decorating the Tabernacle, the Temple (Exod 25:3-9; 1 Chr 29:2), and the priests' clothing (Exod 28:9-14, 20). • *Resin* was used in sacred incense (Exod 30:34).

2:13 *Gihon:* Though unknown, proposals have included the Nile (as in the Greek version of Jer 2:18; Josephus, *Antiquities* 1.1.3), the Jordan, or, according to Jewish tradition, a river that formerly ran through the Kidron Valley (1 Kgs 1:33; 2 Chr 33:14). • Although *Cush* is the name of ancient Ethiopia, Mesopotamian regions associated with Babylon seem to be the immediate setting (see 10:8); Cush is possibly the land of the Kassites, a dynasty ruling in Babylonia.

2:14 *Tigris . . . Euphrates:* These well-known rivers flow from the mountains of eastern Turkey.

2:16
Gen 3:1-3

2:17
Gen 3:1, 16-17
Deut 30:15, 19-20
Rom 6:23
Jas 1:15

2:18
Gen 3:12
Prov 18:22

2:19
Gen 1:20-25

2:22
1 Cor 11:8-9
1 Tim 2:13

2:23
Gen 29:14
Eph 5:28-30

2:24
*Matt 19:5
*1 Cor 6:16
Eph 5:31

2:25
Gen 3:7, 10-11

¹⁶But the LORD God warned him, "You may freely eat the fruit of every tree in the garden—¹⁷except the tree of the knowledge of good and evil. If you eat its fruit, you are sure to die."

Creation of the Woman

¹⁸Then the LORD God said, "It is not good for the man to be alone. I will make a helper who is just right for him." ¹⁹So the LORD God formed from the ground all the wild animals and all the birds of the sky. He brought them to the man to see what he would call them, and the man chose a name for each one. ²⁰He gave names to all the livestock, all the birds of the sky, and all the wild animals. But still there was no helper just right for him.

²¹So the LORD God caused the man to fall into a deep sleep. While the man slept, the LORD God took out one of the man's ribs and closed up the opening. ²²Then the LORD God made a woman from the rib, and he brought her to the man.

²³"At last!" the man exclaimed.

"This one is bone from my bone,
    and flesh from my flesh!
She will be called 'woman,'
    because she was taken from 'man.' "

²⁴This explains why a man leaves his father and mother and is joined to his wife, and the two are united into one.

²⁵Now the man and his wife were both naked, but they felt no shame.

. . . .

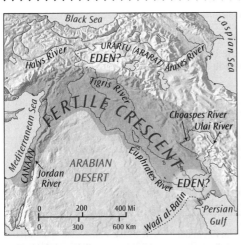

◄ **The Location of Eden (2:8-14).** Eden might have been located in the mountains of Ararat or near the Persian Gulf (see notes on 2:8-14). Possibilities for the four rivers (2:10-14) exist in either location (see note on 2:11). Eden represented God's presence on earth that was withdrawn at the Fall and reinaugurated at Sinai (see Exod 3:1-6; 24:9-18; 40:34-38).

distinctions (cp. 29:14). • Adam declares that "*She will be called 'woman'* (Hebrew *'ishah*) *because she was taken from 'man'* (Hebrew *'ish*)." He understood the nature of their connection (see Eph 5:28-29). Adam had earlier assessed the animals without finding the characteristics he needed in a partner. How different this evaluation is!

2:24 Marriage between a man and a woman is not just a human social construct but is rooted in the created order. • *a man leaves . . . and is joined:* Marriage entails a shift of loyalty from parents to spouse. • *the two are united into one:* Marriage and its commitments make it the most fundamental covenant relationship observed among humans. Marriage is a powerful image of Israel's covenant with God (Hos 2:14-23) and of Christ's relationship to the church (Eph 5:22-32). Marriage is designed as an inseparable, exclusive relationship between a man and a woman. • The family unit it creates is the basic building block of human society.

2:25 *both naked:* Prior to the Fall (ch 3), nakedness reflected innocence and trust. After the Fall, it denoted vulnerability and *shame* (see 9:22-23; Lev 18:1-23; Isa 47:3). Shame is more than embarrassment; it connotes exploitation and humiliation (see Deut 28:48; Isa 58:7; Jas 2:15-16).

2:15 *to tend and watch over:* The garden required maintenance and oversight. Tending the *Garden* was humanity's dignifying work. These roles in God's garden-sanctuary were later applied to God's Tabernacle (see Lev 8:35; Num 3:5-10; 4:46-49).

2:17 *except* (literally *but you must not eat*): This prohibition is given in the same legal format as Israel's Ten Commandments (see Exod 20:1-17; Deut 5:6-21). The Lord built law and obedience into the fabric of his covenant relationship with humanity. • *the knowledge of good and evil:* See note on 2:9. • *you are sure to die:* The consequences of disobedience would be immediate spiritual death (loss of relationship with God) and eventual physical death (see 3:22-23; Eccl 12:6-7).

2:18-23 As human creation was the climax of ch 1, so human intimacy is the high point of ch 2. God's concern for mutual human support and companionship finds no parallel in ancient Near Eastern literature.

2:18 *It is not good:* This is God's first negative assessment of an otherwise excellent creation (1:31). *The LORD God* is portrayed as a father who obtains a bride for his son (cp. 24:1-67). • The answer to the man's need is *a helper who is just right for him*; she is his perfect complement, made in the same image of God (1:26-27), given the same commission (1:28; 2:15), and obligated by the same prohibition (2:17). The man cannot fulfill his created purpose alone.

2:19-20 *to see what he would call them:* Following God's example (1:5, 8, 10), the man *chose a name for each* of the creatures. In so doing, he was exercising his reign over creation (1:26, 28).

2:19 *the man:* Or *Adam,* and so throughout the chapter.

2:21 *took out one of the man's ribs* (or *took a part of the man's side*): Cp. 2:23; Eph 5:28.

2:23 Adam recognized the woman as a "helper just right for him" (2:20). His celebration of her in poetry and song observed his unity with her, not their

The Ruin of God's Creation (3:1-24)
Temptation to Sin

3 The serpent was the shrewdest of all the wild animals the LORD God had made. One day he asked the woman, "Did God really say you must not eat the fruit from any of the trees in the garden?"

²"Of course we may eat fruit from the trees in the garden," the woman replied. ³"It's only the fruit from the tree in the middle of the garden that we are not allowed to eat. God said, 'You must not eat it or even touch it; if you do, you will die.'"

⁴"You won't die!" the serpent replied to the woman. ⁵"God knows that your eyes will be opened as soon as you eat it, and you will be like God, knowing both good and evil."

Man and Woman Rebel against the Creator
⁶The woman was convinced. She saw that the tree was beautiful and its fruit looked delicious, and she wanted the wisdom it would give her. So she took some of the fruit and ate it. Then she gave some to her husband, who was with her, and he ate it, too. ⁷At that moment their eyes were opened, and they suddenly felt shame at their nakedness. So they sewed fig leaves together to cover themselves.

God Interrogates the Man and Woman
⁸When the cool evening breezes were blowing, the man and his wife heard the LORD God walking about in the garden. So they hid from the LORD God among the trees. ⁹Then the LORD God called to the man, "Where are you?"

¹⁰He replied, "I heard you walking in the garden, so I hid. I was afraid because I was naked."

¹¹"Who told you that you were naked?" the LORD God asked. "Have you eaten from the tree whose fruit I commanded you not to eat?"

¹²The man replied, "It was the woman you gave me who gave me the fruit, and I ate it."

¹³Then the LORD God asked the woman, "What have you done?"

3:1
2 Cor 11:3
Rev 12:9; 20:2

3:2
Gen 2:16

3:3
Gen 2:17
Exod 19:12

3:4
John 8:44
2 Cor 11:3

3:5
Gen 2:17; 3:22
Isa 14:14
Ezek 28:2

3:6
2 Cor 11:3
1 Tim 2:14
Jas 1:14-15
1 Jn 2:16

3:8
Lev 26:12
Deut 23:14
Job 31:33

3:9
Gen 4:9; 18:9

3:10
Deut 5:5

3:12
Prov 28:13

3:13
2 Cor 11:3
1 Tim 2:14

. . . .

3:1-24 The rebellion of the man and the woman shattered their unity and harmony with earth, animals, each other, and God.

3:1 Genesis describes the deceiver as a *serpent*, one of the animals God created (see also 3:14 and note). He is later identified as Satan, the great enemy of God's people (Rev 12:9; 20:2). His manipulative language and his disguise as a serpent, *the shrewdest of all* creatures, show him as a master deceiver. Satan has various methods for opposing God's people (see 1 Chr 21:1; Zech 3:1-2); deception remains among his key strategies (cp. 2 Cor 11:3, 14). The Hebrew term for shrewd (*'arum*) can be positive ("prudent," Prov 14:8) or negative ("cunning," as here; Job 5:12). It forms a wordplay with "naked" (*'arummim*) in 2:25. Adam and Eve were naked and vulnerable; the serpent was shrewd and cunning. • Probably the serpent *asked the woman because the prohibition was given to Adam prior to Eve's creation (see 2:16-17).* Adam was probably aware of the serpent's cunning, having assessed and named all the animals before Eve was created (2:19-20, 23). • *Did God really say?* The deceiver began by twisting God's language to cast doubt on God's goodness. God's original prohibition applied to only one tree (2:16-17), not to all (*any*) of them.

3:2-3 The woman attempted to set the record straight; in the process, she belittled the privileges God had given her and her husband in several ways: (1) She reduced God's "freely eat" (2:16) to *may eat*; (2) she downplayed God's emphasis on the availability of fruit from every tree but one (2:17); (3) she added not touching to God's prohibition against eating (2:17); and (4) she softened the certainty of death (2:17).

3:4-5 *You won't die!* This is the exact negation of God's clear and emphatic words: "you are sure to die" (2:17). The serpent capitalizes on the woman's uncertainty by baldly denying the penalty and quickly diverting her attention to the supposed prize—to *be like God, knowing both good and evil.* The deceiver falsely implies that this would be an unqualified good for them. The term rendered God is *Elohim*; it can also mean "divine beings" (i.e., God and the angels; e.g., Ps 29:1; 89:7).

3:6 *She saw . . . she wanted:* The woman made two grave errors. (1) She assumed the right to decide what was and was not good, though God alone has this right; and (2) she coveted God's wisdom (see Deut 5:21). • *her husband . . . with her:* Although Scripture is clear about the woman's central role in the Fall (cp. 1 Tim 2:14), the man was clearly present and culpable as well. He comes to center stage in the verses that follow and in biblical theology. The consequence of his sin for the entire human race was immense. The Good News is that in Jesus Christ, the "second Adam," God has made salvation universally available (Rom 5:12-21).

3:7 *Shame* is opposite to the naked innocence Adam and Eve enjoyed prior to their rebellion (2:25). Their relationship with one another and with God was fractured. • *sewed fig leaves together:* These covered their physical bodies, but not their shame. They could not mend their broken relationships (see also 3:21 and note).

3:8 *When the cool evening breezes were blowing:* The Hebrew has traditionally been interpreted as referring to the cool part of the day, most likely the evening. Others think that the language refers to a powerful manifestation of God's presence (a *theophany;* see Exod 19:16-25; 1 Sam 7:10) as a storm. If this view is correct, the man and the woman were hiding from the sound of the Lord appearing in judgment (see 2 Sam 5:24; Ps 29). • *the man:* Or *Adam,* and so throughout the chapter. • God put *trees* in the garden as an environment for humanity to enjoy fellowship with God. Now the man and woman used them to evade the divine presence.

3:9-10 *Where are you?* The true intent of this rhetorical question is revealed in the man's answer (3:10). The real question was, why are you hiding? (cp. 4:9-10). • *I was afraid because I was naked:* Modesty was not the issue. The shame brought on by rebellion drove Adam and his wife to hide. Possibly they also feared punishment (see note on 3:8).

3:12 *It was the woman you gave me:* Rather than confessing, the man became evasive. He blamed the woman for giving him the fruit and God for giving him the woman.

3:13 *What have you done?* is another rhetorical question that is really an exclamation of horror (cp. 4:10). • *The serpent deceived me:* As the man implicated the woman (3:12), the woman accused the serpent. The serpent did play

3:14
Deut 28:15
Isa 65:25

3:15
John 8:44
Rom 16:20
Heb 2:14
'zera' (2233)
  • Gen 12:7

3:16
1 Cor 11:3
Eph 5:22
1 Tim 2:15

3:17
Job 5:7
Eccl 1:3
Rom 8:20-22

"The serpent deceived me," she replied. "That's why I ate it."

God Indicts and Convicts

¹⁴Then the LORD God said to the serpent,

"Because you have done this, you are cursed
more than all animals, domestic and wild.
You will crawl on your belly,
groveling in the dust as long as you live.
¹⁵ And I will cause hostility between you and the woman,

and between your offspring and her offspring.
He will strike your head,
and you will strike his heel."

¹⁶Then he said to the woman,

"I will sharpen the pain of your pregnancy,
and in pain you will give birth.
And you will desire to control your husband,
but he will rule over you."

¹⁷And to the man he said,

ADAM (2:4–3:24)

Gen 1:26-31;
4:25–5:5
Hos 6:6-7
Luke 3:38
Rom 5:12-21
1 Cor 15:22, 45-49
1 Tim 2:13-14

Adam was the first man, the father of the human race. God created the first couple in his image to populate the earth and rule the created order (1:26-31). God made Adam from earth and breathed life into him (2:7); he was to cultivate the garden (2:15), name the animals (2:19-20), and follow God's instructions (1:28; 2:16-17). God created the woman as a companion and helper for Adam (2:18-22). Eve's creation from Adam's rib portrays the unity that God intended for man and woman in marriage (2:23-25).

After the serpent deceived Eve into rejecting God's rule, Adam also rebelled (3:1-6). Their willful disobedience disrupted their relationship (3:7) and separated them from God. God looked for Adam after his rebellion; he was hiding among the trees, already aware of his alienation (3:8). When God questioned him, Adam blamed Eve and, by implication, God (3:12). Adam's rebellion brought hardship in governing the earth as well as physical and spiritual death (3:17-19, 22). God provided animal skins to cover Adam and Eve (3:21), and promised that Eve's offspring would defeat Satan (3:15; see Rom 16:20; Rev 12:1-9; 20:1-10).

Adam was a historical individual (4:25; 5:1-5; 1 Chr 1:1; Hos 6:7; Luke 3:38; Rom 5:14; 1 Cor 15:22, 45; 1 Tim 2:13-14; Jude 1:14) who represents humanity as a whole. God's mandates (1:26-30) and curses (3:16-19) affected not only Adam and Eve, but the entire human race. Adam represents the separation from God that all humanity experiences.

The apostle Paul contrasted those represented by Adam, the first man, with those who follow Christ, the "last Adam" (1 Cor 15:45-50; see Rom 5:12-21; 8:5-11, 20-22). Those represented by Adam live only in him; they partake of his sin, his alienation from God and creation, and his spiritual death. Those who follow Christ live by faith in him. They are recreated in Christ's image and become "new people" who partake of a new creation (see Rom 8:29; 1 Cor 15:49; 2 Cor 5:17). The barriers Adam raised are removed by Christ (Rom 5:1; 2 Cor 5:19; Gal 3:27-28; 6:15; Eph 2:14-16); Christ restores what Adam lost.

a role and would be punished (3:14), but that did not release the woman or the man from their guilt.

3:14-19 The parties were judged in the order of their transgression—serpent, woman, man. Each received a punishment unique to his or her situation, and each had a key relationship altered. God is principled in judgment, not fickle; each punishment is proportionate to the offense.

3:14 *to the serpent:* Though later revelation identifies the deceiver as Satan, it is the created animal who was cursed, like the ground (3:17). • *Groveling in the dust* is a posture of humiliation and defeat (Ps 72:9; Mic 7:17).

3:15 *hostility:* The prophet Isaiah envisions the day when the Messiah's

kingdom will restore all of creation to a harmonious state like the Garden of Eden before humans sinned (see Isa 11:8). • *her offspring* (literally *her seed*): This collective noun can refer to a single descendant or many. The ancient Near Eastern concept of corporate solidarity (e.g., "you and your descendants," 28:14) is also behind this description of the ongoing hostility that would exist between humans and snakes. The pattern is set using singular terms (*He . . . you*). Christian interpreters have traditionally understood this verse as a prophecy of Christ, the seed of Abraham and the culmination of the woman's seed (Gal 3:16; 4:4). • *strike* (Or *bruise,* in both occurrences): The striking of *his heel* is a reference to the suffering of God's servant (see Isa 53),

while striking the serpent's *head*—a more definitive blow—is ultimately fulfilled in Christ's death, resurrection, and final victory over Satan (1 Cor 15:55-57; Rev 12:7-9; 20:7-10).

3:16 Judgment falls on the woman's unique role of childbearing and on her relationship with her husband. • *And you will desire to control your husband, but he will rule over you* (Or *And though you will have desire for your husband, / he will rule over you*): The marriage relationship now included an element of antagonism rather than just security and fulfillment. New life in Christ allows for the restoration of a man and a woman's marriage relationship (Eph 5:18-32; cp. Matt 20:25-28).

3:17-19 God highlighted his original

"Since you listened to your wife and ate
    from the tree
    whose fruit I commanded you not to
        eat,
    the ground is cursed because of you.
    All your life you will struggle to
        scratch a living from it.
¹⁸ It will grow thorns and thistles for you,
    though you will eat of its grains.
¹⁹ By the sweat of your brow
    will you have food to eat
until you return to the ground
    from which you were made.
For you were made from dust,
    and to dust you will return."

Expulsion and Hope

²⁰Then the man—Adam—named his wife
Eve, because she would be the mother of all
who live. ²¹And the LORD God made clothing from animal skins for Adam and his
wife.

²²Then the LORD God said, "Look, the
human beings have become like us, knowing both good and evil. What if they reach
out, take fruit from the tree of life, and eat
it? Then they will live ᵏforever!" ²³So the
LORD God banished them from the Garden
of Eden, and he sent Adam out to cultivate
the ground from which he had been made.
²⁴After sending them out, the LORD God sta-
tioned mighty ᵃcherubim to the east of the
Garden of Eden. And he placed a flaming
sword that flashed back and forth to guard
the way to the tree of life.

Results of Rebellion (4:1-24)
Cain and Abel

4 Now Adam had sexual relations with
his wife, Eve, and she became pregnant. When she gave birth to Cain, she said,
"With the LORD's help, I have produced a
man!" ²Later she gave birth to his brother
and named him Abel.

When they grew up, Abel became a shepherd, while Cain cultivated the ground.
³When it was time for the harvest, Cain
presented some of his crops as a gift to the
LORD. ⁴Abel also brought a gift—the best
of the firstborn lambs from his flock. The
LORD accepted Abel and his gift, ⁵but he did
not accept Cain and his gift. This made Cain
very angry, and he looked dejected.

⁶"Why are you so angry?" the LORD asked
Cain. "Why do you look so dejected? ⁷You
will be accepted if you do what is right. But
if you refuse to do what is right, then watch
out! Sin is crouching at the door, eager to

3:18
Job 31:40
Heb 6:8

3:19
Gen 2:7
Ps 90:3; 104:29
Eccl 12:7
1 Cor 15:47

3:20
2 Cor 11:3
1 Tim 2:13

3:21
2 Cor 5:2-3

3:22
Gen 1:26
ᵏ*olam* (5769)
› Gen 9:16

3:24
Ezek 10:1
Rev 2:7; 22:2, 14
ᵃ*kerub* (3742)
› Exod 25:18

4:2
Luke 11:50-51

4:3
Lev 2:1-2
Num 18:12

4:4
Exod 13:12
Heb 11:4

4:6
Jon 4:4

4:7
Rom 6:12, 16
Jas 1:15

. . . .

command *not to eat* the fruit by speaking of eating several times in 3:17-19.
The judgment affected humanity's ability to get food, and it was proportionate
to their offense of eating what had been
prohibited. • *the ground is cursed:* The
relationship of the man to the ground
(see note on 2:7) was now antagonistic
as judgment fell on his primary role
(2:5, 15). He must labor and toil to work
the ground, but with diminished productivity. Human sin has broad effects
on creation (see 4:12; 6:7; Lev 26; Deut
11:13-17, 28; Rom 8:22).

3:20-24 Soon after they were judged for
their sin, Adam and Eve were banished
from the garden.

3:20 *Eve* (Hebrew *khawah*) sounds like
a Hebrew term (*khayah*) that means "to
give life." Following God's pronouncement of Adam's impending death (3:19),
Adam expressed hope by giving Eve
a name associated with life. Adam's
naming of Eve in such close proximity
to 3:16 may suggest that the narrator
views it as Adam's first act of ruling over
the woman after the Fall (see note on
2:19-20).

3:21 God mercifully provided more
substantial clothing for Adam and Eve
(cp. 3:7) before expelling them into the
harsh environment outside the garden.

3:22 *human beings:* Or *the man;*
Hebrew reads *ha-'adam.* • *like us:* The
plural probably reflects God's conversation with his angelic court (see note on
1:26). • *the tree of life . . . live forever!*
Mercifully, God prevented humankind
from eating of the tree of life and
having to live forever in a fallen state.
Through Jesus Christ, however, eternal
life is once again made available (see
Rev 2:7; 22:2, 14, 19).

3:23 *So the LORD God banished them
from the Garden of Eden:* Before the
Fall, the garden was a sanctuary in
which humans could move freely in
God's holy presence. Now their sin
required expulsion from that environment. This same principle was behind
the laws that restricted an Israelite's access to God's presence in the Tabernacle
or Temple (e.g., Lev 16:1-2; Num 5:3).

3:24 *Cherubim* are a class of angelic beings that guard access to God's presence
(Exod 26:31; Ezek 28:14). • *east . . . of
Eden:* In Genesis, movement eastward
often implies leaving the presence or
blessing of God, whether in judgment
(see also 4:16), self-aggrandizement
(11:2; 13:11), or estrangement (25:6).

4:1 *Adam:* Or *the man;* also in 4:25.
• *had sexual relations* (literally *knew*):
In certain contexts, the Hebrew term
meaning "to know" is an idiom for
sexual knowledge of another person
(4:17; 19:33, 35). It is never used of animals, which mate by instinct. • *With the*

LORD's help: Eve fulfilled her God-given
role of procreation despite the negative
effects of the Fall (see 3:16, 20). • *I
have produced:* Or *I have acquired. Cain*
(Hebrew *qayin*) sounds like a Hebrew
term (*qanah*) that can mean "produce"
or "acquire."

4:2 *his brother . . . Abel:* The name (Hebrew *habel*) means "breath," "vapor," or
"meaningless," anticipating his tragically
brief life (cp. Eccl 1:2).

4:3 There was nothing wrong with offering grain to the Lord (Lev 2:14; Deut
26:2-4), but Cain brought only a token
gift (*some of his crops*), whereas God
requires the first and best (Exod 23:16,
19; 34:22, 26). Cain's heart attitude
made his offering inferior to Abel's (cp.
Heb 11:4).

4:4-5 *the best of the firstborn lambs:*
Or *the firstborn of his flock and their fat
portions.* Abel was giving God the best
animals and the richest parts. Abel's
offering, in contrast to Cain's, was the
best he had to offer. True worship is a
costly privilege.

4:7 *Sin is crouching at the door . . . you
must subdue it:* Sin is pictured as a vicious animal lying in wait to pounce on
Cain (cp. note on 3:16). Either sin will
dominate Cain, or Cain will resist the
temptation to sin. There is no neutral
ground in that conflict.

4:8
Matt 23:35
1 Jn 3:12

4:9
Gen 3:9

4:10
Num 35:33
Deut 21:1
Heb 12:24

4:11
Deut 27:15-26

4:12
Deut 28:15-24

4:14
Gen 9:6
Job 15:22

4:17
Ps 49:11

control you. But you must subdue it and be its master."

⁸One day Cain suggested to his brother, "Let's go out into the fields." And while they were in the field, Cain attacked his brother, Abel, and killed him.

⁹Afterward the Lord asked Cain, "Where is your brother? Where is Abel?"

"I don't know," Cain responded. "Am I my brother's guardian?"

¹⁰But the Lord said, "What have you done? Listen! Your brother's blood cries out to me from the ground! ¹¹Now you are cursed and banished from the ground, which has swallowed your brother's blood. ¹²No longer will the ground yield good crops for you, no matter how hard you

work! From now on you will be a homeless wanderer on the earth."

¹³Cain replied to the Lord, "My punishment is too great for me to bear! ¹⁴You have banished me from the land and from your presence; you have made me a homeless wanderer. Anyone who finds me will kill me!"

¹⁵The Lord replied, "No, for I will give a sevenfold punishment to anyone who kills you." Then the Lord put a mark on Cain to warn anyone who might try to kill him. ¹⁶So Cain left the Lord's presence and settled in the land of Nod, east of Eden.

The Descendants of Cain

¹⁷Cain had sexual relations with his wife, and she became pregnant and gave birth to

Original Sin (3:1-19)

Gen 8:21
Exod 34:7
Job 4:17-21
Ps 51:5
Prov 22:15
Ezek 36:16-36
John 8:1-11
Rom 1:18–3:20;
5:12-21
1 Cor 15:21-22
Gal 3:22; 5:17-24
Eph 2:1-10
1 Jn 3:14

Genesis 3 describes how human moral innocence collapsed through rebellion (3:11, 17). What God declared as "very good" (1:31) was no longer completely so. Man and woman ate the fruit that promised knowledge of good and evil and thus broke God's command (2:17). Worse, they tried to become like God (3:5) and thus fell from their sinless state. Alienated from God, one another, and creation, they also became subject to death.

The term "original sin" denotes sin's complete, universal infiltration into individual lives and human society as a result of human rebellion. When the first man and woman ate the fruit in disobedience to God, they forfeited their own innocence and that of their children, the entire human race (Rom 5:12-14; 1 Cor 15:21-22, 45-49). All humans are "fallen," born in sin, predisposed to sin (8:21; Job 4:17-21; Ps 51:5; 103:10; 143:2; Prov 20:9), and awaiting death. As people yield to their inherited predisposition to sin, they become responsible for their own wrongdoing (Eccl 7:20; Rom 3:23).

The first man, Adam, introduced sin, but the "second Adam," Jesus Christ, is sin's antidote (1 Cor 15:3; 2 Cor 5:21). When Christ died as Redeemer, he made God's salvation from sin available to all (John 3:16; Rom 1:16).

4:8 The effects of the Fall on human relationships are tragically expressed in the first murder. • The word *brother* is used seven times in 4:2-11, highlighting Cain's fratricide in the face of familial responsibility. • *Let's go out into the fields:* As in Samaritan Pentateuch, Greek and Syriac versions, and Latin Vulgate; Masoretic Text lacks this phrase.

4:9 *Where is your brother?* The questions God asked Cain (4:6, 9, 10) recall those that God asked Cain's parents (3:9-13). In both cases, humans put up evasive answers (cp. 3:12-13). Cain's answer is shockingly defiant—another clue that the problem with his token offering was the attitude that lay behind it.

4:10 *What have you done?* is more an expression of horror and rebuke than a fact-finding question (cp. 3:13). • Abel's *blood* is personified as a legal witness that *cries out* against Cain. • *from the ground:* See note on 4:11-12.

4:11-12 As with his father (cp. 3:9-12, 17-19), Cain's interrogation (4:9-10)

was followed by God's verdict. Adam's sin had already caused *the ground* to be cursed. Now Cain was *cursed* and *banished* from the land he had farmed because he had contaminated it with innocent blood. • *homeless wanderer:* Cain was condemned to ceaseless roving in a land that would provide neither sustenance nor security. The effects of sin were escalating.

4:13-14 For Cain, eviction *from the land*—the domain of his vocation as a farmer (see 4:2; cp. 3:23)—amounted to exile from God's *presence*. The Israelites were warned that unfaithfulness to the Sinai covenant would similarly result in eviction from the Promised Land and from God's presence in the Temple (see, e.g., Lev 26:27-32).

4:13 *My punishment:* Or *My sin*.

4:15 *Sevenfold punishment* was the full weight of justice. Cain complained that his punishment was too great, but the full sentence that would fall on anyone who committed Cain's crime against him shows how gracious the Lord

was to Cain. Cain deserved death (see 9:5-6). • The *mark* graciously provided protection following Cain's judgment (cp. 3:21).

4:16 *Nod* means "wandering." The name speaks more of Cain's fate (see 4:12, 14) than of a specific geographical area (the location is unknown). Cain's sin denied him rest and a sense of belonging. • Cain's exile *east of Eden* is another point of connection with Adam's story (cp. 3:24). Cain did not learn from his father's mistake, so he also suffered estrangement from the ground and exile to the east (see note on 3:24).

4:17–5:32 These back-to-back genealogies do more than list names for the record. They contrast the ways that human culture spread, some in rebellion against God (Cain, 4:17-24) and some in obedience to God (Seth, 4:25–5:32). In Genesis, the history of the rejected branch is generally explained before carrying forward the line that led to Israel. Two points of contrast are especially worth noting: (1) Lamech, the seventh from Adam through the lineage

Enoch. Then Cain founded a city, which he named Enoch, after his son. ¹⁸Enoch had a son named Irad. Irad became the father of Mehujael. Mehujael became the father of Methushael. Methushael became the father of Lamech.

¹⁹Lamech married two women. The first was named Adah, and the second was Zillah. ²⁰Adah gave birth to Jabal, who was the first of those who raise livestock and live in tents. ²¹His brother's name was Jubal, the first of all who play the harp and flute. ²²Lamech's other wife, Zillah, gave birth to a son named Tubal-cain. He became an expert in forging tools of bronze and iron. Tubal-cain had a sister named Naamah. ²³One day Lamech said to his wives,

"Adah and Zillah, hear my voice;
    listen to me, you wives of Lamech.
I have killed a man who attacked me,
    a young man who wounded me.
²⁴ If someone who kills Cain is punished
    seven times,

then the one who kills me will be
    punished seventy-seven times!"

Epilogue: The Birth of Seth (4:25-26)

²⁵Adam had sexual relations with his wife again, and she gave birth to another son. She named him Seth, for she said, "God has granted me another son in place of Abel, whom Cain killed." ²⁶When Seth grew up, he had a son and named him Enosh. At that time people first began to worship the LORD by name.

3. THE ACCOUNT OF ADAM'S DESCENDANTS (5:1–6:8)
Human Identity Restated

5 This is the written account of the descendants of Adam. When God created human beings, he made them to be like himself. ²He created them male and female, and he blessed them and called them "human."

Genealogy: Adam to Noah

³When Adam was 130 years old, he became the father of a son who was just

Cross-references (right margin):

4:23
Lev 19:18
Deut 32:35

4:25
Gen 4:8; 5:3
1 Chr 1:1
Luke 3:38

4:26
Gen 12:8
1 Kgs 18:24
Joel 2:32
Zeph 3:9
Acts 2:21

5:1
Gen 1:26; 6:9
1 Chr 1:1

5:2
Gen 1:27
*Matt 19:4
*Mark 10:6

5:3-32
1 Chr 1:1-3
Luke 3:36-38

5:3
Gen 1:26; 4:25
1 Cor 15:49

. . . .

of Cain, is the main focus of the first genealogy. Like his ancestor, Lamech took human life and had to live in constant fear of death as a consequence (4:23-24). By contrast, Enoch, the seventh from Adam through the lineage of Seth (see 4:25–5:32), lived in a way that pleased God and avoided death altogether (5:24). (2) Advances in human culture and technology came through Cain's line (the first city, livestock, shelter, metallurgy, music), but the effects of sin still dominated. No technological advances are mentioned in Seth's line; instead, people began "to worship the LORD" (4:26) and to find "favor with the LORD" (see 6:8).

4:17 Cain's *wife* was probably one of his sisters (5:4). Cain's marriage to his sister would not have caused genetic problems so early in the development of the human gene pool. • Cain was condemned to be a wanderer. Perhaps he *founded a city* in rebellion against that verdict, seeking to defend himself by enclosing it in walls. Naming it *after his son* reflects a tendency among those who rebel against God to idolize humanity and its achievements.

4:18 *the father of:* Or *the ancestor of,* and so throughout the verse. Hebrew genealogies do not necessarily list every single generation.

4:19 Marrying *two women* was contrary to God's ideal pattern for marriage (2:24), and might be another manifestation of the arrogance and rebellion of Cain's descendants.

4:20-22 Technological advancement

masks increasing self-assertion and distance from God (see note on 4:14–5:32).

4:23-24 Lamech's chilling taunt shows the further escalation of sin's effects on humanity. Cain's line had reached a crescendo of violence with Lamech's contempt for life. In his arrogance, he put his deed into poetic verse. • *punished seventy-seven times!* God warned that anyone who tried to kill Cain would experience the full weight of justice (4:15). Lamech's declaration that anyone who harmed him would receive an even more severe penalty is a claim to be accountable to no one, including God.

4:25–5:32 The story returns to Adam and follows the line of Seth, whose lineage led to Abraham and the Israelite nation.

4:25 *another son . . . in place of Abel:* Cain (4:8-16) and Lamech (4:19-24) illustrate sin's consequences; the birth of Seth brought renewed hope. See also note on 5:1-2. • *Seth* probably means "granted"; the name may also mean "appointed."

4:26 *Enosh* means "humankind." In the OT, the term is often used in poetic texts that emphasize human mortality, frailty, and weakness (e.g., Ps 144:3, "mere mortals"). Enosh was born at the time when people began to *worship the LORD by name* (literally *call on the name of the LORD*). In Genesis, that meant calling on the name of the Lord through sacrifice and prayer (similar Hebrew terminology is found in 12:8; 13:4; 21:33; 26:25).

5:1-32 The genealogies of Genesis go beyond simply recording history. By selective information and by structure, they communicate spiritual truth. The genealogies highlight God's blessing, authenticate the family heritage of important individuals, and hold the Genesis narrative together by showing familial continuity. Adam's genealogy through Seth traces ten generations to Noah (see 1 Chr 1:1-4; Luke 3:36-38), with the flood intervening before another ten generations from Noah to Abram. The number ten indicates completeness (ten plagues, Exod 7:8–11:10; Ten Commandments, Exod 20:2-17). Noah closed history before the flood, and Abram inaugurated a new era.

5:1-2 This is the prologue to the second *account* in Genesis (5:1–6:8; see note on 2:4); it connects God's purpose in creation with Seth's line rather than Cain's (4:17-24).

5:1 *written account:* Although the previous account (2:4–4:26) focused on Adam, Eve, and their first children, it was technically "the account of the heavens and the earth." Genesis 5:1-32 is a more typical genealogy. • *human beings:* Or *man;* Hebrew reads *'adam;* similarly in 5:2. • *like himself:* See 1:26 and note.

5:2 *male and female . . . "human"* (Hebrew *'adam*): See 1:27 and note. • *blessed them:* See 1:28 and note.

5:3 *just like him—in his very image:* The image and likeness of God (see note on 1:26) is preserved in human beings despite sin. Adam's sinful nature was also carried forward (Rom 5:12-14).

5:5
Gen 2:17
Heb 9:27

5:18
Jude 1:14

5:22
Gen 6:9; 48:15

5:24
2 Kgs 2:1, 11
Ps 73:24
Heb 11:5

5:29
Gen 3:17
Rom 8:20

5:32
Gen 7:6; 9:18

6:1
Gen 1:28

6:2
ben 'elohim (1121, 0430)
‣ Job 1:6

6:3
Ps 78:39
1 Pet 3:20

like him—in his very image. He named his son Seth. 4After the birth of Seth, Adam lived another 800 years, and he had other sons and daughters. 5Adam lived 930 years, and then he died.

6When Seth was 105 years old, he became the father of Enosh. 7After the birth of Enosh, Seth lived another 807 years, and he had other sons and daughters. 8Seth lived 912 years, and then he died.

9When Enosh was 90 years old, he became the father of Kenan. 10After the birth of Kenan, Enosh lived another 815 years, and he had other sons and daughters. 11Enosh lived 905 years, and then he died.

12When Kenan was 70 years old, he became the father of Mahalalel. 13After the birth of Mahalalel, Kenan lived another 840 years, and he had other sons and daughters. 14Kenan lived 910 years, and then he died.

15When Mahalalel was 65 years old, he became the father of Jared. 16After the birth of Jared, Mahalalel lived another 830 years, and he had other sons and daughters. 17Mahalalel lived 895 years, and then he died.

18When Jared was 162 years old, he became the father of Enoch. 19After the birth of Enoch, Jared lived another 800 years, and he had other sons and daughters. 20Jared lived 962 years, and then he died.

21When Enoch was 65 years old, he became the father of Methuselah. 22After the

birth of Methuselah, Enoch lived in close fellowship with God for another 300 years, and he had other sons and daughters. 23Enoch lived 365 years, 24walking in close fellowship with God. Then one day he disappeared, because God took him.

25When Methuselah was 187 years old, he became the father of Lamech. 26After the birth of Lamech, Methuselah lived another 782 years, and he had other sons and daughters. 27Methuselah lived 969 years, and then he died.

28When Lamech was 182 years old, he became the father of a son. 29Lamech named his son Noah, for he said, "May he bring us relief from our work and the painful labor of farming this ground that the LORD has cursed." 30After the birth of Noah, Lamech lived another 595 years, and he had other sons and daughters. 31Lamech lived 777 years, and then he died.

32By the time Noah was 500 years old, he was the father of Shem, Ham, and Japheth.

Corruption of the Human Race

6 Then the people began to multiply on the earth, and daughters were born to them. 2The bsons of God saw the beautiful women and took any they wanted as their wives. 3Then the LORD said, "My Spirit will not put up with humans for such a long time,

. . . .

5:5 *he died:* Death indeed came to Adam (see 2:17; 3:18-19) and his descendants (see Rom 5:12-14). Cain's violence is omitted (see 4:8, 15, 23-24) and key figures in Seth's line live in hope (5:29).

5:6 *the father of:* Or *the ancestor of;* also in 5:9, 12, 15, 18, 21, 25. Hebrew genealogies do not necessarily list every single generation.

5:7 *After the birth of:* Or *After the birth of this ancestor of;* also in 5:10, 13, 16, 19, 22, 26 (see note on 5:6).

5:22 *Enoch lived in close fellowship with God* (literally *Enoch walked with God;* also in 5:24): Enoch's position as seventh from Adam in the genealogy strikes a contrast with Lamech, the seventh from Adam in the line of Cain (see note on 4:17–5:32).

5:24 Unlike all other sons of Adam, Enoch did not succumb to death; rather, *he disappeared, because God took him* (cp. 2 Kgs 2:9-12; see also Heb 11:5).

5:27 *969 years:* This statement and the numbers given in 5:25, 28 and 7:6

mean that Methuselah died in the year of the flood.

5:28-29 As with Enoch (5:21-24), the normal genealogical formula is interrupted to highlight important theological information about Noah. *Noah* sounds like a Hebrew term (*nakham*) that can mean "relief" or "comfort," and another term (*nuakh*) that means "rest." As the first person born after Adam's death (see note on 5:5), Noah prompted his father *Lamech* to hope that the curse brought on by Adam's sin (3:17) might be lifted. See 8:21; 2 Cor 1:3-7; 2 Thes 2:16-17.

6:1-8 Human wickedness reached a climax, prompting God to send the flood to destroy all living things. A glimmer of hope appears in God's favor toward Noah (6:8).

6:1-2 The *sons of God* have generally been understood as fallen angels (cp. the same Hebrew phrase in Job 1:6; 2:1; 38:7; Ps 29:1; 89:7). This interpretation is prominent in ancient Jewish and Christian literature (e.g., *1 Enoch* 6:1–7:6; Justin Martyr, *Apology* 2.5) and is apparently supported by

the NT (see 1 Pet 3:18-20; 2 Pet 2:4; Jude 1:6-7). Some interpreters do not believe that God would permit angels to procreate with humans and doubt that the above NT texts should be read in this way. Another possibility is that *sons of God* refers to the righteous descendants of Seth, while the *beautiful women* (6:2, literally *daughters of men;* also in 6:4) were female descendants of Cain's wicked line. This interpretation is in harmony with 4:17–5:32, but is weakened by the language of 6:1-2, which seems to refer to the daughters of humanity in general, not the daughters of Cain specifically. Others believe that *sons of God* refers to tyrannical human kings (possibly demon-possessed) who took Lamech's polygamy (4:19) to a new height of wickedness by seizing the daughters of the righteous. Language reminiscent of 3:6 (*saw . . . took*) shows the rebellious nature of this act.

6:3 *will not put up with* (Greek version reads *will not remain in*): Many think that this is an announcement of God's decision to withdraw the restraining influence of his *Spirit* from human

for they are only mortal flesh. In the future, their normal lifespan will be no more than 120 years."

⁴In those days, and for some time after, giant Nephilites lived on the earth, for whenever the sons of God had intercourse with women, they gave birth to children who became the heroes and famous warriors of ancient times.

⁵The LORD observed the extent of human wickedness on the earth, and he saw that everything they thought or imagined was consistently and totally evil. ⁶So the LORD was sorry he had ever made them and put them on the earth. It broke his heart. ⁷And the LORD said, "I will wipe this human race I have ᶜcreated from the face of the earth. Yes,

and I will destroy every living thing—all the people, the large animals, the small animals that scurry along the ground, and even the birds of the sky. I am sorry I ever made them." ⁸But Noah found favor with the LORD.

4. THE ACCOUNT OF NOAH'S FAMILY (6:9–9:29)
The Story of Noah

⁹This is the account of Noah and his family. Noah was a righteous man, the only ᵈblameless person living on earth at the time, and he walked in close fellowship with God. ¹⁰Noah was the father of three sons: Shem, Ham, and Japheth.

¹¹Now God saw that the earth had become corrupt and was filled with violence.

6:4
Num 13:33
Jude 1:6-7

6:5
Ps 14:1-3

6:6
Exod 32:14
Num 23:19
1 Sam 15:11, 35
2 Sam 24:16

6:7
Deut 29:20
ᶜbara' (1254)
▸ Ps 51:10

6:8
Exod 33:17

6:9
Job 1:1
Ezek 14:14
ᵈtamim (8549)
▸ Gen 17:1

6:11
Deut 31:29
Judg 2:19
Ezek 8:17

NOAH (6:8-22)

Gen 5:28–10:1
1 Chr 1:4
Isa 54:9
Ezek 14:12-20
Matt 24:37-38
Luke 3:36; 17:26-27
Heb 11:7
1 Pet 3:20-21
2 Pet 2:5

Noah was the son of Lamech, a descendant of Seth (5:3-29). Lamech might have hoped that Noah (whose name means "rest" or "relief") would ease the curse of hardship in working the ground (see note on 5:29). God used Noah to help relieve the world of evil.

God intended to destroy creation because of pervasive human wickedness (6:1-7; see Matt 24:37-39; Luke 17:26-27), but he decided to preserve Noah (6:8). God gave Noah, a righteous and blameless man (6:9), precise instructions for building the ark in which only the eight people of his family would be saved, along with every kind of creature (6:14–8:19). When Noah and his family finally emerged from the ark after the flood, Noah pleased God by building an altar and sacrificing burnt offerings. God promised that he would never again flood the whole earth or disrupt the sequence of the seasons, despite human sin (8:20–9:17).

Noah's sons were Shem, Ham, and Japheth. All the nations of the earth descended from them (9:18-19). When Noah became drunk on wine from his vineyard, his sons and their descendants were cursed or blessed in accord with how they responded to him (9:22-27). Noah lived for 950 years, including 350 years after the flood (9:28-29); he is an example of righteousness, obedience, courage, and faith (see Ezek 14:12-20; Heb 11:7; 2 Pet 2:5).

society and allow human wickedness to run its full course. Others think it means that God would withdraw his life-giving breath from humans at an earlier age (*ruakh*, the Hebrew term for "spirit," can also mean "breath"; see 6:17; 7:22; see also Ps 104:29-30). • *normal lifespan will be no more than 120 years* (literally *his days will be 120 years*): It is possible that this was a new restriction on the number of years individuals would generally be allowed to live (so the NLT). However, for generations after the flood, humans lived well beyond 120 years (see, e.g., 11:10-26). An alternative interpretation sees this as a 120-year grace period before the arrival of the flood (see Jon 3:4; Matt 24:37-38; 1 Pet 3:20; 2 Pet 2:5).

6:4 *giant Nephilites* (Hebrew *nepilim*): The term may mean "fallen ones." The context implies that they were the off-spring of the "sons of God" and would be destroyed in the flood. Num 13:31-33 uses the same term to describe other giants who were hostile toward God's

people and would also be destroyed (see also Deut 2:11, which connects the Anakite *nepilim* with another group called the *repa'im*).

6:5 *everything they thought or imagined* (literally *every intention of the thoughts of their hearts*): In the OT, the heart is the core of volition, thought, and morality (see Prov 4:23). Wicked actions stem from a corrupt inner life. • *consistently and totally evil:* Strong language captures the pervasiveness, depth, and persistence of human wickedness. Human nature continued to be corrupt even after the flood (see 8:21).

6:6 *the LORD was sorry:* The extent of human wickedness made the Lord regret having created them (see also 6:7; cp. 1 Sam 15:11, 35). • *It broke his heart:* The evil in humanity's heart (6:5) pained God greatly. Sending the flood was a heart-wrenching act on God's part.

6:7 *wipe . . . from the . . . earth:* As Adam and Eve were banished from the garden-sanctuary (3:23), all of

humankind would be expunged from God's good creation. • *every living thing:* Human sin had so corrupted the earth that judgment fell on the animals and birds over which they had dominion (see 1:28 and note). The special role of humans in the created order (1:28-30) means that nature is affected by human moral choices (see 8:1; Job 38:41; Hos 4:3; Rom 8:19-22).

6:8 *Noah* and his godly life stand in stark contrast to the sinfulness of the rest of the people.

6:9 *the account:* See note on 2:4 • *a righteous man, the only blameless person:* The text does not claim that Noah was without sin (see Rom 5:12-14). Noah's righteousness and blamelessness came about because *he walked in close fellowship with God.* See also 7:1; 17:1; Heb 11:7.

6:11-13 See 6:5-7. • *violence* (Hebrew *khamas*): Murder had especially corrupted the line of Cain (4:8, 23-24).

6:12
Ps 14:1-3

6:13
Isa 34:1-4
Ezek 7:2-3

6:14
Exod 2:3
1 Pet 3:20

6:17
Ps 29:10
2 Pet 2:5

6:18
Gen 9:9-16; 17:7;
19:12

6:20
Gen 7:3

6:21
Gen 1:29

6:22
Gen 7:5
Exod 40:16

7:1
Gen 6:18
Matt 24:38
Luke 17:26-27
Heb 11:7
1 Pet 3:20

7:2
Lev 11:1-47
Deut 14:3-20
Ezek 44:23

7:4
Gen 6:7, 13

7:6
Gen 5:32

7:7
Gen 6:18

¹²God observed all this corruption in the world, for everyone on earth was corrupt. ¹³So God said to Noah, "I have decided to destroy all living creatures, for they have filled the earth with violence. Yes, I will wipe them all out along with the earth!

¹⁴"Build a large boat from cypress wood and waterproof it with tar, inside and out. Then construct decks and stalls throughout its interior. ¹⁵Make the boat 450 feet long, 75 feet wide, and 45 feet high. ¹⁶Leave an 18-inch opening below the roof all the way around the boat. Put the door on the side, and build three decks inside the boat—lower, middle, and upper.

¹⁷"Look! I am about to cover the earth with a flood that will destroy every living thing that breathes. Everything on earth will die. ¹⁸But I will confirm my covenant with you. So enter the boat—you and your wife and your sons and their wives. ¹⁹Bring a pair of every kind of animal—a male and a female—into the boat with you to keep them alive during the flood. ²⁰Pairs of every kind of bird, and every kind of animal, and every kind of small animal that scurries along the ground, will come to you to be kept alive.

²¹And be sure to take on board enough food for your family and for all the animals."

²²So Noah did everything exactly as God had commanded him.

The Universal Flood

7 When everything was ready, the LORD said to Noah, "Go into the boat with all your family, for among all the people of the earth, I can see that you alone are righteous. ²Take with you seven pairs—male and female—of each animal I have approved for eating and for sacrifice, and take one pair of each of the others. ³Also take seven pairs of every kind of bird. There must be a male and a female in each pair to ensure that all life will survive on the earth after the flood. ⁴Seven days from now I will make the rains pour down on the earth. And it will rain for forty days and forty nights, until I have wiped from the earth all the living things I have created."

⁵So Noah did everything as the LORD commanded him.

⁶Noah was 600 years old when the flood covered the earth. ⁷He went on board the boat to escape the flood—he and his wife

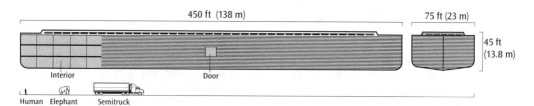

450 ft (138 m)   75 ft (23 m)   45 ft (13.8 m)

Interior   Door

Human   Elephant   Semitruck

▲ **Noah's Ark (6:14-16).** An ark built to the dimensions specified in Genesis would have been immense. Its ratio of length to width (6 to 1) is the most stable known and is used for the design of modern tankers and freight-hauling ships. The ark was able to carry 20,000 tons of cargo; the required number of young adult land animals would have occupied less than half of the available space. The design given was perfect for the ark's function.

6:14 *a large boat:* Traditionally rendered *an ark,* this was a long rectangular barge designed for survival, not for navigation. The Hebrew word *tebah* is used again only of the basket in which the baby Moses was floated on the Nile (Exod 2:3, 5). • *cypress wood:* Or *gopher wood.* It is not clear what kind of wood this was. It was possibly from a conifer, such as cypress.

6:15 The ark's dimensions: Hebrew *300 cubits* [138 meters] *long, 50 cubits* [23 meters] *wide, and 30 cubits* [13.8 meters] *high.* This floating barge displaced around 43,300 tons of water.

6:16 *An 18-inch opening* (Hebrew *an opening of 1 cubit* [46 centimeters]) *below the roof* encircled *the boat,* providing light and air. • Noah was to build a *door* and God would close it (7:16). God was the captain of this peculiar boat

with no sail or rudder. God also brought the animals to Noah (6:20).

6:17 *cover the earth with a flood:* Some propose that the flood might only have covered the ancient Near East as it was known to Noah or Moses. However, the flood's stated purpose—to *destroy every living thing that breathes* (see also 6:7, 11-13; 7:1, 4, 18-23; 8:21)—and its effect of undoing creation (see notes on 1:9-10; 7:11-12) suggest that the flood covered the entire planet (see also 1 Pet 3:20; 2 Pet 2:5; 3:6).

6:18 This first explicit mention of a *covenant* in the Bible refers to the unilateral pact that God made with humankind and the world after the flood (see 9:9, 11, 14-17).

6:19-20 God's instructions to Noah repeat the language of creation (*every kind,* cp. 1:24). • *a male and a female:*

These animals would procreate and repopulate the earth after the flood.

7:2 *of each animal I have approved for eating and for sacrifice* (literally *of each clean animal;* similarly in 7:8): In addition to the animals that were to repopulate the earth, these "clean" animals were for food and for Noah's sacrifice after the flood (8:20-21). This passage does not use the precise technical language that is found in the regulations concerning "clean" and "unclean" given to Israel at Sinai (see Lev 11:1-47; Deut 14:3-12), but the underlying concept is the same (perhaps God revealed it directly to Noah).

7:4 The number *forty* is often associated with affliction, trial, or punishment (see Exod 16:35; Judg 13:1; 1 Kgs 19:8; Ezek 4:6; Jon 3:4; Matt 4:2; Acts 1:3).

7:6 *covered the earth:* See note on 6:17.

and his sons and their wives. ⁸With them were all the various kinds of animals—those approved for eating and for sacrifice and those that were not—along with all the birds and the small animals that scurry along the ground. ⁹They entered the boat in pairs, male and female, just as God had commanded Noah. ¹⁰After seven days, the waters of the flood came and covered the earth.

¹¹When Noah was 600 years old, on the seventeenth day of the second month, all the underground waters erupted from the earth, and the rain fell in mighty torrents from the sky. ¹²The rain continued to fall for forty days and forty nights.

¹³That very day Noah had gone into the boat with his wife and his sons—Shem, Ham, and Japheth—and their wives. ¹⁴With them in the boat were pairs of every kind of animal—domestic and wild, large and small—along with birds of every kind. ¹⁵Two by two they came into the boat, representing every living thing that breathes. ¹⁶A male and female of each kind entered, just as God had commanded Noah. Then the LORD closed the door behind them.

¹⁷For forty days the floodwaters grew deeper, covering the ground and lifting the boat high above the earth. ¹⁸As the waters rose higher and higher above the ground, the boat floated safely on the surface. ¹⁹Finally, the water covered even the highest mountains on the earth, ²⁰rising more than twenty-two feet above the highest peaks. ²¹All the living things on earth died—birds,

domestic animals, wild animals, small animals that scurry along the ground, and all the people. ²²Everything that breathed and lived on dry land died. ²³God wiped out every living thing on the earth—people, livestock, small animals that scurry along the ground, and the birds of the sky. All were destroyed. The only people who survived were Noah and those with him in the boat. ²⁴And the floodwaters covered the earth for 150 days.

The Floodwaters Recede

8 But God ᵉremembered Noah and all the wild animals and livestock with him in the boat. He sent a wind to blow across the earth, and the floodwaters began to recede. ²The underground waters stopped flowing, and the torrential rains from the sky were stopped. ³So the floodwaters gradually receded from the earth. After 150 days, ⁴exactly five months from the time the flood began, the boat came to rest on the mountains of Ararat. ⁵Two and a half months later, as the waters continued to go down, other mountain peaks became visible.

⁶After another forty days, Noah opened the window he had made in the boat ⁷and released a raven. The bird flew back and forth until the floodwaters on the earth had dried up. ⁸He also released a dove to see if the water had receded and it could find dry ground. ⁹But the dove could find no place to land because the water still covered the ground. So it returned to the boat, and

7:9
Gen 6:22
7:11
Ps 78:23
Ezek 26:19
Mal 3:10
7:13
1 Pet 3:20
2 Pet 2:5
7:15
Gen 6:19; 7:9
7:19
Ps 104:6
7:20
2 Pet 3:6
7:23
Matt 24:38-39
Luke 17:26-27
1 Pet 3:20
2 Pet 2:5
7:24
Gen 8:3
8:1
Gen 19:29; 30:22
Exod 2:24; 14:21
Job 12:15
Isa 44:27
ᵉzakar (2142)
▸ Exod 2:24
8:2
Gen 7:4, 12
8:4
Gen 7:20
8:7
Lev 11:15
Deut 14:14
1 Kgs 17:4
Luke 12:24
8:8
Isa 60:8
Hos 11:11
Matt 10:16

. . . .

7:8 See note on 7:2.

7:11-12 *on the seventeenth day of the second month:* Such information gives the flood account a certain solemnity; it reminds readers that this was a true historical event. • *underground waters:* See 2:6. • *rain fell:* The flood undid the boundaries established on the second and third days of creation (1:6-13). Elsewhere, the Bible describes God's judgment as an undoing of creation (see Jer 4:23-26; Amos 7:4). • *forty days and forty nights:* See note on 7:4.

7:16 *the LORD closed the door:* The sovereign Judge took responsibility for the annihilation of all outside the boat and the protection of those within (see also 6:16 and note).

7:17 *floodwaters grew deeper* (literally *waters multiplied):* The same word used for the proliferation of humans and animals during creation (see 1:22, 28) is now used ironically of the water that would annihilate them. • *covering the ground:* The Hebrew word translated *ground*

"ground" or "earth" is mentioned eight times in eight verses (7:17-24). The earth is the domain that humankind had polluted and that was now the object of a cleansing deluge.

7:20 *more than twenty-two feet:* Hebrew *15 cubits* [6.9 meters].

7:22 *Everything that . . . lived:* See note on 6:17.

8:1 *But God remembered:* This structural and theological center of the flood story does not mean that God had at any point forgotten Noah. This is covenant language reflecting God's faithfulness to his promise to ensure the safety of his covenant partner (cp. 6:18; 9:15-16; Exod 2:24; Lev 26:42, 45). • *wind:* The same word is translated "Spirit" in 1:2. This and other parallels (see 9:1-2) suggest that the restoration of the earth after the flood was effectively a new creation.

8:2 *underground waters . . . torrential rains:* See note on 7:11-12.

8:4 *exactly five months from the time the flood began:* Literally *on the seventeenth day of the seventh month;* see 7:11. • *mountains of Ararat:* These mountains might be in the region of Ararat (Urartu) southeast of the Black Sea near Lake Van, which touches parts of eastern Turkey, Armenia, and Iran. There is a Mount Ararat (*Agri Dag*) in Turkey, but this verse only identifies the region, not a specific mountain.

8:5 *Two and a half months later:* Literally *On the first day of the tenth month;* see 7:11 and note on 8:4. • *the waters continued to go down:* Another parallel with the creation week (see 1:9) suggests that the earth's restoration was effectively a new creation (see note on 8:1).

8:7 The *raven* is the largest member of the crow family, and was among Noah's unclean animals (Lev 11:15; Deut 14:14). As a scavenger and carrion eater, it was able to sustain itself without returning to the boat.

8:13
Gen 5:32

8:16
Gen 7:13

8:17
Gen 1:22

8:20
Gen 4:4; 12:7; 13:18;
22:2

8:21
Gen 3:17
Exod 29:18, 25
Lev 1:9, 13
Isa 54:9

Noah held out his hand and drew the dove back inside. [10]After waiting another seven days, Noah released the dove again. [11]This time the dove returned to him in the evening with a fresh olive leaf in its beak. Then Noah knew that the floodwaters were almost gone. [12]He waited another seven days and then released the dove again. This time it did not come back.

[13]Noah was now 601 years old. On the first day of the new year, ten and a half months after the flood began, the floodwaters had almost dried up from the earth. Noah lifted back the covering of the boat and saw that the surface of the ground was drying. [14]Two more months went by, and at last the earth was dry!

Noah's Worship and God's Promise

[15]Then God said to Noah, [16]"Leave the boat, all of you—you and your wife, and your sons and their wives. [17]Release all the animals—the birds, the livestock, and the small animals that scurry along the ground—so they can be fruitful and multiply throughout the earth."

[18]So Noah, his wife, and his sons and their wives left the boat. [19]And all of the large and small animals and birds came out of the boat, pair by pair.

[20]Then Noah built an altar to the LORD, and there he sacrificed as burnt offerings the animals and birds that had been approved for that purpose. [21]And the LORD was pleased with the aroma of the sacrifice

Retribution (6:1–7:24)

Lev 26:14-39
Ps 7:6-17; 57:6;
95:8-11
Prov 6:27-35; 26:27
Mic 2:1-3
Rom 2:5-16
Gal 6:7-8
Heb 10:26-31
12:5-11, 25-29

God gave humans the commission of procreating and caring for the world (1:28). Instead, murder and violence multiplied with humanity's spiritual wickedness (4:8, 23; 6:11-13), resulting in a corrupt world that required cleansing.

The purpose of the flood was to enact God's global cleansing and retribution against evildoers. *Retribution* means "giving what is due" and usually refers to recompense for wrongdoing. Retribution is motivated by the conviction that moral order is woven into the fabric of the world and must be maintained or restored (see Ps 7:14-16; Prov 11:18; 26:27).

God maintains moral order by meting out justice, punishing wickedness, and rewarding right behavior (Gal 6:7). Since God oversees the world, it is never entirely overwhelmed by moral chaos; God holds people accountable for what they do. The judgment and exile of Adam and Eve (3:8-24), Cain's sentence and blood-revenge (4:10-15), and the worldwide flood and annihilation (chs 6–9) are OT examples of God's retribution. They reveal a sovereign God who exacts just punishment in the context of his good intentions for the world (see also Num 16; Deut 30:15-20; Josh 7; Mic 2:1-3).

Retribution is an application of God's righteousness; it purifies the world for his kingdom of peace. Through retribution, the divine King proclaims his universal rule and exercises his justice on all who reject his rule or defy his commands (Deut 7:10; 1 Sam 24:19; Ps 149; Prov 15:25; Mic 5:15; 1 Cor 16:22; Gal 1:8-9; 2 Thes 1:5-10).

For God's people, retribution is his discipline. It is intended to restore covenant fellowship with him (see Isa 44:22; Jer 3:12-14; Lam 3:19-33; Hos 14:1-2; Joel 2:12-13). When God's people experience his chastening, they can respond in hope because God's truth and righteousness will triumph (Ps 58:10-11) and God will redeem and restore his people who trust in him (Lev 26:40-45; Hos 2:2-23).

8:11 Unlike the raven (8:7), the *dove* feeds on vegetation. Since olive trees are not tall, Noah could tell that the water was *almost gone.*

8:13 *On the first day of the new year, ten and a half months after the flood began* (literally *On the first day of the first month;* see 7:11): This was two months after the peaks of the mountains first became visible (8:5).

8:14 *Two more months went by:* Literally *The twenty-seventh day of the second month arrived;* see note on 8:13. • *the earth was dry!* This special word for dry land is uniquely used in connection with the sea to portray God's sov-

ereignty over both domains (see 1:9-10; Exod 14:22, 29; Ps 95:5; Jon 1:9).

8:17 *be fruitful and multiply:* See 9:1.

8:20 This first mention of an *altar* in the Bible (see "Altars" at 35:1-15, p. 91) shows Noah's gratitude for having passed through the judgment. • *sacrificed as burnt offerings:* The same term is used of the whole burnt offering in Leviticus (Lev 1:3-9); however, it can refer to any offering that is burned. Noah gave this offering to thank and worship God, who had delivered him and his family from the flood. • *the animals and birds that had been approved for that purpose:* Literally *every*

clean animal and every clean bird.

8:21 *pleased with the aroma of the sacrifice* (literally *smelled the sweet aroma*): The narrator uses anthropomorphic language (i.e., he describes God's activity in human terms) to show God's acceptance of Noah's offering (see also Exod 29:18; Lev 1:9; Num 15:3). The common ancient Near Eastern notion that the gods ate the sacrifices offered to them is notably absent. • *to himself* (literally *in his heart*): The phrase echoes "broke his heart" (6:6), just as *think or imagine* echoes "everything they thought or imagined" (6:5). God's commitment to a new order replaced

and said to himself, "I will never again curse the ground because of the human race, even though everything they think or imagine is bent toward evil from childhood. I will never again destroy all living things. 22As long as the earth remains, there will be planting and harvest, cold and heat, summer and winter, day and night."

God's Covenant with All Living Creatures

9 Then God blessed Noah and his sons and told them, "Be fruitful and multiply. Fill the earth. 2All the animals of the earth, all the birds of the sky, all the small animals that scurry along the ground, and all the fish in the sea will look on you with fear and terror. I have placed them in your power. 3I have given them to you for food, just as I have given you grain and vegetables. 4But you must never eat any meat that still has the flifeblood in it.

5"And I will require the blood of anyone who takes another person's life. If a wild animal kills a person, it must die. And anyone who murders a fellow human must die. 6If anyone takes a human life, that person's life will also be taken by human hands. For God made human beings in his own image.

7Now be fruitful and multiply, and repopulate the earth."

8Then God told Noah and his sons, 9"I hereby confirm my gcovenant with you and your descendants, 10and with all the animals that were on the boat with you—the birds, the livestock, and all the wild animals—every living creature on earth. 11Yes, I am confirming my covenant with you. Never again will floodwaters kill all living creatures; never again will a flood destroy the hearth."

12Then God said, "I am giving you a sign of my covenant with you and with all living creatures, for all generations to come. 13I have placed my rainbow in the clouds. It is the sign of my covenant with you and with all the earth. 14When I send clouds over the earth, the rainbow will appear in the clouds, 15and I will remember my covenant with you and with all living creatures. Never again will the floodwaters destroy all life. 16When I see the rainbow in the clouds, I will remember the ieternal covenant between God and every living creature on earth." 17Then God said to Noah, "Yes, this rainbow is the sign of the covenant I am confirming with all the creatures on earth."

8:22
Ps 74:17

9:1
Gen 1:22

9:2
Gen 1:26-29
Ps 8:6-8

9:3
Ps 104:14

9:4
Lev 3:17; 7:26; 17:10
Deut 12:16
Acts 15:20, 29
ʾdam (1818)
▸ Gen 49:11

9:5
Exod 21:28-32

9:6
Exod 20:13; 21:12
Num 35:33

9:9
ᵍberith (1285)
▸ Gen 15:18

9:11
Isa 24:5
ʰʾerets (0776)
▸ Gen 12:1

9:12
Gen 17:11

9:13
Ezek 1:28

9:15
Deut 7:9

9:16
ⁱʾolam (5769)
▸ Gen 21:33

. . . .

his grief over the old. • *I will never again curse . . . destroy:* The old curse was not lifted (5:29), but God promised not to add to it, thus establishing new limits for life in a disordered world (cp. Isa 54:9). The flood was to stop violence, not to reform the human heart (6:5). Humankind's *bent toward evil* would be contained to some degree through accountability to a new law (9:5-6).

8:22 God's promise to sustain the rhythm of the seasons reaffirmed the created order (1:14; see also Jer 33:20; Zech 14:7).

9:1-7 God's first post-flood speech opens and closes with blessing (9:1, 7). In it, human and animal relationships are again defined, with some modification of the original created order. The sanctity of life is given special focus.

9:1 *Be fruitful and multiply:* The blessing and mandate first given to Adam (1:28) are now reissued to Noah, the "Adam" of the newly cleansed world in need of repopulation.

9:2-3 There are two modifications to the original created order. (1) Previously, humans reigned over *the animals* (1:28), but now animals would live in *terror* of humans (similar military language is found in Exod 23:27-31; Deut 11:25; 31:8). (2) The animals' terror was related to a change in human diet. Humans were now permitted to eat the meat of animals to supplement their subsis-

tence on grains, fruits, and vegetables (1:29).

9:4 A key restriction is imposed. Since blood was identified with life, it had to be drained from a slain animal before its *meat* could be eaten (see Lev 3:17; 7:26-27; 17:10-14; Deut 12:16, 23). The law of Moses prohibited eating animals that died naturally, since their blood had not been drained (Deut 14:21). God provided animal blood to atone for human sin (Lev 17:11; Heb 9:22).

9:5-6 Violence, including murder, was a major factor in bringing about God's judgment of the flood (4:8; 6:11, 13). At this new beginning for humans, God affirmed the sanctity of human life and established a system of retributive justice for the taking of human life (see also Ps 9:12; "Retribution" at 6:1–7:24, p. 35). The function of law is to restrain human wickedness and preserve moral order. This law was further developed in the law of Moses (Exod 21:12-14; Lev 24:17-22; Num 35:16-34; Deut 17:6-7; 19:15).

9:6 *For God made human beings in his own image:* The death penalty has a theological basis. God's image gives humans a unique status and authority within creation (1:26-28). Since murder destroys a person made in God's image, the ultimate penalty must be imposed on a murderer. See also Exod 21:23-25. We are not to pursue personal revenge

(Rom 12:17-19), but are to uphold the justice of the "governing authorities" that God has established (Rom 13:1-7). • *human beings:* Or *man;* Hebrew reads *ha-ʾadam.*

9:7 *Now be fruitful and multiply, and repopulate* (literally *swarm and fill*): In contrast to those who would destroy human life (9:5-6), God's desire is that human life should abound and flourish.

9:8-17 God's second post-flood speech conveys his promise and plan for preserving creation.

9:9-10 God had promised this *covenant* before the flood (6:18). Its scope extends beyond humanity to include the earth and all animals.

9:11 This promise does not prohibit worldwide judgment, but it restricts the means by which God will do it (see 2 Pet 3:4-13).

9:12 In the Bible, covenants are frequently confirmed by some sort of *sign* (e.g., 17:11; Exod 31:13, 17; Luke 22:20).

9:13-16 God brought cataclysmic judgment through the rainstorm; now, the *rainbow,* a meteorological phenomenon associated with the rainstorm, would be an image of peace for *all the earth* (see 9:17). • "Rainbow" and "bow" are the same term in Hebrew. Since God is sometimes pictured as a warrior who shoots arrows of judgment (see Deut 32:42; Ps 7:12; 18:13-14; Hab 3:9-11),

9:21
Gen 19:35

9:22
Hab 2:15

9:25
Deut 27:16

Noah's Sons; Curse and Blessings

18The sons of Noah who came out of the boat with their father were Shem, Ham, and Japheth. (Ham is the father of Canaan.) 19From these three sons of Noah came all the people who now populate the earth.

20After the flood, Noah began to cultivate the ground, and he planted a vineyard. 21One day he drank some wine he had made, and he became drunk and lay naked inside his tent. 22Ham, the father of Canaan, saw that his father was naked and went outside and told his brothers. 23Then Shem and Japheth took a robe, held it over their shoulders, and backed into the tent to cover their father. As they did this, they looked the other way so they would not see him naked.

24When Noah woke up from his stupor, he learned what Ham, his youngest son, had done. 25Then he cursed Canaan, the son of Ham:

"May Canaan be cursed!
May he be the lowest of servants to
his relatives."

God's Covenant with Noah (9:1-17)

Ezek 14:12-23
Matt 24:37-39
Heb 11:7

The first explicit reference to a covenant in Scripture occurs after the flood (9:1-17). *Covenant* (Hebrew *berith*) means "bond": A covenant is a binding relationship rooted in a commitment that includes promises and obligations. Whether between individuals (e.g., 21:27), whole nations (e.g., Josh 9:15-18), or God and humans, the covenant relationship calls for faithfulness and makes peace and harmony possible.

Here God took the initiative to bind himself again to human beings and to the whole creation despite human faithlessness (see 6:1-7). When God charged Noah to build an ark to escape the impending deluge (6:13-17), he also promised to establish a covenant with him (6:18). The corruption and violence of the human race had provoked God's anger (6:11, 13), but his gracious favor remained with Noah (6:8). Through this covenant, God guaranteed that he would maintain a relationship with one family even as other divine-human relationships were being severed. God's covenant promise to Noah came with his command to build an ark (6:14); Noah's receipt of the covenant blessing depended on his obedience to this divine command (6:22; 7:5).

When Noah made an offering to God after the flood (8:20-22), God elaborated on his covenant with Noah as a universal covenant with humans and with all living creatures (9:8-10). God promised never to send such a flood again as judgment on the world.

This covenant helps us understand God as a covenant-maker. Although human beings deserve punishment because of their wickedness, God withholds ultimate destruction. God's covenant with Noah did not establish an intimate relationship between God and each living being, but it recalibrated moral and ecological life to be as God intended it (9:1-7), leaving open the possibility of a more intimate covenant to come (see 17:1-21). Despite their evil, human beings are allowed to live in God's world and seek a deeper relationship with the world's Creator during their time on earth. God's later covenants with his people made intimacy with him freely available to all (see Acts 2:22-40; 3:17-26).

some think that the imagery in 9:13-17 is of the Divine Warrior hanging up his bow of judgment.

9:18 *Ham is the father of Canaan:* See also 9:20-27; 10:6-20. The text emphasizes Canaan's ancestral connection to Ham to show that the Canaanite identity was inseparably linked to Ham's shameful behavior (9:20-27). The citizens of both Egypt (from which Israel escaped slavery) and Canaan (to which Israel was headed) were Ham's descendants (10:6; see Lev 18:3, 24-26; Ps 105:23, 27; 106:22). Later stories in Genesis emphasize the immoral climate of both Egypt (12:10-20) and Canaan (chs 34, 38). See 9:20-27 and 10:6-20.

9:20-27 The story of Noah begins with him walking in righteousness and obeying the Lord (6:9), but it ends with him lying drunk and naked in his tent and then delivering a curse on Canaan. Even after the great flood, the human race exhibited some of the same sinful characteristics that warranted the judgment in the first place. Special attention is given to the cursed origin of the Canaanites, the corrupt and idolatrous nation Israel would later displace from the Promised Land (see also 15:16 and note; Lev 18:3; 20:23).

9:21 *wine . . . became drunk:* Wine is a gift from God (Deut 14:26; Ps 104:15; Isa 55:1; see Luke 22:14-20; John 2:1-11). Scripture is clear, however, that excessive consumption of alcohol is a perilous sin (Prov 23:20-21, 29-35; 1 Cor 6:10).

9:22 *the father of Canaan:* See note on 9:18. • Ham's behavior was shameful. He gazed upon his naked father and, rather than covering him and keeping the matter secret, robbed him of his dignity by announcing it to his brothers (see Exod 21:15, 17; Lam 4:21; Hab 2:15). An ancient Near Eastern tale says that a son is expected to come to his father's aid when he is drunk (*Tale of Aqhat*; cp. Isa 51:17-18). Ham's neglect of familial duty explains why Noah praised Shem and Japheth but cursed Ham (9:24-27).

9:25 Noah's curse foresaw Ham's actions as morally representative of Ham's descendants through Canaan (see 10:6). • *lowest of servants:* Having refused aid to his family, Ham was condemned to base servitude.

26Then Noah said,

"May the LORD, the God of Shem, be
    blessed,
and may Canaan be his servant!
27 May God expand the territory of
    Japheth!
May Japheth share the prosperity of
    Shem,
and may Canaan be his servant."

28Noah lived another 350 years after the great flood. 29He lived 950 years, and then he died.

5. THE ACCOUNT OF NOAH'S SONS (10:1–11:9)
Nations of the Ancient World (10:1-32)
Superscription

10 This is the account of the families of Shem, Ham, and Japheth, the three sons of Noah. Many children were born to them after the great flood.

Descendants of Japheth

2The descendants of Japheth were Gomer, Magog, Madai, Javan, Tubal, Meshech, and Tiras. 3The descendants of Gomer were Ashkenaz, Riphath, and Togarmah. 4The descendants of Javan were Elishah, Tarshish, Kittim, and Rodanim. 5Their descendants became the seafaring peoples that spread out to various lands, each identified by its own language, clan, and national identity.

Descendants of Ham

6The descendants of Ham were Cush, Mizraim, Put, and Canaan. 7The descendants of Cush were Seba, Havilah, Sabtah, Raamah, and Sabteca. The descendants of Raamah were Sheba and Dedan.

8Cush was also the ancestor of Nimrod, who was the first heroic warrior on earth.

9:26
Gen 14:20

9:27
Gen 10:2-5
Isa 66:19

9:29
Gen 2:17

10:1
Gen 9:18
1 Chr 1:4

10:2
1 Chr 1:5-7
Isa 66:19
Ezek 27:13; 38:2-3, 6

10:3
Jer 51:27
Ezek 27:14

10:4
1 Chr 1:6-7

10:6
1 Chr 1:8-10

10:7
Isa 43:3
Ezek 27:15, 20, 22

. . . .

9:26 Noah refers to God as *the LORD*, who formed the covenant with Israel. *Shem* was the privileged forefather of the Israelites (see 10:21-32).

9:27 *May Japheth share the prosperity of Shem* (literally *May he live in the tents of Shem*): Japheth's descendants would live among Shem's descendants and share Shem's prosperity (cp. Rom 11:17-18).

10:1–11:9 The fifth *account* (10:1) in Genesis (see note on 2:4) unites the Table of Nations (10:2-32) and the Babel story (11:1-9) around the theme of scattering the nations (10:5, 18; 11:4, 8-9). The Table of Nations precedes the Babel story even though the Babel incident caused the geopolitical situation reflected in the Table of Nations. By reversing the order, Genesis links the repopulation of the earth with the blessing conferred upon Noah and his sons (see 9:1 and note) and shows that Abram's call (12:1-3) was God's solution to the problem of human estrangement from God as reflected in the Babel story (11:1-9).

10:1 *Many children were born . . . after the great flood:* This fulfilled the renewed creation mandate (9:1, 9; cp. 1:28).

10:2-32 This section describes the ancestral origin of the nations of the ancient Near East. Ham was at the center (10:6-20), while the descendants of Japheth and Shem spread out to the surrounding regions of Greece, Crete, Asia Minor, Mesopotamia, Madai, the Arabian peninsula, and northeast Africa. The list selectively highlights nations relevant to Israel. The total of seventy (seven times ten) names indicates completeness (see 46:27; Deut 32:8) and symbolizes

the totality of the world, which would later be blessed by the descendants of Abraham (18:18). • Although Shem is mentioned first in 10:1, he is addressed last in the Table because of his connection to Abram (10:21-31; 11:10-32; 12:1). Although God established the boundaries of all nations (see Deut 32:8; Amos 9:7; Acts 17:26), Israel was his special creation—a microcosm of seventy people (46:27) called to be a blessing to a world of seventy nations (see 12:3).

10:2 The seven sons of *Japheth* settled in the region of Anatolia (the western plateau lands of Turkey) and spoke Indo-European languages. • *Gomer* was the ancestor of the later Cimmerians who lived north of the Black Sea. • *Magog* was probably the ancestor of those who settled in the region of Lydia (see Ezek 38:2). • The descendants of *Madai* were the later Medes of northwest Iran (see 2 Kgs 17:6; Jer 51:11; Dan 5:28). • The descendants of *Javan* were the later Ionian Greeks. • The descendants of *Tubal* and *Meshech* were sometimes allies in battle (Ezek 38:2). Both were possibly from the coastal regions of Anatolia (see Ezek 27:13). • The descendants of *Tiras* possibly became the Thracians that lived near the Aegean Sea.

10:3 The *descendants of Gomer* came from near the Upper Euphrates region north of the Black Sea (cp. Ezek 38:1-9). • The descendants of *Ashkenaz* were the later Scythians who inhabited the region between the Black and Caspian Seas. • *Riphath* is near Carchemish. • The descendants of *Togarmah* are associated with Til-garimmu, the capital of Kammanu in modern Armenia (see Ezek 38:6).

10:4 *Elishah* is probably Cyprus. • *Tarshish* is possibly southwest Spain

(see note on Jon 1:3). • The *Kittim* were inhabitants of southern Cyprus. • The *Rodanim* (as in some Hebrew manuscripts and Greek version [see also 1 Chr 1:7]; most Hebrew manuscripts read *Dodanim*) were inhabitants of the island of Rhodes, later a territory of Greece.

10:5 *seafaring peoples . . . various lands:* They settled around the Mediterranean and on various islands. • *language:* This occurred after the Tower of Babel episode (11:1-9; see note on 10:1–11:9).

10:6 The peoples descended from Ham's four sons (Egyptians, Babylonians, Assyrians, Canaanites) were Israel's most hostile neighbors. • *Cush* was possibly in Ethiopia or ancient Nubia (northern Sudan). • *Mizraim* was the ancient name for Egypt (50:11). • *Put* was in Libya. • *Canaan* encompassed southern Syria, Phoenicia, and Palestine west of the Jordan River. In Moses' time, Egypt and Canaan were provinces of the same empire. Ham's descendants were excluded from the blessing of Shem's line (9:20-28).

10:7 The sons of *Cush* and *Raamah* together total seven. • *Seba* was in northern Africa (see Isa 43:3; 45:14). • *Havilah* was in southwest Arabia. • *Sabtah* was in southern Arabia, in ancient Hadramaut, near the Persian Gulf. • *Raamah* was in southwest Arabia near Najran. • *Sabteca* was in ancient Samudake near the Persian Gulf. • *Sheba* was a kingdom in southwest Arabia with commercial colonies (see 1 Kgs 10). • *Dedan* was in northern Arabia.

10:8-12 Special attention is given to the early history of *Babylonia* and *Assyria*, the Mesopotamian empires that would conquer and exile Israel and Judah.

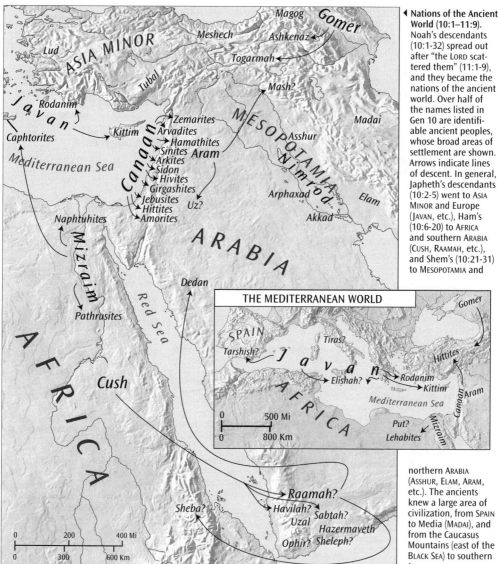

◀ **Nations of the Ancient World (10:1–11:9).** Noah's descendants (10:1-32) spread out after "the Lord scattered them" (11:1-9), and they became the nations of the ancient world. Over half of the names listed in Gen 10 are identifiable ancient peoples, whose broad areas of settlement are shown. Arrows indicate lines of descent. In general, Japheth's descendants (10:2-5) went to Asia Minor and Europe (Javan, etc.), Ham's (10:6-20) to Africa and southern Arabia (Cush, Raamah, etc.), and Shem's (10:21-31) to Mesopotamia and northern Arabia (Asshur, Elam, Aram, etc.). The ancients knew a large area of civilization, from Spain to Media (Madai), and from the Caucasus Mountains (east of the Black Sea) to southern Arabia.

THE MEDITERRANEAN WORLD

Japheth 9:27
Gomer Ezek 38:6
 Ashkenaz Jer 51:27
 Togarmah Ezek 27:14; 38:6
Magog Ezek 38:2; 39:6; Rev 20:8
Madai [Medes] 2 Kgs 17:6; Esth 1:19; Acts 2:9
Javan
 Elishah Ezek 27:7
 Tarshish Ps 72:10; Isa 23:1; 60:9; 66:19; Jer 10:9; Jon 1:3
 Tubal Isa 66:19; Ezek 27:13; 38:2
 Meshech Ps 120:5; Ezek 32:26; 39:1

Ham 14:5; 1 Chr 4:38-41; Ps 105:27
Cush 2:13; Num 12:1; 1 Chr 1:10
 Havilah 25:18; 1 Sam 15:7
 Raamah Ezek 27:22

Sheba 1 Kgs 10:1-13; Isa 60:6; Ezek 27:22-23; Matt 12:42
Dedan 25:3; Jer 25:23; Ezek 25:13; 27:15
Nimrod 1 Chr 1:10; Mic 5:6
Mizraim 50:11
 Caphtorites Deut 2:23
Put Nah 3:9
Canaan 11:31; 12:5-10
 Sidon Josh 13:4-6; 1 Kgs 5:6; 11:33; 16:31; Ezek 28:21-24; Matt 11:21-22; Luke 6:17; Acts 27:3
 Hittites 23:1-20; Num 13:29; Josh 1:4
 Jebusites Josh 15:63; Judg 19:10-11; 2 Sam 5:6-8; Zech 9:7
 Amorites 14:7, 13; Num 21:21-35; Josh 5:1; 10:1-13

Girgashites 15:21; Deut 7:1; Josh 3:10; 24:11; 1 Chr 1:14; Neh 9:8
Hivites 34:1-2; 36:2; Deut 20:17; Josh 9:3-7; 11:3
Arkites Josh 16:2; 2 Sam 15:32
Arvadites Ezek 27:8, 11
Zemarites 2 Chr 13:4
Hamathites 2 Sam 8:9-10; 2 Kgs 14:28; 23:33

Shem
Elam 14:1-9; Ezra 4:9; Isa 22:6; Jer 49:34-39; Ezek 32:24; Dan 8:2; Acts 2:9
Asshur 2:14; 25:3; 25:18; Ezek 27:23
Aram 24:10; 25:20; 28:5–31:21; Num 23:7; Judg 3:8; 2 Sam 8:5-6

⁹Since he was the greatest hunter in the world, his name became proverbial. People would say, "This man is like Nimrod, the greatest hunter in the world." ¹⁰He built his kingdom in the land of Babylonia, with the cities of Babylon, Erech, Akkad, and Calneh. ¹¹From there he expanded his territory to Assyria, building the cities of Nineveh, Rehoboth-ir, Calah, ¹²and Resen (the great city located between Nineveh and Calah). ¹³Mizraim was the ancestor of the Ludites, Anamites, Lehabites, Naphtuhites, ¹⁴Pathrusites, Casluhites, and the Caphtorites, from whom the Philistines came. ¹⁵Canaan's oldest son was Sidon, the ancestor of the Sidonians. Canaan was also the ancestor of the Hittites, ¹⁶Jebusites, Amorites, Girgashites, ¹⁷Hivites, Arkites, Sinites, ¹⁸Arvadites, Zemarites, and Hamathites. The Canaanite clans eventually spread out, ¹⁹and the territory of Canaan extended from Sidon in the north to Gerar and Gaza in the south, and east as far as Sodom, Gomorrah, Admah, and Zeboiim, near Lasha.

²⁰These were the descendants of Ham, identified by clan, language, territory, and national identity.

Descendants of Shem

²¹Sons were also born to Shem, the older brother of Japheth. Shem was the ancestor of all the descendants of Eber. ²²The descendants of Shem were Elam, Asshur, Arphaxad, Lud, and Aram.

10:10 Gen 11:9
10:11 Mic 5:6
10:14 1 Chr 1:12
10:15 Gen 15:20; 23:3 1 Chr 1:13 Jer 47:4
10:16 Gen 15:18-21
10:19 Gen 14:2

. . . .

10:9 *Nimrod* attained great fame by conquest and terror; his empire extended from Babylonia in the south to Assyria in the north (10:10-12). • *the greatest hunter in the world* (literally *a great hunter before the LORD*): Assyrian monarchs glorified their own power, often depicting themselves as valiant hunter-conquerors.

10:10-12 *Babylonia* (Hebrew *Shinar*) is the area surrounding the Tigris and Euphrates in southern Mesopotamia. This *kingdom* eventually reached into northern Mesopotamia (*Assyria*). • Of the cities mentioned, *Babylon* is most important because of its role in building the Tower of Babel (see 11:4 and note). • *Erech* was ancient Uruk and is now Warka in southern Iraq (see Ezra 4:9-10). • *Akkad* was the ancient Agade north of Babylon, home of the famous ruler Sargon (2370–2295 BC). • The location of *Calneh* is uncertain, though it is presumably one of Nimrod's cities located north of Aram-naharaim in southern Mesopotamia (cp. Amos 6:2). • *building . . . Nineveh:* Like Cain, Nimrod built cities (see 4:17 and comments). Nineveh was an ancient Assyrian city on the east bank of the Tigris River in northern Iraq. • *Rehoboth-ir* was a daughter-city of Nineveh or was located nearby. • *Calah* is modern Tell Nimrud, south of Nineveh. • *Resen* is possibly modern Selamiyeh, northwest of Tell Nimrud.

10:11 *From there he expanded his territory to Assyria:* The Hebrew text can also be translated *From that land Assyria went out.*

10:13-14 The *Ludites* were Lydian tribes west of the Nile delta. • The identity of the *Anamites* is uncertain. They were possibly Egyptians near Cyrene, west of Egypt. • The *Lehabites* were possibly a Libyan tribe. • The *Naphtuhites* inhab-ited northern Egypt. • The *Pathrusites* inhabited southern Egypt. • *Casluhites, and the Caphtorites, from whom the Philistines came* (Hebrew text reads *Casluhites, from whom the Philistines came, and Caphtorites;* cp. Jer 47:4; Amos 9:7): The *Casluhites* possibly inhabited an Egyptian district also known as Cyrenaica. The *Caphtorites* were Cretans (see Jer 47:4; Amos 9:7). The *Philistines* from Crete were sea people who lived intermittently in southwest Canaan during the period of the Exodus and later (Exod 13:17; Amos 9:7). They were among Israel's most troublesome enemies during the early monarchy (see 1–2 Sam).

10:15-18 *Sidon* settled in Phoenicia, north of *Canaan.* • *Hittites* (Hebrew *Heth*): The Hittites in Genesis were a coalition of cities within Canaan (see 26:34-35; 27:46; Ezek 16:3). They were probably not the same as the Hittites of Anatolia (Asia Minor), whose empire was one of the great empires of antiquity during the patriarchal period. • The *Jebusites* were ancient inhabitants of Jerusalem (Josh 15:63; Judg 19:10-11; 2 Sam 5:6-9). • The *Amorites* lived throughout the mountains of Palestine in Canaan (see 15:16; 48:22; Num 13:29; Deut 3:8; Josh 10:5; Judg 1:35; 10:8; Ezek 16:3). • Little is known of the *Girgashites,* a Canaanite tribe (15:21; Deut 7:1; Josh 3:10). • The *Hivites* were an uncircumcised Canaanite tribe (34:2, 13-24; Josh 9:1, 7; 11:3; Judg 3:3; 2 Sam 24:7). • The *Arkites* resided in Tell 'Arqa in Lebanon. • The *Sinites* formed a city-state and inhabited Phoenicia. • The *Arvadites* inhabited Ruad in northern Phoenicia, near the El Kebir River. They were known for shipping (cp. Ezek 27:8). • The *Zemarites* inhabited Sumur (modern Sumra), north of Arka on the Phoenician coast. • The *Hamathites* founded what is now Hama on the Orontes River, the northern boundary of Canaan (see Num 34:8; Josh 13:5; 2 Sam 8:9-10; 1 Kgs 8:65; 2 Kgs 14:25-28).

10:19 *The territory of Canaan* is specifically marked off because it would be taken from its inhabitants and given to Israel (see 15:18; Num 34:2-12; Ezek 47:15-20; 48:1-28). • An ancient north-south seacoast highway (the Via Maris) extended from *Sidon . . . to Gerar,* connecting Egypt to Mesopotamia. • Modern *Gaza* is 11 miles northwest of Gerar. • *Sodom* and *Gomorrah* were cities on the border of the land southeast of the Dead Sea. • *Admah* and *Zeboiim* are mentioned 15 times in connection with Sodom and Gomorrah (14:2, 8; Deut 29:23; see Hos 11:8). All four cities were destroyed by God to cleanse the land (see ch 19). • *Lasha* was possibly in the northern region of the Dead Sea.

10:21 *Shem, the older brother of Japheth* (or *Shem, whose older brother was Japheth*), was the father of the Semitic peoples. The descendants listed represent countries east of Israel (modern Iraq, Iran, and Syria). The narrator lists these locations within Mesopotamia since Abram, the father of Israel, originated from this area (see 11:27-32). • *Eber* receives special attention because of his connection with Abram (see note on 10:24).

10:22 The descendants of *Elam* lived in the region of modern southwestern Iran (see 14:1, 9; Ezra 4:9; Isa 11:11). • The descendants of *Asshur* were later Assyrians who lived under Nimrod's jurisdiction (see 10:11). Sumerians descended from Ham were ousted by Mesopotamian Semites. • *Arphaxad* possibly settled northeast of Nineveh; his descendants are further described in 11:12-26. • *Lud* was near the Tigris River; its people were related to the Lydians (see 10:13). • *Aram* was a kingdom of tribes that lived in the Mesopotamian plains.

10:23
Job 1:1
10:24
Luke 3:35
10:32
Gen 9:19; 10:1
11:2
Gen 10:10; 14:1
Isa 11:11
11:3
Gen 14:10
11:4
2 Sam 8:13
11:5
Gen 18:21
Exod 19:11
11:6
Gen 9:19; 11:1

23The descendants of Aram were Uz, Hul, Gether, and Mash.

24Arphaxad was the father of Shelah, and Shelah was the father of Eber.

25Eber had two sons. The first was named Peleg (which means "division"), for during his lifetime the people of the world were divided into different language groups. His brother's name was Joktan.

26Joktan was the ancestor of Almodad, Sheleph, Hazarmaveth, Jerah, 27Hadoram, Uzal, Diklah, 28Obal, Abimael, Sheba, 29Ophir, Havilah, and Jobab. All these were descendants of Joktan. 30The territory they occupied extended from Mesha all the way to Sephar in the eastern mountains.

31These were the descendants of Shem, identified by clan, language, territory, and national identity.

Conclusion

32These are the clans that descended from Noah's sons, arranged by nation according to their lines of descent. All the nations of the earth descended from these clans after the great flood.

The Dispersion at Babel (11:1-9)
The Tower of Babel

11 At one time all the people of the world spoke the same language and used the same words. 2As the people migrated to the east, they found a plain in the land of Babylonia and settled there.

3They began saying to each other, "Let's make bricks and harden them with fire." (In this region bricks were used instead of stone, and tar was used for mortar.) 4Then they said, "Come, let's build a great city for ourselves with a tower that reaches into the sky. This will make us famous and keep us from being scattered all over the world."

The LORD Disperses the Nations

5But the LORD came down to look at the city and the tower the people were building. 6"Look!" he said. "The people are united,

10:23 The patriarchs later interacted with *the descendants of Aram* (see 25:20; 31:20; Deut 26:5). • *Uz* was the chief Aramean tribe, possibly located northeast of the Jordan; it was Job's home (see Job 1:1; see also Lam 4:21). • *Hul* is unknown. He possibly founded Armenia. • *Gether* is unknown; he was possibly the founder of the Syrians. • *Mash* might be associated with Mount Masus in northern Mesopotamia or with a part of the Lebanon Mountains.

10:24 *Arphaxad was the father of Shelah:* Greek version reads *Arphaxad was the father of Cainan, Cainan was the father of Shelah.* Cp. Luke 3:36. • *Shelah* is unknown, but may be short for Methushelah (cp. 38:5, 11). • *Eber* was the ancestor of Abram the Hebrew (11:10-26); his name is at the root of the term "Hebrew" (see 14:13; 39:14; 40:15; 41:12; Exod 2:11; 3:18).

10:25 *Peleg* means *division*, anticipating the separation of people into *language groups* after Babel (11:1-9). Peleg's line led to Abram (see 11:16-26). • *Joktan* was the ancestor of the southern Arabian tribes. The Ishmaelite tribes are in northern Arabia (see 25:13-16).

10:26-32 There were fourteen sons of Shem by Eber through *Joktan*. The placement of the Babel story between the lines of Joktan and Peleg ties Joktan to the judgment of the Babel story (11:1-9) and ties Peleg to Abram (11:27–12:1).

10:26-29 *Almodad* was an ancestor, region, or tribe in modern Yemen. • *Sheleph* was a tribe of Yemen. • *Hazarmaveth* was related to Hadra-

maut in southern Arabia. • *Jerah* is unknown, but was possibly associated with Mount Barach. • *Hadoram* was an Arabian tribe. • *Uzal* was Sana'a, an old capital of Yemen in pre-Islamic times. • *Diklah* was a southern Arabian oasis in Mina. • *Obal* was between Hodeida and Sana'a in southwest Arabia. • *Abimael* was a Sabaean. • *Sheba* was in southern Arabia (see 10:7). • *Ophir* was a region of southern Arabia between Sheba and Havilah; it was a source of gold (Isa 13:12). • *Havilah:* See 10:7. • *Jobab* was possibly Jobebitai in southern Arabia.

10:30 *Mesha* was a region in northern Arabia, south of Hadramaut. • *Sephar* is identified with Isfar, south of Hadramaut in Yemen.

11:1-9 The story of the unfinished tower carries forward themes of language and solidarity from the Table of Nations (ch 10). The builders' desire for autonomy recalls the rebellion in Eden (ch 3) and establishes the need for Abram's redemptive faith in the midst of international disorder (ch 12). The scattering of the nations anticipates the warning to Israel that idolatry would result in their being scattered and their cities devastated (see Num 10:35; Lev 26:33; Deut 4:27; 28:64; 30:3). Chronologically, the story is a flashback that explains the rise of the nations during Peleg's time (see 10:25).

11:1 *At one time:* The events described in 11:1-9 led to the scattering of nations that is reflected in the genealogies of 10:2-30. The reversal of order has a theological purpose (see note on 10:1–11:9).

11:2 *migrated to the east:* See note on

3:24. • *Babylonia* (Hebrew *Shinar*) was located in southern Mesopotamia, the region of Nimrod's later empire and city-building campaign (see 10:10; Isa 11:11; Dan 1:2; Zech 5:11).

11:3 *Stone* was plentiful in Canaan; in Mesopotamia, stone was scarce and brick technology was developed. • *Tar* was made from bitumen, a natural, cement-like, waterproof asphalt (see 6:14; Exod 2:3).

11:4 Far from the original garden (2:15), the first cities of Genesis represent arrogance (4:17), tyranny (10:8-12), and wickedness (18:20-21). The city on the Babylonian plain was a magnet for human pride and idolatry. • *a tower that reaches into the sky:* This was probably a temple-tower (a ziggurat). Common in ancient Babylonian urban culture, ziggurats were regarded as sacred mountains by which deities descended to earth (Jacob's dream in 28:12 possibly reflects this idea). • *This will make us famous* (literally *let us make a name for ourselves*): The tower builders sought fame through idolatrous ambition. God promised to give Abram a famous name because of his humble obedience (12:2).

11:5 *came down:* The tower was a human attempt to ascend to God's realm (see Deut 26:15; Ps 2:4; 103:19; 115:16). The folly of that attempt was exposed by God's "coming down" to see their feeble efforts.

11:6 If left unchecked, the tower builders' solidarity and ambition would allow human wickedness to flourish in unimaginable ways.

and they all speak the same language. After this, nothing they set out to do will be impossible for them! ⁷Come, let's go down and confuse the people with different languages. Then they won't be able to understand each other."

⁸In that way, the LORD scattered them all over the world, and they stopped building the city. ⁹That is why the city was called Babel, because that is where the LORD confused the people with different languages. In this way he scattered them all over the world.

6. THE ACCOUNT OF SHEM'S DESCENDANTS (11:10-26)

¹⁰This is the account of Shem's family.

Two years after the great flood, when Shem was 100 years old, he became the father of Arphaxad. ¹¹After the birth of Arphaxad, Shem lived another 500 years and had other sons and daughters. ¹²When Arphaxad was 35 years old, he became the father of Shelah. ¹³After the birth of Shelah, Arphaxad lived another 403 years and had other sons and daughters. ¹⁴When Shelah was 30 years old, he became the father of Eber. ¹⁵After the birth of Eber, Shelah lived another 403 years and had other sons and daughters.

¹⁶When Eber was 34 years old, he became the father of Peleg. ¹⁷After the birth of Peleg, Eber lived another 430 years and had other sons and daughters. ¹⁸When Peleg was 30 years old, he became the father of Reu. ¹⁹After the birth of Reu, Peleg lived another 209 years and had other sons and daughters. ²⁰When Reu was 32 years old, he became the father of Serug. ²¹After the birth of Serug, Reu lived another 207 years and had other sons and daughters. ²²When Serug was 30 years old, he became the father of Nahor. ²³After the birth of Nahor, Serug lived another 200 years and had other sons and daughters. ²⁴When Nahor was 29 years old, he became the father of Terah. ²⁵After the birth of Terah, Nahor lived another 119 years and had other sons and daughters. ²⁶After Terah was 70 years old, he became the father of Abram, Nahor, and Haran.

7. THE ACCOUNT OF TERAH'S DESCENDANTS (11:27–25:11)
The Family of Terah (11:27-32)

²⁷This is the account of Terah's family. Terah was the father of Abram, Nahor, and Haran; and Haran was the father of Lot. ²⁸But Haran died in Ur of the Chaldeans, the land of his birth, while his father, Terah, was

Cross-references

11:7 Gen 1:26
11:8 Gen 9:19
11:9 Gen 10:10
11:10 Gen 10:22-25; Luke 3:36
11:12 Luke 3:36
11:13 1 Chr 1:17
11:14 Luke 3:35
11:16 Luke 3:35
11:18 Luke 3:35
11:20 Luke 3:35
11:22 Luke 3:34
11:24 Josh 24:2; Luke 3:34
11:26 Gen 22:20; 1 Chr 1:26-27; Luke 3:34
11:29 Gen 17:15; 20:11-12; 22:20
11:30 Gen 16:1; 18:11; 25:21; 1 Sam 1:5; Luke 1:7
11:31 Gen 27:43; Josh 24:2; Acts 7:4

. . . .

11:7 *Come, let's go down:* God addresses his angelic court (see 1:26; 3:22; and notes). • *won't be able to understand each other:* Their inability to communicate would curtail their unified sinful ambition. The God-honoring unity of language on the day of Pentecost was a symbolic reversal of the Babel dispersion (Acts 2:5-13; see Zeph 3:9).

11:8 *the LORD scattered them:* Similarly, Adam and Eve's punishment for grasping at autonomy and Cain's punishment for murder involved banishment and dispersion (3:23; 4:12, 14; 9:19; 10:5, 25, 32).

11:9 *Babel:* Or *Babylon. Babel* sounds like a Hebrew term that means "confusion." The Babylonians viewed their city as the residence or gateway of the gods. The pun that concludes this account accurately reveals Babylon's spiritual confusion. Babylon achieved prominence under Nimrod (10:10) and in later biblical history (see 2 Kgs 25). Its role as an epicenter of arrogance and idolatry make it a fitting image for the anti-God forces associated with the end of time (e.g., Rev 14:8; 16:19; 18:2). • The tower builders had centralized to ascend into God's realm (11:3-4). God descended and *scattered them all over the world* to

frustrate their idolatrous ambition.

11:10 This *account of Shem's family* resumes the line of Shem from 10:21-32, now with special focus on the line leading to Abram. Only Abram and Israel are heirs to Shem's God (see 9:26-27; Deut 32:8-9). The Babel story vividly depicts the culture that Abram was called to abandon (12:1; 24:6-7). Together with the account of Terah's descendants (11:27-32), this second account of Shem's line forms a bridge from the universal history of chs 1–11 to the national history of Israel that begins in ch 12. Abram is the remnant from Babel's confused world. God called him as an act of grace whereby the fractured world of Babel would be blessed (12:3). • *the father of:* Or *the ancestor of;* also in 11:12, 14, 16, 18, 20, 22, 24. Hebrew genealogies do not necessarily list every single generation.

11:11 *After the birth of:* Or *After the birth of this ancestor of;* also in 11:13, 15, 17, 19, 21, 23, 25 (see note on 11:10).

11:12-13 Greek version reads ¹²*When Arphaxad was 135 years old, he became the father of Cainan.* ¹³*After the birth of Cainan, Arphaxad lived another 430 years and had other sons and daughters, and then he died. When*

Cainan was 130 years old, he became the father of Shelah. After the birth of Shelah, Cainan lived another 330 years and had other sons and daughters, and then he died. Cp. Luke 3:35-36.

11:18 *Peleg:* See note on 10:25.

11:27–25:11 *This is the account* (Hebrew *toledoth;* see note on 2:4) *of Terah's family:* What follows are the particulars about the family descended from Terah, notably about Abraham and God's covenant with him, and about Isaac, the child of promise, who carried forward the line and the blessing to the next generation.

11:27-32 This brief section provides a complete summary of Terah's life and accounts for his other sons and their marriages; it also introduces Lot, Abram's nephew, who later played a prominent role. The ancestors, including Terah and his family, were idolatrous, worshiping other gods in Mesopotamia (Josh 24:2).

11:27 *Nahor* was the father of Laban, whose daughters later became Jacob's wives (chs 29–31). • *Lot:* See "Lot," 19:1-38, p. 58.

11:28 The call of Abram occurred in *Ur of the Chaldeans* (15:7; Acts 7:2-4), the

12:1
Gen 15:7
*Acts 7:3
Heb 11:8
i*'erets* (0776)
  ▸ Gen 13:17

12:2
Gen 13:16; 15:5; 17:4;
18:18; 22:17
Zech 8:13
k*barak* (1288)
  ▸ Gen 49:28

12:3
Gen 22:18; 26:4
Exod 23:22
Acts 3:25
*Gal 3:8

12:4
Gen 11:26, 31

still living. ²⁹Meanwhile, Abram and Nahor both married. The name of Abram's wife was Sarai, and the name of Nahor's wife was Milcah. (Milcah and her sister Iscah were daughters of Nahor's brother Haran.) ³⁰But Sarai was unable to become pregnant and had no children.

³¹One day Terah took his son Abram, his daughter-in-law Sarai (his son Abram's wife), and his grandson Lot (his son Haran's child) and moved away from Ur of the Chaldeans. He was headed for the land of Canaan, but they stopped at Haran and settled there. ³²Terah lived for 205 years and died while still in Haran.

The Call of Abram (12:1-9)

12 The LORD had said to Abram, "Leave your native ʲcountry, your relatives, and your father's family, and go to the ʲland that I will show you. ²I will make you into a great nation. I will ᵏbless you and make you famous, and you will be a blessing to others. ³I will bless those who bless you and curse those who treat you with contempt. All the families on earth will be blessed through you."

⁴So Abram departed as the LORD had instructed, and Lot went with him. Abram was seventy-five years old when he left Haran. ⁵He took his wife, Sarai, his nephew Lot,

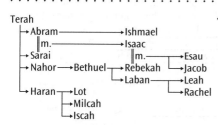

Terah
├→ Abram ──────────→ Ishmael
│ ‖ m. ───────────→ Isaac
├→ Sarai   ‖ m. ──→ Esau
├→ Nahor → Bethuel → Rebekah → Jacob
│   └→ Laban → Leah
└→ Haran → Lot   └→ Rachel
        ├→ Milcah
        └→ Iscah

◀ **Terah's Family (11:27-30),** to four generations. See profiles for ABRAHAM (p. 46), SARAH (p. 55), LOT (p. 58), ISHMAEL (p. 53), ISAAC (p. 63), REBEKAH (p. 69), ESAU (p. 71), JACOB (p. 76), LEAH (p. 79), and RACHEL (p. 78).

main city of Sumer in Mesopotamia near the mouth of the Persian Gulf. The family had moved there perhaps generations before the call. Their ancestral home ("native country," 12:1) was apparently near Haran, in the region of the descendants of Shem (11:10-26); thus they settled there when they left Ur (11:31) and were later described as "Aramaeans" (Deut 26:5). • *land of his birth:* The same Hebrew phrase is repeated in 12:1 ("native country"), making Ur, not Haran, the location of Abram's call (see 15:7; Neh 9:7; Acts 7:2).

11:29 *Sarai* means "princess" in Hebrew. No mention is made of Sarai's parentage, perhaps to add suspense to the Abimelech story, which reveals that she was Abram's half sister (20:9-12). Later, the law prohibited such a marriage (Lev 18:9; 20:17; Deut 27:22). • *Nahor's wife was Milcah:* Milcah was Haran's daughter and Nahor's niece (see 11:29). Her son Bethuel was the father of Rebekah, the wife of Abram's son Isaac (24:10, 15, 24). The name Milcah is related to the Hebrew word meaning "queen." In Akkadian, it is a title of the goddess Ishtar, the moon-god's daughter. Terah's name is related to the word for "moon" in Hebrew; his whole family appears to have worshiped Sin, the moon-god (see Josh 24:14).

11:30 *Sarai*, Rebekah (25:21), and Rachel (29:31) all suffered infertility. Sarai's situation in particular highlights the paradox between the apparent reality and God's promise to give many descendants (12:2). The Israelite nation's origin from barren women fixes its identity in the

sovereignty of God, who miraculously gives children to barren women (see also 1 Sam 1:2; 2:5; Ps 113:9; Isa 54:1).

11:31 *Terah took:* The text is clear that Abram's departure from Ur was prompted by God's calling (see note on 11:28), but the event is described from Terah's perspective, in keeping with the patriarchy of ancient Near Eastern culture. This cultural deference to the oldest male is evidently why Abram did not continue on to Canaan by himself at this time (see Acts 7:2-4). • *Haran* was 550 miles northwest of Ur, near the Syrian-Turkish border. Despite the similar name, there is no connection with Terah's son Haran, who had died in Ur (11:28). • *Haran* means "caravan." Ancient commercial routes converged there, making it a key site for trade. • *Haran* was also well-known for the moon worship to which Terah's family was apparently devoted (see note on 11:29).

11:32 *205 years:* Some ancient versions read *145 years;* cp. 11:26 and 12:4.

12:1-9 Through Abram's faith and family, God began restoring the blessing. God called Abram from a pagan world to begin a new nation; his promises to Abram later became a covenant (ch 15). • God's call to Abram later helped convince the Israelites to leave Egypt and go to the land God promised to Abram. It also reminded the Babylonian exiles of their need to return to their own land (e.g., Isa 51).

12:1-3 These verses are structured around two commands to Abram: *Leave*

and *be a blessing* (see note on 12:2). Each directive is followed by three promises conditioned upon obedience.

12:1 *Abram* knew that he should leave, but he did not know where he was going. Obedience required faith.

12:2 *and you will be a blessing* (or *so that you will be a blessing*): This clause is a command in Hebrew, but it is also a promise conditioned upon Abram's obedience to God's command (12:1): "Go . . . so that you will be a blessing. Be a blessing, so that I can bless and curse others." • *make you famous* (literally *make your name great*): Abram received the fame sought by the builders of Babel (see 11:4 and note).

12:3 Based on Abram's obedience to the command to be a blessing (12:2), God gave him three more promises. • *those who treat you with contempt:* People who disregarded Abram and his covenant were rejecting God's choice and plan. • *All the families on earth will be blessed:* By faith, they could participate in the covenant God was making with Abram. The blessing spread to the whole world through Abraham, Israel, the covenants, the prophets, Scripture, and the Messiah (Gal 3:8, 16; cp. Rom 9:4-5).

12:4-9 Abram's obedience to God's call corresponded to God's commands (see note on 12:1-3). He journeyed to Canaan (12:4-6) and became a blessing (12:5-9).

12:4 *Abram* was middle-aged, settled, prosperous, aristocratic, and polytheistic (see note on 11:27-32). When *the LORD* spoke to him (12:1-3), he obediently left his old ways in Ur to follow God's plan. Since Abram responded in faith, God's promises (12:2-3) could be confirmed in a binding covenant (15:8-21).

12:5 *The people* (Hebrew *hannepesh,* "the lives") *he had taken into his household* were probably converts; Abram first became a blessing by influencing people in his household to join him in following the Lord.

and all his wealth—his livestock and all the people he had taken into his household at Haran—and headed for the land of Canaan. When they arrived in Canaan, [6]Abram traveled through the land as far as Shechem. There he set up camp beside the oak of Moreh. At that time, the area was inhabited by Canaanites.

[7]Then the LORD appeared to Abram and said, "I will give this land to your [a]descendants." And Abram built an altar there and dedicated it to the LORD, who had appeared to him. [8]After that, Abram traveled south and set up camp in the hill country, with Bethel to the west and Ai to the east. There he built another altar and dedicated it to the LORD, and he worshiped the LORD. [9]Then Abram continued traveling south by stages toward the Negev.

Abram and Sarai in Egypt (12:10-20)

[10]At that time a severe famine struck the land of Canaan, forcing Abram to go down

12:6
Gen 33:18; 35:4
Deut 11:30
12:7
Gen 13:15
*Gal 3:16
ª*zera'* (2233)
▸ Gen 26:3
12:8
Gen 4:26; 8:20; 22:9
12:9
Gen 13:1; 20:1
12:10
Gen 26:1; 42:5

God's Covenant Relationships (12:1-9)

Gen 9:1-17; 15:1-21;
17:9-14
Exod 6:2-5;
19:1–24:18
Lev 26:1-46
Deut 7:7-15; 29:2-29
Josh 8:30-35; 24:1-8
2 Sam 7:5-16
Ezra 10:1-17
Isa 59:20-21
Jer 31:31-34; 33:19-
26; 34:12-20
Ezek 16:1-63
Luke 22:20
Gal 4:21-31
Eph 2:11-13
Heb 8:6-13; 10:11-
18; 12:24

The covenant relationships that God established and developed with his people may be the most important theological theme of the OT. The covenant theme in the OT begins with Noah, through whom God made a covenant with all of creation. God promised to uphold the created order and gave the rainbow as the sign of this commitment (9:1-17).

God later established a covenant relationship with Abraham and his family; the sign of this covenant was circumcision (12:1-9; 15:1-21; 17:9-14). God's covenant with Abraham promised descendants, land, and rulers; these promises formed the basis for the covenants God later made with his people.

God's covenant with Israel at Mount Sinai was a national covenant (Exod 19–24) whose sign was the Sabbath; it addressed how Israel would be the chosen descendants of Abraham. This covenant took the form of a suzerain-vassal treaty, an ancient relationship established between a great king and loyal subjects (see note on Exod 20:1–23:33).

The Sinai covenant was renewed in Deuteronomy and Josh 24:1-28. The renewal focused on God's promise of land and how Israel would conduct itself while inhabiting the land. Through his covenant with Israel, God affirmed that he was their God and they were his people, a relationship that required their complete loyalty (Jer 11:4; 24:7; Ezek 11:20; 14:11). God, the great king, would bless and protect the nation Israel. Israel's obligation was to keep God's commands, decrees, and regulations (Exod 19:5, 8; 24:3, 7; Deut 30:15-20).

God later formed a covenant with King David (2 Sam 7:5-16), which provided the line of kings promised to Abraham and Jacob (Gen 17:6, 16; 35:11).

Years later, at a low point in Israel's history, the prophet Jeremiah foretold a "new covenant" in Israel's future (Jer 31:31-33), in which the ideals of the covenants with Abraham and Israel would finally be realized. Jeremiah's prophecy found fulfillment in the person and work of Jesus Christ (see Luke 22:20; Heb 8:6-13; 12:24). This new covenant provides the ultimate fulfillment of the previous promises that were made to God's people.

God's covenants were motivated by God's faithful love (Hebrew *khesed*), which enabled a relationship to continue between God and his people. God initiated this relationship, announced its conditions, and rewarded his people accordingly. These covenants were not rewards but divine gifts. God may exclude people from the covenant relationship (Hos 1:9), but he will not break, revoke, or withdraw his covenants. If broken or annulled by the human parties, the covenant could be renewed only through a reapplication of God's faithful love (Exod 34:6-9; Jer 31:31-33). God's love has preserved the relationship, but his grace must not be mocked (Isa 54:7-10; 55:3; 61:8; 1 Cor 6:9-10; Gal 6:7).

12:6-7 *The oak of Moreh* was apparently a Canaanite shrine; fertile groves of trees were sacred to the Canaanites (cp. Isa 1:29), and *Moreh* means "teacher." Abram proclaimed (Luther: "preached") the Lord's name beside a pagan place of worship and instruction (12:8). • *Abram continued to be a blessing* when he *built an altar* to worship God at *Shechem* and east of Bethel (12:8).

12:7 *The LORD appeared to Abram* at Shechem (12:6) to confirm that *this land* was the Promised Land. Israel was to occupy this land, but sharing in God's promises required their faith (cp. Num 14; Josh 1:6-9). • *to your descendants* (literally *seed*): Abram did not yet possess the land; he lived as a temporary settler.

12:8-9 *Abram* had to keep moving camp because the Canaanites had the fertile land.

12:8 *he worshiped the LORD* (literally *he made proclamation of the LORD by name*): Proclaiming the name (identity and character) of the Lord is central to worship and witness (cp. 4:26; see Exod 34:5-7). Abram had to distinguish his sacrificial worship from that of the pagan Canaanites.

12:11
Gen 29:17

12:12
Gen 20:11

12:16
Gen 20:14; 24:35

12:17
1 Chr 16:21
Ps 105:14

12:18
Gen 20:9-10

12:19
Gen 20:5; 26:9

13:1
Gen 12:9

13:2
Gen 12:5

to Egypt, where he lived as a foreigner. ¹¹As he was approaching the border of Egypt, Abram said to his wife, Sarai, "Look, you are a very beautiful woman. ¹²When the Egyptians see you, they will say, 'This is his wife. Let's kill him; then we can have her!' ¹³So please tell them you are my sister. Then they will spare my life and treat me well because of their interest in you."

¹⁴And sure enough, when Abram arrived in Egypt, everyone noticed Sarai's beauty. ¹⁵When the palace officials saw her, they sang her praises to Pharaoh, their king, and Sarai was taken into his palace. ¹⁶Then Pharaoh gave Abram many gifts because of her—sheep, goats, cattle, male and female donkeys, male and female servants, and camels.

¹⁷But the Lord sent terrible plagues upon Pharaoh and his household because of Sarai, Abram's wife. ¹⁸So Pharaoh summoned Abram and accused him sharply. "What have you done to me?" he demanded. "Why didn't you tell me she was your wife? ¹⁹Why did you say, 'She is my sister,' and allow me to take her as my wife? Now then, here is your wife. Take her and get out of here!" ²⁰Pharaoh ordered some of his men to escort them, and he sent Abram out of the country, along with his wife and all his possessions.

Abram and Lot Separate (13:1-18)

13 So Abram left Egypt and traveled north into the Negev, along with his wife and Lot and all that they owned. ²(Abram was very rich in livestock, silver,

· ·

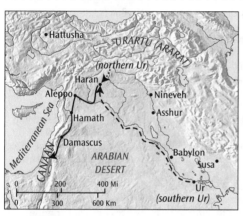

◀ **Abram's Journey to Canaan (12:1-9).** Traditionally, "Ur of the Chaldeans" (11:28, 31; 15:7) has been identified with UR in Mesopotamia (SOUTHERN UR), a chief city of ancient Sumer. Some scholars have proposed a NORTHERN UR to the north of HARAN, where Abram's extended family settled (see 27:43; 28:10; 29:4; Acts 7:2-4).

about Sarai that he could not prevent. His scheme had resulted in a terrible bind that endangered him, Sarai, and the promise. • Abram appeared to prosper from his deception, but the new possessions also caused crises. Abram and Lot had to separate (ch 13), and Hagar, an Egyptian maiden, became the mother of the Ishmaelites, perennial enemies of Israel (ch 16).

12:14-15 *Sarai* was 65 years old, but she lived to be 127; she was like a modern childless woman of about 35. She and Abram came from a noble family (see note on 11:29), so she was regal in her person and dress. Pharaoh was attracted by her physical appearance and her political assets.

12:15 *Pharaoh* was a title, not a personal name (37:36; Exod 1:15).

12:17-19 God's intervention rescued Sarai and preserved the marriage to fulfill the covenant promise. Sarai's restoration to Abram came with a rebuke from Pharaoh on God's behalf (12:18-19).

12:20 No answer to Pharaoh's questions (12:18-19) was needed, because the rebuke was followed by expulsion. Pharaoh's command paralleled God's command to Abram (12:1), but Pharaoh's demand brought shame and disgrace. God was faithful in preserving his promise.

13:1-7 This story is set in conflict amidst God's blessings. In the opening verses, Abram returns to a place where he had built an altar. Previous events are emphasized as Abram's return to the land is described (13:3-4); Abram renewed his worship and again proclaimed the Lord's name (cp. 12:8).

13:2 *Abram* already had powerful resources (12:5); his Egyptian sojourn augmented his wealth and power (12:16).

12:10-20 This episode shows that God would not allow Abram to jeopardize his promises. Just after Abram's obedience to the call, a famine tested his weak faith. God delivered him and his family, even though Abram foolishly used deception rather than trusting in God to preserve him in Egypt. • This story deliberately parallels Israel's later bondage in Egypt. Because of a famine (12:10 // 47:13), Abram/Israel went to Egypt (12:10 // 47:27); there was an attempt to kill the males and save the females (12:12 // Exod 1:22); God plagued Egypt (12:17 // Exod 7:14–11:10); Abram/Israel plundered Egypt (12:16 // Exod 12:35-36); they were expelled (Hebrew *shalakh*, "send"; 12:19-20 // Exod 12:31-33) and ascended to the Negev (13:1 // Num 13:17, 22). Israel was to believe that God would deliver them from bondage in Egypt through the plagues because their ancestor had already been rescued from bondage in Egypt.

12:10-13 Abram's scheme was rooted in fear that jeopardized his family and God's promises. Abram was not walking

by faith when he went to Egypt. He stopped building altars and his deceptiveness took center stage. Deception would plague his family throughout Genesis (26:1-11; 27:1-29; 29:15-30; 30:34-36; 31:6-11; 37:18-35; 39:7-20). • Abram's plan was probably based on a social custom whereby a brother arranged the marriage of his sister (cp. 24:29-61). Abram may have thought that any potential suitor would have to deal with him, giving him time to leave with Sarai. He did not count on Pharaoh's acting without negotiation (12:14-16).

12:10 The Nile River provided ample irrigation, so *Egypt* was often the last region to suffer from *famine*.

12:13 *tell them you are my sister:* This request occurs three times in Genesis (see also 20:2; 26:7). The text explains that this was Abram's usual strategy (20:13), and his son did likewise. This first occasion was outside the land, the second (ch 20) within, showing that God protected his promise in both regions.

12:14-16 Abram was bound by the king's gift to an unwanted agreement

ABRAHAM (11:26–25:11)

Gen 26:2-5
Exod 3:15-16; 6:3;
32:13
Josh 24:2-3
1 Chr 1:27-34
2 Chr 20:7
Isa 29:22; 41:8;
51:1-2
Ezek 33:24
Matt 1:1-2; 3:9;
8:11; 22:31-32
Luke 16:19-31
John 8:31-58
Acts 7:2-8
Rom 4:1-23; 9:5-9;
11:16-17
Gal 3:6-29
Heb 6:13-15; 11:8-
12; 11:17-19
Jas 2:21-23

"By faith . . . Abraham obeyed when God called him to leave home and go to another land. . . . He went without knowing where he was going. . . . By faith . . . Abraham offered Isaac as a sacrifice when God was testing him" (Heb 11:8, 17). These key events in Abraham's life illustrate the faithful obedience for which he is best known.

God called Abram from the city of Ur to become the patriarch of God's people. Abram's family relationships are recorded in Gen 11:26-32. Terah had three sons: Abram, Nahor, and Haran. Terah left Ur with Abram, Abram's wife Sarai, and Lot, whose father, Haran, had died. On his way to Canaan, Terah settled in the city of Haran (11:31). God had called Abram to a new land while he was still in Ur (Acts 7:2-4); God told Abram, "Leave your native country, your relatives, and your father's family, and go to the land that I will show you" (12:1). God blessed Abram by making a covenant with him that included promises of great blessing, numerous descendants, and a new land (12:1-3). These promises later saved Israel from destruction when they repeatedly failed to keep their covenant with God (see Lev 26:40-45).

Abram left Haran at age seventy-five. Entering Canaan, he went first to Shechem, a Canaanite city between Mount Gerizim and Mount Ebal. God appeared to Abram near the oak of Moreh, a Canaanite shrine (see note on 12:6-7). Abram built altars there and near Bethel (12:8), proclaiming the one true God at these centers of false worship. Abram later moved to Hebron by the oaks of Mamre, again building an altar to worship God (13:18).

When God again promised blessings to Abram in a vision (15:1), Abram exclaimed that he was still childless because Sarai was barren (11:30), and that Eliezer of Damascus was his heir (15:2). This obscure statement is clarified by the Nuzi documents. According to Hurrian custom, a childless couple of means could adopt an heir, often a slave who would be responsible for their burial and mourning. A natural son born after the slave-heir's adoption would supplant him. Apparently Abram had adopted Eliezer in this manner, but God promised that Abram's own son would be his heir (15:4).

The hallmark of Abram's life was that he believed the Lord, and the Lord considered him righteous because of his faith (15:6; see Rom 4:3; Gal 3:6; Jas 2:23). Abram's righteousness was not because he never sinned—on several occasions he failed to do what was right, twice he lied about Sarah out of fear, and he took the provision of a son into his own hands with Hagar rather than praying for God to act (16:1-5; cp. 25:21). But he consistently returned to faith as the fundamental principle of his life before God.

Abram was eighty-six years old when Ishmael was born to Sarai's servant Hagar. When Abram was ninety-nine, the Lord appeared to him and reaffirmed his covenant promise of a son and of blessing (ch 17), adding circumcision as the mark of the covenant relationship (17:9-14). God also changed Abram's and Sarai's names to Abraham and Sarah (17:5, 15). Abraham laughed at the promise of another son (17:17). Shortly afterward, the Lord appeared again to Abraham (ch 18) and again announced the promised son. This time, Sarah was caught laughing in disbelief (18:12-15). Abraham was 100 years old and his wife 90 when the Lord did "exactly what he had promised" (21:1). The long-promised son was born and was fittingly named Isaac ("he laughs!").

The supreme test of Abraham's faith came when God commanded him to sacrifice Isaac (ch 22). Abraham obeyed faithfully, trusting that God would not thwart his own purposes (see Heb 11:17-19). Just as the knife was about to fall, the angel of God stopped Abraham and provided a ram for him to sacrifice in Isaac's place (22:13). Abraham's faith was complete (22:12).

Christians understand the sacrifice of Isaac as prefiguring God's provision of his only Son, Jesus Christ, as a sacrifice for the sins of the world. God has fulfilled his covenant with Abraham through Jesus Christ, through whom the blessing of salvation is extended to all who have faith (Rom 4:16-17), and believers become Abraham's spiritual descendants (Gal 3:29). Abraham's life shows that God is faithful and worthy of belief and obedience. The full import of God's promise was realized when the gospel was preached to all nations and people from all families of the earth responded in faith (see Gal 3:6-9).

Abraham was God's friend (2 Chr 20:7; Jas 2:23). All who live by faith are challenged to live as he did, daily venturing into the unknown with trust in God's guidance and sustenance. Abraham is one of many great "witnesses" to a life of faith (Heb 12:1; see Heb 11), inspiring believers to persevere in faith because we know God is faithful.

13:3
Gen 12:8-9

13:5
Gen 12:5

13:6
Gen 12:5; 36:7

13:7
Gen 12:6; 26:20

13:8
Prov 15:18; 20:3

13:9
Gen 20:15

13:10
Gen 2:8-10

13:13
Gen 18:20
Num 32:23
Isa 1:10; 3:9
2 Pet 2:8

13:14
Gen 28:14
Deut 3:27; 34:1-4

13:15
*Gal 3:16
Gen 12:2, 7; 15:18;
17:7-8

13:16
Num 23:10

13:17
Num 13:17-25
ᵇ*erets* (0776)
ᵇ Gen 15:18

13:18
Gen 14:13; 18:1

and gold.) ³From the Negev, they continued traveling by stages toward Bethel, and they pitched their tents between Bethel and Ai, where they had camped before. ⁴This was the same place where Abram had built the altar, and there he worshiped the LORD again.

⁵Lot, who was traveling with Abram, had also become very wealthy with flocks of sheep and goats, herds of cattle, and many tents. ⁶But the land could not support both Abram and Lot with all their flocks and herds living so close together. ⁷So disputes broke out between the herdsmen of Abram and Lot. (At that time Canaanites and Perizzites were also living in the land.)

⁸Finally Abram said to Lot, "Let's not allow this conflict to come between us or our herdsmen. After all, we are close relatives! ⁹The whole countryside is open to you. Take your choice of any section of the land you want, and we will separate. If you want the land to the left, then I'll take the land on the right. If you prefer the land on the right, then I'll go to the left."

¹⁰Lot took a long look at the fertile plains of the Jordan Valley in the direction of Zoar.

The whole area was well watered everywhere, like the garden of the LORD or the beautiful land of Egypt. (This was before the LORD destroyed Sodom and Gomorrah.) ¹¹Lot chose for himself the whole Jordan Valley to the east of them. He went there with his flocks and servants and parted company with his uncle Abram. ¹²So Abram settled in the land of Canaan, and Lot moved his tents to a place near Sodom and settled among the cities of the plain. ¹³But the people of this area were extremely wicked and constantly sinned against the LORD.

¹⁴After Lot had gone, the LORD said to Abram, "Look as far as you can see in every direction—north and south, east and west. ¹⁵I am giving all this land, as far as you can see, to you and your descendants as a permanent possession. ¹⁶And I will give you so many descendants that, like the dust of the earth, they cannot be counted! ¹⁷Go and walk through the ᵇland in every direction, for I am giving it to you."

¹⁸So Abram moved his camp to Hebron and settled near the oak grove belonging to Mamre. There he built another altar to the LORD.

· ·

Age	Event	Reference
10	Sarai is born	17:17; 20:12
75	Abram leaves Haran, moves to Canaan	12:4-6
85	Abram takes Hagar as a secondary wife	16:1-3
86	Ishmael is born	16:15-16
99	Abram is renamed Abraham, is promised a son through Sarah, is given circumcision	17:1–18:15
100	Isaac is born	21:1-7
~103	Isaac is weaned, Ishmael is sent away	21:8-14
137	Sarah dies	23:1
140	Abraham sends his servant to find a wife for Isaac	24:1-9; 25:20
160	Jacob and Esau are born	25:20, 26
175	Abraham dies	25:7-9

▲ **Abraham's Life** (11:26–25:11).

13:5-7 *Lot* was also *wealthy*, with *flocks and herds. Tents* figure prominently in Lot's story (13:12). • The *Canaanites and Perizzites* (see 34:30; Deut 7:1; Judg 1:4; 3:5) held the well-watered land; the quarrel between Abram's and Lot's herdsmen left Abram more vulnerable to attack.

13:8-13 Abram, to whom the land was promised, might have told Lot to find his own place. Abram's generosity was an act of faith; he knew that even if he gave the whole land away, God would still give it to him and his descendants. Abram did not have to cling to things, whereas Lot's choices were self-seeking.

13:8 *Abram* was concerned that there be no *conflict* (Hebrew *meribah*) between them, as they were *close relatives* (literally *brothers*). Moses later reproved Israel over the incident in the wilderness at Meribah (Exod 17:1-7; Num 20:1-13) and instructed them on exercising faith in such situations. Meribah thereafter became a watchword for testing and striving with the Lord in unbelief (see Ps 95).

13:10 What appealed to Lot would be short-lived. In the *garden of the LORD*, Adam and Eve succumbed to their craving for what they saw; Israel was later enslaved in *Egypt. Sodom and Gomorrah* are reminders of putting intense desires ahead of obedience to God (3:5-6; see 1 Jn 2:16). • *Zoar* was a small town in the plain to which Lot and his daughters later fled (19:18-22); it was

previously called Bela (14:2).

13:11-18 The narrator makes numerous contrasts between Lot and Abram.

13:11 Lot's choice was totally selfish, without concern for Abram or faith in the Lord. • The region called *the whole Jordan Valley* (literally *the circle of the Jordan*) is believed to have been near the south end of the Dead Sea, based on descriptions in ancient records that locate cities of the Plain. This area is now very desolate.

13:13 The implication is that Lot would not resist Sodom's influence because he, too, was living for himself.

13:14-17 Abram could give Lot the choice land because he believed in God's promise. Abram waited for God to give him the land; Lot just took what he wanted.

13:15 *descendants:* Literally *seed;* also in 13:16.

13:18 *Hebron* was an Anakite city (Num 13:22) originally called Kiriath-arba ("city of Arba"), located in forested highlands just north of the Negev (12:9; Josh 17:15). Abraham, Isaac, and Jacob all settled there (18:1; 35:27; 37:14), and Sarah, Abraham, Isaac, Rebekah, Jacob, and Leah were buried there (23:19; 35:27-29; 49:29-32; 50:13). • *Mamre* was an Amorite (14:13; 15:16).

Abram's Encounter with Kings (14:1-24)
Abram Rescues Lot

14 About this time war broke out in the region. King Amraphel of Babylonia, King Arioch of Ellasar, King Kedorlaomer of Elam, and King Tidal of Goiim ²fought against King Bera of Sodom, King Birsha of Gomorrah, King Shinab of Admah, King Shemeber of Zeboiim, and the king of Bela (also called Zoar).

³This second group of kings joined forces in Siddim Valley (that is, the valley of the Dead Sea). ⁴For twelve years they had been subject to King Kedorlaomer, but in the thirteenth year they rebelled against him.

⁵One year later Kedorlaomer and his allies arrived and defeated the Rephaites at Ashteroth-karnaim, the Zuzites at Ham, the Emites at Shaveh-kiriathaim, ⁶and the Horites at Mount Seir, as far as El-paran at the edge of the wilderness. ⁷Then they turned back and came to En-mishpat (now called Kadesh) and conquered all the territory of the Amalekites, and also the Amorites living in Hazazon-tamar.

⁸Then the rebel kings of Sodom, Gomorrah, Admah, Zeboiim, and Bela (also called Zoar) prepared for battle in the valley of the Dead Sea. ⁹They fought against King Kedorlaomer of Elam, King Tidal of Goiim, King Amraphel of Babylonia, and King Arioch of Ellasar—four kings against five. ¹⁰As it happened, the valley of the Dead Sea was filled with tar pits. And as the army of the kings of Sodom and Gomorrah fled, some fell into the tar pits, while the rest escaped into the mountains. ¹¹The victorious invaders then plundered Sodom and Gomorrah and headed for home, taking with them all the spoils of war and the food supplies. ¹²They also captured Lot—Abram's nephew who lived in Sodom—and carried off everything he owned.

¹³But one of Lot's men escaped and reported everything to Abram the Hebrew, who was living near the oak grove belonging to Mamre the Amorite. Mamre and his relatives, Eshcol and Aner, were Abram's allies.

¹⁴When Abram heard that his nephew

14:1 Gen 10:10; 11:2
14:2 Gen 10:19; 13:10; Deut 29:23
14:3 Num 34:3, 12; Deut 3:17; Josh 3:16
14:5 Gen 15:20; Deut 2:10, 20; 3:11; Josh 13:19
14:7 Gen 16:14; 20:1; Num 13:26; Deut 1:4; 2 Chr 20:2
14:12 Gen 11:27
14:13 Gen 10:16; 13:18; 39:14
14:14 Gen 12:5; Deut 34:1

◄ The Battle at Siddim Valley (14:1-24). When the kings in the Siddim Valley (the valley of the Dead Sea) rebelled against King Kedorlaomer of Elam (14:4), Kedorlaomer and his Mesopotamian allies followed the King's Highway (see Num 20:17; 21:22) through Transjordan (the region east of the Jordan), then circled around from El-paran through En-mishpat (=Kadesh, 14:7; Num 13:26) to Hazazon-tamar (=En-gedi, 2 Chr 20:2), conquering as they went. They then attacked the five Canaanite kings near Bela. When Abram heard that Lot had been taken captive, he chased after Kedorlaomer, attacked at Dan (=Laish, Josh 19:47), and pursued the fleeing armies north of Damascus to Hobah, and he recovered the captives and their goods. On his return, Abram stopped by the Valley of Shaveh near Salem (=Jerusalem) and was blessed by Melchizedek. • The location of the Siddim Valley is uncertain—it was probably at the south end of the Dead Sea.

an earlier time and put them under tribute for asphalt, olive oil, and copper. *In the thirteenth year* they refused to send it; in the fourteenth year (14:5), the invaders returned to subjugate them again.

14:5-8 The invaders came down the King's Highway on the east side of the Jordan Valley to the Gulf of Aqaba, then circled back to *the valley of the Dead Sea* (Hebrew *Siddim Valley* [see 14:3]; also in 14:10).

14:8-12 The five cities of the plain were close together at the south end of the Dead Sea. The Mesopotamian kings defeated the frail uprising, looted the cities of Sodom and Gomorrah, and carried off Lot with the other captives.

14:13 The word *Hebrew* first occurs here in the Bible. It is not equivalent to the later term *Habiru* from Egyptian texts; the *Habiru* were mercenaries that roamed the land in the era of the judges. • *Mamre:* See note on 13:18. • *relatives:* Or *allies;* literally *brothers.*

14:1-16 In this skirmish typical of ancient politics, powerful kings formed a coalition to subjugate smaller vassal states.

14:1-2 Archaeology has not identified these kings, but similar names from antiquity corroborate the report's accuracy. The Mesopotamian kings were confederates under a suzerain, apparently *Amraphel,* who is mentioned first.

14:1 *Babylonia:* Hebrew *Shinar;* also in 14:9. • *Tidal* apparently ruled a number of city-states (*Goiim,* literally *nations*).

14:3 *Dead Sea:* Literally *Salt Sea.*

14:4-5 This was Kedorlaomer's war. Under the feudal system of tribal affiliations, those in covenant with him had to fight. It was also Abram's battle to rescue Lot, and those under treaty with him had to accompany him.

14:4 *King Kedorlaomer* apparently defeated the Siddim Valley kings at

14:14-16 God could give his people victory over any forces invading the Promised Land. Faithfulness to God was the prerequisite for victory. God promises to bless his people and give them victory over the world. He uses those who respond to his call and can skillfully use weapons of war (cp. Eph 4:8; 6:10-19).

14:14 *Abram . . . mobilized the 318 trained men who had been born into his household:* Abram was a formidable force, an outworking of God's promise to make him great (12:2-3). • *Dan* was a city

14:15
Gen 15:2

14:17
2 Sam 18:18

14:18
Ps 76:2; 110:4
Heb 5:6, 10; 7:1
ᶜ*kohen* (3548)
▸ Exod 18:1

14:19
Gen 27:25; 48:9
Mark 10:16

14:20
Gen 9:26; 24:27
*Heb 7:1-2
ᵈ*elyon* (5945)
▸ Num 24:16
ᵉ*ma'aser* (4643)
▸ Lev 27:30

Lot had been captured, he mobilized the 318 trained men who had been born into his household. Then he pursued Kedorlaomer's army until he caught up with them at Dan. ¹⁵There he divided his men and attacked during the night. Kedorlaomer's army fled, but Abram chased them as far as Hobah, north of Damascus. ¹⁶Abram recovered all the goods that had been taken, and he brought back his nephew Lot with his possessions and all the women and other captives.

Melchizedek Blesses Abram
¹⁷After Abram returned from his victory over Kedorlaomer and all his allies, the king of Sodom went out to meet him in the valley of Shaveh (that is, the King's Valley).

¹⁸And Melchizedek, the king of Salem and a ᶜpriest of God Most High, brought Abram some bread and wine. ¹⁹Melchizedek blessed Abram with this blessing:

"Blessed be Abram by God Most High,
    Creator of heaven and earth.
²⁰ And blessed be God ᵈMost High,
    who has defeated your enemies for you."

Then Abram gave Melchizedek a ᵉtenth of all the goods he had recovered.

Abram Rejects Sodom's Goods (14:21-24)
²¹The king of Sodom said to Abram, "Give back my people who were captured. But you may keep for yourself all the goods you have recovered."

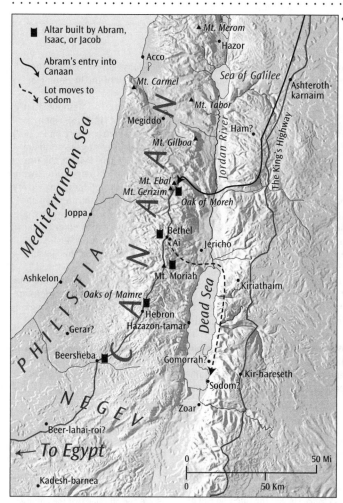

Altar built by Abram, Isaac, or Jacob

Abram's entry into Canaan

Lot moves to Sodom

Mt. Merom
Hazor
Acco
Sea of Galilee
Mt. Carmel
Ashteroth-karnaim
Mt. Tabor
Megiddo
Ham?
Mt. Gilboa
Jordan River
The King's Highway
Mt. Ebal
Mt. Gerizim
Oak of Moreh
Mediterranean Sea
Joppa
CANAAN
Bethel
Ai
Jericho
Ashkelon
Mt. Moriah
Kiriathaim
Oaks of Mamre
Dead Sea
PHILISTIA
Hebron
Gerar?
Hazazon-tamar
Beersheba
Gomorrah?
Kir-hareseth
Sodom?
NEGEV
Zoar
Beer-lahai-roi?
← To Egypt
0   50 Mi
0   50 Km
Kadesh-barnea

◀ **Abram in Canaan (12:1–25:11).** Abram probably entered CANAAN by following the King's Highway—an ancient and well-traveled route that ran just east of Canaan. Philistines had already begun settling along the coast (PHILISTIA; see 10:14; 21:32-34; 26:1-18). Some Canaanite settlements (JERICHO, MEGIDDO, HAZAZON-TAMAR=En-gedi) were very old by this time. Within Canaan, Abram traveled southward along the central ridge of the hill country, building altars at OAK OF MOREH (= Shechem, 12:6-7; see 33:18-19), BETHEL (12:8; 13:3; see 28:10-22; 35:1-15), MOUNT MORIAH (22:1-19), OAKS OF MAMRE (= HEBRON, 13:18; see 23:2), and BEERSHEBA (21:22-34; see 26:23-25; 46:1-7). Lot unwisely chose his portion in SODOM (13:10-13; see 18:16–19:29).

14:15 *Damascus* was 40 miles north of Dan. *Hobah* was about 60 miles *north of Damascus*.

14:17 The *valley of Shaveh* or *King's Valley* was probably the Kidron Valley (see 2 Sam 18:18).

14:18 *Melchizedek* means "king of righteousness," suggesting that he was a righteous servant of God. He was probably a Jebusite priest and king; later authors regarded him as a type of Christ (Ps 110:4; Heb 7:1-19). • *Salem* is Jerusalem (cp. Ps 76:2). • *God Most High:* Hebrew *El-Elyon;* also in 14:19, 20, 22.

14:19-20 By paying a tithe (*a tenth*) to Melchizedek, Abram acknowledged Melchizedek as a spiritual superior (see Heb 7:4) and affirmed that God had given him victory.

14:21-24 Abram knew that accepting the offer of the *king of Sodom* (see note on 14:1-2) could make him his ally or subject, as Lot had been. This would jeopardize the fulfillment of God's promises. Faith looks beyond the riches of the world to the greater blessings that God has in store.

about 150 miles north of Abram's home in Hebron, then named Laish or Leshem (see Josh 19:47 and note; Judg 18:29). Dan, whose descendants migrated north in the days of the judges (Judg 18:1-29), had not yet been born (30:6). An editor apparently updated the text so that later readers could identify this city.

²²Abram replied to the king of Sodom, "I solemnly swear to the LORD, God Most High, Creator of heaven and earth, ²³that I will not take so much as a single thread or sandal thong from what belongs to you. Otherwise you might say, 'I am the one who made Abram rich.' ²⁴I will accept only what my young warriors have already eaten, and I request that you give a fair share of the goods to my allies—Aner, Eshcol, and Mamre."

The LORD's Covenant Promise to Abram (15:1-21)

15 Some time later, the LORD spoke to Abram in a vision and said to him, "Do not be afraid, Abram, for I will ᶠprotect you, and your reward will be great."

²But Abram replied, "O ᵍSovereign LORD, what good are all your blessings when I don't even have a son? Since you've given me no children, Eliezer of Damascus, a servant in my household, will inherit all my wealth. ³You have given me no descendants of my own, so one of my servants will be my heir."

⁴Then the LORD said to him, "No, your servant will not be your heir, for you will have a son of your own who will be your heir." ⁵Then the LORD took Abram outside and said to him, "Look up into the sky and count the stars if you can. That's how many descendants you will have!"

⁶And Abram ʰbelieved the LORD, and the LORD counted him as righteous because of his faith.

14:22
Gen 1:1
14:23
2 Kgs 5:16
15:1
Gen 21:17-18; 26:24
Ps 3:3
ⁱmagen (4043)
▸ Deut 33:29
15:2
ᵍʳadonay Yahweh (0136, 3068)
▸ Deut 3:24
15:4
*Gal 4:28
15:5
Gen 12:2; 22:17; 32:12
*Rom 4:18
15:6
Ps 106:31
*Rom 4:3, 9, 22
*Gal 3:6
ʰaman (0539)
▸ Gen 45:26

MELCHIZEDEK (14:17-24)

Ps 110:4
Heb 5:6-10; 6:20–7:28

Melchizedek is a mysterious biblical personality whose name means "king of righteousness." He was a Canaanite priest and king; there is no record of his family or of the beginning or end of his life.

Abraham met Melchizedek after defeating four Mesopotamian kings. The Mesopotamians had raided Sodom and Gomorrah and captured Abraham's nephew Lot (14:1-16). When Abraham returned from battle, Melchizedek, king of Salem (=Jerusalem; see note on Ps 76:2), was with the grateful kings of the Dead Sea confederacy. When Melchizedek gave Abraham bread, wine, and his blessing, he was acting as "a priest of God Most High" (14:18), the true God who created heaven and earth (see Ps 7:17; 47:2; 57:2; 78:56). Melchizedek correctly understood that Abraham worshiped the true God (14:22), and he praised God for giving victory to Abraham. Abraham received Melchizedek's gifts and gave him his tithe, thus recognizing Melchizedek's higher spiritual rank as a patriarchal priest (see Heb 7:4-7).

Melchizedek is an unusual figure in Genesis, which gives genealogies for its other characters. Melchizedek appears without any such record, and as quickly disappears. Much later in Israel's history, King David was perhaps reflecting on this when he said that the Messiah is "a priest forever in the order of Melchizedek" (Ps 110:4; cp. Heb 7:15-25). The book of Hebrews explains this statement, saying that Melchizedek is remembered as "resembling the Son of God" (Heb 7:3), but was not himself the Son of God. His priesthood lasts forever as an archetype that prefigures the Messiah's priesthood. Like Melchizedek (but unlike the kings of Israel), Jesus is a king who also fulfills priestly functions.

Melchizedek, a royal priest, was superior to Levi, the ancestor of Israel's priests. In the same way, the Messiah, Jesus Christ, is a better priest than the descendants of Aaron. Jesus provides permanent atonement for sins and direct access to his Father through his name (Heb 7:24-28). He guides his people by the Spirit rather than by law (Heb 8:7-13) and lives forever as priest and king for those who trust in him.

14:22 In the words of this oath, Abram may have been clarifying that his God, *the LORD (Yahweh)*, was the *God Most High* that Melchizedek invoked. Perhaps Melchizedek had never heard the name *Yahweh*.

15:1-21 The Lord made a formal covenant with Abram, solemnly confirming the promises made at his call (12:1-3). There would be a long period of slavery for Abram's descendants before these promises would be completely fulfilled.

15:1 *Do not be afraid:* Abram lacked a son to be his heir. The Lord addressed Abram's anxiety about the future with comforting words. • *I will protect you* (literally *I will be your shield*): The Hebrew word for "shield" (*magen*) is from the same root as Melchizedek's word *defeated* (14:20). The Lord who had defeated Abram's enemies would continue to protect him. • *your reward will be great:* The promise of offspring (12:2-3; cp. Ps 127:3) was still unfulfilled.

15:2-3 Using a wordplay, *Abram* expressed his concern that *Eliezer of Damascus* (Hebrew *dammeseq*), a man in Abram's household, would be his *heir* (Hebrew *ben-mesheq*, "son of possession"), as was customary when there was no son.

15:4-6 God affirmed that the promise was for Abram's own offspring and showed him the stars as a promise of the vast number of descendants that he would have (22:17; 26:4). Paul quotes

15:7
Gen 12:1; 13:17
Acts 7:2-4

15:8
Luke 1:18

15:10
Lev 1:17

15:12
Gen 2:21; 28:11

15:13
Exod 12:40
*Acts 7:6
Gal 3:17

15:14
Exod 6:5

15:15
Gen 25:8

15:16
Exod 12:40

⁷Then the LORD told him, "I am the LORD who brought you out of Ur of the Chaldeans to give you this land as your possession."

⁸But Abram replied, "O Sovereign LORD, how can I be sure that I will actually possess it?"

⁹The LORD told him, "Bring me a three-year-old heifer, a three-year-old female goat, a three-year-old ram, a turtledove, and a young pigeon." ¹⁰So Abram presented all these to him and killed them. Then he cut each animal down the middle and laid the halves side by side; he did not, however, cut the birds in half. ¹¹Some vultures swooped down to eat the carcasses, but Abram chased them away.

¹²As the sun was going down, Abram fell into a deep sleep, and a terrifying darkness came down over him. ¹³Then the LORD said to Abram, "You can be sure that your descendants will be strangers in a foreign land, where they will be oppressed as slaves for 400 years. ¹⁴But I will punish the nation that enslaves them, and in the end they will come away with great wealth. ¹⁵(As for you, you will die in peace and be buried at a ripe old age.) ¹⁶After four generations your descendants will return here to this land, for

· ·

God's Covenant with Abraham (15:1-21)

Gen 12:1-3; 17:1-14;
21:1-2; 22:15-18
Exod 2:24
Deut 1:8
Neh 9:7-8
Ps 105:7-45
Luke 3:7-9
Acts 3:24-26; 7:2-8
Rom 4:11-25; 9:7-8;
11:16-17
Gal 3:6-9; 3:29
Heb 6:13-15

The Lord had already established a relationship with Abraham (12:1-9) before he made a formal covenant with him (ch 15). God took all the initiative: He approached Abraham and spoke to him in a vision. God presented the impossible promise that the old man would have a son through whom his descendants would eventually be as numerous as the stars of heaven. Abraham believed God (15:6), and his faith proved to be an act of righteousness—faith is righteousness, and faith produces righteousness in covenant relationship with God (see Hab 2:4; Rom 1:17; 4:3, 17; Gal 3:6, 11; Heb 10:37-38). The covenant of ch 15 includes a royal grant (15:18-21) in which God, the king, gave land to Abraham, his subject, as a possession and an inheritance. (In the ancient Near East, kings sometimes granted land or other gifts to loyal subjects.) At the end of that day, Abraham knew that his own and his descendants' future was firmly in the hands of the covenant God. Later, the grant would be transferred to his descendants.

God later ratified his covenant with Abraham (17:1-22), giving him circumcision as its sign (17:10) and condition (17:4, 9). The almighty God once again took the initiative (17:1) in granting Abraham an extraordinary privilege. The covenant was not a relationship between equals, yet both partners in the covenant assumed responsibilities. God committed himself voluntarily to Abraham and his descendants, while requiring faithfulness from Abraham (17:1, 9-14). The blessing Abraham received as God's covenant partner was embodied in the new name that God gave him (17:5-6).

God's family covenant with Abraham also applied to his descendants (13:15-16; 15:3-5; 17:6-10). It pointed to blessing in the relatively near future when his descendants would possess the land (15:12-16). Much later, Abraham's faith became a blessing to all through his descendant, Jesus Christ, through whom all the families of the earth can share in God's blessing on Abraham (12:3; see Rom 4:11-25; Gal 3:8-9, 16).

· ·

this promise in Rom 4:18 to underscore the strength of Abram's faith.

15:6 *And Abram believed:* God made his covenant with a believer; the statement does not indicate when Abram came to faith. The Hebrew text does not link Abram's belief with the promise of the stars; it just says parenthetically that Abram already believed God. Abram already had faith; his departure from Ur was his first great act that demonstrated it (see Heb 11:8-10). • God *counted him as righteous because of his faith:* This central statement about Abram's saving faith is quoted three times in the NT (Rom 4:3, 22-23; Gal 3:6; Jas 2:23) to support the doctrine of righteousness before God by faith.

15:7-21 With a solemn ceremony, God made a binding covenant with Abram that guaranteed the fulfillment of God's promises to him.

15:10 Obeying God's instructions, *Abram* gathered three herd animals for the ceremony and *cut them in half.* Cutting the animals symbolized the oath, indicating that the covenant maker staked his own life on his word (Jer 34:18).

15:11 *Vultures* are unclean birds of prey that symbolize those who unjustly attack Abraham's heirs (15:13-14).

15:13-16 Not even *400 years* of bondage could interfere with God's plan to fulfill the covenant.

15:13 *oppressed:* The same word is used in Exod 1:11-12. Egypt, like predatory

birds (15:11), would try to destroy Israel and hinder the covenant's fulfillment. • Apparently *400 years* is a round number (also Acts 7:6; cp. Exod 12:40; Gal 3:17). Using the chronology in the Hebrew text, the family moved to Egypt around 1876 BC, and the Exodus occurred around 1446 BC (though many scholars date the Exodus later, around 1270 BC; see "Chronology: Abraham to Joshua," p. 118).

15:16 The reasons for Israel's bondage included God's justice. God would tolerate *the sins of the Amorites* until they fully deserved judgment. • *do not yet warrant their destruction* (literally *are not yet full*): To give the Promised Land to Israel, the Lord would dispossess the land's inhabitants in a way that satisfied

the sins of the Amorites do not yet warrant their destruction."

17After the sun went down and darkness fell, Abram saw a smoking firepot and a flaming torch pass between the halves of the carcasses. 18So the LORD made a icovenant with Abram that day and said, "I have given this jland to your descendants, all the way from the border of Egypt to the great Euphrates River—19the land now occupied by the Kenites, Kenizzites, Kadmonites, 20Hittites, Perizzites, Rephaites, 21Amorites, Canaanites, Girgashites, and Jebusites."

God Provides the Promised Offspring (16:1–22:19)
Hagar and Ishmael

16 Now Sarai, Abram's wife, had not been able to bear children for him. But she had an Egyptian servant named Hagar. 2So Sarai said to Abram, "The LORD has prevented me from having children. Go and sleep with my servant. Perhaps I can have children through her." And Abram agreed with Sarai's proposal. 3So Sarai, Abram's wife, took Hagar the Egyptian servant and gave her to Abram as a wife. (This happened ten years after Abram had settled in the land of Canaan.)

4So Abram had sexual relations with Hagar, and she became pregnant. But when Hagar knew she was pregnant, she began to treat her mistress, Sarai, with contempt. 5Then Sarai said to Abram, "This is all your fault! I put my servant into your arms, but now that she's pregnant she treats me with contempt. The LORD will show who's wrong—you or me!"

6Abram replied, "Look, she is your servant,

15:17
Jer 34:18-19
15:18
Num 34:1-15
Deut 1:7-8
iberith (1285)
▸ Gen 17:2
j'erets (0776)
▸ Gen 28:13
15:19
Num 24:21
15:21
Gen 10:15-16
16:1
Gen 11:30
Gal 4:24-25
16:2
Gen 30:3
16:3
Gen 12:4-5
16:4
Gen 16:15
16:5
Gen 31:53
16:7
Gen 21:17; 22:11, 15

HAGAR (16:1-16)

Gen 21:9-21; 25:12
Gal 4:22-31

Hagar was the Egyptian servant of Sarai, Abram's wife. When God commanded Abram to leave Mesopotamia, he promised him a multitude of descendants who would be given a new land (12:2, 7). After ten childless years in Canaan, Sarai followed the customary Mesopotamian strategy of giving Hagar to Abram as his concubine; any son born of the union of husband and concubine was considered the wife's child (cp. 30:1-6). Hagar bore a son, Ishmael (16:1-16; 21:9-21).

Hagar was so disrespectful to Sarai during her pregnancy (16:4-6) that Sarai dealt harshly with her and Hagar fled into the desert. The angel of the Lord appeared to her at a desert well, telling her to return to Abram's house and submit to Sarai.

Ishmael was born when Abram was eighty-six years old. Fourteen years later, God gave Abraham and Sarah their promised son, Isaac. When Isaac was weaned (at about three years), a traditional feast was held. At this event, Ishmael mocked Isaac (21:9), so Sarah insisted that Abraham send Hagar and Ishmael away. God confirmed this (21:12), so Hagar and Ishmael wandered in the wilderness of Beersheba. When their water was gone, God miraculously rescued them and assured Hagar that Ishmael would father a great nation (21:17-19).

Paul made an analogy (Gal 4:22-31) in which Hagar "represents Mount Sinai," where the old covenant was formed, while Sarah "represents the heavenly Jerusalem," the community of those who receive salvation by faith in Christ. As Isaac was Abraham's son by faith in the divine promise, Christians who are free of the law are spiritual children of Sarah.

his justice. The fulfillment of promises to Israel also brought retributive judgment on people of the land (though individuals were saved by faith; see Josh 2:1-15; 6:23-25; Heb 11:31; Jas 2:25). Until then, God would send the family to Egypt where Israel could become a great nation. Seeing all this in advance was terrifying (15:12), but it was comforting to know that nothing could interfere with God's plan.

15:17-18 *smoking firepot . . . flaming torch:* Fire represented the Lord's cleansing, consuming zeal and unapproachable holiness (cp. Isa 6:3-7). The holy God made (literally *cut*) a unilateral *covenant with Abram*; its promises were absolutely sure because they did not

depend on what Abram or his descendants might do.

15:18-19 God specified the boundaries of the Promised Land. His clear message to Abram was that despite prospects of death and suffering (enslavement), he and his descendants would eventually receive the promises, for God had sworn an oath (see Heb 6:13-14). Nothing can separate God's people from his love or the fulfillment of his plans (see Rom 8:18-39; 2 Pet 1:3-4). • *the border of Egypt:* Literally *the river of Egypt,* referring either to an eastern branch of the Nile River or to the Brook of Egypt in the Sinai (see Num 34:5).

16:1-16 While waiting for their prom-

ised son to be born, Abram and Sarai attempted an alternate plan that was not in keeping with faith.

16:1-3 *Abram* and *Sarai* faced the tension of her being barren and beyond childbearing years. By custom, a barren woman could give her servant to her husband as a slave-wife; the child born to that union was considered the wife's child and could be adopted as the heir. Sarai's suggestion, unobjectionable by custom, set a problematic human plan in motion. God's promises would be fulfilled by faith.

16:4-6 Perhaps *Hagar* expected to become the favored wife instead of *Sarai* (cp. Prov 30:21-23).

ᵏ*mal'ak* (4397)
  ▸ Gen 19:1

16:8
Gen 3:9; 4:9

16:9
Gen 21:12
Eph 6:5

16:10
Gen 17:20

16:11
Gen 16:15
Exod 3:7-8

16:12
Job 39:5-8

16:13
Gen 32:30

16:14
Gen 14:7

16:15
Gen 21:9; 25:12

16:16
Gen 12:4; 16:3

so deal with her as you see fit." Then Sarai treated Hagar so harshly that she finally ran away.

⁷The ᵏangel of the LORD found Hagar beside a spring of water in the wilderness, along the road to Shur. ⁸The angel said to her, "Hagar, Sarai's servant, where have you come from, and where are you going?"

"I'm running away from my mistress, Sarai," she replied.

⁹The angel of the LORD said to her, "Return to your mistress, and submit to her authority." ¹⁰Then he added, "I will give you more descendants than you can count."

¹¹And the angel also said, "You are now pregnant and will give birth to a son. You are to name him Ishmael (which means

'God hears'), for the LORD has heard your cry of distress. ¹²This son of yours will be a wild man, as untamed as a wild donkey! He will raise his fist against everyone, and everyone will be against him. Yes, he will live in open hostility against all his relatives."

¹³Thereafter, Hagar used another name to refer to the LORD, who had spoken to her. She said, "You are the God who sees me." She also said, "Have I truly seen the One who sees me?" ¹⁴So that well was named Beer-lahai-roi (which means "well of the Living One who sees me"). It can still be found between Kadesh and Bered.

¹⁵So Hagar gave Abram a son, and Abram named him Ishmael. ¹⁶Abram was eighty-six years old when Ishmael was born.

· ·

ISHMAEL (16:11-16)

Gen 17:18-26; 21:8-21; 25:9-18; 28:9
Gal 4:21-31

Ishmael was Abraham's first son, born of Hagar, Sarah's Egyptian servant. The boy was born near Hebron when Abraham was 86 years old (13:18; 16:16). God had promised to make a great nation of the childless Abraham (12:2) and assured him that his son would be his heir (15:4). Ishmael was born in Abraham's attempt to fulfill God's promise by human means (see 16:1-16; Gal 4:23), but God would accomplish this through Sarah (see 17:15–18:15; 21:1-7).

When God announced that Sarah would have a son to fulfill the promise (17:15-16), Abraham asked God to accept Ishmael (17:17-18). Ishmael was not the promised son—the covenant would be established with Isaac (17:19)—but God did bless Ishmael and make him the father of a great nation (17:20-21).

At age thirteen, Ishmael was circumcised in witness to God's covenant with Abraham (17:9-14, 22-27). Then, at Isaac's weaning celebration (when Ishmael was about seventeen), Ishmael made fun of Isaac (21:9), and Abraham sent Ishmael and Hagar away with provisions. The angel of God helped Hagar survive in the wilderness, and Ishmael became a wild game hunter. He settled in the wilderness of Paran and married an Egyptian woman (21:20-21). He assisted in Abraham's burial (25:9-10), gave his daughter Mahalath in marriage to Esau (28:9), and died at age 137 (25:17). His twelve sons are named in 25:13-15.

Paul alluded to Ishmael when urging the Galatians to put their faith in God rather than in the law (see Gal 4:21-31). Those who trust the law will not inherit the kingdom, just as the slave woman's son did not inherit with the son of the free woman (Gal 4:30).

· ·

16:7 *The angel of the LORD* was the Lord himself (16:13; 21:17; 22:11-12; 31:11-13; 48:16; Exod 3:2; 32:34; Judg 6:11, 16, 22; 13:22-23; Zech 3:1-2), but was also distinct from the Lord (24:7; 2 Sam 24:16; Zech 1:12). The angel of the LORD was probably a *theophany* (a manifestation of God) or a *Christophony* (an appearance of the pre-incarnate Messiah; see 18:1-2; 19:1; Num 22:22; Judg 2:1-4; 5:23; Zech 12:8), speaking with the authority of the Lord himself.

16:8-12 The angel's rhetorical questions encouraged *Hagar* to pour out her heart to God. When she did, God commanded her to *return* and *submit* (16:9), promising that her son would have innumerable descendants. The angel of the Lord never referred to Hagar as Abram's wife, only as Sarai's servant. She would have Abram's child, but *Ishmael* was not

central to God's covenant with Abram.

16:10-12 Hagar's son would become the father of a great but wild and hostile nation living in the Arabian Desert as perennial enemies of Israel (cp. 25:18). God blessed *Ishmael* as Abram's descendant, but not as the line chosen to carry on the covenant. That blessing was reserved for Abram's chosen heir.

16:11 Names in Genesis often capture the message of a passage and aid the remembrance of the events and their significance in the history of the faith. The name *Ishmael*, which means "*God hears*," commemorates that *the LORD . . . heard* Hagar's *cry of distress* (see also note on 16:14-15). This name would have greatly comforted Hagar; God listened to her prayers and acknowledged her complaint.

16:13 Hagar responded to God's mes-

sages by faith, in her words and in her obedience. • *the God who sees me* (Hebrew *El-roi*): God knew Hagar's plight and watched over her.

16:14-15 The names *Beer-lahai-roi*, which means "*well of the Living One who sees me*," and *Ishmael* (see 16:11) were a message and a rebuke for Abram and Sarai. God sees affliction and hears the cries of those in need. Sarai and Abram should have prayed rather than taking the fulfillment of the promise into their own hands by following social custom (cp. 25:21). Giving children to the barren woman is God's work (Ps 113:9; cp. 1 Sam 1:1-28; Luke 1:1-25); impossible difficulties cannot be resolved by human intervention. The Lord hears the afflicted, sees them in their need, and will miraculously provide for them.

The Covenant Confirmed:
Abram Is Named Abraham

17 When Abram was ninety-nine years old, the LORD appeared to him and said, "I am El-Shaddai—'God ªAlmighty.' Serve me faithfully and live a ᵇblameless life. ²I will make a ᶜcovenant with you, by which I will guarantee to give you countless descendants."

³At this, Abram fell face down on the ground. Then God said to him, ⁴"This is my covenant with you: I will make you the father of a multitude of nations! ⁵What's more, I am changing your name. It will no longer be Abram. Instead, you will be called Abraham, for you will be the father of many nations. ⁶I will make you extremely fruitful. Your descendants will become many nations, and kings will be among them!

⁷"I will confirm my covenant with you and your descendants after you, from generation to generation. This is the everlasting

17:1
Gen 12:7; 28:3; 35:11;
48:3
Deut 18:13
Matt 5:48
ª*shadday* (7706)
▸ Gen 28:3
ᵇ*tamim* (8549)
▸ Exod 12:5

17:2
Gen 12:2; 15:18
ᶜ*berith* (1285)
▸ Exod 19:5

17:3
Gen 17:17; 18:2

- -

Circumcision (17:9-14)

Gen 17:23-27; 21:4;
34:1-26
Exod 4:24-26; 12:48
Lev 12:3
Josh 5:2-8
Jer 9:25-26
Ezek 44:7-9
Luke 1:59; 2:21
Acts 15:1-31; 16:1-5
Rom 2:25-29
1 Cor 7:17-19
Gal 5:1-6; 5:11-12;
6:12-16
Eph 2:11-18
Phil 3:2-7
Col 2:11; 3:11

Circumcision is the removal of the male foreskin. It was practiced by some cultures in the ancient world (see Jer 9:25-26); the Bible uses it to symbolize the removal of sin and an old identity, accompanied by inclusion in the covenant community.

God chose circumcision as the sign of a covenant that focuses on descendants. God had promised to make Abraham and his descendants into a great nation (17:7, 13, 19) and to use them to redeem the Gentile nations (12:3; 17:4-6; see Gal 3:8-9). Circumcision was God's signature in flesh; it would identify Abraham and his descendants as God's own people (17:9-14) and remind them to live in faithfulness to the covenant.

Although circumcision was applied to adult males when they joined the covenant community (17:23-27; Exod 12:48; Josh 5:3-7), it was usually performed on infants (21:4; Lev 12:3), who received God's promises and membership in the covenant community through their parents. Faith was required in order to receive God's blessings, however, as can be seen in the differentiation between Ishmael and Isaac, Esau and Jacob, and Joseph and his brothers. Non-Israelites could also obligate themselves to Israel's covenant (Exod 12:48; cp. Gen 34:15-24); circumcision marked their inclusion into the worshiping community (e.g., Exod 12:44).

Circumcision would help Israel recognize and remember that they must lay aside natural impurity. God's people had to be loyal to the covenant, to the family, and to their own marriages. Intermarriage with uncircumcised people who were not of the covenant was a violation of the covenant. Any man who refused to be circumcised (cut physically in this symbolic way) would be cut off from the covenant people because of his disobedience to God's command (17:14).

Circumcision is a symbol of separation from the world, of purity, and of loyalty to the covenant. It provides the powerful metaphor of "circumcision of the heart," which designates a heart that is committed to God and is inwardly set apart to God, rather than being stubbornly resistant (Jer 9:26; Lev 26:41; Deut 30:6; Jer 4:4; Eph 2:11). Circumcision of the heart evidences salvation and fellowship with God (see Ezek 18:31-32; 36:25-27; Rom 2:28-29; 4:11).

When Jesus Christ established God's new covenant, he fulfilled the requirements of the old covenant, so a new sign was given to identify members of the covenant community. Thus baptism replaces circumcision, and it too must be accompanied by faith. It is not necessary for Gentile believers to be circumcised, since they are incorporated into the people of God through faith in Christ (Acts 15:1-29; Rom 2:25-29; Gal 2:1-10; 6:15; Col 2:11-12). One must turn in confidence to God and his promises, lay aside natural strength and the customs of the world, and live a new life by faith (see Jer 31:33-34; Rom 8:1-17; Gal 5:16–6:10).

- -

17:1-27 God now gave the family signs that the promises would be fulfilled. He changed Abram's name to Abraham (17:1-8), instituted the rite of circumcision as the sign of the covenant (17:9-14, 23-27), and changed Sarai's name to Sarah (17:15-22).

17:1 *El-Shaddai:* This name for God emphasizes his power (see also 28:3; 35:11; 43:14; 48:3; 49:25). • *Serve me faithfully and live a blameless life:* Being a bless-

ing to the nations required obedience from Abram; his conduct would be guided by Almighty God.

17:4-5 God guaranteed his promise by changing Abram's name. *Abram* means "exalted father"; *Abraham* sounds like a Hebrew term that means "father of many" (*'ab hamon*). "Abram" referred to his noble lineage, as Terah was the "exalted father" (11:27). His new name was a wordplay on the promise of his

own progeny (see also John 8:31-59; Rom 4:16-17; Gal 3:7, 15-19, 29). Whenever the new name was used, he and his household would remember that a multitude of nations would issue from him.

17:6 *kings will be among them!* This is the first indication that Israel would become a monarchy (see also 35:11; 36:31; Num 24:7; Deut 17:14-18; 28:36).

17:7-8 The land of Canaan was to be an

17:5
Neh 9:7
*Rom 4:17

17:6
Gen 35:11

17:7
Gen 15:18
Lev 11:45; 26:12
Ps 105:8-11
*Gal 3:16

17:9
Exod 19:5

17:10
John 7:22
Acts 7:8

17:11
Exod 12:48
Josh 5:2

17:12
Gen 21:4
Lev 12:3
Luke 1:59; 2:21

17:14
Exod 30:33
Lev 7:20

17:15
Gen 17:5

17:16
Gen 18:10

17:17
Gen 17:3; 18:11-13

covenant: I will always be your God and the God of your descendants after you. 8And I will give the entire land of Canaan, where you now live as a foreigner, to you and your descendants. It will be their possession forever, and I will be their God."

The Mark of the Covenant

9Then God said to Abraham, "Your responsibility is to obey the terms of the covenant. You and all your descendants have this continual responsibility. 10This is the covenant that you and your descendants must keep: Each male among you must be circumcised. 11You must cut off the flesh of your foreskin as a sign of the covenant between me and you. 12From generation to generation, every male child must be circumcised on the eighth day after his birth. This applies not only to members of your family but also to the servants born in your household and the foreign-born servants whom you have purchased. 13All must be circumcised. Your bodies will bear the mark of my everlasting covenant. 14Any male who fails to be circumcised will be cut off from the covenant family for breaking the covenant."

The Promise Affirmed: Sarai Is Named Sarah

15Then God said to Abraham, "Regarding Sarai, your wife—her name will no longer be Sarai. From now on her name will be Sarah. 16And I will bless her and give you a son from her! Yes, I will bless her richly, and she will become the mother of many nations. Kings of nations will be among her descendants."

17Then Abraham bowed down to the ground, but he laughed to himself in disbelief. "How could I become a father at the age of 100?" he thought. "And how can Sarah have a baby when she is ninety years old?" 18So Abraham said to God, "May Ishmael live under your special blessing!"

SARAH (17:15-22)

Gen 11:29-31;
12:10-20; 16:1-6;
18:10-15; 21:1-10;
23:1-2
Isa 51:2
Rom 4:19; 9:9
Gal 4:21-31
Heb 11:11-12
1 Pet 3:6

Sarah is among the women in Scripture who were barren but miraculously bore a son (see also 30:22-24; 1 Sam 1:11, 19-20; 2 Kgs 4:14-17; Luke 1:5-25). Because Sarah was ninety years old when this happened (cp. 17:17; 21:1-5), she testifies to God's ability to do what is humanly impossible. She was Abraham's wife and the mother of Isaac, through whom God promised to multiply the Israelite nation (12:2; 17:19). Jesus was born from her descendants. Her name Sarai was changed to Sarah when Isaac's birth was promised (see note on 17:15-16). Sarah is honored for her faithfulness, even though she laughed at the prediction of Isaac's birth (18:10-15), twenty-five years after God's original promise to Abraham.

Sarah was also Abraham's half sister (11:29; 20:12). Sarah accompanied Abraham from Ur to Haran to Canaan (11:31; 12:5). On two occasions, in Egypt (12:10-20) and Gerar (20:1-18), Abraham asked Sarah to say that she was his sister rather than his wife because he was afraid that he would be killed as her husband. In both cases, despite Abraham's lack of faith, God protected Sarah, preserving her as Isaac's mother and preventing any doubt as to who Isaac's father was when he was born (21:1-5) about a year after his birth was promised (17:21; 18:10-14). God thus preserved his chosen line.

Sarah died at age 127 and was buried in the cave that Abraham purchased (ch 23) at Machpelah. She is known as the mother of the nation of Israel (Isa 51:2), just as Abraham is its father. She is a key player in accounts of Abraham's faith (Rom 4:19). She represents the freedom that Christians have, as children of Sarah the free woman, through faith in Christ (see Gal 4:21-31). Peter cites her as an example of holy submission (1 Pet 3:6). Sarah believed in God's ability to keep his promises, and her life shows that he does (Rom 9:6-9; Heb 11:11-12).

---

everlasting possession for the descendants of Abraham; the Lord would be their *God* forever (see Jer 31:31-40; Zech 8:8; Luke 1:68-79; Rev 21:1-4).

17:7 descendants: Literally *seed*; also in 17:8, 9, 10, 19.

17:9-14 God gave circumcision as a confirming sign that reminded all households of loyalty to *the covenant*.

17:14 will be cut off: This punishment seems to have several applications. A

person could be exiled from society or put to death by the community; most often it warned that a person might die prematurely as God cut him off from the land of the living (see Exod 31:14; Lev 7:20-27; 17:3-4; 20:17-18; 23:28-29; Num 15:30-31; see also Ps 31:22; Ezek 21:4; Rom 9:3; 11:22). Failure to be circumcised was a serious violation (see Exod 4:24-26; cp. Gal 5:2-4).

17:15-16 *Sarai* and *Sarah* both mean "princess"; the change in spelling may

reflect the difference in dialect between Ur and Canaan. The new name, fitting for one who would be the mother of kings, was a milestone in Sarah's calling and brought attention to the promise.

17:17-18 Abraham *laughed* (Hebrew *yitskhaq*) because the promise seemed unbelievable; he had begun to believe that his line would come through *Ishmael*. But Abraham and Sarah would have a son of their own.

¹⁹But God replied, "No—Sarah, your wife, will give birth to a son for you. You will name him Isaac, and I will confirm my covenant with him and his descendants as an everlasting covenant. ²⁰As for Ishmael, I will bless him also, just as you have asked. I will make him extremely fruitful and multiply his descendants. He will become the father of twelve princes, and I will make him a great nation. ²¹But my covenant will be confirmed with Isaac, who will be born to you and Sarah about this time next year." ²²When God had finished speaking, he left Abraham.

Abraham Accepts the Covenant

²³On that very day Abraham took his son, Ishmael, and every male in his household, including those born there and those he had bought. Then he circumcised them, cutting off their foreskins, just as God had told him. ²⁴Abraham was ninety-nine years old when he was circumcised, ²⁵and Ishmael, his son, was thirteen. ²⁶Both Abraham and his son, Ishmael, were circumcised on that same day, ²⁷along with all the other men and boys of the household, whether they were born there or bought as servants. All were circumcised with him.

A Son Is Promised to Sarah

18 The LORD appeared again to Abraham near the oak grove belonging to Mamre. One day Abraham was sitting at the entrance to his tent during the hottest part of the day. ²He looked up and noticed three men standing nearby. When he saw them, he ran to meet them and welcomed them, bowing low to the ground.

³"My lord," he said, "if it pleases you, stop here for a while. ⁴Rest in the shade of this tree while water is brought to wash your feet. ⁵And since you've honored your servant with this visit, let me prepare some food to refresh you before you continue on your journey."

"All right," they said. "Do as you have said."

⁶So Abraham ran back to the tent and said to Sarah, "Hurry! Get three large measures of your best flour, knead it into dough, and bake some bread." ⁷Then Abraham ran out to the herd and chose a tender calf and gave it to his servant, who quickly prepared it. ⁸When the food was ready, Abraham took some yogurt and milk and the roasted meat, and he served it to the men. As they ate, Abraham waited on them in the shade of the trees.

⁹"Where is Sarah, your wife?" the visitors asked.

"She's inside the tent," Abraham replied.

¹⁰Then one of them said, "I will return to you about this time next year, and your wife, Sarah, will have a son!"

Sarah was listening to this conversation from the tent. ¹¹Abraham and Sarah were both very old by this time, and Sarah was long past the age of having children. ¹²So she laughed silently to herself and said, "How could a worn-out woman like me enjoy such pleasure, especially when my master—my husband—is also so old?"

¹³Then the LORD said to Abraham, "Why did Sarah laugh? Why did she say, 'Can an old woman like me have a baby?' ¹⁴Is anything too hard for the LORD? I will return

17:19
Gen 21:2; 26:2-5
17:20
Gen 25:12-16
17:21
Gen 18:10, 14
17:22
Gen 18:33; 35:13
17:23
Gen 14:14
17:24
Rom 4:11
17:25
Gen 16:16
18:1
Gen 12:7; 13:18
18:2
Gen 32:24
Josh 5:13
Judg 13:6-11
18:4
Gen 19:2; 24:32
18:5
Judg 6:18-19;
13:15-16
18:10
*Rom 9:9
18:11
Gen 17:17
18:12
1 Pet 3:6
18:14
Gen 18:10
Jer 32:17, 27
*Rom 9:9

17:19 The name *Isaac* means "he laughs" (Hebrew *yitskhaq*); it would constantly recall Abraham's disbelieving laughter when he heard the promise. It was also a reminder of God's favor and his pleasure in the birth (cp. 21:6).

17:20-21 *Ishmael* would not be abandoned; his family would prosper (see 25:13-16), but the *covenant* promises were for *Isaac*.

17:23-27 Having received God's word about Isaac, Abraham immediately complied with God's instructions. He implemented the rite of circumcision as an act of faith; it signified their participation in the covenant (cp. Rom 4:11-12; Gal 5:2-6, 11; 6:15; Phil 3:2-3; Col 2:11-12; 1 Pet 3:21).

18:1-15 The Lord's visit to Abraham set the time for Isaac's birth. The three visitors were probably the Lord and two angels (see note on 16:7). Abraham's peaceful and generous reception of the

visitors contrasts sharply with the chaos and corruption of Sodom (ch 19). Eating together was important in making or confirming covenants; when God was ready to fulfill the covenant promise, he came in person to share a meal with Abraham. Fellowship with God has always been signified by a communal meal (see Exod 24:9-11; Matt 26:17-30 // Luke 22:7-38; Acts 2:42; 1 Cor 11:20-34).

18:2-8 Abraham received his visitors as very important guests, perhaps realizing that they were messengers from God.

18:3 *My lord:* The Hebrew text uses *'adonay* ("Lord"), the word that is usually reserved for God. In Hebrew tradition, it was spoken in places where the holy name Yahweh (the LORD) was in the text. Perhaps the text uses *'adonay* rather than the more common *'adoni* to show that this was the angel of the Lord—i.e., the Lord himself (see note on 16:7). We don't know whether Abraham knew his

visitors' identity at the outset, but by the story's end Abraham certainly knew he had been talking with God.

18:6 *three large measures:* Hebrew *3 seahs*, about 15 quarts or 18 liters.

18:9 The visitors' rhetorical question focuses attention on *Sarah*, whom the visitors knew by name.

18:10 *I will return:* The Hebrew verb means "to intervene in someone's life to change their destiny." The statement announced a coming dramatic change.

18:13-15 Sarah thought her disbelieving laughter was hidden, but God knows human hearts (see Ps 69:5; Prov 20:27; Mark 4:22; Luke 8:43-48; Heb 4:13), whether they stagger at the promises or step out in faith (see Heb 11:11-12).

18:14 *Is anything too hard for the LORD?* The question is rhetorical. God is able to do marvelous things. Nothing is incredible to those in covenant fellowship

18:16
Gen 18:22; 19:1
18:17
Gen 19:24
18:18
Gen 12:2-3
*Gal 3:18
18:19
Neh 9:7
18:20
Gen 19:13
18:21
Gen 11:5
Exod 3:8
18:22
Gen 18:16; 19:1
18:23
Exod 23:7
18:25
Deut 1:16-17; 32:4
Ps 58:11
ᵈshapat (8199)
 ▸ Exod 2:14
ᵉmishpat (4941)
 ▸ Ps 9:16
18:27
Gen 2:7
Job 30:19; 42:6
18:30
Exod 32:32
18:33
Gen 17:22; 35:13
19:1
Gen 18:2
ᶠmal'ak (4397)
 ▸ Gen 28:12

about this time next year, and Sarah will have a son."

¹⁵Sarah was afraid, so she denied it, saying, "I didn't laugh."

But the LORD said, "No, you did laugh."

Abraham Intercedes for Sodom

¹⁶Then the men got up from their meal and looked out toward Sodom. As they left, Abraham went with them to send them on their way.

¹⁷"Should I hide my plan from Abraham?" the LORD asked. ¹⁸"For Abraham will certainly become a great and mighty nation, and all the nations of the earth will be blessed through him. ¹⁹I have singled him out so that he will direct his sons and their families to keep the way of the LORD by doing what is right and just. Then I will do for Abraham all that I have promised."

²⁰So the LORD told Abraham, "I have heard a great outcry from Sodom and Gomorrah, because their sin is so flagrant. ²¹I am going down to see if their actions are as wicked as I have heard. If not, I want to know."

²²The other men turned and headed toward Sodom, but the LORD remained with Abraham. ²³Abraham approached him and said, "Will you sweep away both the righteous and the wicked? ²⁴Suppose you find fifty righteous people living there in the city—will you still sweep it away and not spare it for their sakes? ²⁵Surely you wouldn't do such a thing, destroying the righteous along with the wicked. Why, you would be treating the righteous and the wicked exactly the same! Surely you wouldn't do that! Should not the ᵈJudge of all the earth do what is ᵉright?"

²⁶And the LORD replied, "If I find fifty righteous people in Sodom, I will spare the entire city for their sake."

²⁷Then Abraham spoke again. "Since I have begun, let me speak further to my Lord, even though I am but dust and ashes. ²⁸Suppose there are only forty-five righteous people rather than fifty? Will you destroy the whole city for lack of five?"

And the LORD said, "I will not destroy it if I find forty-five righteous people there."

²⁹Then Abraham pressed his request further. "Suppose there are only forty?"

And the LORD replied, "I will not destroy it for the sake of the forty."

³⁰"Please don't be angry, my Lord," Abraham pleaded. "Let me speak—suppose only thirty righteous people are found?"

And the LORD replied, "I will not destroy it if I find thirty."

³¹Then Abraham said, "Since I have dared to speak to the Lord, let me continue—suppose there are only twenty?"

And the LORD replied, "Then I will not destroy it for the sake of the twenty."

³²Finally, Abraham said, "Lord, please don't be angry with me if I speak one more time. Suppose only ten are found there?"

And the LORD replied, "Then I will not destroy it for the sake of the ten."

³³When the LORD had finished his conversation with Abraham, he went on his way, and Abraham returned to his tent.

Sodom and Gomorrah Destroyed

19 That evening the two ᶠangels came to the entrance of the city of Sodom. Lot was sitting there, and when he saw them,

. . . .

with the Lord, because nothing is too difficult for him.

18:16-33 God took Abraham into his confidence as his prophet (18:16-21; see 20:7); Abraham, in turn, interceded for Sodom (18:23-32; see Heb 7:23-26). God is able to do whatever he chooses to do; this passage affirms that it will be just and right.

18:17-19 Abraham was responsible for teaching his descendants righteousness and justice so that they might enjoy God's blessings. It was important for Abraham to know how God's righteousness was at work in judgment.

18:20-21 The omniscient God was cautious in his judgment: He knew the sins of Sodom and Gomorrah, but this close scrutiny communicated God's justice in human terms—he would not destroy the people of the plain unless he was absolutely sure they were wicked.

18:20 *a great outcry:* See Ezek 16:49-50.

18:22-33 Abraham probably thought there were more righteous people in Sodom and Gomorrah than there were (see note on 19:14). In his concern for them, he approached the Lord with a legal appeal based on God's justice. His prayer seems too bold at times, as though he were bargaining with God, but he approached God with genuine humility and reverence. He did not try to talk God into doing something against his will, but prayed for the well-being of others (contrast Lot's prayer, 19:18-23). God is a righteous judge; righteousness exalts a nation (Prov 14:34), and righteous people help to preserve society (cp. Matt 5:13).

19:1-38 The Canaanites were an evil, corrupting people. God judged their morally bankrupt civilization and warned others against becoming like them. It was difficult to get Lot and

his family out of Sodom; it was more difficult to get Sodom out of Lot and his family. This chapter helped later Israelites to understand the moral and spiritual threat of the peoples living in and around the Promised Land, such as the Canaanites and Lot's descendants, the Moabites and the Ammonites (see Num 22–25; Deut 23:3-6; Josh 24:9; Judg 10:7-9; 11:4-5; 1 Sam 10:27; 1 Kgs 11:1-3; 2 Kgs 24:2).

19:1-14 *The two angels* who were with the Lord at Mamre (cp. 18:2, 22) visited *Sodom* reluctantly, knowing what kind of people lived there. Despite Lot's hospitality, they preferred lodging in the square to entering Lot's house.

19:1 No longer living in tents next to Sodom (13:12), Lot had become a citizen and leader in Sodom, *sitting there* at the entrance of the city. Community leaders (elders) usually congregated in the gates, where legal and business

he stood up to meet them. Then he welcomed them and bowed with his face to the ground. ²"My lords," he said, "come to my home to wash your feet, and be my guests for the night. You may then get up early in the morning and be on your way again."

"Oh no," they replied. "We'll just spend the night out here in the city square."

³But Lot insisted, so at last they went home with him. Lot prepared a feast for them, complete with fresh bread made without yeast, and they ate. ⁴But before they retired for the night, all the men of Sodom, young and old, came from all over the city and surrounded the house. ⁵They shouted to Lot, "Where are the men who came to spend the night with you? Bring them out to us so we can have sex with them!"

⁶So Lot stepped outside to talk to them,

shutting the door behind him. ⁷"Please, my brothers," he begged, "don't do such a wicked thing. ⁸Look, I have two virgin daughters. Let me bring them out to you, and you can do with them as you wish. But please, leave these men alone, for they are my guests and are under my protection."

⁹"Stand back!" they shouted. "This fellow came to town as an outsider, and now he's acting like our judge! We'll treat you far worse than those other men!" And they lunged toward Lot to break down the door.

¹⁰But the two angels reached out, pulled Lot into the house, and bolted the door. ¹¹Then they blinded all the men, young and old, who were at the door of the house, so they gave up trying to get inside.

¹²Meanwhile, the angels questioned Lot. "Do you have any other relatives here in

19:2
Gen 18:4
19:3
Gen 18:6-8
19:4
Gen 13:13; 18:20
19:5
Lev 18:22
Judg 19:22
19:8
Deut 23:17
19:9
Exod 2:14
19:10
Gen 19:1
19:11
Deut 28:28-29
2 Kgs 6:18
Acts 13:11

LOT (19:1-38)

Gen 11:27, 31;
12:4-5; 13:1-14;
14:12-16
Deut 2:9, 17-19
Ps 83:4-8
Luke 17:28-33
2 Pet 2:6-9

Lot was Abraham's nephew and the ancestor of the Moabites and Ammonites. Like Abraham, Lot was born in Ur and accompanied Terah to Haran (11:27-32). After Terah's death, he joined Abraham in journeying to Canaan and Egypt.

When Lot and Abraham returned from Egypt to Canaan, their flocks and herds grew too numerous for them to live together. Abraham gave Lot his choice of land on which to settle. Lot chose the fertile plain of the Jordan that was like "the garden of the Lord" (13:10), and eventually he took up residence in Sodom. His increasing involvement with the completely corrupt cities of the plain contaminated Lot and resulted in the loss of all his wealth.

While Lot lived in Sodom, four Mesopotamian kings defeated the kings of five towns in the area; in the subsequent plundering, they carried off Lot, his family, and his possessions (14:1-12). When word of this reached Abraham, he launched a rearguard action against the invaders and recovered the prisoners and property (14:13-16). Later, two angelic visitors called on Lot in Sodom to hasten his departure from the doomed city (ch 19). The homosexual attack on the visitors illustrates the city's depravity, and Lot's willingness to sacrifice his daughters shows how corrupt and compromised he had become. Lot was reluctant to leave Sodom. No one but his immediate family accompanied him, and his wife was destroyed when she turned back. His daughters, despairing of finding husbands, got Lot drunk enough to have sexual relations with them. Their two sons, Moab and Ben-ammi, were ancestors of the Moabites and Ammonites (19:30-38), two nations that became inveterate enemies of Israel (see Deut 23:3-6).

Lot was a fool and a hypocrite to the people of the town, and on his journey out of Sodom he was still bargaining with God. His drunkenness and incest with his two daughters also reveals his character. Despite his waywardness, Peter declares that Lot was a "righteous man who was tormented in his soul by the wickedness he saw and heard day after day" (see 2 Pet 2:6-9).

transactions were publicly finalized (cp. 23:18; Job 29:7, 12-17). As a righteous man (2 Pet 2:7-8), Lot tried to modify the townspeople's wickedness by giving advice on good living (cp. 19:9). Although he denounced gross evil, Lot preferred Sodom's sumptuous lifestyle to life in the hills (cp. 13:10-11), where there was clean living but no "good life." As long as the Lord left Lot and his family alone in Sodom, he lived comfort-

ably there and kept his personal belief in God; but finally, he could not hold to both. Sodom would have destroyed Lot if the Lord had not destroyed Sodom.
• This account showed Israel that God is the righteous judge of the whole earth (18:25) who will judge evildoers with justice and equity. In wicked societies, moral and ethical failures lead to social injustice.

19:4-5 The townsmen's vileness was matched by Lot's hypocrisy (19:6-9).

19:6-9 Lot opposed homosexuality and rape and rebuked their wicked plans,

but he was hypocritically willing to sacrifice his daughters to fend off the townsmen's vice. Lot had originally pitched his tent next to Sodom; now Sodom controlled his life.

19:9 The men of the city were enraged by Lot's attempts to curtail their wickedness. Lot had apparently not condemned them before, since they were amazed that he now judged them.

19:10 *angels:* Literally *men;* also in 19:12, 16. They first appeared to Abraham as men (18:2); the text identifies two of them as angels (19:1).

19:13
Gen 18:20
1 Chr 21:15
Jude 1:7

19:14
Exod 9:21
Jer 5:12; 43:1-2

19:17
Gen 13:10; 19:26
Jer 48:6

19:22
Gen 13:10

19:24
Luke 17:29
Jude 1:7

19:25
Deut 29:23
Isa 13:19
Lam 4:6
2 Pet 2:6

19:26
Gen 19:17
Luke 17:32

19:27
Gen 18:22

19:28
Rev 9:2

19:29
Deut 7:8; 9:5
2 Pet 2:7-8

19:30
Gen 13:10

the city?" they asked. "Get them out of this place—your sons-in-law, sons, daughters, or anyone else. 13For we are about to destroy this city completely. The outcry against this place is so great it has reached the Lord, and he has sent us to destroy it."

14So Lot rushed out to tell his daughters' fiancés, "Quick, get out of the city! The Lord is about to destroy it." But the young men thought he was only joking.

15At dawn the next morning the angels became insistent. "Hurry," they said to Lot. "Take your wife and your two daughters who are here. Get out right now, or you will be swept away in the destruction of the city!"

16When Lot still hesitated, the angels seized his hand and the hands of his wife and two daughters and rushed them to safety outside the city, for the Lord was merciful. 17When they were safely out of the city, one of the angels ordered, "Run for your lives! And don't look back or stop anywhere in the valley! Escape to the mountains, or you will be swept away!"

18"Oh no, my lord!" Lot begged. 19"You have been so gracious to me and saved my life, and you have shown such great kindness. But I cannot go to the mountains. Disaster would catch up to me there, and I would soon die. 20See, there is a small village nearby. Please let me go there instead;

don't you see how small it is? Then my life will be saved."

21"All right," the angel said, "I will grant your request. I will not destroy the little village. 22But hurry! Escape to it, for I can do nothing until you arrive there." (This explains why that village was known as Zoar, which means "little place.")

23Lot reached the village just as the sun was rising over the horizon. 24Then the Lord rained down fire and burning sulfur from the sky on Sodom and Gomorrah. 25He utterly destroyed them, along with the other cities and villages of the plain, wiping out all the people and every bit of vegetation. 26But Lot's wife looked back as she was following behind him, and she turned into a pillar of salt.

27Abraham got up early that morning and hurried out to the place where he had stood in the Lord's presence. 28He looked out across the plain toward Sodom and Gomorrah and watched as columns of smoke rose from the cities like smoke from a furnace.

29But God had listened to Abraham's request and kept Lot safe, removing him from the disaster that engulfed the cities on the plain.

Lot and His Daughters

30Afterward Lot left Zoar because he was afraid of the people there, and he went to

. . . .

◀ **The Destruction of Sodom and Gomorrah (18:16–19:38).** The two angels apparently traveled, as shown, from Abraham's camp at the OAKS OF MAMRE to destroy SODOM and GOMORRAH. Lot and his daughters took refuge at ZOAR, then moved eastward into the mountains of MOAB. Lot fathered two sons by his daughters; the two sons became the nations of MOAB (see Num 21:10-20; 22:1–25:3; Deut 23:3, 6; Judg 3:12-30; Ruth 1:1-6) and AMMON (see Num 21:24; Deut 2:19-37; 23:3; Judg 10:6–12:3; 1 Sam 10:27–11:11).

mercifully spared Lot for Abraham's sake (18:23; 19:29). Lot deserved judgment for his way of life, but he was a believer at heart and the Lord rescued him (2 Pet 2:7-8). • Lot is not alone in his conflicted lifestyle. Countless believers fall in with a corrupt world rather than flee a doomed society. God's people, living in a pagan world, must remain separate (1 Jn 2:15-17). The corrupt world system awaits God's coming judgment, which will be far greater than the destruction of Sodom and Gomorrah (Matt 11:23-24).

19:18-22 Lot demanded a concession from the angels even after he was

19:14 Lot's warning words were not taken seriously because of his hypocrisy. It seemed that there would not be even ten righteous people in the city.

19:15-23 Lot escaped judgment by God's grace, but his heart was still in Sodom. Israel would forever remember Lot as lingering, halting, and being dragged to safety by angels. The Lord

delivered. He wanted to live in the small town of Zoar (*little place*).

19:23-25 Cp. Luke 17:29. The eruption of Vesuvius and the destruction of Pompeii in 79 AD, as well as recent natural disasters, show how quickly a thorough catastrophe like this could happen.

19:26 *looked back:* The verb indicates prolonged, intense gazing toward the world she loved, not a curious glance (15:5; Exod 33:8; Num 21:9; 1 Sam 2:32; cp. Exod 3:6). *Lot's wife* was too attached to Sodom to follow God's call of grace, so she was included in the judgment as she lingered on the valley slopes. Christ's return to judge the world will be as sudden and devastating as the destruction of Sodom (Luke 17:32-37). Those who crave the life of this wicked world will lose this world and the next.

19:29 God honored Abraham's intercession (cp. 18:23-32), but Lot's entire world was gone because he lived by instinct and desire, not by faith in God. He could no longer live in the good land he selfishly chose for himself (13:10-13; cp. Matt 16:26; 2 Cor 5:7).

19:30-38 The poverty of the cave contrasts with the wealth Lot shared with Abram and the good life he lived

live in a cave in the mountains with his two daughters. ³¹One day the older daughter said to her sister, "There are no men left anywhere in this entire area, so we can't get married like everyone else. And our father will soon be too old to have children. ³²Come, let's get him drunk with wine, and then we will have sex with him. That way we will preserve our family line through our father."

³³So that night they got him drunk with wine, and the older daughter went in and had intercourse with her father. He was unaware of her lying down or getting up again.

³⁴The next morning the older daughter said to her younger sister, "I had sex with our father last night. Let's get him drunk with wine again tonight, and you go in and have sex with him. That way we will preserve our family line through our father." ³⁵So that night they got him drunk with wine again, and the younger daughter went in and had intercourse with him. As before, he was unaware of her lying down or getting up again.

³⁶As a result, both of Lot's daughters became pregnant by their own father. ³⁷When the older daughter gave birth to a son, she named him Moab. He became the ancestor of the nation now known as the Moabites. ³⁸When the younger daughter gave birth

to a son, she named him Ben-ammi. He became the ancestor of the nation now known as the Ammonites.

Abraham Deceives Abimelech

20 Abraham moved south to the Negev and lived for a while between Kadesh and Shur, and then he moved on to Gerar. While living there as a foreigner, ²Abraham introduced his wife, Sarah, by saying, "She is my sister." So King Abimelech of Gerar sent for Sarah and had her brought to him at his palace.

³But that night God came to Abimelech in a dream and told him, "You are a dead man, for that woman you have taken is already married!"

⁴But Abimelech had not slept with her yet, so he said, "Lord, will you destroy an innocent nation? ⁵Didn't Abraham tell me, 'She is my sister'? And she herself said, 'Yes, he is my brother.' I acted in complete innocence! My hands are clean."

⁶In the dream God responded, "Yes, I know you are innocent. That's why I kept you from sinning against me, and why I did not let you touch her. ⁷Now return the woman to her husband, and he will pray for you, for he is a ^gprophet. Then you will live. But if you don't return her to him, you can be sure that you and all your people will die."

19:33
Gen 9:21

19:37
Gen 36:35
Exod 15:15
Num 21:29
Deut 2:9
Ruth 1:1

19:38
Num 21:24
Deut 2:19

20:1
Gen 14:7; 26:1

20:2
Gen 12:13

20:3
Gen 28:12; 31:24;
37:5

20:4
Gen 18:23-25

20:5
Gen 12:19
1 Kgs 9:4
Ps 7:8; 26:6

20:7
1 Sam 7:5
Job 42:8
^gnabi' (5030)
   ›Exod 7:1

. . . .

in Sodom. Abraham would father a righteous nation (17:1), but Lot and his daughters gave birth to a new Sodom.

19:30-35 The character of Lot's *daughters* was formed by Sodom's culture more than by their father's heritage, so they had no qualms about having children by their drunk father (cp. 9:21-22). They saw no other way to carry on their line.

19:36-38 The daughters' plan worked, and they each *became pregnant by their own father*. From these two incest-born sons came two perennial enemies of Israel, the nations of Moab and Ammon. Their grotesque wickedness was due in part to their origin. • Both daughters chose ambiguous names that hinted at their actions without raising the suspicions of those who did not know the stories. *Moab* sounds like a Hebrew term that means "from father." *Ben-ammi* means "son of my kinsman."

20:1-18 This second "sister story" in Genesis (cp. 12:10-20) occurred shortly before Sarah became pregnant with Isaac (ch 21). On both occasions, God protected Abraham and Sarah's marriage in purity for the sake of the covenant promises. Participation in God's

plan requires separation from worldly corruption. • This story took place in the Promised Land; it showed Israel how God intervened in people's lives to fulfill his plan, how God continued to protect them against threats from other tribes, and how God used his chosen people to mediate his relationship with the nations. • God's preventing the destruction of Abraham's marriage by adultery reminded the Israelites to keep their marriages morally and racially pure (Ezra 9:1-4; Neh 13:23-27; Mal 2:10-17); they should not allow any opportunity for temptation (Exod 20:14, 17; Lev 20:10; 21:13-15). Adultery would eventually destroy the covenant and covenant people.

20:1 *Gerar* was near the coast in Philistine land, about twelve miles south of Gaza and fifty miles southwest of Hebron.

20:2 *Abraham* told the same lie to Abimelech that he had told to Pharaoh (12:13); Isaac would later do the same (26:1-11), probably having learned this tactic from his father. • *Abimelech* (literally *my father the king*) was probably a title like "Pharaoh" (37:36; Exod 1:15), not a proper name (see note on 26:1).

20:3-7 *God* gave *Abimelech* a stern warning against committing adultery; it was a capital offense (cp. Exod 20:14), viewed throughout the ancient Near East as a "great sin" (20:9).

20:3 *that night God came . . . in a dream:* God urgently intervened to stop *Abimelech* from violating Sarah's purity shortly before God's promise was fulfilled (18:10; 21:1-3).

20:4-5 *Abimelech* was *innocent* (20:6); his conscience was clear. Nonetheless, he was about to commit adultery, and ignorance does not excuse guilt (Lev 4:13-14). • *will you destroy an innocent nation?* Abimelech's appeal to God echoes Abraham's earlier words (cp. 18:23-32) and rebukes Abraham's lack of faith on this occasion.

20:6 Because Abimelech acted with a clear conscience, God *kept* him *from sinning.* God will graciously help those who try to do what is right. When people act with reverence toward God, God gives them more revelation and draws them into more specific faith (see Acts 10).

20:7 Abraham's prayer saved the king's life and restored his family (20:17-18).

20:9
Gen 12:18
20:11
Gen 12:12; 42:18
20:13
Gen 12:1
20:14
Gen 12:16
20:16
Gen 23:15
20:17
Num 12:13; 21:7
ʰ*palal* (6419)
▸ Deut 9:26
20:18
Gen 12:17
21:1
Gen 17:16, 21
21:2
Gen 18:10
Gal 4:22
Heb 11:11
21:3
Gen 17:19
21:4
Gen 17:10, 12
21:5
Gen 12:4
Heb 6:15
21:6
Isa 54:1
21:7
Gen 18:13
21:8
1 Sam 1:23
21:9
Gal 4:29
21:10
*Gal 4:30

⁸Abimelech got up early the next morning and quickly called all his servants together. When he told them what had happened, his men were terrified. ⁹Then Abimelech called for Abraham. "What have you done to us?" he demanded. "What crime have I committed that deserves treatment like this, making me and my kingdom guilty of this great sin? No one should ever do what you have done! ¹⁰Whatever possessed you to do such a thing?"

¹¹Abraham replied, "I thought, 'This is a godless place. They will want my wife and will kill me to get her.' ¹²And she really is my sister, for we both have the same father, but different mothers. And I married her. ¹³When God called me to leave my father's home and to travel from place to place, I told her, 'Do me a favor. Wherever we go, tell the people that I am your brother.'"

¹⁴Then Abimelech took some of his sheep and goats, cattle, and male and female servants, and he presented them to Abraham. He also returned his wife, Sarah, to him. ¹⁵Then Abimelech said, "Look over my land and choose any place where you would like to live." ¹⁶And he said to Sarah, "Look, I am giving your 'brother' 1,000 pieces of silver in the presence of all these witnesses. This is to compensate you for any wrong I may have done to you. This will settle any claim against me, and your reputation is cleared."

¹⁷Then Abraham ʰprayed to God, and God healed Abimelech, his wife, and his female servants, so they could have children. ¹⁸For the LORD had caused all the women to be infertile because of what happened with Abraham's wife, Sarah.

The Birth of Isaac

21 The LORD kept his word and did for Sarah exactly what he had promised. ²She became pregnant, and she gave birth to a son for Abraham in his old age. This happened at just the time God had said it would. ³And Abraham named their son Isaac. ⁴Eight days after Isaac was born, Abraham circumcised him as God had commanded. ⁵Abraham was 100 years old when Isaac was born.

⁶And Sarah declared, "God has brought me laughter. All who hear about this will laugh with me. ⁷Who would have said to Abraham that Sarah would nurse a baby? Yet I have given Abraham a son in his old age!"

Hagar and Ishmael Are Sent Away

⁸When Isaac grew up and was about to be weaned, Abraham prepared a huge feast to celebrate the occasion. ⁹But Sarah saw Ishmael—the son of Abraham and her Egyptian servant Hagar—making fun of her son, Isaac. ¹⁰So she turned to Abraham and demanded, "Get rid of that slave woman and her son. He is not going to share the inheritance with my son, Isaac. I won't have it!"

¹¹This upset Abraham very much because Ishmael was his son. ¹²But God told

. . . .

Abimelech learned that Abraham's God was sovereign, and that Abraham, God's **prophet**, had received God's revelation and would intercede for others (see Num 12:13; Deut 9:20), even if he did not always live up to the office.

20:8-10 Abraham had earned rebukes from Abimelech and from God (cp. 12:17-19). Abimelech was angry that Abraham's deception had made him guilty **of this great sin** (see note on 20:3-7). He knew that taking a married woman into his harem was wrong.

20:11-13 Abraham's duplicity was not a momentary loss of faith. Despite the rebuke he received in Egypt, he practiced this strategy **wherever** he went (cp. 12:12-13). Living by faith requires perseverance.

20:14-16 Abimelech secured his **reputation** as a good man (see note on 20:4-5) and demonstrated his integrity. He made amends by allowing Abraham to live in the region, and by giving him slaves, livestock (cp. 21:27), and *1,000 pieces of silver* (Hebrew *1,000 [shekels] of silver*, about 25 pounds or 11.4 kilo-

grams in weight) to *compensate . . . for any wrong* done to Sarah.

20:17-18 Sarah's barrenness suggests that some time had passed. God controls births; he opens and closes wombs (25:21; 29:31; 30:2, 17, 22-23; 1 Sam 1:19-20; Ps 113:9; 127:3; Luke 1:13).

21:1-2 See 18:10.

21:3-4 *Abraham* responded in faith by naming his *son Isaac* and circumcising him according to the terms of the covenant (see 17:9-14).

21:5 Isaac was born twenty-five years after the promise was first given (cp. 12:4).

21:6-7 *Sarah* was filled with joy and praise for this amazing event—only *God* could enable her to have a child.

21:6 The name *Isaac* (Hebrew *yitskhaq*) means "he laughs." Sarah's wordplay shows that the laughter of unbelief when the promise was given (18:12) had changed to the laughter of joy at its fulfillment. Isaac's name could refer to the pleasure of God and of his parents

at his birth. Sarah knew that everyone who heard about this would *laugh with* her and rejoice at the news.

21:8-21 God used the incident of Ishmael's mocking Isaac to separate Ishmael and Hagar from the family and the child of promise. They would constantly threaten the promised descendant if they remained with the family.

21:8-9 The *feast* for Isaac's weaning probably occurred when he was three and *Ishmael* about seventeen years old (16:16). Sarah saw Ishmael *making fun of her son, Isaac* (as in Greek version and Latin Vulgate; Hebrew lacks *of her son, Isaac*). The verb *metsakheq* ("making fun of") is related to the word for "laughter"; this theme (21:6) is given a sour twist by Ishmael's mockery.

21:10 Earlier, Sarah mistreated Hagar and pressured her to flee (16:6); when Hagar's son mistreated Isaac, Sarah demanded that *that slave woman and her son* leave.

21:11-13 Abraham was *upset* by Sarah's demand to oust Hagar and *Ishmael*.

Abraham, "Do not be upset over the boy and your servant. Do whatever Sarah tells you, for Isaac is the son through whom your descendants will be counted. ¹³But I will also make a nation of the descendants of Hagar's son because he is your son, too."

¹⁴So Abraham got up early the next morning, prepared food and a container of water, and strapped them on Hagar's shoulders. Then he sent her away with their son, and she wandered aimlessly in the wilderness of Beersheba.

¹⁵When the water was gone, she put the boy in the shade of a bush. ¹⁶Then she went and sat down by herself about a hundred yards away. "I don't want to watch the boy die," she said, as she burst into tears.

¹⁷But God heard the boy crying, and the angel of God called to Hagar from heaven, "Hagar, what's wrong? Do not be afraid! God has heard the boy crying as he lies there. ¹⁸Go to him and comfort him, for I will make a great nation from his descendants."

¹⁹Then God opened Hagar's eyes, and she saw a well full of water. She quickly filled her water container and gave the boy a drink.

²⁰And God was with the boy as he grew up in the wilderness. He became a skillful archer, ²¹and he settled in the wilderness of Paran. His mother arranged for him to marry a woman from the land of Egypt.

Abraham's Covenant with Abimelech

²²About this time, Abimelech came with Phicol, his army commander, to visit Abraham. "God is obviously with you, helping you in everything you do," Abimelech said. ²³"Swear to me in God's name that you will never deceive me, my children, or any of my descendants. I have been loyal to you, so now swear that you will be loyal to me and to this country where you are living as a foreigner."

²⁴Abraham replied, "Yes, I swear to it!" ²⁵Then Abraham complained to Abimelech about a well that Abimelech's servants had taken by force from Abraham's servants.

²⁶"This is the first I've heard of it," Abimelech answered. "I have no idea who is responsible. You have never complained about this before."

²⁷Abraham then gave some of his sheep, goats, and cattle to Abimelech, and they made a treaty. ²⁸But Abraham also took seven additional female lambs and set them off by themselves. ²⁹Abimelech asked, "Why have you set these seven apart from the others?"

³⁰Abraham replied, "Please accept these seven lambs to show your agreement that I dug this well." ³¹Then he named the place Beersheba (which means "well of the oath"), because that was where they had sworn the oath.

21:12 *Rom 9:7 *Heb 11:18
21:13 Gen 16:10; 21:18; 25:12-18
21:14 Gen 16:1
21:16 Jer 6:26
21:17 Exod 3:7 Deut 26:7 Ps 6:8
21:18 Gen 26:24
21:20 Gen 28:15
21:21 Gen 25:18
21:22 Gen 26:26
21:23 Gen 24:3
21:25 Gen 26:15
21:27 Gen 26:31
21:30 Gen 31:44
21:31 Gen 21:14; 26:33

God told him to comply, assuring Abraham that Ishmael would also have a future as Abraham's offspring.

21:14-21 God again rescued Hagar *in the wilderness* and guaranteed her future (cp. 16:7-14). This passage is similar to ch 16, but the differences are great. Here, Hagar and Ishmael are rescued, but there is no commemorative naming. God's earlier promise to Hagar is reiterated, but this time Hagar is not told to return to Sarah. The repeated motifs on the two occasions confirm God's sovereign plan for Hagar and Ishmael. As Joseph told Pharaoh, the twofold event showed that God confirmed it (41:32). God did not abandon Hagar and Ishmael but met them in their despair (cp. 16:7), provided sustenance for them, and promised again that Ishmael would found a great nation (21:13; cp. 16:11-12). Paul uses this event in his letter to the Galatians to illustrate how God's people must relinquish all that threatens the fulfillment of God's promise (Gal 4:21-31).

21:16 *a hundred yards* (literally *a bow-shot*): This description connects with Ishmael's vocation (21:20).

21:22-34 This passage, at its climax,

explains the name of *Beersheba*, Abraham's home (21:31-34). Beersheba reflected the covenant Abraham made with the residents of the land, which enabled him to dwell there in peace and prosperity. God's promise was coming to fruition (12:7; 13:14-17; 15:7, 18-21; 17:8).

21:22-23 *Abimelech* pressed for the treaty so that *Abraham* would not cheat or *deceive* him. Abimelech knew that God was blessing Abraham even though Abraham was not entirely trustworthy (20:9-10). This sad contradiction made the treaty necessary. By contrast, God's faithful people are exhorted to speak the truth (Eph 4:15, 25), and Jesus warned against manipulating truth by the clever use of oaths (Matt 5:37; Jas 5:12).

21:25 The motif of the *well* appears again (cp. 16:14; 21:19). God provided water (a symbol of blessing) in the barren wilderness, and later even brought water out of a rock for Israel (Exod 15:22-27; 17:1-7; Num 20:1-13).

21:27-31 Abraham's gifts to Abimelech (cp. 20:14) secured his legal right to dwell peaceably in the land and to claim ownership of the well. *Beersheba*

marked one more step toward the fulfillment of God's promise.

21:32 *The Philistines* in Genesis are different from the Philistines of Judges through Kings. The earlier Philistines had Semitic names (e.g., Abimelech) and Canaanite culture. The later Philistines were apparently of Greek origin, with Greek customs and culture. They seem to have arrived in Canaan by sea from the Aegean area around 1200 BC, during the time of the judges. Probably the name of the later Philistines was used here simply to describe the region's earlier inhabitants.

21:33-34 *A tamarisk tree* requires a lot of water; this act indicated Abraham's security in his land rights and his faith that God would provide water in this desert area. He settled *as a foreigner* in the land, but dwelling under his tree was a sign of peaceful security (cp. Zech 3:10). • *there he worshiped the LORD:* See note on 12:8. • *the Eternal God:* Hebrew *El-Olam.*

22:1-2 The greatest test in Abraham's life came after he had received the promised child following a long wait. He had grown to love Isaac and had enjoyed his presence for a number of years.

21:33
1 Sam 22:6; 31:13
Ps 90:2
Isa 9:6; 40:28
'olam (5769)
  ▸ Deut 33:15

22:1
Exod 15:25; 16:4
Deut 8:2, 16

22:2
2 Chr 3:1
John 3:16

22:5
khawah (7812)
  ▸ Gen 42:6

³²After making their covenant at Beer-sheba, Abimelech left with Phicol, the commander of his army, and they returned home to the land of the Philistines. ³³Then Abraham planted a tamarisk tree at Beer-sheba, and there he worshiped the Lᴏʀᴅ, the ⁱEternal God. ³⁴And Abraham lived as a foreigner in Philistine country for a long time.

Abraham's Faith Tested

22 Some time later, God tested Abraham's faith. "Abraham!" God called. "Yes," he replied. "Here I am."

²"Take your son, your only son—yes, Isaac, whom you love so much—and go to the land of Moriah. Go and sacrifice him as a burnt offering on one of the mountains, which I will show you."

³The next morning Abraham got up early. He saddled his donkey and took two of his servants with him, along with his son, Isaac. Then he chopped wood for a fire for a burnt offering and set out for the place God had told him about. ⁴On the third day of their journey, Abraham looked up and saw the place in the distance. ⁵"Stay here with the donkey," Abraham told the servants. "The boy and I will travel a little farther. We will ʲworship there, and then we will come right back."

ISAAC (21:1-12)

Gen 17:19-21;
22:1-19; 24:1-8,
14, 62-67; 25:5-11,
19-28; 26:1–28:9;
31:42; 35:12, 27-28;
48:15-16; 49:31
Exod 3:6
Josh 24:3-4
Rom 9:6-10
Gal 4:21-31
Heb 11:8-9, 17-20

At Isaac's birth, his parents, Abraham and Sarah, were beyond childbearing age. God had promised Abraham a son (15:4-6), but no son had come. Ishmael had been born through Hagar (16:1-16), but he was not the promised son.

Isaac means "he laughs," reflecting the circumstances of his birth. When God promised that Isaac would be born, both Abraham and Sarah first laughed in disbelief (17:15-19; 18:9-15). When he was born, they laughed for joy (21:6-7).

During Isaac's adolescence, God tested Abraham by telling him to sacrifice Isaac (22:1-19). Abraham's faith remained firm; he obeyed, and Isaac submitted to his father. God then intervened to provide a sacrificial ram in Isaac's place. Abraham's faith in God was rewarded with the promise of great blessings (22:15-18).

Isaac married Rebekah and was ready to carry on the chosen line, but Rebekah was unable to bear children (25:21). Rather than take matters into his own hands as his father had done (see 16:1-16), Isaac "pleaded with the Lᴏʀᴅ" and Rebekah bore twin sons. Isaac favored Esau, the older son, while Rebekah preferred Jacob. Favoritism remained a problem among Isaac's descendants (see notes on 29:30; 33:1-2; 37:4) and led to Isaac's being deceived by his son Jacob when he was old and blind (ch 27).

Isaac followed his father Abraham's example in relating to surrounding nations. When visiting another kingdom during a famine, he fearfully claimed that his wife was his sister (26:1-11; cp. 12:10-20; 20:1-18). Like his father, Isaac became prosperous in that land and was asked to leave (26:12-16; cp. 12:16-20); he experienced conflict over water and land with other herdsmen (26:17-22; cp. 21:25-31); and he made a treaty with the king of the Philistines (26:26-31; cp. 21:22-31). When Isaac worshiped the Lord at Beersheba, he was given the same promise that his father had received (26:2-5, 23-25; cp. 21:32-33; 22:16-18).

Isaac continued God's covenant with Abraham and linked Abraham with Jacob (see Acts 7:8; Heb 11:9-20). As the child of promise, Isaac represents all who are children of Abraham by faith in Christ and are thereby free to live as God's children rather than as slaves (see Gal 4:21–5:1).

22:1 *Some time later:* Abraham had sent Ishmael away and settled in the land. Now *God tested Abraham's faith* by telling him to give up Isaac. This pushed the limits of logic and of Abraham's knowledge of God. Would he still obey when God seemed to be working against him and against the covenant? Would he cling to the boy or surrender him to God (see Exod 13:11-13)? Did he believe that God would still keep his word and bless the world through Abraham's offspring?

22:2 Obedience to God's earlier call (12:1-3) was rewarded with great bless-ing; now Abraham had the opportunity to show even greater obedience. • *Take your son . . . Isaac, whom you love so much:* By this detailed description of Isaac, God reminded Abraham that the young man was his beloved son, and intensified his awareness of the cost of the sacrifice. • The name *Moriah* is explained by the Chronicler (2 Chr 3:1) as the place of the later Temple Mount in Jerusalem. • *Go:* By wording the command in this way, God helped Abraham to obey by recalling his former call (cp. 12:1-3).

22:3 Abraham's immediate, unques-tioning obedience is almost as astounding as the test.

22:5 *We will worship there, and then we will come* (or *We will worship there so that we may come back*): Abraham's amazing statement makes us wonder what he was thinking. Abraham knew that God had planned the future of the covenant around Isaac, and that God wanted him to sacrifice Isaac. He could not reconcile these things in his mind; he could only do what God commanded him to do, and leave the future to God (cp. Heb 11:17-19).

⁶So Abraham placed the wood for the burnt offering on Isaac's shoulders, while he himself carried the fire and the knife. As the two of them walked on together, ⁷Isaac turned to Abraham and said, "Father?"

"Yes, my son?" Abraham replied.

"We have the fire and the wood," the boy said, "but where is the sheep for the burnt offering?"

⁸"God will provide a sheep for the burnt offering, my son," Abraham answered. And they both walked on together.

⁹When they arrived at the place where God had told him to go, Abraham built an altar and arranged the wood on it. Then he tied his son, Isaac, and laid him on the altar on top of the wood. ¹⁰And Abraham picked up the knife to kill his son as a sacrifice. ¹¹At that moment the angel of the LORD called to him from heaven, "Abraham! Abraham!"

"Yes," Abraham replied. "Here I am!"

¹²"Don't lay a hand on the boy!" the angel said. "Do not hurt him in any way, for now I know that you truly fear God. You have not withheld from me even your son, your only son."

¹³Then Abraham looked up and saw a ram caught by its horns in a thicket. So he took the ram and sacrificed it as a burnt offering in place of his son. ¹⁴Abraham named the place Yahweh-Yireh (which means "the LORD will provide"). To this day, people still use that name as a proverb: "On the mountain of the LORD it will be provided."

¹⁵Then the angel of the LORD called again to Abraham from heaven. ¹⁶"This is what the LORD says: Because you have obeyed me and have not withheld even your son, your only son, I swear by my own name that ¹⁷I will certainly bless you. I will multiply your descendants beyond number, like the stars in the sky and the sand on the seashore. Your descendants will conquer the cities of their enemies. ¹⁸And through your descendants all the nations of the earth will be blessed—all because you have obeyed me."

¹⁹Then they returned to the servants and traveled back to Beersheba, where Abraham continued to live.

Nahor's Family (22:20-24)

²⁰Soon after this, Abraham heard that Milcah, his brother Nahor's wife, had borne Nahor eight sons. ²¹The oldest was named Uz, the next oldest was Buz, followed by

22:6
John 19:17
22:7
Gen 8:20
Exod 29:38-42
John 1:29, 36
Rev 13:8
22:9
Heb 11:17-19
Jas 2:21
22:11
Gen 16:7; 21:17
22:12
Heb 11:17
22:13
Gen 8:20
22:14
Gen 22:7-8
22:16
*Heb 6:13-14
22:17
Gen 12:2; 15:5; 26:4
*Heb 6:14
22:18
*Acts 3:25
*Gal 3:8, 16
22:19
Gen 21:14
22:20
Gen 11:29

. . . .

22:7-8 In response to Isaac's question, *Abraham* again showed his faith in the Lord, saying *God will provide,* although he was not sure how. This theme is central to the entire narrative.

22:9-19 God's intervention was dramatic and instructive, confirming that he never intended for Isaac to be sacrificed. God later made it clear that child sacrifice was an abomination to him (see Lev 18:21; 20:1-5; Deut 18:10; 2 Kgs 16:2-3; Isa 57:5; Jer 32:35). God wanted Abraham to sacrifice his own will and surrender it to God, and when he did, God intervened. This passage sets a pattern for all sacrificial worshipers. Like Abraham, true worshipers of God know that everything belongs to God—it all came from God and must therefore be acknowledged as God's possession. A true worshiper holds nothing back but obediently gives God what he asks, trusting that God will provide for all his needs, and then discovering through experience that God always does so.

22:11 *The angel of the LORD* stopped Abraham just as he was ready to plunge the knife into his son.

22:12 Now God knew that Abraham would hold nothing back from him, that he did *truly fear God.* To fear the Lord means to reverence him as sovereign, trust him implicitly, and obey him without protest. The sacrifice that pleases God is a heart broken of self-will,

surrendered to God (Ps 40:6-8; 51:17) and offering its best to God. • *You have not withheld:* Cp. Rom 8:32, which uses the same verb ("spare") as the Greek OT uses here. If God gave us his dearest possession, he will surely provide all things for us.

22:13 God provided *a ram caught by its horns in a thicket* for the sacrifice. God graciously allowed Abraham to substitute an animal sacrifice *in place of* Isaac. Later, all Israel would offer animals to the Lord, knowing that God's grace had provided this substitution (Exod 29:10; Lev 4:15; 16:20-22). In the NT, God substituted his only son for all humanity; the perfect sacrifice was made once and for all (Isa 53:6, 10; John 1:29; Heb 7:27; 10:1-14; 1 Pet 3:18).

22:14 As with many patriarchal narratives, the heart of the matter is retained through commemorative naming. *Yahweh-Yireh . . . means "the LORD will provide"* (see 22:8). That Abraham used the holy name in this act shows that the patriarchs knew the name *Yahweh* (cp. Exod 6:2-3), but not its full meaning (see note on Exod 6:2-3). • *To this day:* Later Israelites understood this passage as a lesson about their own worship in Jerusalem. Abraham's sacrifice took place *on the mountain of the LORD,* later the location of the Temple in Jerusalem (see note on 22:2). Three times a year, the people of Israel brought their best

to God as a sacrifice, trusting that he would continue to provide for their needs.

22:15-19 After the event, God again confirmed his covenant with Abraham (cp. 15:5, 18-21; 17:3-8). His descendants would be numerous *like the stars in the sky* (cp. 26:4), like the *sand on the seashore* (cp. 32:12), and like the dust of the earth (cp. 13:16; 28:14).

22:16 *by my own name:* There is no higher name by which God can *swear* (Heb 6:13-17).

22:17 *descendants:* Literally *seed;* also in 22:18. • Joshua and OT Israel partially fulfilled the promise that Abraham's descendants would *conquer the cities* (literally *take possession of the gates*) of God's *enemies;* this will be fulfilled fully by the church (cp. Matt 16:18 and note).

22:18–25:11 Abraham passed the test of faith; from this point, his task was to pass the covenant blessings to Isaac. He purchased a burial plot (ch 23), acquired a wife for Isaac (ch 24), and distributed his property (25:1-11).

22:20-24 A report came from the east that Abraham's brother Nahor (see 11:27-29) was flourishing. The actors in the following narrative are introduced here.

22:20 *Milcah,* Nahor's wife, was also his niece (see 11:29).

22:21 *Uz* might have been Job's forefather (Job 1:1).

22:23
Gen 24:15

23:2
Josh 14:15

23:3
Gen 10:15

23:4
Lev 25:23
1 Chr 29:15
Ps 39:12
Heb 11:9

23:6
Gen 14:14-16

23:8-9
Gen 25:9

23:10
Ruth 4:1, 11

23:15
Exod 30:13

23:16
Jer 32:9

23:17-18
Gen 25:9; 49:29-30;
50:13

Kemuel (the ancestor of the Arameans), [22]Kesed, Hazo, Pildash, Jidlaph, and Bethuel. [23](Bethuel became the father of Rebekah.) In addition to these eight sons from Milcah, [24]Nahor had four other children from his concubine Reumah. Their names were Tebah, Gaham, Tahash, and Maacah.

The Burial of Sarah:
Abraham's Land Purchase (23:1-20)

23 When Sarah was 127 years old, [2]she died at Kiriath-arba (now called Hebron) in the land of Canaan. There Abraham mourned and wept for her.

[3]Then, leaving her body, he said to the Hittite elders, [4]"Here I am, a stranger and a foreigner among you. Please sell me a piece of land so I can give my wife a proper burial."

[5]The Hittites replied to Abraham, [6]"Listen, my lord, you are an honored prince among us. Choose the finest of our tombs and bury her there. No one here will refuse to help you in this way."

[7]Then Abraham bowed low before the Hittites [8]and said, "Since you are willing to help me in this way, be so kind as to ask Ephron son of Zohar [9]to let me buy his cave at Machpelah, down at the end of his field. I will pay the full price in the presence of witnesses, so I will have a permanent burial place for my family."

[10]Ephron was sitting there among the others, and he answered Abraham as the others listened, speaking publicly before all the Hittite elders of the town. [11]"No, my lord," he said to Abraham, "please listen to me. I will give you the field and the cave. Here in the presence of my people, I give it to you. Go and bury your dead."

[12]Abraham again bowed low before the citizens of the land, [13]and he replied to Ephron as everyone listened. "No, listen to me. I will buy it from you. Let me pay the full price for the field so I can bury my dead there."

[14]Ephron answered Abraham, [15]"My lord, please listen to me. The land is worth 400 pieces of silver, but what is that between friends? Go ahead and bury your dead."

[16]So Abraham agreed to Ephron's price and paid the amount he had suggested— 400 pieces of silver, weighed according to the market standard. The Hittite elders witnessed the transaction.

[17]So Abraham bought the plot of land belonging to Ephron at Machpelah, near Mamre. This included the field itself, the cave that was in it, and all the surrounding trees. [18]It was transferred to Abraham as his permanent possession in the presence of the Hittite elders at the city gate. [19]Then Abraham buried his wife, Sarah, there in Canaan, in the cave of Machpelah, near Mamre (also called Hebron). [20]So the field and the cave were transferred from the Hittites to Abraham for use as a permanent burial place.

22:22-23 *Bethuel* was the youngest of Nahor's eight sons by Milcah; he was *the father of Rebekah*, Isaac's future wife (see 24:15, 67). Rebekah would follow Sarah as matriarch of the clan (23:1-2).

23:1-20 When *Sarah . . . died*, Abraham acquired a parcel of land for a burial place. This transaction was the first sign that a permanent transition had taken place, as people were normally buried in their ancestral homeland (cp. 49:29–50:13). In burying Sarah, Abraham detached from his just-mentioned ancestral home (where his relatives still lived, 22:20-24); his future would be in Canaan, where his descendants would realize the promise.

23:1 *Sarah was 127 years old:* Isaac was 37 at this time (cp. 17:17). • *Hebron:* See note on 13:18.

23:3-4 Abraham bargained with local *Hittite elders* for a *piece of land* for a burial site. These Hittites had apparently migrated south to Canaan from the great Hittite empire in eastern Asia Minor (modern Turkey; cp. 10:15). • Abraham was *a stranger and a foreigner* among these people; his hope was in God's promise that he would eventually possess the land.

23:5-6 *my lord, you are an honored prince:* Either Abraham was highly regarded by these people, or they were politely appealing to his generosity. • *Choose the finest. . . . No one here will refuse:* They were willing to accommodate his request, especially if they could legally obligate him to themselves (23:11).

23:7-16 Abraham wanted to *buy* Ephron's *cave at Machpelah*, but *Ephron* wanted him to buy the entire field.

23:9 This would be a *permanent burial place* for Abraham's *family*. The site was near Mamre (23:19), where Abraham lived (see 13:18; 14:13; 18:1). Abraham and Sarah, Isaac and Rebekah, and Jacob and Leah would all be buried in this cave (23:19; 25:9; 35:27-29; 49:29-31; 50:13), their permanent place in the Promised Land.

23:11 Ephron did not intend to *give* the cave to Abraham; Abraham was expected to "give" the full price in return. Ephron wanted to sell as much as he could to avoid responsibility for caring for the cave and to receive as high a price as possible.

23:12-13 Abraham didn't want the whole field, but he was willing to take it to get the cave.

23:15 *400 pieces* (Hebrew *400 shekels*, about 10 pounds or 4.6 kilograms in weight; also in 23:16) *of silver* was a very high price. Ephron's politeness was typical of the bargaining process.

23:16-20 Abraham *paid the amount* and finalized the transaction, avoiding indebtedness by accepting no gifts from the people (cp. 14:21-24). The *Hittite elders witnessed the transaction*, ensuring that no one could challenge Abraham's full ownership of the land. The transaction took place *at the city gate*, where public legal and business dealings were conducted (cp. 19:1). The land became Abraham's *permanent possession*, a down payment on God's promise to give him the land. Abraham knew that God's promise was not fulfilled (12:7) by this acquisition, so he planned for the future. By buying land for his dead, he declared that God's promises do not end with this life. This is the hope of all who die in faith.

A Wife for Isaac from Nahor's Family (24:1-67)

Commission to Find a Wife

24 Abraham was now a very old man, and the LORD had blessed him in every way. ²One day Abraham said to his oldest servant, the man in charge of his household, "Take an oath by putting your hand under my thigh. ³Swear by the LORD, the God of heaven and earth, that you will not allow my son to marry one of these local Canaanite women. ⁴Go instead to my homeland, to my relatives, and find a wife there for my son Isaac."

⁵The servant asked, "But what if I can't find a young woman who is willing to travel so far from home? Should I then take Isaac there to live among your relatives in the land you came from?"

⁶"No!" Abraham responded. "Be careful never to take my son there. ⁷For the LORD, the God of heaven, who took me from my father's house and my native land, solemnly promised to give this land to my descendants. He will send his angel ahead of you, and he will see to it that you find a wife there for my son. ⁸If she is unwilling to come back with you, then you are free from this oath of mine. But under no circumstances are you to take my son there."

Dependence on God's Leading

⁹So the servant took an oath by putting his hand under the thigh of his master, Abraham. He swore to follow Abraham's instructions. ¹⁰Then he loaded ten of Abraham's camels with all kinds of expensive gifts from his master, and he traveled to distant Aram-naharaim. There he went to the town where Abraham's brother Nahor had settled. ¹¹He made the camels kneel beside a well just outside the town. It was evening, and the women were coming out to draw water.

¹²"O LORD, God of my master, Abraham," he prayed. "Please give me success today, and show unfailing love to my master, Abraham. ¹³See, I am standing here beside this spring, and the young women of the town are coming out to draw water. ¹⁴This is my request. I will ask one of them, 'Please give me a drink from your jug.' If she says, 'Yes, have a drink, and I will water your camels, too!'—let her be the one you have selected as Isaac's wife. This is how I will know that you have shown unfailing love to my master."

¹⁵Before he had finished praying, he saw a young woman named Rebekah coming out with her water jug on her shoulder. She was the daughter of Bethuel, who was the son of Abraham's brother Nahor and his wife, Milcah. ¹⁶Rebekah was very beautiful and old enough to be married, but she was still a virgin. She went down to the spring, filled her jug, and came up again. ¹⁷Running over to her, the servant said, "Please give me a little drink of water from your jug."

¹⁸"Yes, my lord," she answered, "have a drink." And she quickly lowered her jug from her shoulder and gave him a drink. ¹⁹When she had given him a drink, she said, "I'll draw water for your camels, too, until they have had enough to drink." ²⁰So she quickly emptied her jug into the watering trough and ran back to the well to draw water for all his camels.

²¹The servant watched her in silence, wondering whether or not the LORD had given him success in his mission. ²²Then at last, when the camels had finished drinking, he

24:1
Gen 12:2; 24:35
24:2
Gen 47:29
24:3
Gen 14:19
24:4
Gen 12:1
24:5
Gen 24:39
24:7
Gen 12:1, 7; 16:7;
22:11
Rom 4:13
*Gal 3:16
24:10
Gen 11:29
Deut 23:4
24:11
Gen 24:42
24:12
Gen 24:27, 48
24:14
Judg 6:17
1 Sam 14:10
24:15
Gen 22:20-24
24:16
Gen 12:11; 29:17
24:17
1 Kgs 17:10
John 4:7
24:19
Gen 24:14
24:22
Gen 24:47

. . . .

24:1-67 Isaac's marriage to Rebekah ensured that God's plan would continue into the next generation. God showed covenant faithfulness by working through his faithful people (24:12, 27, 49).

24:1-9 Confident in the Lord's promise, Abraham had his chief servant (probably Eliezer, 15:2) *swear* to *find a wife* among Abraham's *relatives* in his *homeland*, some 450 miles away. Abraham was faithful to the covenant by preparing for Isaac's future.

24:2 Putting his *hand under* Abraham's *thigh* (cp. 47:29), the servant took a very solemn oath, assuming the burden of completing this mission.

24:3 Isaac knew how wicked and threatening the *local Canaanite* people were, so he maintained separation from them (cp. 26:34-35; 27:46; 28:8-9).

24:6-8 *Under no circumstances* was the servant to take Isaac from the Promised Land to seek a wife. Abraham ensured Isaac's safety and secured God's promises in the land of blessing.

24:7 *descendants:* Literally *seed;* also in 24:60.

24:10-60 The servant faithfully carried out the mission, and he glorified God for displaying faithful covenant love for Abraham's family by bringing all the details together. God sovereignly worked behind the scenes to accomplish his will through the circumstances of those acting responsibly in faith.

24:10-27 The servant obeyed his master's instructions and trusted God to lead him to the right woman.

24:10 *Aram-naharaim* ("Aram of the two rivers") was also called *Paddan-*

aram ("the field of Aram," cp. 25:20). It was a two-week journey in each direction, so the servant had *ten . . . camels* for provisions and *gifts* (24:22, 53).

24:14 Abraham's future daughter-in-law manifested hospitality and industry like Abraham's (see 18:1-8). Ten thirsty camels could drink 250 gallons of water, so a woman who would work that hard for a stranger was certainly not lazy, but generous and hospitable.

24:15-22 The servant received a precise, immediate answer to his prayer for guidance.

24:22 The servant showed his gratitude by giving the girl expensive jewelry. • *a gold ring for her nose and two large gold bracelets:* Hebrew *a gold nose-ring weighing a half shekel* [0.2 ounces or 6 grams] *and two gold bracelets weighing 10 shekels* [4 ounces or 114 grams].

24:24
Gen 24:15

24:26
Exod 4:31

24:27
Gen 14:20; 24:12, 48

24:28
Gen 29:12

24:29
Gen 25:20; 29:5

24:30
Gen 24:10

24:31
Gen 26:29

24:34
Gen 15:2; 24:2

24:35
Gen 12:2

24:36
Gen 21:1-7; 25:5

24:37
Gen 24:2-4

24:40
Gen 24:7

took out a gold ring for her nose and two large gold bracelets for her wrists.

²³"Whose daughter are you?" he asked. "And please tell me, would your father have any room to put us up for the night?"

²⁴"I am the daughter of Bethuel," she replied. "My grandparents are Nahor and Milcah. ²⁵Yes, we have plenty of straw and feed for the camels, and we have room for guests."

²⁶The man bowed low and worshiped the LORD. ²⁷"Praise the LORD, the God of my master, Abraham," he said. "The LORD has shown unfailing love and faithfulness to my master, for he has led me straight to my master's relatives."

The Success of the Mission

²⁸The young woman ran home to tell her family everything that had happened. ²⁹Now Rebekah had a brother named Laban, who ran out to meet the man at the spring. ³⁰He had seen the nose-ring and the bracelets on his sister's wrists, and had heard Rebekah tell what the man had said. So he rushed out to the spring, where the man was still standing beside his camels. ³¹Laban said to him, "Come and stay with us, you who are blessed by the LORD! Why are you standing here outside the town when I have a room all ready for you and a place prepared for the camels?"

³²So the man went home with Laban, and Laban unloaded the camels, gave him straw for their bedding, fed them, and provided water for the man and the camel drivers to wash their feet. ³³Then food was served. But Abraham's servant said, "I don't want to eat until I have told you why I have come."

"All right," Laban said, "tell us."

³⁴"I am Abraham's servant," he explained. ³⁵"And the LORD has greatly blessed my master; he has become a wealthy man. The LORD has given him flocks of sheep and goats, herds of cattle, a fortune in silver and gold, and many male and female servants and camels and donkeys.

³⁶"When Sarah, my master's wife, was very old, she gave birth to my master's son, and my master has given him everything he owns. ³⁷And my master made me take an oath. He said, 'Do not allow my son to marry one of these local Canaanite women. ³⁸Go instead to my father's house, to my relatives, and find a wife there for my son.'

³⁹"But I said to my master, 'What if I can't find a young woman who is willing to go back with me?' ⁴⁰He responded, 'The LORD, in whose presence I have lived, will send his angel with you and will make your mission successful. Yes, you must find a wife for my son from among my relatives, from my father's family. ⁴¹Then you will have fulfilled your obligation. But if you go to my relatives and they refuse to let her go with you, you will be free from my oath.'

⁴²"So today when I came to the spring, I prayed this prayer: 'O LORD, God of my master, Abraham, please give me success on this mission. ⁴³See, I am standing here beside this spring. This is my request. When a young woman comes to draw water, I will say to her, "Please give me a little drink of water from your jug." ⁴⁴If she says, "Yes, have a drink, and I will draw water for your camels, too," let her be the one you have selected to be the wife of my master's son.'

. . . .

◀ **Journeys to Paddan-aram (24:1-67; 28:1–29:14; 31:1–33:20).** When Abraham's servant traveled to PADDAN-ARAM (=Aram-naharaim? cp. 24:10; 25:20) to find a wife for Isaac, he probably followed the same route that he had previously traveled from Haran (11:28–12:9). Jacob later made the same trip to and from Haran (28:1–29:14; 31:1–33:20; see "Jacob's Family in Canaan" at 32:1–38:30, p. 87).

24:25 Rebekah again showed kindness by offering lodging for the servant and food for his camels.

24:26 The servant *bowed* to the ground and *worshiped the LORD* for his loyal love and faithfulness in guiding him to the exact family he sought.

These words express this chapter's message (cp. 24:48). Believers can trust the Lord's leading because he is sovereign in all things. He never leaves his people to their own resources in carrying out his covenant work.

24:29-31 *Laban . . . ran:* He was not going to miss the chance to marry his sister off and receive more gifts. Laban's response to the servant's wealth foreshadows his avaricious character (see 24:54-56 and note; 29:21-27; 30:27-36; 31:1-13).

24:33-48 The *servant* was not diverted from his mission; he insisted on telling his story before he would eat. He recounted his mission and acknowledged God's providence in directing him to Rebekah before attending to his personal needs. The servant wanted everyone to know that this was God's work, not a chance or humanly arranged meeting.

24:23-24 God led the servant to Abraham's family.

24:27 *The LORD has shown unfailing love and faithfulness to my master:*

45"Before I had finished praying in my heart, I saw Rebekah coming out with her water jug on her shoulder. She went down to the spring and drew water. So I said to her, 'Please give me a drink.' 46She quickly lowered her jug from her shoulder and said, 'Yes, have a drink, and I will water your camels, too!' So I drank, and then she watered the camels.

47"Then I asked, 'Whose daughter are you?' She replied, 'I am the daughter of Bethuel, and my grandparents are Nahor and Milcah.' So I put the ring on her nose, and the bracelets on her wrists.

48"Then I bowed low and worshiped the LORD. I praised the LORD, the God of my master, Abraham, because he had led me straight to my master's niece to be his son's wife. 49So tell me—will you or won't you show unfailing love and faithfulness to my master? Please tell me yes or no, and then I'll know what to do next."

50Then Laban and Bethuel replied, "The LORD has obviously brought you here, so there is nothing we can say. 51Here is Rebekah; take her and go. Yes, let her be the wife of your master's son, as the LORD has directed."

52When Abraham's servant heard their answer, he bowed down to the ground and worshiped the LORD. 53Then he brought out silver and gold jewelry and clothing and presented them to Rebekah. He also gave expensive presents to her brother and mother. 54Then they ate their meal, and the servant and the men with him stayed there overnight.

But early the next morning, Abraham's servant said, "Send me back to my master."

55"But we want Rebekah to stay with us at least ten days," her brother and mother said. "Then she can go."

56But he said, "Don't delay me. The LORD has made my mission successful; now send me back so I can return to my master."

57"Well," they said, "we'll call Rebekah and ask her what she thinks." 58So they called Rebekah. "Are you willing to go with this man?" they asked her.

And she replied, "Yes, I will go."

59So they said good-bye to Rebekah and sent her away with Abraham's servant and his men. The woman who had been Rebekah's childhood nurse went along with her. 60They gave her this blessing as she parted:

"Our sister, may you become
　the mother of many millions!
May your descendants be strong
　and conquer the cities of their
　enemies."

61Then Rebekah and her servant girls mounted the camels and followed the man. So Abraham's servant took Rebekah and went on his way.

The Marriage of Isaac and Rebekah

62Meanwhile, Isaac, whose home was in the Negev, had returned from Beer-lahai-roi. 63One evening as he was walking and meditating in the fields, he looked up and saw the camels coming. 64When Rebekah looked up and saw Isaac, she quickly dismounted from her camel. 65"Who is that man walking through the fields to meet us?" she asked the servant.

And he replied, "It is my master." So Rebekah covered her face with her veil. 66Then the servant told Isaac everything he had done.

67And Isaac brought Rebekah into his mother Sarah's tent, and she became his wife. He loved her deeply, and she was a special comfort to him after the death of his mother.

24:45
1 Sam 1:12
24:47
Gen 24:23-24
24:49
Gen 47:29
24:50
Ps 118:23
24:52
Gen 24:26
24:54
Gen 30:25
24:55
Judg 19:4
24:59
Gen 35:8
24:60
Gen 17:16; 22:17
24:62
Gen 16:14
24:63
Ps 119:15, 27, 48
24:67
Gen 23:1-2; 25:20; 29:18

. . . .

24:48 The way that God directed this event from behind the scenes is different than in most of Genesis, but it is true to how the life of faith normally works. Faith, expressed in personal prayer and obedience, looks for evidence of God's working. Believers usually have to make wise choices and remain faithful to the covenant, trusting that God will guide them through the circumstances of life to accomplish his will.

24:50-51 Following his testimony about God's guidance, the servant secured the family's blessing and permission to take *Rebekah* to his master's son, Isaac.

24:53 The servant gave expensive gifts to *Rebekah,* her *mother,* and *her brother*

to conclude the arrangements.

24:54-56 It was hard for Rebekah's family to let her go so suddenly, and Laban may have hoped to gain more wealth. However, the servant had sworn an oath and would not rest until it was completed. There was no reason for him to stay.

24:57-58 Rebekah's decision to leave immediately to be with her new husband settled the impasse. *Rebekah* submitted to the Lord's obvious leading. Young women were normally eager to marry (not to marry was a catastrophe), and later accounts of Laban suggest why Rebekah preferred to leave (cp. 31:14-15). Rebekah displayed faithful love to the servant, Abraham's family, and Isaac

by going to be Isaac's wife.

24:60 At Rebekah's departure, her family invoked the blessing that she would be a *mother of many millions* and that her descendants would *conquer . . . their enemies.* Rebekah's marriage to Isaac was part of God's plan to bless all humankind (12:1-3).

24:62 *Isaac* lived *in the Negev,* in the southern part of Canaan.

24:67 *Isaac* was 40 years old when he married *Rebekah* (25:20), so Abraham was 140 (21:5).

25:1-11 Though Abraham had sons by another wife, he safeguarded Isaac's inheritance and blessing.

25:1-4
//1 Chr 1:32-33
25:5
Gen 24:35-36
25:7
Gen 12:4
25:8
Gen 15:15; 25:17;
35:29; 49:29, 33
25:9-10
Gen 23:17-18; 49:29;
50:13
25:11
Gen 12:2; 24:62
25:12-16
//1 Chr 1:29-31

Abraham's Final Days (25:1-11)
Abraham's Family with Keturah

25 Abraham married another wife, whose name was Keturah. ²She gave birth to Zimran, Jokshan, Medan, Midian, Ishbak, and Shuah. ³Jokshan was the father of Sheba and Dedan. Dedan's descendants were the Asshurites, Letushites, and Leummites. ⁴Midian's sons were Ephah, Epher, Hanoch, Abida, and Eldaah. These were all descendants of Abraham through Keturah.

Isaac Receives the Inheritance

⁵Abraham gave everything he owned to his son Isaac. ⁶But before he died, he gave gifts to the sons of his concubines and sent them off to a land in the east, away from Isaac.

The Death of Abraham

⁷Abraham lived for 175 years, ⁸and he died at a ripe old age, having lived a long and satisfying life. He breathed his last and joined his ancestors in death. ⁹His sons Isaac and Ishmael buried him in the cave of Machpelah, near Mamre, in the field of Ephron son of Zohar the Hittite. ¹⁰This was the field Abraham had purchased from the Hittites and where he had buried his wife Sarah. ¹¹After Abraham's death, God blessed his son Isaac, who settled near Beer-lahai-roi in the Negev.

8. THE ACCOUNT OF ISHMAEL'S DESCENDANTS (25:12-18)

¹²This is the account of the family of Ishmael, the son of Abraham through Hagar, Sarah's Egyptian servant. ¹³Here is a list, by their names and clans, of Ishmael's descendants: The oldest was Nebaioth, followed by Kedar, Adbeel, Mibsam, ¹⁴Mishma, Dumah, Massa, ¹⁵Hadad, Tema, Jetur, Naphish, and Kedemah. ¹⁶These twelve sons of Ishmael became the founders of twelve tribes

. . . .

REBEKAH (24:12-67)

Gen 22:23; 25:20-
28; 26:7-8, 35; 27:5-
17, 42-46; 29:12;
35:8; 49:31
Rom 9:10-13

Genesis 24 describes the mission of Abraham's servant to find a wife for Isaac. At Abraham's command, he went to Haran in Aram-naharaim (northwest Mesopotamia), to Abraham's relatives, because Abraham did not want Isaac to marry a local Canaanite. The servant prayed that the young woman God had selected to be Isaac's wife would answer his request for a drink by immediately giving it and watering his camels as well (24:12-14). Such a young woman would readily exercise hospitality and be willing to work hard (see note on 24:14). God abundantly answered his prayer with Rebekah, the daughter of Bethuel (22:23; 25:20), the son of Abraham's brother Nahor (11:27-32).

When Abraham's servant described how God had led him (24:34-49), Rebekah's father and brother recognized it as God's hand, but they were reluctant to let her go immediately (24:50-56). Rebekah, however, demonstrated faith in God's plan; she was willing to leave her family without delay to marry Isaac (24:57-58). Rebekah's faith was richly rewarded; the blessing her womenfolk gave her in parting (24:59-60) came true when she bore to Isaac the next generation of God's chosen line.

Rebekah bore twins, Esau and Jacob (25:20-26). She preferred Jacob, the younger, whom God had told her would be the stronger and the leader of the two (25:23). Rebekah helped Jacob seize the blessing of the firstborn by deceiving Isaac (27:1-40). Afterward, she arranged for Jacob to be sent to Haran to get away from his brother's anger over the stolen blessing (27:41–28:5). Rebekah's deceptive scheme created a lasting schism in the family, and she apparently never saw her favorite son again. She was, however, buried beside her husband in the family burial site (49:31), and she fulfilled God's plan as the mother of Jacob, the founding father of Israel.

. . . .

25:1 Exactly when *Abraham married . . . Keturah* is unknown. It was probably, but not necessarily, after Sarah's death.

25:2-4 The birth of these nations from Abraham partially fulfilled God's promise to him (12:2; 17:4).

25:3 *Sheba and Dedan:* Cp. 10:7. Abraham's descendants probably settled in these regions and became identified by their names, along with people of other lineage.

25:5-6 *Abraham* loved all his sons, so

before he died, he *gave* them *gifts* and *sent them* away as he had sent Ishmael (21:8-14). In this way, he preserved Isaac's position as his heir.

25:7-8 Abraham's death is recorded before the births of Jacob and Esau, but he lived until they were fifteen years old (25:19-26; cp. 21:5; 25:26). This literary arrangement closes Abraham's story before focusing on Isaac's family.

25:11 God's blessing transferred to Isaac; Abraham's other sons had been

sent away. Isaac lived *near Beer-lahai-roi*—a special place where God had answered prayer (16:14) and where Isaac waited on the Lord (24:62).

25:12-18 This record lists Ishmael's descendants before tracing Isaac's (25:19–35:29), which is in keeping with the literary arrangement of Genesis (see Introduction to Genesis: "Summary," p. 15).

25:16 Ishmael's *twelve sons* fulfilled God's promise of blessing (17:20).

named after them, listed according to the places they settled and camped. 17Ishmael lived for 137 years. Then he breathed his last and joined his ancestors in death. 18Ishmael's descendants occupied the region from Havilah to Shur, which is east of Egypt in the direction of Asshur. There they lived in open hostility toward all their relatives.

9. THE ACCOUNT OF ISAAC'S DESCENDANTS (25:19–35:29)
The Births of Esau and Jacob (25:19-26)

19This is the account of the family of Isaac, the son of Abraham. 20When Isaac was forty years old, he married Rebekah, the daughter of Bethuel the Aramean from Paddan-aram and the sister of Laban the Aramean.

21Isaac pleaded with the LORD on behalf of his wife, because she was unable to have children. The LORD answered Isaac's prayer, and Rebekah became pregnant with twins. 22But the two children struggled with each other in her womb. So she went to ask the LORD about it. "Why is this happening to me?" she asked.

23And the LORD told her, "The sons in your womb will become two nations. From the very beginning, the two nations will be rivals. One nation will be stronger than the other; and your older son will serve your younger son."

24And when the time came to give birth, Rebekah discovered that she did indeed have twins! 25The first one was very red at

25:17
Gen 25:8
25:18
Gen 16:12; 20:1
25:21
Gen 21:2
25:23
Gen 17:2-4; 27:29; 48:19
Num 20:14
Deut 2:4, 8
*Rom 9:11-12
25:25
Gen 27:11

Infertility (25:21)

Gen 16:1-6; 17:15-21; 20:17-18; 29:31; 30:1-2; 30:22-24
Exod 23:25-26
Deut 7:12-15
Judg 13:2-5
1 Sam 1:2-28; 2:5-7
Ps 113:5-9
Isa 54:1-3
Luke 1:5-25
Rom 4:19-22
Gal 4:24-28
Heb 11:11-12

With the possible exception of Leah, each of the patriarchs' wives suffered infertility for a time before having children (11:30; 25:21; 29:31; see also 1 Sam 1:1-18). Children continued the family line, helped protect the tribe, and provided labor. They ensured that hereditary property would stay within the family, guaranteed assistance in old age, and enacted the proper funeral rites. Infertility was therefore a crushing stigma for a woman (Ps 113:9; Prov 30:15-16; Isa 54:1), who understood herself to be created as a vessel of life (1:28; 3:20). It was considered a denial of blessing, design, and desire (1:28), and it brought shame (1 Sam 1:7), ridicule (16:4), and vicious jealousy (30:1).

In the OT, childlessness is a theological issue. Fertility is controlled by the Creator (20:17-18; 30:2, 23; 1 Sam 1:6, 27), who causes fertility and infertility according to his purpose and his promises (17:19; 30:2; Ps 113:9; Luke 1:11-20; Rom 4:19). God often chose infertility as a precursor to the birth of a promised or unique child, marking the birth as God's own work. Childlessness is thus a trial of patience that prompts prayer and faith (25:21; 1 Sam 1:11). Abraham learned to nurture faith in God's promise long before his child arrived (15:4-6; 17:15-21; Rom 4:20-22). When a couple has been infertile, a child's arrival is marked as a special display of God's faithfulness and creative authority.

God's delays are not necessarily denials, but they remind longing parents to use trials for growth and to see children as a gift that cannot be taken for granted. A childless home can be filled with devotion as human expectations submit to future glory (see, e.g., Luke 2:36-37).

25:18 *Havilah* was a region in north-central Arabia. • *Shur* was a region between Beersheba and Egypt. • *in open hostility toward all their relatives:* The meaning of the Hebrew is uncertain, but the wording is close to that of 16:12.

25:19–35:29 This *account of the family of Isaac,* the chosen *son of Abraham,* mostly recounts Jacob's struggle for the blessing (25:27-34; chs 27–33).

25:19-26 Jacob's struggle for supremacy began before the twins were born (see Hos 12:3).

25:19-20 *Isaac . . . married Rebekah:* Isaac's marriage tied him and his family even more closely to Abraham's ancestors. Had he married a Canaanite, the covenant faith would have been imperiled by this corrupt, syncretistic people.

25:21 For twenty years, Rebekah was

barren (cp. 25:20, 26), like Sarah (see 16:1). This condition tested their faith (see note on 16:1-3). How could they be childless when God promised that nations would issue from them? • *Isaac pleaded with the LORD* and *the LORD answered Isaac's prayer.* Isaac apparently learned from his father's mistake and responded in faith.

25:22 When the pregnancy was difficult, Rebekah *went to ask the LORD about it,* probably by visiting a prophet—perhaps Abraham (20:7; see note on 25:7-8).

25:23 *rivals:* Jacob and Esau fought in the womb, and their descendants (Israel and Edom) fought continuously throughout their history. In their many conflicts, Israel achieved supremacy over Edom. • *your older son will serve your younger son:* God's choice of the

younger son over the elder ran against natural order (cp. 48:12-14; see Mal 1:1-3; Rom 9:11-16).

25:24-26 When the twins were born, the unusual circumstances inspired each boy's name and hinted at what would happen to him in the future.

25:25 Two wordplays anticipate Esau's later life. *Esau* sounds like a Hebrew term that means "hair" (Hebrew *se'ar*); Esau's later homeland, Edom, was known as *Seir* ("hairy") because it was wooded (as though covered with hair). • *red* (Hebrew *'admoni*) sounds like Esau's other name, Edom (25:27-34); Edom had red soil. • Esau's *hair* was *like* the *fur coat* of an animal, foreshadowing his unspiritual character (25:34; Heb 12:16; cp. Lev 26:22; Deut 7:22; 1 Cor 15:32). The description of the child uses words that highlight the Edomites' nature.

25:26
Hos 12:3

25:30
Gen 36:1, 8

25:31
Deut 21:16-17
1 Chr 5:1-2

25:33
Gen 27:36
Heb 12:16

birth and covered with thick hair like a fur coat. So they named him Esau. ²⁶Then the other twin was born with his hand grasping Esau's heel. So they named him Jacob. Isaac was sixty years old when the twins were born.

Esau Sells His Birthright (25:27-34)

²⁷As the boys grew up, Esau became a skillful hunter. He was an outdoorsman, but Jacob had a quiet temperament, preferring to stay at home. ²⁸Isaac loved Esau because he enjoyed eating the wild game Esau brought home, but Rebekah loved Jacob.

²⁹One day when Jacob was cooking some stew, Esau arrived home from the wilderness exhausted and hungry. ³⁰Esau said to Jacob, "I'm starved! Give me some of that red stew!" (This is how Esau got his other name, Edom, which means "red.")

³¹"All right," Jacob replied, "but trade me your rights as the firstborn son."

³²"Look, I'm dying of starvation!" said Esau. "What good is my birthright to me now?"

³³But Jacob said, "First you must swear that your birthright is mine." So Esau swore

. . . .

ESAU (25:21-34)

Gen 26:34-35; 27:1-
42; 28:6-9; 32:3-20;
33:1-16; 35:28-29;
36:1-43
Deut 2:1-8, 12,
22, 29
Josh 24:4
Mal 1:2-5
Rom 9:6-13
Heb 11:20; 12:16-17

Esau, the son of Isaac and Rebekah, was Jacob's older twin brother (25:24-26), so named because his body was hairy at birth. His descendants were called Edom ("red") on account of his reddish color at birth, the red lentil soup he received from Jacob (25:30), and the reddish color of the land in which he settled (see note on 25:25).

Esau was a proficient hunter who brought tasty wild meat to his father. Isaac enjoyed its strong flavor more than the mild meat Jacob provided from the family flocks. One day Esau returned home very hungry from an unsuccessful hunt, and Jacob persuaded Esau to surrender his birthright in exchange for food (25:29-34). Esau had little regard for his birthright and was controlled by his carnal desires (see Heb 12:16). He also married two local women who were not Abraham's descendants (26:34-35), which may be why Rebekah coached Jacob in obtaining the patriarchal blessing that would normally have belonged to the elder brother (ch 27). Esau's anger on discovering his brother's deception prompted Jacob to flee for Haran. The brothers were reunited 20 years later because of Esau's gracious forgiveness (33:1-16).

Jacob was born grasping Esau's heel; this omen was interpreted to mean that Esau's Edomite descendants would be subject to Jacob's offspring. The subservient relationship between the Edomites and the Israelites in David's time (2 Sam 8:11-15; 1 Chr 18:13) continued until the reign of Jehoram (2 Kgs 8:20-22; 2 Chr 21:8-10). Following a rebellion in 845 BC, the Edomites briefly gained their independence but were conquered again by Amaziah (796–767 BC). They regained their freedom in 735 BC and then remained independent of Judah.

In the NT, Esau represents the line of Abraham's descendants who lacked the gift of faith and were rejected by God as recipients of his promised blessings (see Rom 9:6-24).

. . . .

25:26 The name *Jacob* (Hebrew *ya'aqob*) sounds like the Hebrew words for "heel" and "deceiver" (from Hebrew *'aqeb*). The name was originally positive, meaning "protect" (like a rear guard), but it took on the negative meaning of "heel grabber" or "deceiver" in the context of Jacob's deceptive, grasping, usurping character (see 27:36).

25:27-34 Jacob and Esau each developed in accord with his initial characteristics (25:24-26). Esau, the reddish, hairy man, cared about physical things rather than spiritual things (see Heb 12:16); he was finally overcome by physical appetites and sold his birthright. Jacob, the heel grabber, knew the birthright's value and drove a ruthless bargain to gain it presumptuously from his brother.

25:27 *Esau* was a *skillful hunter* and *an outdoorsman*—a wild man who loved wild country. Jacob had a *quiet* (or *even*)

temperament and preferred *to stay at home* (literally *dwelling in tents*)—i.e., he was civilized.

25:28 The parents each practiced favoritism. • *because:* Isaac's love for Esau was conditioned upon his son's performance. Rebekah's love for Jacob was constant and unconditional.

25:29 Ironically, *Jacob* proved the more cunning hunter. The word *cooking* (Hebrew *wayyazed*, "boiling") sounds like the word for "hunter" (Hebrew *tsayid*). While boiling stew, Jacob was laying a trap for the hairy red animal. He may have waited a long time for this opportunity. This word for "boil" was also used for presumptuous action (like water boiling over the rim of the pot). Jacob overstepped his boundaries when he seized the promise for himself. By contrast, Abraham knew the promise was his and was secure in giving the land away (see note on 13:8-13). • *Esau*

was *exhausted and hungry*, but his life was not in danger (25:32; see note on 25:33-34).

25:30 *Esau* was preoccupied with his appetite. Being driven by one's appetites leaves no place for spiritual values. The text emphasizes this by using a Hebrew word (translated *give*) that was normally used for feeding animals. • *Edom, which means "red"*: See note on 25:25.

25:31-33 *Jacob* was the better hunter on this occasion, but great danger lay in exercising such strong ambition. God's people should desire the things of God, but they must not seek them "in the flesh" (see Zech 4:6; Gal 5:16-17; Eph 6:10-12). The Lord dealt severely with Jacob to purge him of carnal methods. He later received the promise not as crafty Jacob the usurper, but as Israel (meaning, "God fights"), with God fighting on his behalf (32:28).

an oath, thereby selling all his rights as the firstborn to his brother, Jacob.

³⁴Then Jacob gave Esau some bread and lentil stew. Esau ate the meal, then got up and left. He showed contempt for his rights as the firstborn.

Isaac and Abimelech (26:1-35)
Isaac Deceives Abimelech

26 A severe famine now struck the land, as had happened before in Abraham's time. So Isaac moved to Gerar, where Abimelech, king of the Philistines, lived. ²The LORD appeared to Isaac and said, "Do not go down to Egypt, but do as I tell you. ³Live here as a foreigner in this land, and I will be with you and bless you. I hereby confirm that I will give all these lands to you and your ᵏdescendants, just as I solemnly promised Abraham, your father. ⁴I will cause your descendants to become as numerous as the stars of the sky, and I will give them all these lands. And through your descendants all the nations of the earth will be blessed. ⁵I will do this because Abraham listened to me and obeyed all my requirements, commands, decrees, and instructions." ⁶So Isaac stayed in Gerar.

⁷When the men who lived there asked Isaac about his wife, Rebekah, he said, "She is my sister." He was afraid to say, "She is my wife." He thought, "They will kill me to get her, because she is so beautiful." ⁸But some time later, Abimelech, king of the Philistines, looked out his window and saw Isaac caressing Rebekah.

⁹Immediately, Abimelech called for Isaac and exclaimed, "She is obviously your wife! Why did you say, 'She is my sister'?"

"Because I was afraid someone would kill me to get her from me," Isaac replied.

¹⁰"How could you do this to us?" Abimelech exclaimed. "One of my people might easily have taken your wife and slept with her, and you would have made us guilty of great sin."

¹¹Then Abimelech issued a public proclamation: "Anyone who touches this man or his wife will be put to death!"

Conflict over Water Rights

¹²When Isaac planted his crops that year, he harvested a hundred times more grain than he planted, for the LORD blessed him. ¹³He became a very rich man, and his wealth continued to grow. ¹⁴He acquired so many flocks of sheep and goats, herds of cattle, and servants that the Philistines became jealous of him. ¹⁵So the Philistines filled up all of Isaac's wells with dirt. These were the wells that had been dug by the servants of his father, Abraham.

¹⁶Finally, Abimelech ordered Isaac to leave the country. "Go somewhere else," he

26:1
Gen 12:10; 20:1-2
26:2
Gen 12:1, 7
26:3
Gen 12:7
ᵏ*zera'* (2233)
▸Gen 35:12
26:4
Gen 15:5; 22:17
Exod 32:13
*Acts 3:25
*Gal 3:8
26:7
Gen 12:11-13;
20:2, 12
26:10
Gen 20:7-10
26:12
Gen 26:3
26:13
Gen 24:35; 25:5
26:15
Gen 21:25
26:16
Exod 1:9

. . . .

25:33-34 *Esau* eagerly took Jacob's bait and fell into the trap. He ate and left too quickly to have been near death (25:32). The final comment on the passage explains that Esau *showed contempt for* his birthright, considering it worthless (Heb 12:16). It is foolish to sacrifice spiritual blessings to satisfy physical appetites (cp. 3:6).

26:1-35 In this digression from Jacob's story, Isaac's prosperity (ch 26) shows that the blessing had passed to him (cp. 25:11) despite his failures of faith.

26:1 This *Abimelech* is probably not the man in ch 20, for these events could have been 90 years apart. Possibly Abimelech was a dynastic name or title (a later King Achish, 1 Sam 21:10, was also called Abimelech, Ps 34:TITLE).

26:2-5 The Lord assured Isaac that the covenant promises (cp. 12:2-3; 15:5-8; 17:3-8; 22:15-18; 28:13-14) would pass to him because Abraham faithfully *listened* to God and *obeyed all* his *requirements, commands, decrees, and instructions*. These terms were later used in Deuteronomy to describe God's full legal covenant with Israel. An Israelite reader would immediately think of the complete Torah when hearing these words and be prompted to obey God's

law as Abraham did, though Abraham had only a few commands from the Lord. Through these words, the text emphasizes that Abraham would have obeyed the later commands if he had had them, because he was an obedient servant of the Lord.

26:3 *descendants:* Literally *seed;* also in 26:4, 24.

26:6-11 While staying in Gerar, Isaac, like his father, deceived people into believing that his wife was his sister. Some suppose that this story duplicates the stories of Abraham's deception (12:10-20; 20:1-18), but the differences are greater than the similarities, and the son's repetition of his father's lie is natural. Through numerous parallels with Abraham, ch 26 shows how God's plan continued with Isaac. Even when Isaac jeopardized the covenant as his father had, God prevented disaster and preserved the marriage. Abraham's descendants would be blessed because of Abraham, but they had to exercise their own faith to enjoy the blessings. Genuine faith in God's promises engenders a fearless walk with him; cowering in fear endangers the blessing and mocks the faith.

26:8 *Abimelech . . . saw Isaac caressing*

Rebekah: The word for "caressing" (Hebrew *metsakheq*) is the same as the word used for Ishmael's "making fun of" Isaac (21:9); the word is related to the name "Isaac" (Hebrew *yitskhaq*). It is as though Isaac's lapse of faith made fun of Abimelech and made a mockery of Rebekah and the great promise embodied in Isaac's name.

26:10-11 Isaac, like his father, was rebuked by *Abimelech* (see note on 20:1-18). This legal wording would remind Israel of how important it was to preserve marital purity. Abimelech recognized the danger to his own people. Though his decree preserved his own society, it was also a word from God that preserved the sanctity of Isaac's and Israel's marriages. If Isaac's marriage had ended here, there would have been no Israelite society.

26:12-13 *Isaac* lived in the land as a temporary settler, enjoying abundant prosperity because of God's blessing; *his crops* flourished and he became *very rich*.

26:14-16 *The Philistines* envied Isaac's prosperity and *filled* his *wells with dirt*. The king then *ordered Isaac to leave* that region because he was *too powerful* for them (cp. 21:22-23).

26:19
John 4:10-11

26:22
Ps 4:1; 18:19
Isa 54:2

26:23
Gen 22:19

26:24
Gen 17:7; 22:17
Exod 3:6

26:25
Gen 12:7-8; 13:4

26:26
Gen 21:22

26:27
Gen 26:16

26:28
Gen 21:22-23

26:30
Gen 31:54

26:31
Gen 21:31

26:33
Gen 21:31

26:34
Gen 28:8

26:35
Gen 27:46

27:1
Gen 25:25; 48:10

27:2
Gen 47:29

27:3
Gen 25:27

27:4
Gen 24:60; 27:19; 48:9

said, "for you have become too powerful for us."

17So Isaac moved away to the Gerar Valley, where he set up their tents and settled down. 18He reopened the wells his father had dug, which the Philistines had filled in after Abraham's death. Isaac also restored the names Abraham had given them.

19Isaac's servants also dug in the Gerar Valley and discovered a well of fresh water. 20But then the shepherds from Gerar came and claimed the spring. "This is our water," they said, and they argued over it with Isaac's herdsmen. So Isaac named the well Esek (which means "argument"). 21Isaac's men then dug another well, but again there was a dispute over it. So Isaac named it Sitnah (which means "hostility"). 22Abandoning that one, Isaac moved on and dug another well. This time there was no dispute over it, so Isaac named the place Rehoboth (which means "open space"), for he said, "At last the LORD has created enough space for us to prosper in this land."

23From there Isaac moved to Beersheba, 24where the LORD appeared to him on the night of his arrival. "I am the God of your father, Abraham," he said. "Do not be afraid, for I am with you and will bless you. I will multiply your descendants, and they will become a great nation. I will do this because of my promise to Abraham, my servant." 25Then Isaac built an altar there and worshiped the LORD. He set up his camp at that place, and his servants dug another well.

Isaac's Covenant with Abimelech
26One day King Abimelech came from Gerar with his adviser, Ahuzzath, and also Phicol, his army commander. 27"Why have you come here?" Isaac asked. "You obviously hate me, since you kicked me off your land."

28They replied, "We can plainly see that the LORD is with you. So we want to enter into a sworn treaty with you. Let's make a covenant. 29Swear that you will not harm us, just as we have never troubled you. We have always treated you well, and we sent you away from us in peace. And now look how the LORD has blessed you!"

30So Isaac prepared a covenant feast to celebrate the treaty, and they ate and drank together. 31Early the next morning, they each took a solemn oath not to interfere with each other. Then Isaac sent them home again, and they left him in peace.

32That very day Isaac's servants came and told him about a new well they had dug. "We've found water!" they exclaimed. 33So Isaac named the well Shibah (which means "oath"). And to this day the town that grew up there is called Beersheba (which means "well of the oath").

Esau's Hittite Wives (26:34-35)
34At the age of forty, Esau married two Hittite wives: Judith, the daughter of Beeri, and Basemath, the daughter of Elon. 35But Esau's wives made life miserable for Isaac and Rebekah.

Jacob Steals Esau's Blessing (27:1-40)
27 One day when Isaac was old and turning blind, he called for Esau, his older son, and said, "My son."

"Yes, Father?" Esau replied.

2"I am an old man now," Isaac said, "and I don't know when I may die. 3Take your bow and a quiver full of arrows, and go out into the open country to hunt some wild game for me. 4Prepare my favorite dish, and bring it here for me to eat. Then I will pronounce the blessing that belongs to you, my firstborn son, before I die."

. . . .

26:17-22 *Isaac moved . . . to the Gerar Valley* (away from the city of Gerar itself, 26:6, but probably still within ten miles) and *reopened* his father's *wells*. Isaac was also opposed there, but chose not to fight back; he relinquished one well after another until God's blessing outdid the opposition. Whenever Isaac reopened a well, and regardless of how often enemies caused them to cave in, he found water. God was blessing Isaac and that blessing could not be hindered. Finally, the Philistines left Isaac alone.

26:23-25 At *Beersheba, . . . the LORD appeared to* Isaac to confirm his covenant (cp. 21:31-33). *Isaac* responded in faith as his father had done by building *an altar* to the Lord and proclaiming the

Lord's identity and nature (see note on 12:8; 21:33).

26:26-33 This *treaty* is similar to the one an earlier king had made with Abraham (cp. 21:22-31). This king acknowledged that God was blessing Isaac and realized that a treaty with Isaac would benefit him. No opposition can hinder God's blessing—it will flourish, and other nations will see it and seek peace with God's people to share in the blessing.

26:33 Since the earlier treaty was renewed with Isaac, the name of the well was also renewed by the oath.

26:34-35 Esau's marriages illustrate how unfit he was to lead the covenant people into God's blessings, and how foolish was Isaac's later attempt to bless

Esau (27:1-40). Esau later married a third wife in vain attempt to do the right thing (28:6-9).

27:1-40 Jacob got his father Isaac's blessing through deception. In this story, an entire family tries to carry out their responsibilities by physical means rather than by faith. Faith would have provided Rebekah and Jacob a more honorable solution to the crisis.

27:1-4 The first scene sets up the chapter's crisis. Isaac knew of God's oracle (25:22-23), yet he thwarted or ignored it by trying to bless Esau. • *Isaac was old and turning blind:* He was losing his senses, both physically and spiritually.

27:3-4 Like Esau, Isaac allowed his palate to govern his heart (cp. 25:28-34).

⁵But Rebekah overheard what Isaac had said to his son Esau. So when Esau left to hunt for the wild game, ⁶she said to her son Jacob, "Listen. I overheard your father say to Esau, ⁷'Bring me some wild game and prepare me a delicious meal. Then I will bless you in the LORD's presence before I die.' ⁸Now, my son, listen to me. Do exactly as I tell you. ⁹Go out to the flocks, and bring me two fine young goats. I'll use them to prepare your father's favorite dish. ¹⁰Then take the food to your father so he can eat it and bless you before he dies."

¹¹"But look," Jacob replied to Rebekah, "my brother, Esau, is a hairy man, and my skin is smooth. ¹²What if my father touches me? He'll see that I'm trying to trick him, and then he'll curse me instead of blessing me."

¹³But his mother replied, "Then let the curse fall on me, my son! Just do what I tell you. Go out and get the goats for me!"

¹⁴So Jacob went out and got the young goats for his mother. Rebekah took them and prepared a delicious meal, just the way Isaac liked it. ¹⁵Then she took Esau's favorite clothes, which were there in the house, and gave them to her younger son, Jacob. ¹⁶She covered his arms and the smooth part of his neck with the skin of the young goats. ¹⁷Then she gave Jacob the delicious meal, including freshly baked bread.

¹⁸So Jacob took the food to his father. "My father?" he said.

"Yes, my son," Isaac answered. "Who are you—Esau or Jacob?"

¹⁹Jacob replied, "It's Esau, your firstborn son. I've done as you told me. Here is the wild game. Now sit up and eat it so you can give me your blessing."

²⁰Isaac asked, "How did you find it so quickly, my son?"

"The LORD your God put it in my path!" Jacob replied.

²¹Then Isaac said to Jacob, "Come closer so I can touch you and make sure that you really are Esau." ²²So Jacob went closer to his father, and Isaac touched him. "The voice is Jacob's, but the hands are Esau's," Isaac said.

²³But he did not recognize Jacob, because Jacob's hands felt hairy just like Esau's. So Isaac prepared to bless Jacob. ²⁴"But are you really my son Esau?" he asked.

"Yes, I am," Jacob replied.

²⁵Then Isaac said, "Now, my son, bring me the wild game. Let me eat it, and then I will give you my blessing." So Jacob took the food to his father, and Isaac ate it. He also drank the wine that Jacob served him. ²⁶Then Isaac said to Jacob, "Please come a little closer and kiss me, my son."

²⁷So Jacob went over and kissed him. And when Isaac caught the smell of his clothes, he was finally convinced, and he blessed his son. He said, "Ah! The smell of my son is like the smell of the outdoors, which the LORD has blessed!

²⁸ "From the dew of heaven
    and the richness of the earth,
may God always give you abundant
        harvests of grain
    and bountiful new wine.
²⁹ May many nations become your
        servants,
    and may they bow down to you.
May you be the master over your
        brothers,
    and may your mother's sons bow
        down to you.
All who curse you will be cursed,
    and all who bless you will be blessed."

³⁰As soon as Isaac had finished blessing Jacob, and almost before Jacob had left his father, Esau returned from his hunt. ³¹Esau prepared a delicious meal and brought it to his father. Then he said, "Sit up, my father, and eat my wild game so you can give me your blessing."

³²But Isaac asked him, "Who are you?"

Esau replied, "It's your son, your firstborn son, Esau."

³³Isaac began to tremble uncontrollably and said, "Then who just served me wild game? I have already eaten it, and I blessed him just before you came. And yes, that blessing must stand!"

27:5-6
Gen 25:27-28
27:8
Gen 27:13, 43
27:11
Gen 25:25
27:12
Gen 9:25; 27:21-22
27:13
Gen 27:8
27:15
Gen 27:27
27:19
Gen 27:31
27:21
Gen 27:12
27:23
Gen 27:16
27:25
Gen 27:4
27:27
Ps 65:10
Heb 11:20
27:28
Deut 7:13; 33:13, 28
Zech 8:12
27:29
Gen 9:25-27; 12:3
Isa 45:14
27:31
Gen 27:4
27:32
Gen 27:18
27:33
Gen 27:35

. . . .

27:5-17 The blessing seemed to be in jeopardy. In scene two, Rebekah and Jacob sought to achieve God's blessing by deception, without faith or love. Rebekah planned to deceive the old man into thinking that he was blessing Esau when he was actually blessing Jacob.

27:5 *Esau* agreed to Isaac's plan, thus breaking the oath he had sworn to Jacob (25:33).

27:11-12 *Jacob* had no qualms about this deception; he only feared that it might not work and that he would be cursed for trying.

27:18-29 In scene three, Jacob deceives his father and receives the blessing.

27:18-20 *Jacob* lied about his identity, and then came close to blasphemy by lying about *God*.

27:20-27 *Isaac* voiced his suspicion

three times, but was finally deceived by his senses, which were not functioning well (see note on 27:1-4).

27:30-40 In scene four, everything is discovered and the family becomes even more divided.

27:33 When he realized what had happened, *Isaac began to tremble uncontrollably*; he had been tampering with God's plan, and God had overruled him.

27:34
Heb 12:17

27:35
Gen 27:19

27:36
Gen 25:26

27:37
Gen 27:28-29

27:38
Heb 12:17

27:39
Heb 11:20

27:40
2 Kgs 8:20-22

27:41
Gen 32:3-11; 37:4

27:43
Gen 27:8

27:44
Gen 31:41

27:46
Gen 26:34-35

28:1
Gen 24:3

28:2
Gen 25:20

28:3
Gen 17:16; 35:11
ᵃshadday (7706)
▸ Gen 35:11
ᵇqahal (6951)
▸ Gen 35:11

28:4
Gen 12:1-3; 15:7;
35:11

34When Esau heard his father's words, he let out a loud and bitter cry. "Oh my father, what about me? Bless me, too!" he begged.

35But Isaac said, "Your brother was here, and he tricked me. He has taken away your blessing."

36Esau exclaimed, "No wonder his name is Jacob, for now he has cheated me twice. First he took my rights as the firstborn, and now he has stolen my blessing. Oh, haven't you saved even one blessing for me?"

37Isaac said to Esau, "I have made Jacob your master and have declared that all his brothers will be his servants. I have guaranteed him an abundance of grain and wine—what is left for me to give you, my son?"

38Esau pleaded, "But do you have only one blessing? Oh my father, bless me, too!" Then Esau broke down and wept.

39Finally, his father, Isaac, said to him,

"You will live away from the richness of
the earth,
and away from the dew of the heaven
above.
40 You will live by your sword,
and you will serve your brother.
But when you decide to break free,
you will shake his yoke from your
neck."

Jacob Flees to Paddan-Aram (27:41–28:5)

41From that time on, Esau hated Jacob because their father had given Jacob the blessing. And Esau began to scheme: "I will soon be mourning my father's death. Then I will kill my brother, Jacob."

42But Rebekah heard about Esau's plans. So she sent for Jacob and told him, "Listen, Esau is consoling himself by plotting to kill you. 43So listen carefully, my son. Get ready and flee to my brother, Laban, in Haran. 44Stay there with him until your brother cools off. 45When he calms down and forgets what you have done to him, I will send for you to come back. Why should I lose both of you in one day?"

46Then Rebekah said to Isaac, "I'm sick and tired of these local Hittite women! I would rather die than see Jacob marry one of them."

28 So Isaac called for Jacob, blessed him, and said, "You must not marry any of these Canaanite women. 2Instead, go at once to Paddan-aram, to the house of your grandfather Bethuel, and marry one of your uncle Laban's daughters. 3May God aAlmighty bless you and give you many children. And may your descendants multiply and become bmany nations! 4May God pass on to you and your descendants the blessings he promised to Abraham. May you own this land where you are now living as a foreigner, for God gave this land to Abraham."

5So Isaac sent Jacob away, and he went to Paddan-aram to stay with his uncle Laban, his mother's brother, the son of Bethuel the Aramean.

. . . .

27:34-35 *Esau* was very *bitter*, and angry enough to kill (27:41).

27:36 *Esau* began to realize Jacob's true nature, saying *he has cheated me* (or *tripped me up*, or *deceived me) twice*, by taking the birthright (the right of inheritance, Hebrew *bekorah; 25:27-34*) and by deceiving their father to receive the *blessing* (the spoken pronouncement of the inheritance, Hebrew *berakah*).
• *Jacob* sounds like the Hebrew words for "heel" and "deceiver." Esau's assessment of Jacob was correct, but he failed to see his own ungodliness in these transactions (see note on 27:5; Heb 12:16).

27:37 There was no going back. *Isaac* had declared an oracle from God, who had *made Jacob* to be Esau's *master* (see Rom 9:11-13).

27:39-40 All that remained for Esau was a promise of hardship and struggle (cp. 3:17-19; 16:11-12).

27:41-45 Rebekah and Jacob got the blessing but reaped hatred from Esau

and separation from one another; there is no indication that Rebekah and Jacob ever saw each other again. They gained nothing that God was not already going to give them, and their methods were costly. Jacob fled from home to escape Esau's vengeance.

27:42–33:17 Jacob met the Lord on a route that Abraham had taken 125 years earlier. The story follows a chiastic structure that centers on Jacob's exile:
A: Jacob flees Esau (27:42–28:9)
  B: Angels of God meet Jacob at
     Bethel (28:10-22)
    C: Jacob is exiled in Paddan-
       aram (29:1–31:55)
  B': Angels of God meet Jacob at
      Mahanaim (32:1-2)
A': Jacob is reconciled to Esau
    (32:3–33:17)

27:46 *Rebekah* manipulated *Isaac* into sending *Jacob* away. Like Isaac, Jacob took a wife from among his relatives in the east.

28:1-2 *Isaac* remained in the land, but *Jacob* had to leave it. God would deal

with Jacob under the hand of *Laban*, his *uncle* (see note on 29:1–31:55).
• Believers in any age must remain spiritually pure by marrying other believers (2 Cor 6:14-18). The Canaanite people incorporated dozens of groups and clans into their society and religion by wars, treaties, and marriages (see 34:20-23). Abraham's family was to resist such mixing (cp. 24:3; ch 34); they were to marry within their clan to maintain the purity of the line and of the faith that identified them as the chosen seed. The surest way to lose their distinctiveness was to intermarry with people of other tribal backgrounds and beliefs (see Ezra 9–10; Neh 13:23-29).

28:3-5 Before Jacob departed, Isaac gave him a pure, legitimate blessing. He did not hold back, because he now knew what God wanted him to do. Isaac clearly passed on the blessing *God Almighty* (Hebrew *El-Shaddai*; see 17:1) had given to Abraham and to him regarding prosperity and the land (cp. 15:5, 18-20).

28:4 *descendants*: Literally *seed*; also in 28:13, 14.

JACOB (27:1–35:29)

Gen 25:19-34;
37:1-35; 42:1-4,
29-38; 43:1-13;
45:25–50:14
Exod 1:1-5
Num 23:7-10, 20-23;
24:5-9, 17-19
Deut 26:5
Josh 24:4, 32
Hos 12:2-14
Mal 1:2
John 4:5-6, 12
Acts 7:8-16
Rom 9:10-13
Heb 11:8-9, 20-21

Jacob, younger twin son of Isaac and Rebekah, struggled with his twin brother Esau in the womb and was born grasping his heel (25:24-26). God told Rebekah that the boys represented two nations and that the older son would serve the younger (25:23).

Isaac favored Esau, an outdoorsman; Rebekah preferred Jacob, who was happier at home. Once, Esau returned famished from hunting and Jacob bought his birthright with some red stew he had cooked (25:27-34; see Heb 12:16). Later, Isaac asked Esau to prepare wild game so he could eat and bless him (27:1-4; cp. 25:28). Rebekah sent Jacob to deceive Isaac into blessing him instead, and her ploy was successful (27:5-29). Jacob's ruse was soon discovered (27:30-35), but legally valid blessings were irrevocable promises (27:33). So Isaac gave Esau a lesser blessing (27:36-40), and Esau plotted to kill Jacob (27:41). Rebekah convinced Isaac to send Jacob away to her brother Laban so that Jacob would marry among relatives (27:46).

So Isaac transferred the covenant promises to Jacob and sent him to Haran (28:1-5). Along the way, God appeared to Jacob in a dream and affirmed the promises of land and descendants that he had given to Abraham and Isaac (28:10-15). Jacob worshiped the Lord and named the place Bethel ("house of God").

At Haran, Jacob began to serve his uncle Laban (chs 29–31). Jacob loved Laban's daughter Rachel and worked seven years to marry her, but Laban deceived him by substituting his older daughter Leah on Jacob's wedding night. Jacob worked seven more years for Rachel and an additional six years to acquire flocks for himself (30:25-43; see also 31:38-42). Despite many hardships, he had thirteen children and became very prosperous.

After twenty years, God told Jacob to return to Canaan (31:3). Fearing reprisals from Laban and his sons (31:1-2), Jacob organized his caravan and left while Laban was away (31:4-21). Laban gave chase, but God prevented him from harming Jacob (31:22-24, 29). Laban instead upbraided Jacob for leaving stealthily and for stealing his idols (31:25-30; see also 31:19). Jacob let Laban search his tents, but the idols were not found (31:33-35), and Jacob became angry (31:36-42). Though their conflict remained unresolved (31:43), the two men made a peace covenant (31:44-54); the location formed the lasting boundary between Israel and Aram.

Jacob now faced Esau and God. When Esau came to meet him with 400 men, Jacob sought God's protection and sent gifts to pacify his estranged brother (32:3-21). During a night that symbolized his whole life, Jacob wrestled alone with a man who dislocated his hip and gave him the blessing he sought (32:22-32). God changed his name to Israel ("God fights").

Jacob met Esau and the two were reconciled (33:1-11); Esau was gracious and forgiving, and Jacob shared some of his blessing. Esau then returned to Seir while Jacob continued to Canaan. In Shechem, Jacob bought land and built an altar (33:16-20), then moved to Bethel and expelled all foreign idols from his household (35:1-8). God reaffirmed Jacob's new name, Israel, and renewed his promises of land and descendants (35:9-15).

Jacob's favoritism for Rachel extended to her son Joseph, whom Jacob intended to anoint as the firstborn and heir (37:1-4), a plan that God confirmed through dreams (37:5-11). But then Joseph's brothers sold him as a slave (Gen 37:9-28) and for over twenty years Jacob believed he was dead. Only after letting Benjamin go to Egypt in Judah's care did Jacob learn that Joseph was alive and would be the source of famine relief for his family (43:1-14; 45:24-28). Jacob's spirits revived. He moved to Egypt and joyously reunited with his favorite son at Goshen (Gen 46:28-30), where he prospered for seventeen more years.

When Jacob approached death at age 147, he arranged for the future of his family. He made Joseph swear to bury him in Canaan (47:29-31; 49:29-32). He gave Joseph's sons his prime blessing (48:1-20) and put Ephraim, the younger son, first. He gave assurance that the family would return to Canaan (48:21-22), then blessed each of his sons and prophesied the future of their descendants (49:1-28). He died (49:33) and was buried at the cave of Machpelah, accompanied by his sons and a large Egyptian procession. His death marked the end of the patriarchal age and the beginning of Israel's growth as a nation in Egypt until they returned to live again in the Promised Land (see Exodus—Joshua).

The name "Jacob" became synonymous with the nation of Israel (see Num 23:7, 21; 24:5; Hos 12:2). God called the nation to serve him as their forefathers had done (Hos 12:3-13). He promised Israel the same love that he had shown toward Jacob (Mal 1:2). And he promised that a conquering ruler would come from Jacob's descendants (Gen 49:8-12; Num 24:17-19).

28:6
Gen 28:1

28:8
Gen 26:35

28:9
Gen 36:2

28:10
Gen 26:23

28:12
Gen 20:3
Num 12:6
*John 1:51
ᶜmal'ak (4397)
▸ Gen 48:16

28:13
ᵈ'erets (0776)
▸ Num 13:27

28:14
Gen 12:2; 13:14;
22:17

28:15
Gen 48:21
Deut 7:9; 31:6, 8

28:17
Exod 3:5
Ps 68:35

28:18
Gen 35:14

28:19
Gen 12:8; 35:6; 48:3

28:21
Exod 15:2

Esau's Ishmaelite Wives (28:6-9)

⁶Esau knew that his father, Isaac, had blessed Jacob and sent him to Paddan-aram to find a wife, and that he had warned Jacob, "You must not marry a Canaanite woman." ⁷He also knew that Jacob had obeyed his parents and gone to Paddan-aram. ⁸It was now very clear to Esau that his father did not like the local Canaanite women. ⁹So Esau visited his uncle Ishmael's family and married one of Ishmael's daughters, in addition to the wives he already had. His new wife's name was Mahalath. She was the sister of Nebaioth and the daughter of Ishmael, Abraham's son.

Jacob's Dream at Bethel:
The Blessing Confirmed (28:10-22)

¹⁰Meanwhile, Jacob left Beersheba and traveled toward Haran. ¹¹At sundown he arrived at a good place to set up camp and stopped there for the night. Jacob found a stone to rest his head against and lay down to sleep. ¹²As he slept, he dreamed of a stairway that reached from the earth up to heaven. And he saw the ᶜangels of God going up and down the stairway.

¹³At the top of the stairway stood the LORD, and he said, "I am the LORD, the God of your grandfather Abraham, and the God of your father, Isaac. The ᵈground you are lying on belongs to you. I am giving it to you and your descendants. ¹⁴Your descendants will be as numerous as the dust of the earth! They will spread out in all directions—to the west and the east, to the north and the south. And all the families of the earth will be blessed through you and your descendants. ¹⁵What's more, I am with you, and I will protect you wherever you go. One day I will bring you back to this land. I will not leave you until I have finished giving you everything I have promised you."

¹⁶Then Jacob awoke from his sleep and said, "Surely the LORD is in this place, and I wasn't even aware of it!" ¹⁷But he was also afraid and said, "What an awesome place this is! It is none other than the house of God, the very gateway to heaven!"

¹⁸The next morning Jacob got up very early. He took the stone he had rested his head against, and he set it upright as a memorial pillar. Then he poured olive oil over it. ¹⁹He named that place Bethel (which means "house of God"), although it was previously called Luz.

²⁰Then Jacob made this vow: "If God will indeed be with me and protect me on this journey, and if he will provide me with food and clothing, ²¹and if I return safely to my

. . . .

Age	Event	Reference
15	Abraham dies	21:5; 25:7, 26
91	Joseph is born	See "Joseph's Life," p. 99
108	Joseph is sold into slavery	37:2
120	Isaac dies	25:26; 35:28
130	Jacob moves to Egypt	47:7-9
147	Jacob dies, is buried in Canaan	47:28

▲ Jacob's Life (27:1–35:29).

28:6-9 *Esau*, the unchosen son still trying to please *his father*, married a woman from the unchosen line of *Ishmael*, which he thought would be more acceptable. He did not understand the uniqueness of the covenant family.

28:10-22 Despite Jacob's previous means of securing the blessing, God assured him of protection and provision. The God of Abraham and Isaac was also the God of Jacob. The revelation dramatically changed Jacob's outlook and brought faith into clearer focus.

28:11 The *good place* where Jacob *set up camp* was apparently a protected area at the foot of a hill. The *stone to rest his head against* was probably large, more for protection than for a pillow.

28:12-15 The point of the vision was that God and his angels were with Jacob on his journey. God reiterated to Jacob the covenant promises made to Abraham and Isaac, promising him land, descendants numerous as the dust (cp. 13:16; 22:17), and universal blessing through him (cp. 12:2-3; 15:5, 18; 17:3-8; 22:15-18; 35:11-12). God also promised to be with Jacob and watch over him until he returned.

28:12-13 *stairway* (traditionally *ladder*): This word occurs nowhere else in Scripture. The imagery probably reminded readers of a staircase or ramp up the front of a ziggurat that signified communication between heaven and earth (see note on 11:4). God initiated a divine communication between heaven and earth to guide and protect Jacob, the steward of his covenant (28:13-15; see Ps 91:11-15). • Jesus said that he himself is the stairway between heaven and earth (John 1:51).

28:14 Jacob inherited Abraham's entire covenant (see 22:17), which confirmed Isaac's blessing (28:3-4) and stipulated a temporary exile (28:15; see 15:12-16).

28:15 *I am with you:* The promise of God's presence meant that God would *protect* and provide for Jacob in a special way. God's promise to be with his people is repeated throughout Scripture (see also 26:24), prompting a response of worship and confidence in those who have faith (28:16-22).

28:16-22 The second half of the passage gives Jacob's response to the revelation. He felt reverential fear and awe in the Lord's presence, and his acts of devotion became archetypes of Israel's worship. When God graciously visits his people and promises to be with them and make them a blessing to the world, his people respond in faith with reverential fear, worship, offerings, and vows. They preserve their faith in memory for future worshipers.

28:18 Anointing with *oil* became a way of setting something apart for divine use in Israel's worship (Exod 29:1-7; 40:9; Lev 2:1; 1 Sam 10:1).

28:19 *Bethel* later became a holy site for Israel (see Judg 20:18-27; 1 Sam 7:16; 10:3; 1 Kgs 12:26–13:10; 2 Kgs 2:2-3).

28:20-22 In view of what God would do for him, Jacob vowed to do certain things for God. He believed the Lord's words and responded in gratitude. Jacob's *vow* influenced Israel's way of making commitments to God in worship.

father's home, then the LORD will certainly be my God. ²²And this memorial pillar I have set up will become a place for worshiping God, and I will present to God a tenth of everything he gives me."

Jacob in Paddan-Aram (29:1–31:55)
Jacob Meets Rachel and Laban

29 Then Jacob hurried on, finally arriving in the land of the east. ²He saw a well in the distance. Three flocks of sheep and goats lay in an open field beside it, waiting to be watered. But a heavy stone covered the mouth of the well.

³It was the custom there to wait for all the flocks to arrive before removing the stone and watering the animals. Afterward the stone would be placed back over the mouth of the well. ⁴Jacob went over to the shepherds and asked, "Where are you from, my friends?"

"We are from Haran," they answered.

⁵"Do you know a man there named Laban, the grandson of Nahor?" he asked.

"Yes, we do," they replied.

⁶"Is he doing well?" Jacob asked.

"Yes, he's well," they answered. "Look, here comes his daughter Rachel with the flock now."

⁷Jacob said, "Look, it's still broad daylight—too early to round up the animals. Why don't you water the sheep and goats so they can get back out to pasture?"

⁸"We can't water the animals until all the flocks have arrived," they replied. "Then the shepherds move the stone from the mouth of the well, and we water all the sheep and goats."

⁹Jacob was still talking with them when Rachel arrived with her father's flock, for she was a ^eshepherd. ¹⁰And because Rachel was his cousin—the daughter of Laban, his mother's brother—and because the sheep and goats belonged to his uncle Laban, Jacob went over to the well and moved the stone from its mouth and watered his uncle's flock. ¹¹Then Jacob kissed Rachel, and he wept aloud. ¹²He explained to Rachel that

28:22
Gen 14:20; 35:7
Deut 14:22

29:1
Judg 6:3, 33

29:2
Gen 24:10-11

29:4
Gen 28:10

29:5
Gen 11:29

29:6
Exod 2:16

29:9
^ero'ah (7462)
▶ Gen 48:15

29:10
Exod 2:17

29:11
Gen 33:4

29:12
Gen 28:5

RACHEL (29:6–30:24)

Gen 31:4-19, 31-35;
33:1-7; 35:16-20;
46:19-22; 48:7
Ruth 4:11
1 Sam 10:2
Jer 31:15
Matt 2:18

Rachel, Laban's beautiful younger daughter, was Jacob's favorite wife. He first met her as he arrived at Paddan-aram in Haran, when he helped Rachel remove the stone from the well and watered her father's sheep (29:10). Jacob agreed to work seven years for Laban in order to have Rachel as his wife, and the time seemed like only a few days because of his great love for her.

Laban deceptively required Jacob to marry Leah, his older, less attractive daughter, before finally giving him Rachel. Unlike Leah, Rachel was barren in the early years of her marriage to Jacob (30:1). She gave her servant Bilhah to Jacob in order to have children, and Dan and Naphtali were born (30:3-8). In time, Rachel conceived and bore Joseph (30:22-25), and Jacob took his wives, children, and possessions away from Haran.

Somewhere between Bethel and Bethlehem, Rachel died while giving birth to Benjamin (35:16-20). Jacob set up a pillar over her tomb that was a landmark even in Saul's time (1 Sam 10:2). Rachel and Leah are highly regarded for having built up the house of Israel (Ruth 4:11). In Jer 31:15, Rachel is pictured as crying for her children being carried off into captivity, and Matthew recalls Jeremiah's words at Herod's slaughter of the male infants (Matt 2:18).

28:22 *I will present to God a tenth:* By paying a tithe (*a tenth*) as an act of worship, a person acknowledges that everything is a gift from God and belongs to God (see 14:19-20; Num 18:21-32; Deut 14:22-29; 2 Chr 31:5-6; Mal 3:7-12; Matt 23:23).

29:1–31:55 These chapters tell how God kept his promise by abundantly blessing Jacob with family and possessions. God also disciplined Jacob, leaving him to struggle with Laban for many years. Laban was Jacob's match in deception, and thus a means of correction. • The story of Jacob and Laban parallels Israel's later sojourn in Egypt. Jacob struggled while serving his uncle, but finally emerged with a large family

(the founders of the twelve tribes) and great wealth. In Egypt, the Israelites suffered under their oppressors, but they also flourished, becoming a great nation of twelve large tribes and escaping with great riches.

29:1 *Jacob hurried on:* The Hebrew text says that he "picked up his feet" as if he felt the wind at his back; he continued his journey with fresh enthusiasm. His changed outlook was the direct result of the vision he received at Bethel, a marvelous revelation that God was going to protect and bless him. He now sought the fulfillment of God's promises to him, not just an escape from Esau. Jacob's attitude had become positive and magnanimous to the point

of being naive and vulnerable.

29:2-12 Jacob's meeting Rachel at the well was providentially timed by the sovereign God who was leading Jacob to fulfillment of the promises (cp. 24:12-20). The well was a reminder of God's blessing (cp. 16:13-14; 21:19; 26:19-25, 33).

29:10 In contrast to the lazy, unhelpful shepherds (29:7-8), Jacob is portrayed as generous, industrious, and energetic. • *Jacob . . . watered his uncle's flock:* Laban's flocks would flourish under Jacob's care.

29:11 *Jacob kissed Rachel:* Kissing relatives was a proper greeting (29:13; cp. Song 8:1).

29:14
Judg 9:2
2 Sam 5:1

29:15
Gen 30:28; 31:7, 41

29:16
Gen 29:25-26

29:17
Gen 12:11

29:18
Gen 24:67
Hos 12:12

29:20
Song 8:7

29:22
Judg 14:10

29:23
Gen 24:65; 38:14

29:24
Gen 30:9

29:25
Gen 12:18

he was her cousin on her father's side—the son of her aunt Rebekah. So Rachel quickly ran and told her father, Laban.

¹³As soon as Laban heard that his nephew Jacob had arrived, he ran out to meet him. He embraced and kissed him and brought him home. When Jacob had told him his story, ¹⁴Laban exclaimed, "You really are my own flesh and blood!"

Jacob Marries Leah and Rachel

After Jacob had stayed with Laban for about a month, ¹⁵Laban said to him, "You shouldn't work for me without pay just because we are relatives. Tell me how much your wages should be."

¹⁶Now Laban had two daughters. The older daughter was named Leah, and the younger one was Rachel. ¹⁷There was no sparkle in Leah's eyes, but Rachel had a beautiful figure and a lovely face. ¹⁸Since

Jacob was in love with Rachel, he told her father, "I'll work for you for seven years if you'll give me Rachel, your younger daughter, as my wife."

¹⁹"Agreed!" Laban replied. "I'd rather give her to you than to anyone else. Stay and work with me." ²⁰So Jacob worked seven years to pay for Rachel. But his love for her was so strong that it seemed to him but a few days.

²¹Finally, the time came for him to marry her. "I have fulfilled my agreement," Jacob said to Laban. "Now give me my wife so I can sleep with her."

²²So Laban invited everyone in the neighborhood and prepared a wedding feast. ²³But that night, when it was dark, Laban took Leah to Jacob, and he slept with her. ²⁴(Laban had given Leah a servant, Zilpah, to be her maid.)

²⁵But when Jacob woke up in the morning— it was Leah! "What have you done to me?"

· ·

LEAH (29:14-35)

Gen 30:9-21; 31:4-16; 33:1-7; 34:1; 46:8-15; 49:31
Ruth 4:11

Leah was Laban's first daughter, Jacob's unloved first wife, and Rachel's older sister.

After Jacob deceived his father Isaac into giving him the blessing intended for Esau (27:1-40), Jacob went to his uncle Laban in Mesopotamia to find a wife (27:46–28:2) and escape Esau's revenge (27:41-42). He fell in love with his cousin Rachel and arranged with her father to marry her after seven years of work (29:17-18). At the wedding feast, Laban deceived Jacob by giving him Leah instead of Rachel (29:21-25), claiming that custom required the older daughter to marry first (29:26). Leah's eyes were not beautiful, but Rachel "had a beautiful figure and a lovely face" (29:17).

Jacob's love for Rachel (29:20) induced him to work another seven years to marry her. In the intense rivalry between the two sisters, Jacob favored Rachel, so the Lord blessed Leah with six sons and a daughter (Reuben, Simeon, Levi, Judah, Issachar, Zebulun, and Dinah) before Rachel was given any children (29:31–30:22). This barrenness became a great burden for Rachel. At one point she bargained with Leah for mandrakes, a plant believed to ensure conception, in exchange for conjugal rights. This increased her sister's advantage, because Leah conceived and bore her fifth son (30:14-17).

Leah was the mother of two tribes that played significant roles in Israelite history. The tribe of Levi was the tribe of the priesthood, and the tribe of Judah became the tribe of royalty through which the promised seed (3:15; 12:2-3; 2 Sam 7:16; Matt 1:1) came in the person of Jesus Christ.

· ·

29:14a *You really are my own flesh and blood!* Laban welcomed Jacob into his house and treated him much like a son.

29:14b-30 Jacob's joyful prospect of marriage to the lovely Rachel became an occasion for Laban's shrewdness and Jacob's discipline. Jacob and his mother had deceived his father and brother to gain the blessing; now his mother's brother deceived him. Jacob received a dose of his own duplicity through twenty years of labor, affliction, and deception in Laban's service (31:38). In God's justice, people harvest what they plant (Gal 6:7). Laban's deception was perfectly designed to make Jacob aware

of his own craftiness. God often brings people into the lives of believers to discipline them. But Jacob was tenacious, and God blessed him abundantly with a large family and many possessions (30:25-43) during this time of service.

29:17 *There was no sparkle in Leah's eyes:* Or *Leah had dull eyes,* or *Leah had soft eyes.* The meaning of the Hebrew is uncertain.

29:18 *Seven years* of service was a high bride-price in the ancient world, but Rachel was beautiful (like Sarah and Rebekah), and *Jacob was in love* with her.

29:23-26 Like Isaac, Jacob was plied with food and wine (cp. 27:25), deprived

of sight in the darkness (cp. 27:1), baffled by clothing (cp. 27:15), and misled by touch (cp. 27:23). The marriage had been consummated (29:23; see 2:24), so Jacob was bound to Leah, but Jacob only acknowledged Rachel as his wife (44:27) and her children as his own (42:38). • *It's not our custom here to marry off a younger daughter ahead of the firstborn:* Laban's words are a reminder of what Jacob did when he, the younger son, pretended to be his older brother to gain the blessing (ch 27). Now Leah, the older sister, pretended to be the younger sister to get a husband. God gave the deceiver a dose of his own deception as a discipline in his life.

Jacob raged at Laban. "I worked seven years for Rachel! Why have you tricked me?"

26"It's not our custom here to marry off a younger daughter ahead of the firstborn," Laban replied. 27"But wait until the bridal week is over, then we'll give you Rachel, too—provided you promise to work another seven years for me."

28So Jacob agreed to work seven more years. A week after Jacob had married Leah, Laban gave him Rachel, too. 29(Laban gave Rachel a servant, Bilhah, to be her maid.) 30So Jacob slept with Rachel, too, and he loved her much more than Leah. He then stayed and worked for Laban the additional seven years.

Children Born to Leah and Rachel

31When the LORD saw that Leah was unloved, he enabled her to have children, but Rachel could not conceive. 32So Leah became pregnant and gave birth to a son. She named him Reuben, for she said, "The LORD has noticed my misery, and now my husband will love me."

33She soon became pregnant again and gave birth to another son. She named him Simeon, for she said, "The LORD heard that I was unloved and has given me another son."

34Then she became pregnant a third time and gave birth to another son. She named

him Levi, for she said, "Surely this time my husband will feel affection for me, since I have given him three sons!"

35Once again Leah became pregnant and gave birth to another son. She named him Judah, for she said, "Now I will praise the LORD!" And then she stopped having children.

30 When Rachel saw that she wasn't having any children for Jacob, she became jealous of her sister. She pleaded with Jacob, "Give me children, or I'll die!"

2Then Jacob became furious with Rachel. "Am I God?" he asked. "He's the one who has kept you from having children!"

3Then Rachel told him, "Take my maid, Bilhah, and sleep with her. She will bear children for me, and through her I can have a family, too." 4So Rachel gave her servant, Bilhah, to Jacob as a wife, and he slept with her. 5Bilhah became pregnant and presented him with a son. 6Rachel named him Dan, for she said, "God has vindicated me! He has heard my request and given me a son." 7Then Bilhah became pregnant again and gave Jacob a second son. 8Rachel named him Naphtali, for she said, "I have struggled hard with my sister, and I'm winning!"

9Meanwhile, Leah realized that she wasn't getting pregnant anymore, so she took her

29:27	Judg 14:12
29:29	Gen 30:3
29:30	Gen 29:16
29:31	Deut 21:15-17
29:32	Gen 30:23; 37:21; 46:8
29:33	Deut 21:15
29:34	Gen 49:5
29:35	Gen 49:8; Matt 1:2-3
30:1	1 Sam 1:5-6
30:2	Gen 20:18; 29:31
30:3-4	Gen 16:2-4
30:6	Gen 30:23
30:8	Gen 32:28

. . . .

29:28-30 After the bridal week ended (29:27), Jacob also received Rachel as his wife, though he then would have to work an *additional seven years* (cp. 31:41). Laban seemed to have gained the upper hand.

29:30 Jacob *loved* Rachel *much more than Leah:* Favoritism was an ongoing cause of dysfunction in Jacob's family (cp. 25:28; 37:3). Jacob's favoritism had lasting effects: his family was never together, and their descendants, the tribes of Israel, were rarely unified.

29:31–30:24 The rivalry between these sisters explains much of the later rivalry among their sons, and then among the tribes, just as the rivalry between Jacob and Laban foreshadowed conflict between Israel and the Arameans of Damascus (2 Sam 8:5-6; 10:8-19; 1 Kgs 20:1-34; 2 Kgs 5–8; 13; Isa 7:1-9). • God champions the cause of the poor and oppressed; he exalted Leah, the despised first wife, as the first to become a mother. Judah's kingly tribe and Levi's priestly line came through her despite Jacob's favoritism for Rachel and her children. Despite the tension and jealousy resulting from Laban's treachery and Jacob's favoritism, God still built Jacob's family and brought about the births of the tribal ancestors.

29:31-35 Leah's first four sons were born in rapid succession, but *Rachel could not conceive.* She was barren, like Sarah and Rebekah (cp. 16:1; 25:21; see also 1 Sam 1:1-28; Luke 1:5-25). • Each name is a memorable wordplay on Leah's experience and hopes.

29:32 *Reuben* (Hebrew *re'uben*) means "Look, a son!" It also sounds like the Hebrew for "He has seen my misery" (*ra'ah be'onyi*). His birth gave Leah consolation from God and hope for Jacob's love. Jacob seems not to have seen her misery, but God did (cp. 16:14; 24:62; 25:11). The name was a reminder of God's intervention.

29:33 Leah named her second son *Simeon. Simeon* probably means "one who hears." *The LORD heard that* Leah *was unloved.* The name suggests that she had cried out to the Lord (cp. 16:11).

29:34 *Levi* sounds like a Hebrew term that means "being attached" or "feeling affection for." Leah named her third son Levi, hoping that her *husband* would become attached to her since she had *given him three sons.* This hope was not fulfilled.

29:35 Leah reconciled herself to the reality that nothing would turn Jacob's affections toward her. She named her fourth son *Judah* with the sentiment,

"I will praise the LORD" (Judah is related to the Hebrew term for "praise"). She seems to have given up on Jacob, taking her consolation from the Lord.

30:1-8 Rachel's naming of sons through Bilhah does not reflect faith as Leah's namings had. Rachel felt wronged over the marriage and her barrenness. The names of Bilhah's sons reflect Rachel's bitter struggle with her sister and her feeling of some victory.

30:1-2 In that culture, it was like death for a woman not to have children (cp. 1 Sam 1); only God could open Rachel's womb.

30:3-4 Rachel's decision to have children through her servant, and Jacob's compliance, recall Sarai's use of Hagar (16:1-4). • *bear children for me:* Literally *bear children on my knees.*

30:5-6 *Dan* means "he judged" or "he vindicated." Rachel felt *vindicated* (Hebrew *dananni*) by Dan's birth.

30:7-8 *Naphtali* means "my struggle"; it is related to the clause *I have struggled hard* (Hebrew *naptule 'elohim niptalti,* "I have struggled the struggles of God"). This word for God expresses the superlative.

30:9 When Leah saw that she had stopped bearing children, she coun-

30:11
Gen 35:26; 46:16;
49:19

30:14
Song 7:13

30:17
Gen 25:21

30:18
Gen 49:14

30:22
1 Sam 1:19-20

30:23
Luke 1:25

30:24
Gen 35:17

30:26
Gen 29:18
Hos 12:12

30:27
Gen 39:2-5

30:28
Gen 29:15; 31:7

30:32
Gen 31:8, 12

servant, Zilpah, and gave her to Jacob as a wife. ¹⁰Soon Zilpah presented him with a son. ¹¹Leah named him Gad, for she said, "How fortunate I am!" ¹²Then Zilpah gave Jacob a second son. ¹³And Leah named him Asher, for she said, "What joy is mine! Now the other women will celebrate with me."

¹⁴One day during the wheat harvest, Reuben found some mandrakes growing in a field and brought them to his mother, Leah. Rachel begged Leah, "Please give me some of your son's mandrakes."

¹⁵But Leah angrily replied, "Wasn't it enough that you stole my husband? Now will you steal my son's mandrakes, too?"

Rachel answered, "I will let Jacob sleep with you tonight if you give me some of the mandrakes."

¹⁶So that evening, as Jacob was coming home from the fields, Leah went out to meet him. "You must come and sleep with me tonight!" she said. "I have paid for you with some mandrakes that my son found." So that night he slept with Leah. ¹⁷And God answered Leah's prayers. She became pregnant again and gave birth to a fifth son for Jacob. ¹⁸She named him Issachar, for she said, "God has rewarded me for giving my servant to my husband as a wife." ¹⁹Then Leah became pregnant again and gave birth to a sixth son for Jacob. ²⁰She named him Zebulun, for she said, "God has given me a good reward. Now my husband will treat me with respect, for I have given him six sons." ²¹Later she gave birth to a daughter and named her Dinah.

²²Then God remembered Rachel's plight and answered her prayers by enabling her to have children. ²³She became pregnant and gave birth to a son. "God has removed my disgrace," she said. ²⁴And she named him Joseph, for she said, "May the LORD add yet another son to my family."

Jacob's Wealth Increases

²⁵Soon after Rachel had given birth to Joseph, Jacob said to Laban, "Please release me so I can go home to my own country. ²⁶Let me take my wives and children, for I have earned them by serving you, and let me be on my way. You certainly know how hard I have worked for you."

²⁷"Please listen to me," Laban replied. "I have become wealthy, for the LORD has blessed me because of you. ²⁸Tell me how much I owe you. Whatever it is, I'll pay it."

²⁹Jacob replied, "You know how hard I've worked for you, and how your flocks and herds have grown under my care. ³⁰You had little indeed before I came, but your wealth has increased enormously. The LORD has blessed you through everything I've done. But now, what about me? When can I start providing for my own family?"

³¹"What wages do you want?" Laban asked again.

Jacob replied, "Don't give me anything. Just do this one thing, and I'll continue to tend and watch over your flocks. ³²Let me inspect your flocks today and remove all the sheep and goats that are speckled or spotted, along with all the black sheep. Give these to me as my wages. ³³In the future, when you check on the animals you have given me as my wages, you'll see that I have been honest. If you find in my flock

. . . .

tered Rachel's effort by giving **her servant . . . to Jacob as a wife** even though she already had four sons.

30:10-13 Gad means "good fortune" and was the name of a god of fortune. *Asher* means "happy" and was the name of a god of luck. These names reflect Leah's pagan background, but there is no indication that she believed in these gods.

30:14-17 *Mandrakes* were considered an aphrodisiac and aid to procreation (see Song 7:13). Rachel thought they would help her get pregnant and so traded Jacob for a night to get them. In the process, Leah got pregnant, not Rachel.

30:18 *Issachar* sounds like a Hebrew term that means "reward." The name captures the sense of Jacob's being hired (30:16) and of the Lord's rewarding Leah (Hebrew *sekari*, "my hire").

30:19-20 *Zebulun* probably means "honor"; it also means "gift," as in a

dowry or tribute. Leah thought that God gave her Zebulun so that her husband would honor her. This hope never fully left her.

30:21 *Dinah* was Jacob's only daughter. See ch 34.

30:22-24 Rachel finally *gave birth to* her own *son*, Joseph. His birth was brought about by God's intervention, not by superstitious practices (30:14-16) or the social custom of giving servants as wives. • *Removed* (Hebrew *'asap*, "take away") sounds similar to *Joseph* (Hebrew *yosep*). *Joseph* means "may he add." Rachel rejoiced over Joseph's birth, yet she prayed that the Lord would *add yet another son to* her *family*.

30:25-34 After his fourteen years of service, Jacob asked Laban for permission to go home. The two bedouin leaders negotiated politely but remained cautiously on guard. Laban wanted to get more out of Jacob. Jacob wanted to gain

his wages by selective breeding.

30:27 *I have become wealthy, for* (or *I have learned by divination that*): God had prospered Laban through Jacob's presence (see 22:18). Laban may have looked for omens, or simply have perceived what was happening. Since dark-colored sheep (30:32) were rare, a large number of them was considered an omen of God's blessing.

30:30-33 Jacob agreed that God had blessed Laban through him, so he made a plan to gain something for himself. He proposed for his wages the rare black and multicolored goats and the speckled and spotted sheep that were born.

30:32 As Abraham had done with Lot (13:9), Jacob gave Laban what he valued most. White sheep were more common and more valuable than dark or multicolored sheep; as a man of faith, Jacob was willing to take the rejects (cp. 1 Cor 1:26).

any goats without speckles or spots, or any sheep that are not black, you will know that I have stolen them from you."

³⁴"All right," Laban replied. "It will be as you say." ³⁵But that very day Laban went out and removed the male goats that were streaked and spotted, all the female goats that were speckled and spotted or had white patches, and all the black sheep. He placed them in the care of his own sons, ³⁶who took them a three-days' journey from where Jacob was. Meanwhile, Jacob stayed and cared for the rest of Laban's flock.

³⁷Then Jacob took some fresh branches from poplar, almond, and plane trees and peeled off strips of bark, making white streaks on them. ³⁸Then he placed these peeled branches in the watering troughs where the flocks came to drink, for that was where they mated. ³⁹And when they mated in front of the white-streaked branches, they gave birth to young that were streaked, speckled, and spotted. ⁴⁰Jacob separated those lambs from Laban's flock. And at mating time he turned the flock to face Laban's animals that were streaked or black. This is how he built his own flock instead of increasing Laban's.

⁴¹Whenever the stronger females were ready to mate, Jacob would place the peeled branches in the watering troughs in front of them. Then they would mate in front of the branches. ⁴²But he didn't do this with the weaker ones, so the weaker lambs belonged to Laban, and the stronger ones were Jacob's. ⁴³As a result, Jacob became

very wealthy, with large flocks of sheep and goats, female and male servants, and many camels and donkeys.

Jacob Flees from Laban

31 But Jacob soon learned that Laban's sons were grumbling about him. "Jacob has robbed our father of everything!" they said. "He has gained all his ᶠwealth at our father's expense." ²And Jacob began to notice a change in Laban's attitude toward him.

³Then the LORD said to Jacob, "Return to the land of your father and grandfather and to your relatives there, and I will be with you."

⁴So Jacob called Rachel and Leah out to the field where he was watching his flock. ⁵He said to them, "I have noticed that your father's attitude toward me has changed. But the God of my father has been with me. ⁶You know how hard I have worked for your father, ⁷but he has cheated me, changing my wages ten times. But God has not allowed him to do me any harm. ⁸For if he said, 'The speckled animals will be your wages,' the whole flock began to produce speckled young. And when he changed his mind and said, 'The striped animals will be your wages,' then the whole flock produced striped young. ⁹In this way, God has taken your father's animals and given them to me.

¹⁰"One time during the mating season, I had a dream and saw that the male goats mating with the females were streaked, speckled, and spotted. ¹¹Then in my dream,

30:43
Gen 13:2; 24:35; 26:13

31:1
ᶠ*kabod* (3519)
▸ Exod 16:10

31:3
Gen 28:15; 32:9

31:6
Gen 30:29

31:7
Gen 29:25; 31:41

31:8
Gen 30:32

31:11
Gen 16:7-11; 22:11, 15

30:34-36 *Laban* verbally agreed with Jacob's plan, but he tried to prevent Jacob from accruing wealth by removing animals from the flock that would fulfill the agreement. • Laban's deception with his *goats* reminds us of Jacob's deception of Esau (cp. 27:9; see note on 29:14b-30).

30:37-43 God blessed Jacob despite Laban's duplicity. Not to be outwitted, Jacob used selective breeding to acquire a flock, following the traditional belief that peeled sticks influenced the kind of animal that would be born. The peeled branches seemingly made his animals produce streaked and spotted young; Jacob later acknowledged that God had prospered him (31:7-12). Jacob gained *stronger* animals for himself and *weaker ones* for Laban (30:41-42).

30:37 *making white streaks:* A clever wordplay captures the meaning of this whole section. When Jacob exposed the white (Hebrew *laban*) streaks of

wood underneath, he played the "white" game (the *Laban* game) and won. As he outwitted Laban ("Whitey"), Jacob's flocks flourished and Jacob prospered.

30:42 Laban now received due recompense for his treatment of Jacob. Laban's attempt to defraud Jacob resulted in Jacob's coming out ahead, because God was at work in his life.

30:43 *Jacob became very wealthy*, in fulfillment of God's promises to him (27:28; 28:13-15).

31:1-21 Jacob's return journey precipitated a confrontation with Laban that set a permanent boundary between Israel (Jacob) and Aram (Laban). God kept his word to Jacob by prospering him in Paddan-aram and protecting him on his journey home.

31:1-2 The animosity of *Laban's sons* against *Jacob* grew because his flocks were multiplying faster than Laban's. They were jealous of God's blessing on Jacob and afraid that he would completely overrun them.

31:3 *The land of your father and grandfather* was the land of Canaan, to which Abraham had previously been called (12:1-7; 17:8). • *Return . . . I will be with you:* See notes on 26:2-5; 28:12-15. God protected Jacob ("Israel," 32:28) as he brought his family back to the land that was promised to them. God later brought Israel back to Canaan after long years of service in Egypt. That great return had many elements similar to this passage: God defeated foreign gods and beliefs, used dreams for rescue and protection, gave victory over those who threatened them, and established boundaries between nations and tribes (see Deut 32:8).

31:4-13 Jacob explained to his wives how God had blessed him despite Laban's opposition. He was not sure they would want to leave Laban and go to Canaan. He wanted to take a willing family, so he had to make an effective appeal. He rehearsed God's leading and provision over the years, and then told them that he had to keep the vow he had made at Bethel (28:20-22).

31:12
Gen 30:32
Exod 3:7

31:13
Gen 28:10-22

31:15
Gen 29:20, 27

31:18
Gen 25:20

31:19
Judg 17:5

31:20
Gen 31:27

31:21
Gen 37:25
Num 32:1

31:22
Gen 30:36

31:24
Gen 25:20

31:28
Gen 31:55

31:31
Gen 20:11

31:32
Gen 44:9

the angel of God said to me, 'Jacob!' And I replied, 'Yes, here I am.'

12"The angel said, 'Look up, and you will see that only the streaked, speckled, and spotted males are mating with the females of your flock. For I have seen how Laban has treated you. 13I am the God who appeared to you at Bethel, the place where you anointed the pillar of stone and made your vow to me. Now get ready and leave this country and return to the land of your birth.' "

14Rachel and Leah responded, "That's fine with us! We won't inherit any of our father's wealth anyway. 15He has reduced our rights to those of foreign women. And after he sold us, he wasted the money you paid him for us. 16All the wealth God has given you from our father legally belongs to us and our children. So go ahead and do whatever God has told you."

17So Jacob put his wives and children on camels, 18and he drove all his livestock in front of him. He packed all the belongings he had acquired in Paddan-aram and set out for the land of Canaan, where his father, Isaac, lived. 19At the time they left, Laban was some distance away, shearing his sheep. Rachel stole her father's household idols and took them with her. 20Jacob outwitted Laban the Aramean, for they set out secretly and never told Laban they were leaving. 21So Jacob took all his possessions with him and crossed the Euphrates River, heading for the hill country of Gilead.

Dispute between Laban and Jacob

22Three days later, Laban was told that Jacob had fled. 23So he gathered a group of his relatives and set out in hot pursuit. He caught up with Jacob seven days later in the hill country of Gilead. 24But the previous night God had appeared to Laban the Aramean in a dream and told him, "I'm warning you—leave Jacob alone!"

25Laban caught up with Jacob as he was camped in the hill country of Gilead, and he set up his camp not far from Jacob's. 26"What do you mean by deceiving me like this?" Laban demanded. "How dare you drag my daughters away like prisoners of war? 27Why did you slip away secretly? Why did you deceive me? And why didn't you say you wanted to leave? I would have given you a farewell feast, with singing and music, accompanied by tambourines and harps. 28Why didn't you let me kiss my daughters and grandchildren and tell them good-bye? You have acted very foolishly! 29I could destroy you, but the God of your father appeared to me last night and warned me, 'Leave Jacob alone!' 30I can understand your feeling that you must go, and your intense longing for your father's home. But why have you stolen my gods?"

31"I rushed away because I was afraid," Jacob answered. "I thought you would take your daughters from me by force. 32But as for your gods, see if you can find them, and let the person who has taken them die! And if you find anything else that belongs to you, identify it before all these relatives of ours, and I will give it back!" But Jacob did not know that Rachel had stolen the household idols.

33Laban went first into Jacob's tent to search there, then into Leah's, and then

. . . .

31:13 the God who appeared to you at Bethel: As in Greek version and an Aramaic Targum; Hebrew reads the God of Bethel.

31:14-16 The women responded immediately that they would go with Jacob because God had blessed him. They were very willing to leave Laban, who had squandered their wealth (the property that would have provided for them). They knew that what God had given to Jacob would also be theirs.

31:17-21 Jacob left Laban secretly out of fear of reprisal (31:31).

31:19-20 Rachel stole her father's household idols: Rachel probably wanted to regain some of the assets Laban had squandered; possibly she also worshiped idols (cp. 35:2-4). To have the idols may have signified claiming the family inheritance, as customs in subsequent periods indicate. Laban apparently felt vulnerable without them.

Whatever her reasons, Rachel's theft almost brought disaster on the fleeing family when Laban caught up with them. • A wordplay shows that Rachel and Jacob were very much alike—Rachel stole (Hebrew wattignob) Laban's household gods, and Jacob outwitted (Hebrew wayyignob, "stole the heart of, deceived") Laban.

31:21 The journey took the family from Haran southwest to the land of Gilead, just east of the Jordan River in the north of today's kingdom of Jordan. • the Euphrates River: Literally the river.

31:22-23 The theft of the idols (31:19) was probably the main reason that Laban and his men chased Jacob. It was one thing for Jacob to take his family and flocks—Laban probably still believed they were all his—but another matter entirely to take his household gods. Laban may have feared that Jacob would return someday to claim all of

Laban's estate. When he failed to find the gods, he asked for a treaty to keep Jacob away (31:43-53). • It took Laban seven days to catch up with Jacob.

31:24 leave Jacob alone! (literally Do not speak to Jacob either good or evil): God commanded Laban not to take justice into his own hands. When we try to enact our own sense of good and evil apart from God's command, we always do evil (see note on 2:9).

31:25-30 The dispute between the two men used the language of legal controversies and lawsuits (see also 31:36). In his first argument, Laban presented himself as a wounded party that Jacob had robbed.

31:32 Jacob, so convinced that he didn't have the gods, used an oath that unwittingly put Rachel under a death sentence.

31:33-35 Laban searched for the idols but found nothing. Laban never

the tents of the two servant wives—but he found nothing. Finally, he went into Rachel's tent. 34But Rachel had taken the household idols and hidden them in her camel saddle, and now she was sitting on them. When Laban had thoroughly searched her tent without finding them, 35she said to her father, "Please, sir, forgive me if I don't get up for you. I'm having my monthly period." So Laban continued his search, but he could not find the household idols.

36Then Jacob became very angry, and he challenged Laban. "What's my crime?" he demanded. "What have I done wrong to make you chase after me as though I were a criminal? 37You have rummaged through everything I own. Now show me what you found that belongs to you! Set it out here in front of us, before our relatives, for all to see. Let them judge between us!

38"For twenty years I have been with you, caring for your flocks. In all that time your sheep and goats never miscarried. In all those years I never used a single ram of yours for food. 39If any were attacked and killed by wild animals, I never showed you the carcass and asked you to reduce the count of your flock. No, I took the loss myself! You made me pay for every stolen animal, whether it was taken in broad daylight or in the dark of night.

40"I worked for you through the scorching heat of the day and through cold and sleepless nights. 41Yes, for twenty years I slaved in your house! I worked for fourteen years earning your two daughters, and then six more years for your flock. And you changed my wages ten times! 42In fact, if the God of my father had not been on my side—the God of Abraham and the fearsome God of Isaac—you would have sent me away empty-handed. But God has seen your abuse and

my hard work. That is why he appeared to you last night and rebuked you!"

Jacob's Treaty with Laban

43Then Laban replied to Jacob, "These women are my daughters, these children are my grandchildren, and these flocks are my flocks—in fact, everything you see is mine. But what can I do now about my daughters and their children? 44So come, let's make a covenant, you and I, and it will be a witness to our commitment."

45So Jacob took a stone and set it up as a monument. 46Then he told his family members, "Gather some stones." So they gathered stones and piled them in a heap. Then Jacob and Laban sat down beside the pile of stones to eat a covenant meal. 47To commemorate the event, Laban called the place Jegar-sahadutha (which means "witness pile" in Aramaic), and Jacob called it Galeed (which means "witness pile" in Hebrew).

48Then Laban declared, "This pile of stones will stand as a witness to remind us of the covenant we have made today." This explains why it was called Galeed—"Witness Pile." 49But it was also called Mizpah (which means "watchtower"), for Laban said, "May the LORD keep watch between us to make sure that we keep this covenant when we are out of each other's sight. 50If you mistreat my daughters or if you marry other wives, God will see it even if no one else does. He is a witness to this covenant between us.

51"See this pile of stones," Laban continued, "and see this monument I have set between us. 52They stand between us as witnesses of our vows. I will never pass this pile of stones to harm you, and you must never pass these stones or this monument to harm me. 53I call on the God of our ancestors—the God of your grandfather Abraham and the

31:37
Gen 31:33

31:38
Gen 27:44

31:39
Exod 22:10-13

31:41
Gen 29:30

31:42
Gen 29:32

31:44
Gen 21:27, 30

31:45
Gen 28:18
Josh 24:26-27

31:48
Gen 21:30

31:49
Judg 10:17; 11:29

31:50
Judg 11:10
1 Sam 12:5
Jer 29:23; 42:5

31:52
Gen 31:29, 42

31:53
Gen 24:12

. . . .

dreamed that a woman having her *monthly period* would desecrate the idols by *sitting on them* (cp. Lev 15:19-24).

31:36-42 Jacob retaliated by accusing Laban of false charges and humiliation. Laban now became the defendant, for his charges were demeaning and apparently groundless.

31:40 Jacob, who preferred domestic life (25:27), had for twenty years endured the rigors of the outdoors that Esau had loved.

31:42 *on my side . . . and the fearsome God of Isaac* (or *and the Fear of Isaac*): The God that Isaac feared was with Jacob (31:3), had seen his *hard work*

and faithfulness despite Laban's *abuse*, and had rewarded Jacob. Laban's dream only proved to Jacob that he was in the right.

31:43-44 *Laban* pushed for a treaty to settle the dispute—he felt vulnerable, so he wanted to secure the borders. Jacob did not need a treaty, since God had provided for him and protected him.

31:45-48 The *stone* and the *heap* of stones were a *monument* to the border treaty between the two men, as a witness to future generations. Each man named the monument *witness pile* in his native language. It remained the perpetual border between Israel and the kingdom of Aram (Syria), two nations often at war.

31:49 The witness pile was also called *watchtower*. God would watch over Jacob and Laban and keep them apart, for they could not trust each other.

31:50-53 Laban added some face-saving stipulations to the treaty, using many words to cover up his own untrustworthiness and portray Jacob as the unethical party. He even took credit for the monument Jacob had erected (*this monument I have set*, 31:51). The women and children would be much safer and better cared for with Jacob than they ever were with Laban.

31:53 *the fearsome God of his father, Isaac:* Or *the Fear of his father, Isaac.* See note on 31:42.

31:54
Exod 18:12

31:55
Gen 31:28

32:1
Gen 16:11
2 Kgs 6:16-17

32:2
Josh 13:26; 21:38
2 Sam 2:8

32:3
Gen 27:41-42

32:4
Gen 31:41

32:7
Gen 33:1

32:9
Gen 28:13-15; 31:13

32:10
Gen 24:27

32:11
Gen 27:41

32:12
Gen 28:14

32:18
Gen 32:13

32:20
1 Sam 25:19

God of my grandfather Nahor—to serve as a judge between us."

So Jacob took an oath before the fearsome God of his father, Isaac, to respect the boundary line. 54Then Jacob offered a sacrifice to God there on the mountain and invited everyone to a covenant feast. After they had eaten, they spent the night on the mountain.

55Laban got up early the next morning, and he kissed his grandchildren and his daughters and blessed them. Then he left and returned home.

Jacob Returns Home (32:1–33:20)
Angels Meet Jacob

32 As Jacob started on his way again, angels of God came to meet him. 2When Jacob saw them, he exclaimed, "This is God's camp!" So he named the place Mahanaim.

Jacob Sends Gifts to Esau

3Then Jacob sent messengers ahead to his brother, Esau, who was living in the region of Seir in the land of Edom. 4He told them, "Give this message to my master Esau: 'Humble greetings from your servant Jacob. Until now I have been living with Uncle Laban, 5and now I own cattle, donkeys, flocks of sheep and goats, and many servants, both men and women. I have sent these messengers to inform my lord of my coming, hoping that you will be friendly to me.'"

Jacob Prepares to Meet Esau

6After delivering the message, the messengers returned to Jacob and reported, "We met your brother, Esau, and he is already on his way to meet you—with an army of 400 men!" 7Jacob was terrified at the news. He divided his household, along with the flocks and herds and camels, into two groups. 8He thought, "If Esau meets one group and attacks it, perhaps the other group can escape."

9Then Jacob prayed, "O God of my grandfather Abraham, and God of my father, Isaac—O LORD, you told me, 'Return to your own land and to your relatives.' And you promised me, 'I will treat you kindly.' 10I am not worthy of all the unfailing love and faithfulness you have shown to me, your servant. When I left home and crossed the Jordan River, I owned nothing except a walking stick. Now my household fills two large camps! 11O LORD, please rescue me from the hand of my brother, Esau. I am afraid that he is coming to attack me, along with my wives and children. 12But you promised me, 'I will surely treat you kindly, and I will multiply your descendants until they become as numerous as the sands along the seashore—too many to count.'"

13Jacob stayed where he was for the night. Then he selected these gifts from his possessions to present to his brother, Esau: 14200 female goats, 20 male goats, 200 ewes, 20 rams, 1530 female camels with their young, 40 cows, 10 bulls, 20 female donkeys, and 10 male donkeys. 16He divided these animals into herds and assigned each to different servants. Then he told his servants, "Go ahead of me with the animals, but keep some distance between the herds."

17He gave these instructions to the men leading the first group: "When my brother, Esau, meets you, he will ask, 'Whose servants are you? Where are you going? Who owns these animals?' 18You must reply, 'They belong to your servant Jacob, but they are a gift for his master Esau. Look, he is coming right behind us.'"

19Jacob gave the same instructions to the second and third herdsmen and to all who followed behind the herds: "You must say the same thing to Esau when you meet him. 20And be sure to say, 'Look, your servant Jacob is right behind us.'"

Jacob thought, "I will try to appease him by sending gifts ahead of me. When I see

---

31:55 Verse 31:55 is numbered 32:1 in Hebrew text.

32:1-32 Verses 32:1-32 are numbered 32:2-33 in Hebrew text.

32:1 God assured *Jacob* of his protection at a time when Jacob most needed such consolation. His journey was both a physical return to his homeland and a spiritual return to the land of God's promised blessing. God protects his people and fulfills his plan.

32:2 *This is God's camp!* Jacob must have seen the *angels* that revealed God's presence as a sign of protec-

tion, as with the earlier vision when he was departing the land (28:10-22).
• *Mahanaim* means "two camps." Jacob's company and the company of angels were together in one place.

32:3-5 Apparently inspired by the vision of angels (32:1, Hebrew *mal'akim*), *Jacob sent messengers* (*mal'akim*) into Edom to meet Esau.

32:7-8 Jacob *divided* his company *into two groups* or camps (Hebrew *makhanoth*, related to "Mahanaim" in 32:2) because he was afraid, remembering Esau's character and his threat to kill Jacob (see 25:25; 27:41).

32:9-12 Jacob's prayer is a wonderful example of how to address God. He based his appeal on God's will, reminding God of his relationship with him, his command for him to return to the land, and his promise (32:9). He had a correct attitude of genuine humility and total dependence on God (32:10). Finally, he asked that God *rescue* him from his brother, and he repeated God's promises (see 22:17).

32:13-21 Taking a large portion of the wealth God had blessed him with (some 550 animals), Jacob prepared a gift to appease Esau's anger and gain his favor.

him in person, perhaps he will be friendly to me." 21So the gifts were sent on ahead, while Jacob himself spent that night in the camp.

Jacob Wrestles with God and Becomes Israel

22During the night Jacob got up and took his two wives, his two servant wives, and his eleven sons and crossed the Jabbok River with them. 23After taking them to the other side, he sent over all his possessions.

24This left Jacob all alone in the camp, and a man came and wrestled with him until the dawn began to break. 25When the man saw that he would not win the match, he touched Jacob's hip and wrenched it out of its socket. 26Then the man said, "Let me go, for the dawn is breaking!"

But Jacob said, "I will not let you go unless you bless me."

27"What is your name?" the man asked.

He replied, "Jacob."

28"Your name will no longer be Jacob," the man told him. "From now on you will be called Israel, because you have fought with God and with men and have won."

29"Please tell me your name," Jacob said.

"Why do you want to know my name?" the man replied. Then he blessed Jacob there.

30Jacob named the place Peniel (which means "face of God"), for he said, "I have seen God face to face, yet my life has been spared." 31The sun was rising as Jacob left Peniel, and he was limping because of the injury to his hip. 32(Even today the people of Israel don't eat the tendon near the hip socket because of what happened that night when the man strained the tendon of Jacob's hip.)

couldn't enter P.L. til he acknow-ledged the limits of his self-sufficiency

Jacob and Esau Make Peace

33 Then Jacob looked up and saw Esau coming with his 400 men. So he divided the children among Leah, Rachel, and

(handwritten marginal notes:)
Gen 18:2
32:22 Deut 3:16 / Josh 12:2
32:24 Gen 18:2
32:26 Hos 12:3-4
32:28 Gen 35:10 / 1 Kgs 18:31
32:29 Exod 3:13 / Judg 13:17
32:30 Gen 16:13 / Exod 24:10; 33:20 / Num 12:8 / Deut 5:24; 34:10 / Judg 6:22 / John 1:18
32:31 Judg 8:8-9
33:1 Gen 32:6-7

. . . . _(humble dependance)_ . . . . . _disprit need for God's_ _blessing_

32:22-32 Before Jacob returned to the land God had promised him, God met him, crippled him, and blessed him, changing his name to Israel. This episode was a significant turning point for him.

32:22-24 *The Jabbok River* flows westward to the Jordan Valley, dividing the region of Bashan on the north from Gilead on the south. Wordplays on Jacob's name and character preserve the memory of this encounter. *Jacob* (Hebrew *ya'aqob*), while at *Jabbok* (Hebrew *yabboq*), *wrestled* (Hebrew *way ye'abeq*). Through his fight with an adversary to receive the blessing, Jacob's name would be changed, and his deceptive striving would partially give way to faith as his way of life.

32:24 *a man came:* The narrative unfolds as the event did for Jacob. No details are given about the assailant, who later refused to identify himself (32:29). • *until the dawn:* The darkness fit Jacob's situation and increased the fear and uncertainty that seized him. In the darkness he had no idea who it was—it might have been one of Esau's men, or Laban's.

32:25 *he touched Jacob's hip and wrenched it out of its socket:* Jacob, the deceitful fighter, could fight no more. When his assailant fought him as man to man, Jacob could hold his own. But like so many of his own rivals, he had now more than met his match.

32:26 At daybreak, the significance of this fight began to dawn on Jacob. He realized who his assailant was, and since it was futile to fight, he held on to obtain God's blessing.

32:27 *What is your name?* The Lord's

question was really about Jacob's character, not his identity (cp. 3:9; 4:9). By giving his name, *Jacob* confessed his nature, his way of doing things as "Heel-grabber, Deceiver, Usurper." Before God would bless him, he had to acknowledge who he was, and then God would change his identity.

32:28 *Jacob* sounds like the Hebrew words for "heel" and "deceiver." *Israel* means "God fights." God first had to fight with him, but now God would fight for him. Jacob's name was thus full of promise for Jacob and his descendants. • *you have fought with God and with men:* Through his entire life, Jacob had been seizing God's blessing by his own abilities and by any means possible. Jacob knew the importance of the blessing, but he was too self-sufficient and proud to let the blessing be given to him. He had been fighting God long before this encounter. • *and have won:* He had prevailed in his struggles with Esau and with Laban; now he prevailed in obtaining God's blessing.

32:29 *Jacob* knew who was with him (32:30); the request was his attempt to regain some control. God would not reveal his *name*, which cannot be had on demand.

32:30 *Peniel (which means "face of God"):* The name shows that Jacob recognized the man as a manifestation of God (a *theophany*). • *yet my life has been spared* (or *and I have been rescued*): The saying probably meant that Jacob realized that his prayer to be rescued from Esau (32:11) had been answered, for if he could meet God like this and walk away, he had nothing to fear from Esau. The saying may also

reflect an ancient understanding that no one could see God and live (see Exod 33:20).

32:31 *Peniel:* Hebrew *Penuel,* a variant spelling of Peniel. • *he was limping:* God injured Jacob's hip, thus curtailing his proud self-sufficiency. Since the Lord had restricted his natural strength, Jacob would have to rely on the Lord with greater faith. He had thought that returning to his land would be a matter of outwitting his brother once again (32:3-21), but here at the land's threshold he met its true proprietor. He would get the land, but only if God fought for him. Self-sufficiency—trying to achieve the blessing by our own strength or by the ways of the world—will not suffice. If we persist, God may have to cripple our self-sufficiency to make us trust him more.

32:32 The story includes a dietary restriction for Israel that became a custom but was not put into law. This custom helped preserve the memory of the story. Observant Jews still refuse to eat the tendons of an animal's hindquarters.

33:1-17 Jacob's long-anticipated meeting with his brother Esau turned out far better than he had feared. Esau's changed heart is an example of how "God fights" (32:28). Earlier, he had cared little about the birthright (25:32-34); now he cared little for old grudges. Jacob recognized that God had intervened.

33:1-2 Jacob's identity had been changed (32:27-28), but he had not yet learned to live up to the new name; he still showed the favoritism that divides families. He lined up his family and his possessions in the order of their

33:3
Gen 18:2; 42:6
33:4
Gen 45:14-15
33:5
Gen 48:9
33:8
Gen 32:14-16

his two servant wives. ²He put the servant wives and their children at the front, Leah and her children next, and Rachel and Joseph last. ³Then Jacob went on ahead. As he approached his brother, he bowed to the ground seven times before him. ⁴Then Esau ran to meet him and embraced him, threw his arms around his neck, and kissed him. And they both wept.

⁵Then Esau looked at the women and children and asked, "Who are these people with you?"

"These are the children God has graciously given to me, your servant," Jacob replied. ⁶Then the servant wives came forward with their children and bowed before him. ⁷Next came Leah with her children,

and they bowed before him. Finally, Joseph and Rachel came forward and bowed before him.

⁸"And what were all the flocks and herds I met as I came?" Esau asked.

Jacob replied, "They are a gift, my lord, to ensure your friendship."

⁹"My brother, I have plenty," Esau answered. "Keep what you have for yourself."

¹⁰But Jacob insisted, "No, if I have found favor with you, please accept this gift from me. And what a relief to see your friendly smile. It is like seeing the face of God! ¹¹Please take this gift I have brought you, for God has been very gracious to me. I have more than enough." And because Jacob insisted, Esau finally accepted the gift.

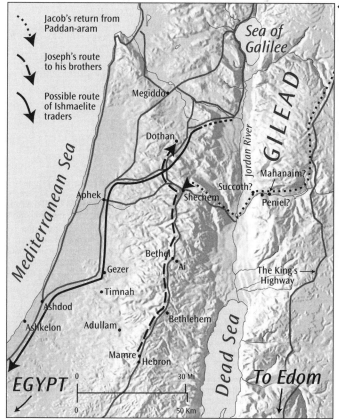

◀ **Jacob's Family in Canaan (32:1–38:30).** When Jacob returned to Canaan from Haran, after making a treaty with Laban at Mizpah (31:48-49), he met angels at MAHANAIM (32:1-2) and wrestled with God at PENIEL (32:22-32). After making peace with Esau (33:1-16), Jacob traveled to SUCCOTH (33:17) and then SHECHEM (33:18-20; cp. 12:6-7). After the conflict with the people of Shechem (ch 34), at God's instruction Jacob moved to BETHEL (35:1-15; cp. 12:8; 13:1-4; 28:10-22). After Jacob left Bethel, Rachel died in childbirth on the way to Ephrath (=BETHLEHEM, 35:16-20; cp. 1 Sam 10:2; Jer 31:15). Jacob continued to HEBRON (35:27), where he was reunited with his father. There he settled, and from there Joseph later went to find his brothers (37:14). Joseph's route to SHECHEM and then DOTHAN is shown (37:14-17), as is the possible route of the Ishmaelite traders from GILEAD to EGYPT (37:25-36). ADULLAM, where Judah moved (38:1), is also shown.

and to Esau as his lord (33:8, 13-15); Esau called Jacob "my brother" (33:9). Jacob was cautiously warding off any possible retaliation by reversing the words of the oracle (25:23).

33:7 Among Jacob's sons, only *Joseph* is named; he was Jacob's favorite son and the recipient of the blessing.

33:10 Jacob knew that Esau's friendly greeting was God's work, secured at Peniel when he saw God face to face.

33:11 *this gift I have brought you* (literally *my blessing*): Jacob perceived Esau as a threat and tried to appease him with a gift (cp. 2 Kgs 17:3-4; 18:7, 14; 2 Chr 28:21), perhaps in a guilty attempt to undo the past. Jacob would not take no for an answer.

importance to him, with the slave wives and their children in front (to face danger first), Leah's group behind them, and Rachel and Joseph in the back, where it was safest.

33:3-13 Even though Jacob had nothing to fear, he was afraid and tried to appease his brother. He assumed the role of a servant before royalty by bowing

(33:3), using an honorific title (33:8, 13), making introductions (33:6-7), and presenting gifts (33:8).

33:4 Esau's friendly greeting was an answer to prayer (32:11). God had rescued Jacob from Esau's revenge.

33:5 *your servant:* In talking with his brother, Jacob continued to refer to himself as Esau's servant (also 33:14)

12"Well," Esau said, "let's be going. I will lead the way."

13But Jacob replied, "You can see, my lord, that some of the children are very young, and the flocks and herds have their young, too. If they are driven too hard, even for one day, all the animals could die. 14Please, my lord, go ahead of your servant. We will follow slowly, at a pace that is comfortable for the livestock and the children. I will meet you at Seir."

15"All right," Esau said, "but at least let me assign some of my men to guide and protect you."

Jacob responded, "That's not necessary. It's enough that you've received me warmly, my lord!"

16So Esau turned around and started back to Seir that same day. 17Jacob, on the other hand, traveled on to Succoth. There he built himself a house and made shelters for his livestock. That is why the place was named Succoth (which means "shelters").

Jacob Moves to Shechem

18Later, having traveled all the way from Paddan-aram, Jacob arrived safely at the town of Shechem, in the land of Canaan. There he set up camp outside the town. 19Jacob bought the plot of land where he camped from the family of Hamor, the fa-

ther of Shechem, for 100 pieces of silver. 20And there he built an altar and named it El-Elohe-Israel.

The Danger of Intermarriage (34:1-31)
Dinah Is Defiled

34 One day Dinah, the daughter of Jacob and Leah, went to visit some of the young women who lived in the area. 2But when the local prince, Shechem son of Hamor the Hivite, saw Dinah, he seized her and raped her. 3But then he fell in love with her, and he tried to win her affection with tender words. 4He said to his father, Hamor, "Get me this young girl. I want to marry her."

5Soon Jacob heard that Shechem had defiled his daughter, Dinah. But since his sons were out in the fields herding his livestock, he said nothing until they returned. 6Hamor, Shechem's father, came to discuss the matter with Jacob. 7Meanwhile, Jacob's sons had come in from the field as soon as they heard what had happened. They were shocked and furious that their sister had been raped. Shechem had done a disgraceful thing against Jacob's family, something that should never be done.

Intermarriage with Shechem Negotiated

8Hamor tried to speak with Jacob and his sons. "My son Shechem is truly in love with

33:14 Gen 32:3
33:17 Judg 8:5, 14; Ps 60:6
33:18 Gen 12:6; 25:20
33:19 Josh 24:32; John 4:5
34:1 Gen 30:21
34:2 Deut 21:14; 2 Sam 13:14
34:4 Gen 21:21
34:7 2 Sam 13:12

. . . .

33:12-15 Despite Esau's apparent magnanimity, Jacob was wary and cleverly avoided traveling with his brother. • *I will meet you at Seir:* Jacob's lie manifests his old character, living by deception rather than by faith.

33:16-17 Instead of following *Esau* south *to Seir* as promised, *Jacob* again deceived his brother, then headed in the opposite direction *to Succoth,* east of the Jordan River and north of the Jabbok.

33:18-20 These verses form an epilogue to Jacob's adventures outside the land. He returned in peace with a large family and many possessions. • *Jacob,* like Abraham, *built an altar* at *Shechem* (see 12:6-8) and purchased land *from the family of Hamor.*

33:19 *100 pieces of silver:* Hebrew *100 kesitahs;* the value or weight of the kesitah is no longer known.

33:20 *El-Elohe-Israel* means "God, the God of Israel." The name of the altar commemorated Jacob's relationship with God. Jacob publicly proclaimed that God was his God, and that God had led him back to the land he would inherit.

34:1-31 Once Jacob and his family settled in the land, the Canaanite pres-

ence became a threat. This account is a stern warning to the Israelites about the possibility of their being defiled by the Canaanites. The nation of Israel was later commanded not to intermarry or make treaties with them, for they were a corrupt and corrupting people. This chapter implicitly warns against becoming familiar with the way they lived (34:1-2). It also taught Israel that in dealing with the Canaanites, they were to keep their integrity and not use the holy things of the covenant for deception and slaughter (34:13); Israel's reputation was at stake in the land (34:30). For their ruthless violence, Simeon and Levi were passed over in the birthright blessing (49:5-7).

34:1-2 As far as we know, *Dinah* was Jacob's only daughter (30:21). Her seemingly innocent but unguarded *visit* to *some of the young women who lived in the area* was actually naive and foolish, because the local Hivites were very corrupt, not safe or trustworthy. • *Shechem . . . seized her and raped her:* Shechem violated and debased Dinah, so she had no chance for a proper marriage.

34:3-4 While Shechem's intense feelings for Dinah made him willing to undergo significant hardship (34:11-12, 17-18, 24), the way he showed his "love" for her was selfish, impetuous, and in viola-

tion of customary decency (cp. Judg 14:2; see 1 Cor 13:4-7; 1 Jn 4:10). His character illustrated why Israel needed to remain separate from the Canaanites.

34:5-7 Jacob's response to this crime is surprising. When he *heard* that Dinah had been *defiled,* he said nothing about it until *his sons* came home. Because Jacob did not act, his sons did, though without the wisdom and integrity necessary for justice. Dinah's full brothers *were shocked and furious* that Shechem had done such a *disgraceful thing against Jacob's family* (literally *a disgraceful thing in Israel;* this is the first use of the name *Israel* to describe the family). This sexual crime was an outrage against the community of God's people and deserved punishment, but the leader of the clan did nothing.

34:8-10 *Hamor* proposed an alliance of intermarriage with the prospect of mutual economic benefit, but God had already promised Jacob everything, including the land (34:10; see 14:21-24). Hamor wanted to gain control of Israel's wealth (34:23); no good could come of trusting the defiling Canaanites. For some of these reasons, intermarriage with Canaanites was not allowed under the law (see Exod 23:27-33; Deut 7:1-5)—unless, of course, they came to faith (see Josh 2:1-15; 6:23-25; Matt 1:5).

34:10
Gen 33:19

34:12
Exod 22:16

34:13
Gen 27:36

34:14
Gen 17:14

34:19
Gen 29:20

34:22
Gen 34:15

34:25
Gen 49:5-7
Josh 5:8

34:28
Gen 43:18

34:30
Gen 13:7; 49:5-7
Exod 5:21
2 Sam 10:6
1 Chr 16:19

35:1
Gen 12:8; 28:19

your daughter," he said. "Please let him marry her. 9In fact, let's arrange other marriages, too. You give us your daughters for our sons, and we will give you our daughters for your sons. 10And you may live among us; the land is open to you! Settle here and trade with us. And feel free to buy property in the area."

11Then Shechem himself spoke to Dinah's father and brothers. "Please be kind to me, and let me marry her," he begged. "I will give you whatever you ask. 12No matter what dowry or gift you demand, I will gladly pay it—just give me the girl as my wife."

13But since Shechem had defiled their sister, Dinah, Jacob's sons responded deceitfully to Shechem and his father, Hamor. 14They said to them, "We couldn't possibly allow this, because you're not circumcised. It would be a disgrace for our sister to marry a man like you! 15But here is a solution. If every man among you will be circumcised like we are, 16then we will give you our daughters, and we'll take your daughters for ourselves. We will live among you and become one people. 17But if you don't agree to be circumcised, we will take her and be on our way."

18Hamor and his son Shechem agreed to their proposal. 19Shechem wasted no time in acting on this request, for he wanted Jacob's daughter desperately. Shechem was a highly respected member of his family, 20and he went with his father, Hamor, to present this proposal to the leaders at the town gate.

21"These men are our friends," they said. "Let's invite them to live here among us and trade freely. Look, the land is large enough to hold them. We can take their daughters as wives and let them marry ours. 22But they will consider staying here and becoming one people with us only if all of our men are circumcised, just as they are. 23But if we do

this, all their livestock and possessions will eventually be ours. Come, let's agree to their terms and let them settle here among us."

Jacob's Sons Destroy Shechem

24So all the men in the town council agreed with Hamor and Shechem, and every male in the town was circumcised. 25But three days later, when their wounds were still sore, two of Jacob's sons, Simeon and Levi, who were Dinah's full brothers, took their swords and entered the town without opposition. Then they slaughtered every male there, 26including Hamor and his son Shechem. They killed them with their swords, then took Dinah from Shechem's house and returned to their camp.

27Meanwhile, the rest of Jacob's sons arrived. Finding the men slaughtered, they plundered the town because their sister had been defiled there. 28They seized all the flocks and herds and donkeys—everything they could lay their hands on, both inside the town and outside in the fields. 29They looted all their wealth and plundered their houses. They also took all their little children and wives and led them away as captives.

30Afterward Jacob said to Simeon and Levi, "You have ruined me! You've made me stink among all the people of this land—among all the Canaanites and Perizzites. We are so few that they will join forces and crush us. I will be ruined, and my entire household will be wiped out!"

31"But why should we let him treat our sister like a prostitute?" they retorted angrily.

Jacob's Return to Bethel (35:1-15)

35 Then God said to Jacob, "Get ready and move to Bethel and settle there. Build an altar there to the God who appeared to you when you fled from your brother, Esau."

34:13-17 Dinah's brothers *responded* to the proposal without waiting for Jacob to respond, and they acted *deceitfully*. They may not have thought that *Shechem* and his people would ever agree to the rite of circumcision, but they knew what they would do if the Canaanites accepted (34:25).

34:18-24 The Canaanites accepted the stipulation and *every male in the town was circumcised*. This was not just to allow Shechem to marry Dinah, but to give them the opportunity to acquire everything that Jacob possessed (34:23).

34:25-29 When *Simeon and Levi* used

circumcision to deceive and slaughter the Canaanites, they showed disdain for the sign of the covenant. Their slaughter of all the males and their plunder of the city was not justice, but brutal and excessive revenge. In their moral outrage and desire to right the wrong, they should have demanded compensation (see Exod 22:16-17; Deut 22:28-29). Instead, their passionate act of rage cost them their birthright blessing (49:5-7).

34:30 *Jacob* responded again out of fear of what would happen to him, but God caused *the people of this land* to fear him instead (35:5).

35:1-29 This chapter highlights God's promises, Jacob's vow, and the transition to Jacob's sons' carrying on the covenant. Deborah, Rachel, and Isaac all died, marking the end of an era and of the account of Isaac's family (25:19–35:29). • Idols were removed (35:1-4) and pure worship was established (35:6-7). During this transition, the faith had to be revitalized so that the covenant could be carried forward by Jacob's sons.

35:1-7 *Jacob* returned *to Bethel*, about fifteen miles south of Shechem, to complete the vows he had made at Bethel (28:20-22).

²So Jacob told everyone in his household, "Get rid of all your pagan idols, purify yourselves, and put on clean clothing. ³We are now going to Bethel, where I will build an altar to the God who answered my prayers when I was in distress. He has been with me wherever I have gone."

⁴So they gave Jacob all their pagan idols and earrings, and he buried them under the great tree near Shechem. ⁵As they set out, a terror from God spread over the people in all the towns of that area, so no one attacked Jacob's family.

⁶Eventually, Jacob and his household arrived at Luz (also called Bethel) in Canaan. ⁷Jacob built an altar there and named the place El-bethel (which means "God of Bethel"), because God had appeared to him there when he was fleeing from his brother, Esau.

⁸Soon after this, Rebekah's old nurse, Deborah, died. She was buried beneath the oak tree in the valley below Bethel. Ever since, the tree has been called Allon-bacuth (which means "oak of weeping").

⁹Now that Jacob had returned from Paddan-aram, God appeared to him again at Bethel. God blessed him, ¹⁰saying, "Your name is Jacob, but you will not be called Jacob any longer. From now on your name will be Israel." So God renamed him Israel.

¹¹Then God said, "I am El-Shaddai—'God ᵍAlmighty.' Be fruitful and multiply. You will become a great nation, even ʰmany nations. Kings will be among your descendants! ¹²And I will give you the land I once gave to Abraham and Isaac. Yes, I will give it to you and your ⁱdescendants after you." ¹³Then God went up from the place where he had spoken to Jacob.

¹⁴Jacob set up a stone pillar to mark the place where God had spoken to him. Then he poured wine over it as an offering to God and anointed the pillar with olive oil. ¹⁵And Jacob named the place Bethel (which means "house of God"), because God had spoken to him there.

Jacob Moves to Mamre (35:16-29)
Rachel Dies in Childbirth
¹⁶Leaving Bethel, Jacob and his clan moved on toward Ephrath. But Rachel went into labor while they were still some distance away. Her labor pains were intense. ¹⁷After a very hard delivery, the midwife finally exclaimed, "Don't be afraid—you have another son!" ¹⁸Rachel was about to die, but with her last breath she named the baby Ben-oni (which means "son of my sorrow"). The baby's father, however, called him Benjamin (which means "son of my right hand"). ¹⁹So Rachel died and was buried on the way to Ephrath (that is, Bethlehem). ²⁰Jacob set up a stone monument over Rachel's grave, and it can be seen there to this day.

Reuben's Transgression
²¹Then Jacob traveled on and camped beyond Migdal-eder. ²²While he was living there, Reuben had intercourse with Bilhah, his father's concubine, and Jacob soon heard about it.

35:2
Gen 31:19
35:3
Gen 28:15-22
35:4
Exod 32:3
Judg 8:24
Hos 2:13
35:5
Exod 15:16
35:6
Gen 28:19
35:7
Gen 28:19
35:8
Gen 24:59
35:9
Gen 28:13
35:10
Gen 32:28
35:11
Gen 12:2; 17:1, 6
ᵍshadday (7706)
▸ Gen 48:3
ʰqahal (6951)
▸ Deut 23:2
35:12
Gen 13:15; 28:13
ⁱzera' (2233)
▸ Gen 48:4
35:13
Judg 6:21; 13:20
35:14
Gen 28:18-19
35:16
Ruth 4:11
35:17
Gen 30:22-24
35:18
Gen 49:27
35:19
Gen 48:7
35:22
Gen 49:4
Lev 18:8
1 Chr 5:1

· ·

35:2-4 Jacob had vowed wholehearted devotion to the Lord (28:20-22); establishing this required that his family remove all *pagan idols* and cease their devotion to other gods. God permits no rivals; only the Lord was to be their God (cp. Josh 5:1-9).

35:3 *He has been with me wherever I have gone:* God had fulfilled his promises (28:15; 31:3), so Jacob must fulfill his vow.

35:5 *a terror from God:* People had heard about the massacre of Shechem (34:25-30).

35:6-7 Jacob *built an altar* at *Bethel* as God had instructed (35:1; cp. 12:8).

35:9-15 *At Bethel*, God confirmed the promise he had made there earlier; he reiterated Jacob's change of *name* from *Jacob* to *Israel* as proof that the blessing had been given.

35:10 Jacob's name change is reiterated and confirmed (cp. 41:32). • *Jacob* sounds like the Hebrew words for "heel" and "deceiver." *Israel* means "God fights."

35:11-12 God's reference to himself as *God Almighty* assured Jacob that his promise could and would be fulfilled. At Bethel, God had promised that Jacob would have descendants in the land (cp. 28:13-14); here he added that his descendants would include *kings* (see 17:6).

35:14-15 In fulfilling his vow (28:20-22), Jacob's actions were almost identical to his actions in the earlier experience at Bethel (cp. 28:16-19).

35:16-20 Benjamin's birth completed the family, but it was a sorrowful event because *Rachel died* in childbirth (see note on 31:32).

35:18 *Rachel* found the name *son of my sorrow* appropriate to the situation, but Jacob did not want such a sad name for his son, so he changed it to *son of my right hand*. Jacob thus turned the day of sorrow into a day of hope that gave his son the prospect of success.

35:19 Jacob did not carry Rachel's body to the family tomb at Machpelah

(23:1-20; 25:9; 49:30; 50:13), but buried her in the territory that would be Benjamin's (see Josh 18:21-28; 1 Sam 10:2).

35:20 *it can be seen there to this day:* This seems to be a later editorial comment by someone who was living in the land after the conquest and giving directions to the tomb (see Introduction to Genesis: "Composition," p. 16).

35:21 *Jacob:* Hebrew *Israel;* also in 35:22a. The names "Jacob" and "Israel" are often interchanged throughout the Old Testament, referring sometimes to the individual patriarch and sometimes to the nation.

35:22 *Reuben had intercourse with Bilhah,* thus defiling his father's marriage bed. Perhaps Reuben, as the oldest son, was trying to replace his father as head of the clan by a pagan procedure (cp. 2 Sam 16:15-22), but by this action he lost his birthright (see 49:3-4). • *Jacob soon heard about it,* but he again delayed his response (see 49:3-4; cp. 34:5).

35:23-26
//1 Chr 2:1-2
35:23
Gen 29:31-35;
30:18-20
35:24
Gen 30:24
35:25
Gen 30:5-8
35:26
Gen 30:10-13
35:27
Gen 13:18; 23:2
35:28
Gen 25:7-8, 20
36:1
Gen 25:30
36:2
Gen 26:34
1 Chr 1:40
36:3
Gen 25:13

The Twelve Sons of Jacob

These are the names of the twelve sons of Jacob:

23The sons of Leah were Reuben (Jacob's oldest son), Simeon, Levi, Judah, Issachar, and Zebulun.

24The sons of Rachel were Joseph and Benjamin.

25The sons of Bilhah, Rachel's servant, were Dan and Naphtali.

26The sons of Zilpah, Leah's servant, were Gad and Asher.

These are the names of the sons who were born to Jacob at Paddan-aram.

Jacob Returns to Isaac; Isaac's Death

27So Jacob returned to his father, Isaac, in Mamre, which is near Kiriath-arba (now called Hebron), where Abraham and Isaac had both lived as foreigners. 28Isaac lived for 180 years. 29Then he breathed his last and died at a ripe old age, joining his ancestors in death. And his sons, Esau and Jacob, buried him.

10. THE ACCOUNT OF ESAU'S DESCENDANTS (36:1–37:1)

Esau's Life

36 This is the account of the descendants of Esau (also known as Edom). 2Esau married two young women from Canaan: Adah, the daughter of Elon the Hittite; and Oholibamah, the daughter of Anah and granddaughter of Zibeon the Hivite. 3He also married his cousin Basemath, who was the daughter of Ishmael and the

. . . .

Altars (35:1-15)

Gen 8:20-21; 12:7-8;
22:9-14; 26:25;
33:20
Exod 20:24-26; 24:4-
5; 27:1-8
Josh 22:10-34
1 Kgs 18:20-40
2 Kgs 23:10-20
Hos 8:11
Matt 5:23-24
Heb 13:10-14
Rev 6:9; 8:3-5

The first recorded altar was built by Noah (8:20-21), though Cain and Abel gave the first offerings (4:3-4). The patriarchs built numerous altars (see 8:20-21; 12:7-8; 13:4, 18; 22:9; 26:25; 33:20; 35:1, 14-15). These altars designated sacred sites of divine revelation and personal land claims in the Promised Land, both north (in Shechem) and south (in Beersheba). Altars were made of stone, earth, brick, or metal and wood. Their table-like form allowed smoke to rise unhindered. Intended as memorials or places for sacrifice, an altar was the most common image of worship in the OT and in the wider ancient world. The typical altar was on a raised platform accessed by a ramp or stairway; this elevated the sacrificial worship toward heaven. The four horns on the corners of the altar marked off the sacred space of meeting between divine and human realms. Through sacrifice and burning, the offering was transferred from the visible to the invisible world. Altars were both religious monuments and places of refuge where fugitives could find asylum (see Exod 21:14).

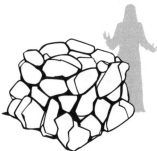

Jesus unites the various aspects of the altar imagery in himself as high priest, sacrificial lamb, and altar (see Heb 4:14-15; 7:24, 27; 9:14, 26; 10:10; 13:10, 12). Jesus anticipated his own sacrifice in his reference to the blood of martyrs (see Matt 23:35; Luke 11:51). The enthroned Lamb in Revelation removes the need for temple and altar (Rev 21:22). The cross is the final altar; Jesus' death is the new covenant memorial and his body is the place of sanctuary (Heb 13:10).

◄ **Altars of the Patriarchs (35:1-15).** Several of the patriarchs built altars, including Noah (8:20), Abraham (12:7, 8; 13:18; 22:9), Isaac (26:25), and Jacob (33:20; 35:7). These altars were probably made of piles of uncut stone, as God later instructed Israel (Exod 20:25; Deut 27:5-6; cp. Josh 8:30-31).

. . . .

35:23-26 The twelve sons became leaders of the twelve tribes of Israel. Their names are the firstfruits of the nation.

35:27-29 *Esau and Jacob* (listed here in ordinary birth order) came together—probably for the first time since they had reconciled (33:16-17)—to bury *Isaac* in *Hebron* (see 13:18; 23:1-2, 17-19).

36:1-43 The book turns to the accounts of Isaac's sons, concluding the unchosen line of Esau (ch 36) before proceeding with the chosen line of Jacob (ch 37).

36:1-8 The *account* of *Esau* stresses

two points. First, Esau's sons were *born . . . in the land of Canaan* (36:5) before he moved to *Seir* (36:8). Jacob's children, by contrast, were almost all born outside the land but then moved into it. God was giving the land to Jacob and his descendants and so made room for them by providing for Esau in a different place. Second, Esau's other name was *Edom*. Israel often struggled with the Edomites (see 1 Sam 21:7; 22:9-22; Obad 1:1-21; see also "Herod the Great" at Matt 2:1-20, p. 1578).

36:2-3 Esau's three wives—*Adah, Oholibamah,* and *Basemath*—are listed. Two of these wives' names are different from those listed earlier (26:34; 28:9). Perhaps the others died, or Esau favored these three among a total of six, or these were just different names for the same three. There is not enough information to decide.

36:2 *Oholibamah* was a great-granddaughter of Seir the Horite, whose descendants lived in Edom when Esau went to live there (36:20, 25).

sister of Nebaioth. 4Adah gave birth to a son named Eliphaz for Esau. Basemath gave birth to a son named Reuel. 5Oholibamah gave birth to sons named Jeush, Jalam, and Korah. All these sons were born to Esau in the land of Canaan.

6Esau took his wives, his children, and his entire household, along with his livestock and cattle—all the wealth he had acquired in the land of Canaan—and moved away from his brother, Jacob. 7There was not enough land to support them both because of all the livestock and possessions they had acquired. 8So Esau (also known as Edom) settled in the hill country of Seir.

Esau's Descendants

9This is the account of Esau's descendants, the Edomites, who lived in the hill country of Seir.

10These are the names of Esau's sons: Eliphaz, the son of Esau's wife Adah; and Reuel, the son of Esau's wife Basemath.

11The descendants of Eliphaz were Teman, Omar, Zepho, Gatam, and Kenaz. 12Timna, the concubine of Esau's son Eliphaz, gave birth to a son named Amalek. These are the descendants of Esau's wife Adah.

13The descendants of Reuel were Nahath, Zerah, Shammah, and Mizzah. These are the descendants of Esau's wife Basemath.

14Esau also had sons through Oholibamah, the daughter of Anah and granddaughter of Zibeon. Their names were Jeush, Jalam, and Korah.

15These are the descendants of Esau who became the leaders of various clans:

The descendants of Esau's oldest son, Eliphaz, became the leaders of the clans of Teman, Omar, Zepho, Kenaz, 16Korah, Gatam, and Amalek. These are the clan leaders in the land of Edom who descended from Eliphaz. All these were descendants of Esau's wife Adah.

17The descendants of Esau's son Reuel became the leaders of the clans of Nahath, Zerah, Shammah, and Mizzah. These are the clan leaders in the land of Edom who descended from Reuel. All these were descendants of Esau's wife Basemath.

18The descendants of Esau and his wife Oholibamah became the leaders of the clans of Jeush, Jalam, and Korah. These are the clan leaders who descended from Esau's wife Oholibamah, the daughter of Anah.

19These are the clans descended from Esau (also known as Edom), identified by their clan leaders.

Original Peoples of Edom

20These are the names of the tribes that descended from Seir the Horite. They lived in the land of Edom: Lotan, Shobal, Zibeon, Anah, 21Dishon, Ezer, and Dishan. These were the Horite clan leaders, the descendants of Seir, who lived in the land of Edom.

22The descendants of Lotan were Hori and Hemam. Lotan's sister was named Timna.

23The descendants of Shobal were Alvan, Manahath, Ebal, Shepho, and Onam.

24The descendants of Zibeon were Aiah and Anah. (This is the Anah who discovered the hot springs in the wilderness while he was grazing his father's donkeys.)

25The descendants of Anah were his son, Dishon, and his daughter, Oholibamah.

26The descendants of Dishon were Hemdan, Eshban, Ithran, and Keran.

27The descendants of Ezer were Bilhan, Zaavan, and Akan.

28The descendants of Dishan were Uz and Aran.

29So these were the leaders of the Horite clans: Lotan, Shobal, Zibeon, Anah, 30Dishon, Ezer, and Dishan. The Horite clans are named after their clan leaders, who lived in the land of Seir.

Rulers of Edom

31These are the kings who ruled in the land of Edom before any king ruled over the Israelites:

36:4
1 Chr 1:35
36:5
Gen 36:18
36:7
Gen 13:6
36:8
Gen 14:6; 25:30
36:9
Gen 36:43
36:10-14
//1 Chr 1:35-37
36:19
1 Chr 1:35
36:20-28
//1 Chr 1:38-42
36:20
Gen 14:6
Deut 2:12, 22
36:25
Gen 36:2, 5, 14, 18
1 Chr 1:41
36:27
1 Chr 1:38, 42
36:29-30
Gen 36:20
36:31-43
//1 Chr 1:43-54

. . . .

36:7-8 *Esau*, like Lot, left for the eastern land (cp. 13:5-6).

36:9-43 This passage begins a second *account of Esau's descendants* (36:1); it traces the family to subsequent generations and alliances.

36:9-14 The *descendants* of Esau's five sons are named.

36:15-19 Thirteen of Esau's descendants had positions as *leaders of various clans*. A picture begins to emerge of Esau as a grand overlord of tribes (cp. 36:40-43).

36:20-30 *Seir the Horite* was an early inhabitant of the land; his descendants populated the region until Esau moved in and displaced them (Deut 2:12).

36:26 Hebrew *Dishan*, a variant spelling of Dishon; cp. 36:21, 28.

36:31-39 It is not clear how these *kings* of *Edom* were related to Esau. The clans in Edom followed the same pattern of organization as the later tribes of Israel. They eventually chose a king from one of their tribes and carried on a line of succession from him.

36:31 *before any king ruled over the Israelites* (Or *before an Israelite king ruled over them*): This editorial note was

37:1
Gen 17:8; 28:4
37:2
Gen 35:22-26; 41:46
37:3
Gen 37:23, 32; 44:20
37:4
Gen 27:41
37:5
Gen 28:12
Num 12:6
Dan 2:1

³²Bela son of Beor, who ruled in Edom from his city of Dinhabah. ³³When Bela died, Jobab son of Zerah from Bozrah became king in his place. ³⁴When Jobab died, Husham from the land of the Temanites became king in his place. ³⁵When Husham died, Hadad son of Bedad became king in his place and ruled from the city of Avith. He was the one who defeated the Midianites in the land of Moab. ³⁶When Hadad died, Samlah from the city of Masrekah became king in his place. ³⁷When Samlah died, Shaul from the city of Rehoboth-on-the-River became king in his place. ³⁸When Shaul died, Baal-hanan son of Acbor became king in his place. ³⁹When Baal-hanan son of Acbor died, Hadad became king in his place and ruled from the city of Pau. His wife was Mehetabel, the daughter of Matred and granddaughter of Me-zahab.

⁴⁰These are the names of the leaders of the clans descended from Esau, who lived in the places named for them: Timna, Alvah, Jetheth, ⁴¹Oholibamah, Elah, Pinon, ⁴²Kenaz, Teman, Mibzar, ⁴³Magdiel, and Iram. These are the leaders of the clans of Edom, listed according to their settlements in the land they occupied. They all descended from Esau, the ancestor of the Edomites.

Recapitulation and Contrast with Jacob

37 So Jacob settled again in the land of Canaan, where his father had lived as a foreigner.

11. THE ACCOUNT OF JACOB'S DESCENDANTS (37:2–50:26)
Joseph's Dreams of Prominence (37:2-11)

²This is the account of Jacob and his family. When Joseph was seventeen years old, he often tended his father's flocks. He worked for his half brothers, the sons of his father's wives Bilhah and Zilpah. But Joseph reported to his father some of the bad things his brothers were doing.

³Jacob loved Joseph more than any of his other children because Joseph had been born to him in his old age. So one day Jacob had a special gift made for Joseph—a beautiful robe. ⁴But his brothers hated Joseph because their father loved him more than the rest of them. They couldn't say a kind word to him.

⁵One night Joseph had a dream, and when he told his brothers about it, they hated him more than ever. ⁶"Listen to this dream," he

---

probably inserted into the text during Israel's monarchy (see note on 35:20).

36:39 Hadad: As in some Hebrew manuscripts, Samaritan Pentateuch, and Syriac version (see also 1 Chr 1:50); most Hebrew manuscripts read *Hadar.*

36:40-43 These chiefs descended from Esau, who was a great and powerful overlord. As father of the Edomites, he ruled over clans and regions, with eleven chiefs descended from him. By separating from Jacob, Esau was beginning to shake Jacob's yoke from his neck (27:39-40).

37:1 In ch 36, Esau was well on his way to power and prosperity; by contrast, *Jacob,* still waiting for the promise, *settled* in the land *as a foreigner,* like *his father.* He was still a temporary resident with a single family. Worldly greatness often comes more swiftly than spiritual greatness. Waiting for the promised spiritual blessing while others prosper is a test of patience, faith, and perseverance.

37:2–50:26 The story of Joseph and his brothers comprises a separate unit in Genesis, distinct in tone and emphasis from the preceding material. It traces one continuous series of episodes with Joseph at their center. • Cycles of repeated motifs structure the entire Joseph account. The themes are closely related to those found in wisdom books such as Proverbs, Ecclesiastes, and Daniel. Wisdom literature assures the faithful that God brings good out of evil and joy out of pain—if not in this life, then certainly in the life to come. Though the wicked may prosper for a time, the righteous should hold fast to their integrity because a higher, more enduring principle of life is realized through obedience to God. Everyone who aspires to leadership in God's plan should observe how wisdom led to Joseph's success. Christ Jesus embodied the life of wisdom portrayed here as no one else could, for he is the wisdom of God. • Judah is also an important character in the story. He began as irresponsible and mean-spirited as his brothers; but he truly repented, put his life on the line to ransom a child for his father, and received a very important inheritance.

37:2 *The account of Jacob and his family* tells of *Joseph* and his brothers. Jacob is still prominent, but the focus is on Joseph, who is introduced as an obedient seventeen-year-old son. • *Joseph reported . . . the bad things his brothers were doing:* Bringing a bad report has never been popular, but it was the right thing to do and shows that Joseph was faithful from the beginning. As the story progresses, we see more of his brothers' wickedness displayed until, like Cain, they tried to eliminate the brother who pleased God.

37:3 Jacob: Hebrew *Israel;* also in 37:13. See note on 35:21. • Jacob *loved Joseph more* because *Joseph had been born to him in his old age* and because he was the first son of his favorite wife, Rachel. • *A beautiful robe* (traditionally rendered *a coat of many colors;* the exact meaning of the Hebrew is uncertain): Jacob gave Joseph this robe to demonstrate that he intended to grant him the largest portion of the inheritance.

37:4 Jacob's favoritism toward Joseph inflamed his other sons' hatred of their brother. Just as Isaac's and Rebekah's favoritism had separated their family, Jacob's favoritism would separate him from his son Joseph.

37:5-11 God confirmed his choice of this faithful son as the eventual leader of the whole family through two symbolic dreams. This is the first of three *dream* sequences in chs 37–50 (see 40:1–41:36; cp. 15:13; 20:3; 28:12-15; 31:24). Dreams carried weight as a form of divine communication, especially if the dream revelation was given twice. Everyone would have taken Joseph's dreams seriously.

said. 7"We were out in the field, tying up bundles of grain. Suddenly my bundle stood up, and your bundles all gathered around and bowed low before mine!"

8His brothers responded, "So you think you will be our king, do you? Do you actually think you will reign over us?" And they hated him all the more because of his dreams and the way he talked about them.

9Soon Joseph had another dream, and again he told his brothers about it. "Listen, I have had another dream," he said. "The sun, moon, and eleven stars bowed low before me!"

10This time he told the dream to his father as well as to his brothers, but his father scolded him. "What kind of dream is that?" he asked. "Will your mother and I and your brothers actually come and bow to the ground before you?" 11But while his brothers were jealous of Joseph, his father wondered what the dreams meant.

Joseph Sold into Slavery in Egypt (37:12-36)

12Soon after this, Joseph's brothers went to pasture their father's flocks at Shechem. 13When they had been gone for some time, Jacob said to Joseph, "Your brothers are pasturing the sheep at Shechem. Get ready, and I will send you to them."

"I'm ready to go," Joseph replied.

14"Go and see how your brothers and the flocks are getting along," Jacob said. "Then come back and bring me a report." So Jacob sent him on his way, and Joseph traveled to Shechem from their home in the valley of Hebron.

15When he arrived there, a man from the area noticed him wandering around the countryside. "What are you looking for?" he asked.

16"I'm looking for my brothers," Joseph replied. "Do you know where they are pasturing their sheep?"

17"Yes," the man told him. "They have moved on from here, but I heard them say, 'Let's go on to Dothan.' " So Joseph followed his brothers to Dothan and found them there.

18When Joseph's brothers saw him coming, they recognized him in the distance. As he approached, they made plans to kill him. 19"Here comes the dreamer!" they said. 20"Come on, let's kill him and throw him into one of these cisterns. We can tell our father, 'A wild animal has eaten him.' Then we'll see what becomes of his dreams!"

21But when Reuben heard of their scheme, he came to Joseph's rescue. "Let's not kill him," he said. 22"Why should we shed any blood? Let's just throw him into this empty cistern here in the wilderness. Then he'll die without our laying a hand on him." Reuben was secretly planning to rescue Joseph and return him to his father.

23So when Joseph arrived, his brothers ripped off the beautiful robe he was wearing. 24Then they grabbed him and threw him into the cistern. Now the cistern was empty; there was no water in it. 25Then,

37:7
Gen 42:6, 9; 43:26

37:8
Deut 33:16

37:10
Gen 27:29

37:11
Luke 2:19, 51
Acts 7:9
qana' (7065)
› Exod 20:5

37:13
Gen 33:19

37:14
Gen 35:27

37:17
2 Kgs 6:13

37:20
Gen 37:33

37:21
Gen 42:22

37:22
Gen 37:29

37:23
Gen 37:3

37:24
Jer 38:6; 41:7

37:25
Gen 31:21; 37:28
Jer 8:22; 46:11

. . . .

37:7 The *bundles of grain* hint at how Joseph's authority over his family would be achieved (see 42:1-3).

37:8 The brothers' angry response to the revelation, in contrast to Joseph's honesty and faithfulness, clearly demonstrates why they were not chosen for leadership: Leaders in God's plan cannot be consumed with jealousy and hatred. In their anger, they missed an important part of the revelation—they too would be rulers (stars, 37:9) who would productively bind their sheaves (37:7).

37:9 *The sun, moon, and eleven stars:* Astrological symbols often represent rulers. The dream predicted Joseph's elevation to a position of authority over the whole clan of Israel.

37:10 *your mother and I:* Joseph's birth mother, Rachel, was dead (35:19). Leah was now the matriarch of the clan.

37:11 *His brothers* hated Joseph because they *were jealous* of him. Rather than recognize the hand of God, the brothers tried to prevent the dream

from being fulfilled (37:18-36). These actions show that they were not fit to lead the household of faith. God's sovereign choice of a leader, especially if the one chosen is young or appears unqualified, often brings out the true colors of those who refuse to submit to that leader's authority. The brothers represent people throughout history who have been driven by envy and malice because they were not committed to doing the Lord's will. • Jacob *wondered what the dreams meant* because he knew that God would choose the next leader, that God could choose the younger son to rule over the older sons, and that God could reveal all this in dreams.

37:12-13 It was foolish for *Jacob* to *send* Joseph on such a mission, knowing how the brothers felt about him. *Joseph* obeyed his father by going to find his brothers despite their hatred for him.

37:14-17 The *brothers* ranged far and wide. *Shechem* was about fifty miles from *Hebron*, and *Dothan* another fifteen miles beyond Shechem.

37:18-20 *When Joseph's brothers saw him coming,* they devised a plot *to kill . . . the dreamer* and end *his dreams.* Earlier, they had unjustly killed the men of Shechem to avenge their sister (ch 34); in the region of Shechem, they now plotted unjustly to kill their own brother out of envy.

37:21-24 *Reuben* was perhaps trying to get back into his father's good graces (35:22) by exercising the leadership of the firstborn (cp. 42:22). Reuben succeeded in saving Joseph's life, but he failed to earn his father's favor (37:29-30).

37:23 The recurring motif of changed clothes signifies changes in status, position, and authority (see 37:3, 23; 38:14, 19; 39:15-18; 41:14, 42).

37:25-28 The *Ishmaelite traders* were descendants of the slave child who was cast out for mocking Isaac. Now they would enslave Joseph. When he was sold for *twenty pieces of silver* and carried *to Egypt,* he was at least preserved alive.

37:28
Gen 39:1; 45:4-5
Lev 27:5
Judg 8:22-24
Acts 7:9

37:29
Gen 37:34; 44:13
Num 14:6

37:30
Gen 42:13, 36

37:32
Luke 15:22

37:33
Gen 37:20; 44:28

37:34
Gen 37:29
k*'abal* (0056)
▸ Exod 33:4

37:35
Gen 44:29
2 Sam 12:17
Ps 77:2
a*she'ol* (7585)
▸ Num 16:30

37:36
Gen 39:1; 40:3

38:1
Josh 15:35
1 Sam 22:1

38:2
Gen 24:3; 34:2; 38:12

38:3
Gen 46:12
Num 26:19

38:6
Matt 1:3

38:7
Gen 6:5; 13:13; 19:13;
38:10
1 Chr 2:3

38:8
Num 36:8
Deut 25:5-10
*Matt 22:24
*Mark 12:19

just as they were sitting down to eat, they looked up and saw a caravan of camels in the distance coming toward them. It was a group of Ishmaelite traders taking a load of gum, balm, and aromatic resin from Gilead down to Egypt.

26Judah said to his brothers, "What will we gain by killing our brother? We'd have to cover up the crime. 27Instead of hurting him, let's sell him to those Ishmaelite traders. After all, he is our brother—our own flesh and blood!" And his brothers agreed. 28So when the Ishmaelites, who were Midianite traders, came by, Joseph's brothers pulled him out of the cistern and sold him to them for twenty pieces of silver. And the traders took him to Egypt.

29Some time later, Reuben returned to get Joseph out of the cistern. When he discovered that Joseph was missing, he tore his clothes in grief. 30Then he went back to his brothers and lamented, "The boy is gone! What will I do now?"

31Then the brothers killed a young goat and dipped Joseph's robe in its blood. 32They sent the beautiful robe to their father with this message: "Look at what we found. Doesn't this robe belong to your son?"

33Their father recognized it immediately. "Yes," he said, "it is my son's robe. A wild animal must have eaten him. Joseph has clearly been torn to pieces!" 34Then Jacob tore his clothes and dressed himself in burlap. He kmourned deeply for his son for a long time. 35His family all tried to comfort him, but he refused to be comforted. "I will go to my agrave mourning for my son," he would say, and then he would weep.

36Meanwhile, the Midianite traders arrived in Egypt, where they sold Joseph to Potiphar, an officer of Pharaoh, the king of Egypt. Potiphar was captain of the palace guard.

Judah, Tamar, and the Birth of Judah's Offspring (38:1-30)

38 About this time, Judah left home and moved to Adullam, where he stayed with a man named Hirah. 2There he saw a Canaanite woman, the daughter of Shua, and he married her. When he slept with her, 3she became pregnant and gave birth to a son, and he named the boy Er. 4Then she became pregnant again and gave birth to another son, and she named him Onan. 5And when she gave birth to a third son, she named him Shelah. At the time of Shelah's birth, they were living at Kezib.

6In the course of time, Judah arranged for his firstborn son, Er, to marry a young woman named Tamar. 7But Er was a wicked man in the LORD's sight, so the LORD took his life. 8Then Judah said to Er's brother Onan, "Go and marry Tamar, as our law requires of the brother of a man who has died. You must produce an heir for your brother."

. . . .

37:26 *Judah* began to exercise leadership that he would continue to develop as events unfolded (see 43:8-10). • *cover up the crime:* Literally *cover his blood.*

37:28 *the Ishmaelites, who were Midianite traders* (literally *the Midianite traders*): Ishmaelites were descendants of Abraham through Hagar (16:5), while Midianites were descendants of Abraham through Keturah (25:1-2). The term *Ishmaelite* may have described bedouin tribes generally. The Midianites might also have been traveling with a separate caravan of *Ishmaelite traders* (37:27). • *Twenty pieces:* Hebrew *20 shekels,* about 8 ounces or 228 grams in weight. • *Kidnapping* (see 40:15) was a capital offense (see Exod 21:16).

37:29-30 When *Reuben returned*, he *tore his clothes in grief*. His attempt to restore his relationship with his father by saving Joseph had gone awry.

37:31-35 The old family propensity for deception seized the brothers' imagination. Jacob had *killed a young goat* to deceive Isaac (27:5-17); now Jacob's sons deceived him with a goat (see note on 30:34-36).

37:32 *your son:* In their cold hatred, the brothers did not refer to Joseph by name or acknowledge him as their brother (see 21:10).

37:33 *recognized:* Cp. 27:23.

37:34-35 *Jacob tore his clothes and dressed himself in burlap:* These were signs of great distress and mourning (see 44:13; Job 1:20; 16:15). Jacob was devastated and *refused to be comforted*. The treachery that affected everyone in his family. • *go to my grave:* Hebrew *go down to Sheol.*

37:36 *the Midianite traders:* As in the Greek version; Hebrew reads *the Medanites.* The relationship between the Midianites and Medanites is unclear; cp. 37:28. See also 25:2. • *sold Joseph to Potiphar:* Joseph found himself in a place of service that seemed congruent with his rise to authority, yet he still faced more testing.

38:1-30 The story of *Judah* and *Tamar* is a carefully placed interlude; it reports what was happening in the family of Judah, who would later rise to prominence, and it shows the beginnings of assimilation with the people of the land

to help explain why God sent the family to Egypt (chs 39–47). The Egyptians were strict separatists (43:32); the Israelites would retain their unique identity better in Egypt than in Canaan.

38:7-10 In this story, *the LORD* is mentioned as the sovereign judge who took the lives of Judah's *evil* sons.

38:7 That *Er was a wicked man* is not surprising, since his mother was a Canaanite and his father a wayward Israelite.

38:8 *as our law requires. . . . You must produce an heir for your brother:* The custom that informs this episode is the law for levirate marriage (Latin *levir,* "husband's brother"). By this custom, which was later incorporated into God's law for Israel (Deut 25:5-10), if a man died childless, his brother or nearest relative would marry his widow to produce a child who would carry on the family name of the deceased and inherit his property. Apparently, the near kinsman had a right to refuse, but he would be disgraced in the family for refusing to perpetuate his brother's name.

⁹But Onan was not willing to have a child who would not be his own heir. So whenever he had intercourse with his brother's wife, he spilled the semen on the ground. This prevented her from having a child who would belong to his brother. ¹⁰But the Lord considered it evil for Onan to deny a child to his dead brother. So the Lord took Onan's life, too.

¹¹Then Judah said to Tamar, his daughter-in-law, "Go back to your parents' home and remain a widow until my son Shelah is old enough to marry you." (But Judah didn't really intend to do this because he was afraid Shelah would also die, like his two brothers.) So Tamar went back to live in her father's home.

¹²Some years later Judah's wife died. After the time of mourning was over, Judah and his friend Hirah the Adullamite went up to Timnah to supervise the shearing of his sheep. ¹³Someone told Tamar, "Look, your father-in-law is going up to Timnah to shear his sheep."

¹⁴Tamar was aware that Shelah had grown up, but no arrangements had been made for her to come and marry him. So she changed out of her widow's clothing and covered herself with a veil to disguise herself. Then she sat beside the road at the entrance to the village of Enaim, which is on the road to Timnah. ¹⁵Judah noticed her and thought she was a prostitute, since she had covered her face. ¹⁶So he stopped and propositioned her. "Let me have sex with you," he said, not realizing that she was his own daughter-in-law.

"How much will you pay to have sex with me?" Tamar asked.

¹⁷"I'll send you a young goat from my flock," Judah promised.

"But what will you give me to guarantee that you will send the goat?" she asked.

¹⁸"What kind of guarantee do you want?" he replied.

She answered, "Leave me your identification seal and its cord and the walking stick you are carrying." So Judah gave them to her. Then he had intercourse with her, and she became pregnant. ¹⁹Afterward she went back home, took off her veil, and put on her widow's clothing as usual.

²⁰Later Judah asked his friend Hirah the Adullamite to take the young goat to the woman and to pick up the things he had given her as his guarantee. But Hirah couldn't find her. ²¹So he asked the men who lived there, "Where can I find the shrine prostitute who was sitting beside the road at the entrance to Enaim?"

"We've never had a shrine prostitute here," they replied.

²²So Hirah returned to Judah and told him, "I couldn't find her anywhere, and the men of the village claim they've never had a shrine prostitute there."

²³"Then let her keep the things I gave her," Judah said. "I sent the young goat as we agreed, but you couldn't find her. We'd be the laughingstock of the village if we went back again to look for her."

²⁴About three months later, Judah was told, "Tamar, your daughter-in-law, has acted like a prostitute. And now, because of this, she's pregnant."

"Bring her out, and let her be burned!" Judah demanded.

²⁵But as they were taking her out to kill her, she sent this message to her father-in-law: "The man who owns these things made me pregnant. Look closely. Whose seal and cord and walking stick are these?"

²⁶Judah recognized them immediately and said, "She is more righteous than I am, because I didn't arrange for her to marry

38:11
Ruth 1:13
38:12
Gen 31:19
Josh 15:10, 57
38:16
Lev 18:15
2 Sam 13:11
38:17
Gen 38:20
38:18
Gen 41:42
38:24
Lev 20:10; 21:9
38:26
1 Sam 24:17

. . . .

38:9-10 *Onan* married Tamar, but *was not willing* to provide an *heir* for his brother. He would have sex with Tamar but not fulfill his responsibility to his dead brother (38:8).

38:11 *Judah* is now presented as the model for his sons' behavior—he, too, was unfaithful to his levirate responsibility to Tamar as next kinsman (see note on 38:8). Judah and his sons were far too Canaanite in their ways (see note on 38:27-30; contrast Boaz, Ruth 3–4).

38:12-13 Without a marriage, the family's future was in jeopardy.
• *Judah's wife died:* This made Judah available to fulfill the responsibility of providing an heir.

38:14-19 *Tamar* realized that she

would have to take matters into her own hands if the family were to have a future. Tamar acted in keeping with the levirate custom (see note on 38:8) out of loyalty to her deceased husband. She had a legal right to an heir by Judah's son or by Judah, so she lured her father-in-law into having sex with her. Jacob's family was deceived again, this time by a Canaanite daughter-in-law.

38:17 It would be normal for Tamar to ask for a pledge if the man did not have the money to pay. A woman in such a position would not trust anyone to send the money.

38:18 *identification seal:* A stone or metal cylinder was engraved with

distinctive designs and was usually worn around the neck on a *cord*; when rolled onto clay or wax, it left a distinct impression.

38:20-23 *Judah* had gone in to Tamar as a regular prostitute (Hebrew *zonah*, 38:15), whereas *Hirah* was mistakenly looking for a *shrine prostitute* (Hebrew *qedeshah*), of which there were none.

38:24-26 *Judah* played the hypocrite when he condemned *Tamar* to death for adultery. When she produced the *seal and cord and walking stick* that identified him as the father, he withdrew the condemnation.

38:26 *She is more righteous than I am:* Judah acknowledged that he had shirked his responsibility to provide an

38:27
Gen 25:24

38:29
Gen 46:12
Num 26:20-21
Ruth 4:12
1 Chr 2:4
Matt 1:3
Luke 3:33

39:1
Gen 37:25

39:2
Acts 7:9

39:4
Gen 40:4
Prov 22:29

39:5
Deut 28:3-4, 11

39:6
1 Sam 16:12, 18
Acts 7:20

39:7
Prov 7:15-20

39:8
Gen 39:4-5
Prov 6:23-24

39:9
b*khata'* (2398)
▸ Exod 10:16

39:10
1 Thes 5:22

39:12
Prov 7:13
2 Tim 2:22

39:17
Exod 20:16; 23:1
Ps 55:3

my son Shelah." And Judah never slept with Tamar again.

27When the time came for Tamar to give birth, it was discovered that she was carrying twins. 28While she was in labor, one of the babies reached out his hand. The midwife grabbed it and tied a scarlet string around the child's wrist, announcing, "This one came out first." 29But then he pulled back his hand, and out came his brother! "What!" the midwife exclaimed. "How did you break out first?" So he was named Perez. 30Then the baby with the scarlet string on his wrist was born, and he was named Zerah.

Joseph's Rise to Power in Egypt (39:1–41:57)
Joseph's Rise in Potiphar's House

39 When Joseph was taken to Egypt by the Ishmaelite traders, he was purchased by Potiphar, an Egyptian officer. Potiphar was captain of the guard for Pharaoh, the king of Egypt.

2The LORD was with Joseph, so he succeeded in everything he did as he served in the home of his Egyptian master. 3Potiphar noticed this and realized that the LORD was with Joseph, giving him success in everything he did. 4This pleased Potiphar, so he soon made Joseph his personal attendant. He put him in charge of his entire household and everything he owned. 5From the day Joseph was put in charge of his master's household and property, the LORD began to bless Potiphar's household for Joseph's sake. All his household affairs ran smoothly, and his crops and livestock flourished. 6So Potiphar gave Joseph complete administrative responsibility over everything he owned. With Joseph there,

he didn't worry about a thing—except what kind of food to eat!

Potiphar's Wife
Joseph was a very handsome and well-built young man, 7and Potiphar's wife soon began to look at him lustfully. "Come and sleep with me," she demanded.

8But Joseph refused. "Look," he told her, "my master trusts me with everything in his entire household. 9No one here has more authority than I do. He has held back nothing from me except you, because you are his wife. How could I do such a wicked thing? It would be a great bsin against God."

10She kept putting pressure on Joseph day after day, but he refused to sleep with her, and he kept out of her way as much as possible. 11One day, however, no one else was around when he went in to do his work. 12She came and grabbed him by his cloak, demanding, "Come on, sleep with me!" Joseph tore himself away, but he left his cloak in her hand as he ran from the house.

13When she saw that she was holding his cloak and he had fled, 14she called out to her servants. Soon all the men came running. "Look!" she said. "My husband has brought this Hebrew slave here to make fools of us! He came into my room to rape me, but I screamed. 15When he heard me scream, he ran outside and got away, but he left his cloak behind with me."

16She kept the cloak with her until her husband came home. 17Then she told him her story. "That Hebrew slave you've brought into our house tried to come in and fool around with me," she said. 18"But when I screamed, he ran outside, leaving his cloak with me!"

. . . .

heir. It was sinful for Judah to go to a prostitute, but Tamar had a legal right to be the mother of Judah's child and had acted on that right. In the book of Ruth, the elders analogously blessed the marriage of Boaz and Ruth, praying that God would make Ruth like Tamar (Ruth 4:12; cp. Matt 1:3, 5).

38:27-30 Judah's line continued because of Tamar. The *twins* replaced Judah's two slain sons (38:7, 10); their birth was similar to the birth of Jacob and Esau (25:21-26) in that the "red" one was born first, but the other son pushed past him in later life. Jacob's gaining the right to rule over his older brother (27:29) seemed to be relived in Judah's line. The line was carried on through Perez and not through the elder son Shelah, whom he had gone to such lengths to protect (38:11; see 1 Chr 4:21), nor through the elder twin Zerah

(see Ruth 4:13-22; Matt 1:3).

38:29-30 *Perez* means "breaking out." He pushed past his brother, just as Joseph would soon do in relation to his brothers (chs 39–47). • *Zerah* means "scarlet" or "brightness."

39:1–47:31 Joseph began as a slave, alienated from his brothers and separated from his father; he ended as Pharaoh's viceroy. Through the trips to Egypt, the covenant family went from the brink of apostasy, divided by jealousy and deception, to being reconciled and united by Judah's intercession and Joseph's forgiveness. • God is mentioned for the first time (apart from 38:7-10) since Jacob built his altar in Bethel (35:1-15); his covenant name, "the LORD," is used for the first time since Jacob left Laban (31:49).

39:1-23 Joseph's integrity in Potiphar's service contrasts with Judah's moral

failure (ch 38). God was with Joseph (39:2-3, 21, 23) and enabled him to prosper and be a blessing (see notes on 12:1-9; 28:16-22) despite his slavery and imprisonment.

39:5 God *began to bless* Egypt through Joseph (see 22:18).

39:6-10 One of the major motifs of wisdom literature (see note on 37:2–50:26) is to warn young people that immorality will lead them to disaster (cp. Prov 5–7). Joseph was able to resist temptation because he had godly wisdom—he was guided by the fear of the Lord (Prov 1:7; 9:10).

39:14 Though Potiphar's wife was addressing slaves, she appealed to them as fellow Egyptians (*us*) to enlist them as witnesses against the despised *Hebrew* (see 43:32) who had won Potiphar's trust.

Joseph Put in Prison

¹⁹Potiphar was furious when he heard his wife's story about how Joseph had treated her. ²⁰So he took Joseph and threw him into the prison where the king's prisoners were held, and there he remained. ²¹But the LORD was with Joseph in the prison and showed him his faithful love. And the LORD made Joseph a favorite with the prison warden. ²²Before long, the warden put Joseph in charge of all the other prisoners and over everything that happened in the prison. ²³The warden had no more worries, because Joseph took care of everything. The LORD was with him and caused everything he did to succeed.

Joseph Interprets Two Prisoners' Dreams

40 Some time later, Pharaoh's chief cup-bearer and chief baker offended their royal master. ²Pharaoh became angry with these two officials, ³and he put them in the prison where Joseph was, in the palace of the captain of the guard. ⁴They remained in prison for quite some time, and the captain of the guard assigned them to Joseph, who looked after them.

⁵While they were in prison, Pharaoh's cup-bearer and baker each had a dream one night, and each dream had its own meaning. ⁶When Joseph saw them the next morning, he noticed that they both looked upset. ⁷"Why do you look so worried today?" he asked them.

⁸And they replied, "We both had dreams last night, but no one can tell us what they mean."

"Interpreting dreams is God's business," Joseph replied. "Go ahead and tell me your dreams."

⁹So the chief cup-bearer told Joseph his dream first. "In my dream," he said, "I saw a grapevine in front of me. ¹⁰The vine had three branches that began to bud and blossom, and soon it produced clusters of ripe grapes. ¹¹I was holding Pharaoh's wine cup in my hand, so I took a cluster of grapes and squeezed the juice into the cup. Then I placed the cup in Pharaoh's hand."

¹²"This is what the dream means," Joseph said. "The three branches represent three days. ¹³Within three days Pharaoh will lift you up and restore you to your position as his chief cup-bearer. ¹⁴And please remember me and do me a favor when things go well for you. Mention me to Pharaoh, so he might let me out of this place. ¹⁵For I was kidnapped from my homeland, the land of the Hebrews, and now I'm here in prison, but I did nothing to deserve it."

¹⁶When the chief baker saw that Joseph had given the first dream such a positive interpretation, he said to Joseph, "I had a dream, too. In my dream there were three baskets of white pastries stacked on my head. ¹⁷The top basket contained all kinds of pastries for Pharaoh, but the birds came and ate them from the basket on my head."

¹⁸"This is what the dream means," Joseph told him. "The three baskets also represent three days. ¹⁹Three days from now Pharaoh will lift you up and impale your body on a pole. Then birds will come and peck away at your flesh."

²⁰Pharaoh's birthday came three days later, and he prepared a banquet for all his officials and staff. He summoned his chief cup-bearer and chief baker to join the other officials. ²¹He then restored the chief cup-bearer to his former position, so he could again hand Pharaoh his cup. ²²But Pharaoh impaled the chief baker, just as Joseph had predicted when he interpreted his dream.

39:20 Gen 40:1-3, 15; 41:10
Ps 105:18
39:21 Ps 105:19
Acts 7:9
39:22 Gen 39:4
39:23 Gen 39:3
40:1 Neh 1:11
40:4 Gen 37:36; 39:4
40:5 Gen 20:3; 41:11
40:8 Gen 41:15-16
Dan 2:27-28
40:12 Gen 41:12
40:13 Gen 40:19-20
40:14 1 Sam 20:14
40:15 Gen 37:26-28; 39:20
40:18 Gen 40:12
40:19 Deut 21:22-23
40:22 Gen 40:19

. . . .

39:19-20 This was the second time that *Joseph*, while faithfully doing the right thing, was thrown into bondage with his clothing used deceptively as evidence (cp. 37:23-24, 31-33).

39:21-23 *Joseph* thrived in *prison* because God was with him. Each time Joseph prospered, he was put *in charge* of something.

40:1-23 Joseph did not lose faith in God's promises, as evidenced by his readiness to interpret the dreams of two prisoners. He was still convinced that God's revelation in his own two dreams (37:5-11) was true, and he had not abandoned hope that they would be fulfilled. When the fellow prisoners' dreams were fulfilled exactly as Joseph said, this confirmed that his previous dreams were from God.

40:1-4 *Joseph* was so faithful and trustworthy that *the captain of the guard* trusted him with the care of two of Pharaoh's *chief . . . officials*.

40:5-8 *Pharaoh's cup-bearer and baker* looked *worried* because they knew that their futures were somehow bound up in these ominous and disturbing dreams that they could not understand. • Joseph still had faith that *interpreting dreams is God's business*, and that he would understand them with God's help. He knew he had not misinterpreted his own dreams.

40:9-19 Joseph listened to the dreams and offered their interpretations. These dreams were not trivial; they were ominous warnings from God about what everyone was going to face. These two dreams prepared for Pharaoh's two dreams, which revealed the periods of life and death that the nation would soon experience.

40:14-15 Because he knew that the chief cup-bearer was going back into Pharaoh's personal service, Joseph saw an opportunity to seek his own release from prison.

40:20-22 The interpretations Joseph gave the prisoners proved true. The death of the *chief baker* speaks of the harsh realities of life in ancient Egypt, with a king whose word was his land's highest law. • *He summoned:* Literally *He lifted up the head of.*

40:23
Gen 40:14

41:5
2 Kgs 4:42

41:6
Ezek 19:12

23Pharaoh's chief cup-bearer, however, forgot all about Joseph, never giving him another thought.

Pharaoh's Dreams

41 Two full years later, Pharaoh dreamed that he was standing on the bank of the Nile River. 2In his dream he saw seven fat, healthy cows come up out of the river and begin grazing in the marsh grass. 3Then he saw seven more cows come up behind them from the Nile, but these were scrawny and thin. These cows stood beside the fat cows on the riverbank. 4Then the scrawny, thin cows ate the seven healthy, fat cows! At this point in the dream, Pharaoh woke up.

5But he fell asleep again and had a second dream. This time he saw seven heads of grain, plump and beautiful, growing on a single stalk. 6Then seven more heads of grain appeared, but these were shriveled

JOSEPH (39:1–45:28)

Gen 30:22-24;
37:2-36; 48:1-22;
49:22-26; 50:1-26
Exod 13:19
Deut 33:13-17
Josh 24:32
Ps 105:16-22
Acts 7:9-14

Joseph is known for his dreams and for the beautiful coat his father Jacob gave him. He is an example of faith, prudence, and administrative ability. Despite overwhelming difficulties, Joseph saved Canaan, Egypt, and his own family from starvation during seven years of drought.

Joseph was Jacob's eleventh son, the first child of Jacob's favorite wife, Rachel. Joseph's name means "may he add," expressing Rachel's desire that God give her another son (30:24). Rachel later died at the birth of Benjamin, Joseph's only full brother.

Joseph's brothers resented him because of his dreams. They sold him to a passing caravan and led Jacob to believe an animal had killed him. In Egypt, Joseph quickly became prominent until he was jailed when his master's wife falsely accused him. Having correctly interpreted dreams for fellow inmates, he was summoned when Pharaoh couldn't understand his dreams. Joseph said they predicted seven good years followed by seven lean years, and Pharaoh directed him to prepare for famine. When Joseph's family had to buy grain in Egypt, Joseph eventually disclosed his identity. The family was reconciled and reunited when Jacob came to live in Egypt.

Because Jacob blessed Joseph's sons, Ephraim and Manasseh, and took them as his own (48:5-20), each was considered a separate tribe later in Israel. Ephraim, whom Jacob put first and to whom he gave the birthright (48:17-20), became one of the strongest tribes of Israel and the leading tribe in the northern kingdom after the division during Rehoboam's reign (see 1 Kgs 11:26–12:33). Several of the prophets refer to the northern kingdom under the names Ephraim (e.g., Ezek 37:15-19; Hos 5:3-5) and Joseph (e.g., Obad 1:18).

Age	Event	Reference
17	Joseph is sold into slavery	37:2, 18-36
30	Joseph begins serving Pharaoh	41:46
39	Joseph is reunited with his brothers, Jacob moves to Egypt	45:3-6
56	Jacob dies, is buried in Canaan	47:28
110	Joseph dies in Egypt	50:26

▲ Joseph's Life (39:1–45:28).

Joseph's dying wish (which Moses later honored) was that his bones be buried in Canaan (Exod 13:19; Josh 24:32). Joseph's story dramatizes the life of a man of faith and godly character who fulfilled God's plan. His name is mentioned frequently in Scripture, showing that he was highly regarded by later Israelites. His story is summarized in the Psalms (Ps 105:16-22) and in Stephen's speech just prior to his martyrdom (Acts 7:9-14).

Joseph's life confirms God's control of the long course of history even when bad things happen (50:20). God expresses his sovereign power through his provident, faithful love for his people. Joseph also models for us a firm faith in the sovereign God and personal integrity in the face of adversity.

40:23 The *cup-bearer . . . forgot all about Joseph,* but God did not forget him. Joseph's faith was about to be rewarded (ch 41).

41:1-46 God had used two dreams to identify Joseph as a leader among his brothers (37:5-11). He used two dreams to test Joseph's faith in prison (40:5-14). Now he would use two dreams to elevate Joseph from prison to preeminence. Joseph had repeatedly proven faithful in small matters; now he would be put in charge of great things.

41:1-4 Pharaoh's first dream was about *cows.* Cows liked to stand half-submerged among the reeds in the Nile River to take refuge from the heat and flies. They would come out of the water to find pasture. The second cows disturbed Pharaoh because they were scrawny yet able to swallow the *fat cows.*

41:5-7 Pharaoh's *second dream* carried a similar message. Seven *plump heads of grain* on *a single stalk* were *swallowed up* by seven *shriveled and withered* heads that sprouted after them.

and withered by the east wind. 7And these thin heads swallowed up the seven plump, well-formed heads! Then Pharaoh woke up again and realized it was a dream.

8The next morning Pharaoh was very disturbed by the dreams. So he called for all the magicians and wise men of Egypt. When Pharaoh told them his dreams, not one of them could tell him what they meant.

9Finally, the king's chief cup-bearer spoke up. "Today I have been reminded of my failure," he told Pharaoh. 10"Some time ago, you were angry with the chief baker and me, and you imprisoned us in the palace of the captain of the guard. 11One night the chief baker and I each had a dream, and each dream had its own meaning. 12There was a young Hebrew man with us in the prison who was a slave of the captain of the guard. We told him our dreams, and he told us what each of our dreams meant. 13And everything happened just as he had predicted. I was restored to my position as cup-bearer, and the chief baker was executed and impaled on a pole."

Joseph's Interpretation and Counsel
14Pharaoh sent for Joseph at once, and he was quickly brought from the prison. After he shaved and changed his clothes, he went in and stood before Pharaoh. 15Then Pharaoh said to Joseph, "I had a dream last night, and no one here can tell me what it means. But I have heard that when you hear about a dream you can interpret it."

16"It is beyond my power to do this," Joseph replied. "But God can tell you what it means and set you at ease."

17So Pharaoh told Joseph his dream. "In my dream," he said, "I was standing on the bank of the Nile River, 18and I saw seven fat, healthy cows come up out of the river and begin grazing in the marsh grass. 19But then I saw seven sick-looking cows, scrawny and

thin, come up after them. I've never seen such sorry-looking animals in all the land of Egypt. 20These thin, scrawny cows ate the seven fat cows. 21But afterward you wouldn't have known it, for they were still as thin and scrawny as before! Then I woke up.

22"Then I fell asleep again, and I had another dream. This time I saw seven heads of grain, full and beautiful, growing on a single stalk. 23Then seven more heads of grain appeared, but these were blighted, shriveled, and withered by the east wind. 24And the shriveled heads swallowed the seven healthy heads. I told these dreams to the magicians, but no one could tell me what they mean."

25Joseph responded, "Both of Pharaoh's dreams mean the same thing. God is telling Pharaoh in advance what he is about to do. 26The seven healthy cows and the seven healthy heads of grain both represent seven years of prosperity. 27The seven thin, scrawny cows that came up later and the seven thin heads of grain, withered by the east wind, represent seven years of famine.

28"This will happen just as I have described it, for God has revealed to Pharaoh in advance what he is about to do. 29The next seven years will be a period of great prosperity throughout the land of Egypt. 30But afterward there will be seven years of famine so great that all the prosperity will be forgotten in Egypt. Famine will destroy the land. 31This famine will be so severe that even the memory of the good years will be erased. 32As for having two similar dreams, it means that these events have been decreed by God, and he will soon make them happen.

33"Therefore, Pharaoh should find an intelligent and wise man and put him in charge of the entire land of Egypt. 34Then

41:8
Exod 7:11-12
Dan 2:1-3; 4:5-7

41:9
Gen 40:14

41:10
Gen 40:2

41:11
Gen 40:5

41:12
Gen 40:12

41:13
Gen 40:22

41:14
Ps 105:20

41:15
Dan 2:25

41:16
Gen 40:8

41:17
Gen 41:1

41:27
2 Kgs 8:1

41:29
Gen 41:47

41:30
Gen 47:13

41:33
Gen 41:39

. . . .

41:8 The *magicians and wise men* belonged to a guild of supposed experts in spiritual matters, including dreams and visions (cp. Exod 8:18-19; Dan 2:10-11), but they could not interpret these dreams. God used an Israelite slave to confound the wisdom of the world (cp. Dan 2). However powerful a nation becomes, it is still under God's sovereign control (Dan 2:20-23).

41:9-13 The *chief cup-bearer* finally remembered Joseph and testified that his interpretations were true.

41:14-15 *Pharaoh* immediately summoned *Joseph* from prison to interpret his dreams. • *he shaved:* As was the Egyptian custom.

41:16 *Joseph* knew that only *God* could tell what Pharaoh's dreams meant (cp. 40:8), and he was confident that God would do so, because he had given the dreams for a purpose (41:25, 28).

41:17-24 *Pharaoh* recounted his dreams and testified that no human wisdom could interpret them.

41:25-32 Both dreams predicted that *seven years* of abundant crops would be followed by *seven years* of severe *famine*.

41:32 The *two similar dreams* confirmed that the message was *decreed by God* and would *soon . . . happen*, just as the dreams of the two prisoners were

quickly fulfilled (40:5-23). Joseph's own two dreams (37:5-11) were about to come true as well (41:37-46; 42:6-9).

41:33-36 God's revelation demanded a response—it was not given just to satisfy curiosity about the future. Joseph's advice about planning and preparing showed that he was the kind of *intelligent and wise man* that Pharaoh needed (41:37-40). • Joseph instituted central planning and control with a supervisor, local managers, a 20 percent tax on grain, and a rationing system. Later wisdom literature (see note on 37:2–50:26) teaches the principle of planning ahead rather than living just for the moment (see Prov 6:6-8; 27:12).

41:36
Gen 47:14

41:38
Dan 4:8, 18; 5:11, 14

41:39
Gen 41:33

41:40
Gen 39:9
Ps 105:21
Acts 7:10

41:41
Esth 8:2
Dan 6:3

41:42
Esth 3:10; 6:8

41:44
Gen 45:8
Ps 105:22

41:45
Ezek 30:17

41:46
Gen 37:2

41:51
Gen 48:1
Deut 33:17

41:52
Gen 17:6

41:54
Gen 41:30
Ps 105:16
Acts 7:11

41:55
Gen 41:41

Pharaoh should appoint supervisors over the land and let them collect one-fifth of all the crops during the seven good years. 35Have them gather all the food produced in the good years that are just ahead and bring it to Pharaoh's storehouses. Store it away, and guard it so there will be food in the cities. 36That way there will be enough to eat when the seven years of famine come to the land of Egypt. Otherwise this famine will destroy the land."

Pharaoh Promotes Joseph to Power

37Joseph's suggestions were well received by Pharaoh and his officials. 38So Pharaoh asked his officials, "Can we find anyone else like this man so obviously filled with the spirit of God?" 39Then Pharaoh said to Joseph, "Since God has revealed the meaning of the dreams to you, clearly no one else is as intelligent or wise as you are. 40You will be in charge of my court, and all my people will take orders from you. Only I, sitting on my throne, will have a rank higher than yours."

41Pharaoh said to Joseph, "I hereby put you in charge of the entire land of Egypt." 42Then Pharaoh removed his signet ring from his hand and placed it on Joseph's finger. He dressed him in fine linen clothing and hung a gold chain around his neck. 43Then he had Joseph ride in the chariot reserved for his second-in-command. And wherever Joseph went, the command was shouted, "Kneel down!" So Pharaoh put Joseph in charge of all Egypt. 44And Pharaoh said to him, "I am Pharaoh, but no one will lift a hand or foot in the entire land of Egypt without your approval."

45Then Pharaoh gave Joseph a new Egyptian name, Zaphenath-paneah. He also gave him a wife, whose name was Asenath. She was the daughter of Potiphera, the priest of On. So Joseph took charge of the entire land of Egypt. 46He was thirty years old when he began serving in the court of Pharaoh, the king of Egypt. And when Joseph left Pharaoh's presence, he inspected the entire land of Egypt.

God Provides through Joseph and for Joseph

47As predicted, for seven years the land produced bumper crops. 48During those years, Joseph gathered all the crops grown in Egypt and stored the grain from the surrounding fields in the cities. 49He piled up huge amounts of grain like sand on the seashore. Finally, he stopped keeping records because there was too much to measure.

50During this time, before the first of the famine years, two sons were born to Joseph and his wife, Asenath, the daughter of Potiphera, the priest of On. 51Joseph named his older son Manasseh, for he said, "God has made me forget all my troubles and everyone in my father's family." 52Joseph named his second son Ephraim, for he said, "God has made me fruitful in this land of my grief."

The Beginning of the Famine

53At last the seven years of bumper crops throughout the land of Egypt came to an end. 54Then the seven years of famine began, just as Joseph had predicted. The famine also struck all the surrounding countries, but throughout Egypt there was plenty of food. 55Eventually, however, the famine spread throughout the land of Egypt as well. And when the people cried out to Pharaoh for food, he told them, "Go to Joseph, and do whatever he tells you." 56So with severe famine everywhere, Joseph opened up

. . . .

41:37-40 Pharaoh recognized that Joseph was the man for the job; he had *the spirit of God* and was *intelligent* and *wise.* God showed his sovereign rule in Egypt; Israelites who later read the account could be confident that God would save them as he had promised.

41:41-46 Joseph was made the acting ruler or manager of Egypt.

41:42 Pharaoh's *signet ring* had a seal used for signing documents. The seal was impressed in soft clay, which hardened and left a permanent impression of the ruler's signature, which carried his authority. Numerous seals of this type have been found in archaeological digs. • The *linen clothing* and *gold chain* signified Joseph's new status as ruler.

41:43-44 Pharaoh made Joseph *second-in-command*; all the people had to submit to him. Cp. Ps 105:16-22.

41:45 As token of Joseph's new status, *Pharaoh gave* him an *Egyptian name* and *a wife* from a high-ranking family. • *Zaphenath-paneah* probably means "God speaks and lives." • *On:* Greek version reads *Heliopolis;* also in 41:50. On was a center for sun worship that came to be known as Heliopolis ("sun city").

41:46 *He was thirty years old:* It had been approximately thirteen years since his brothers had sold Joseph into slavery (37:2). • *he inspected the entire land of Egypt:* As a wise manager, his first priority was to learn the scope of his responsibilities.

41:47-57 Pharaoh's dreams were fulfilled in keeping with Joseph's interpretation.

41:50-52 In spite of his position and authority, *Joseph* never abandoned his heritage; he gave Hebrew names to his *two sons.* • *Manasseh* sounds like a Hebrew term that means "causing to forget." Joseph's prosperity and success made him forget the misery of separation from his family. • *Ephraim* sounds like a Hebrew term that means "fruitful." In so naming him, Joseph proclaimed his gratitude to God for the fruitfulness he was experiencing in Egypt.

41:53-57 Joseph's wisdom paid off, for the seven years of plenty were followed by seven years of severe famine, *but throughout Egypt there was plenty of food.* Joseph had grain to sell to the Egyptians and to people from other countries as well.

the storehouses and distributed grain to the Egyptians, for the famine was severe throughout the land of Egypt. ⁵⁷And people from all around came to Egypt to buy grain from Joseph because the famine was severe throughout the world.

Israel Moves to Egypt (42:1–47:31)
Joseph's Brothers Go to Egypt

42 When Jacob heard that grain was available in Egypt, he said to his sons, "Why are you standing around looking at one another? ²I have heard there is grain in Egypt. Go down there, and buy enough grain to keep us alive. Otherwise we'll die."

³So Joseph's ten older brothers went down to Egypt to buy grain. ⁴But Jacob wouldn't let Joseph's younger brother, Benjamin, go with them, for fear some harm might come to him. ⁵So Jacob's sons arrived in Egypt along with others to buy food, for the famine was in Canaan as well.

⁶Since Joseph was governor of all Egypt and in charge of selling grain to all the people, it was to him that his brothers came. When they arrived, they ᶜbowed before him with their faces to the ground. ⁷Joseph recognized his brothers instantly, but he pretended to be a stranger and spoke harshly to them. "Where are you from?" he demanded.

"From the land of Canaan," they replied. "We have come to buy food."

Joseph Accuses His Brothers to Have Benjamin Brought

⁸Although Joseph recognized his brothers, they didn't recognize him. ⁹And he remembered the dreams he'd had about them many years before. He said to them, "You are spies! You have come to see how vulnerable our land has become."

¹⁰"No, my lord!" they exclaimed. "Your servants have simply come to buy food. ¹¹We are all brothers—members of the same family. We are honest men, sir! We are not spies!"

¹²"Yes, you are!" Joseph insisted. "You have come to see how vulnerable our land has become."

¹³"Sir," they said, "there are actually twelve of us. We, your servants, are all brothers, sons of a man living in the land of Canaan. Our youngest brother is back there with our father right now, and one of our brothers is no longer with us."

¹⁴But Joseph insisted, "As I said, you are spies! ¹⁵This is how I will test your story. I swear by the life of Pharaoh that you will never leave Egypt unless your youngest brother comes here! ¹⁶One of you must go and get your brother. I'll keep the rest of you here in prison. Then we'll find out whether or not your story is true. By the life of Pharaoh, if it turns out that you don't have a younger brother, then I'll know you are spies."

¹⁷So Joseph put them all in prison for three days. ¹⁸On the third day Joseph said to them, "I am a God-fearing man. If you do as I say, you will live. ¹⁹If you really are honest men, choose one of your brothers to remain in prison. The rest of you may go home with grain for your starving families. ²⁰But you must bring your youngest brother back to me. This will prove that you are telling the truth, and you will not die." To this they agreed.

²¹Speaking among themselves, they said, "Clearly we are being punished because of what we did to Joseph long ago. We saw his anguish when he pleaded for his life, but we wouldn't listen. That's why we're in this trouble."

²²"Didn't I tell you not to sin against the boy?" Reuben asked. "But you wouldn't

41:57 Gen 42:5; 47:15
Ps 105:16
42:1 Acts 7:12
42:2 Gen 43:2, 4
42:3 Gen 43:20
42:4 Gen 35:24
42:5 Gen 41:57
Acts 7:11
42:6 Ps 105:16-21
ᶜkhawah (7812)
▸ Exod 4:31
42:7 Gen 42:30
42:8 Gen 37:2
42:9 Gen 42:16, 30-34
42:10 Gen 37:6-9
42:11 Gen 42:19, 31-34
42:13 Gen 37:30-33; 44:20; 46:31
42:14 Gen 42:9
42:17 Gen 40:4
42:18 Gen 20:11
Lev 25:43
42:20 Gen 42:34; 43:15
42:21 Gen 37:23-28; 45:3-5
42:22 Gen 9:5-6; 37:21-22

. . . .

42:1–47:31 God used the famine to bring Israel to Egypt under Joseph's rule, thus fulfilling two prophecies (15:13; 37:7-11).

42:1–44:34 Joseph did several unusual things to his brothers when they came looking for grain. The last time Joseph had been with them, they were filled with jealousy, hatred, and anger; they attempted to destroy their brother, and they deceived their father. Joseph put them through various tests, similar to the trying situations they had put him through, to see if they had changed.

42:4 *Jacob* may have believed that *Benjamin* would not be safe with his brothers.

42:5 *Jacob's:* Hebrew *Israel's.* See note on 35:21.

42:6-7 Joseph's first dream (37:5-11) was partially fulfilled when his brothers *bowed* down to him without recognizing him (see also 43:26; 44:14). It was totally fulfilled in 50:18. Joseph recognized his brothers immediately, but he could not reveal himself because he did not yet trust them to be the honest men they claimed to be (42:10).

42:8 *they didn't recognize him:* Joseph was a grown man, not a boy. He was not wearing a beard, was dressed in Egyptian clothes, and was in an unexpected position, speaking to them through an interpreter (42:23).

42:9 *You are spies!* The brothers had considered Joseph a spy for their father and had treated him roughly (37:2, 14, 18-28). Joseph was putting them in a

similar situation to see how they would respond.

42:11 Joseph knew that they had not always been the *honest men* they claimed to be.

42:15-17 Joseph put the brothers in jail for three days to see if they had a conscience functioning about what they had done (42:21-23). The brothers had similarly thrown Joseph into a cistern-prison while they decided what to do with him (37:24).

42:18-20 Rather than keep all but one, Joseph would release all but one to take *grain* home to their *starving families.*

42:21-23 *Clearly we are being punished:* The brothers sensed that having to bring Benjamin back to Egypt against their

42:24
Gen 43:14, 23
42:25
Gen 44:1
42:28
Gen 43:23
ᵈleb (3820)
▸ Exod 15:8
42:30
Gen 42:7
42:31
Gen 42:11
42:32
Gen 42:13

listen. And now we have to answer for his blood!"

²³Of course, they didn't know that Joseph understood them, for he had been speaking to them through an interpreter. ²⁴Now he turned away from them and began to weep. When he regained his composure, he spoke to them again. Then he chose Simeon from among them and had him tied up right before their eyes.

²⁵Joseph then ordered his servants to fill the men's sacks with grain, but he also gave secret instructions to return each brother's payment at the top of his sack. He also gave them supplies for their journey home. ²⁶So the brothers loaded their donkeys with the grain and headed for home.

²⁷But when they stopped for the night and one of them opened his sack to get grain for his donkey, he found his money in the top of his sack. ²⁸"Look!" he exclaimed to his brothers. "My money has been returned; it's here in my sack!" Then their ᵈhearts sank. Trembling, they said to each other, "What has God done to us?"

The Brothers Report to Jacob

²⁹When the brothers came to their father, Jacob, in the land of Canaan, they told him everything that had happened to them. ³⁰"The man who is governor of the land spoke very harshly to us," they told him. "He accused us of being spies scouting the land. ³¹But we said, 'We are honest men, not spies. ³²We are twelve brothers, sons of

Famine (41:56-57)

Gen 12:10; 26:1;
41:33-36; 45:6-7
Lev 26:19-20
Deut 8:3;
11:16-17
Ruth 1:1
2 Sam 21:1
1 Kgs 18:1-2
2 Kgs 8:1-2
Jer 14:11-16
Ezek 34:29-31;
36:28-32
Joel 1:1-20
Amos 8:11-14
Hag 1:1-11
Luke 6:21
John 6:32-35
Acts 11:28-30
Rev 7:16

Famine occurred early in the lives of Abraham (12:10) and Isaac (26:1). When famine afflicted Jacob's family (41:56-57), God had already placed Joseph in Egypt to provide for his people through the disaster (45:5, 7). This famine was particularly severe, but famines were not uncommon in the ancient world (see 12:10; 26:1; see also Ruth 1:1; 2 Sam 21:1; 1 Kgs 18:1-2; Hag 1:1-11; Acts 11:28). Dependence on rainfall caused some people to stockpile food against possible famine. In Egypt, Joseph implemented a grain ration that saved the people, supplied seed, and filled Pharaoh's royal storehouses (41:33-36; 47:23-24). Israel's temple also contained storerooms (1 Chr 26:15; 2 Chr 31:11; Neh 10:37-39).

Famine was a devastating catastrophe in an agrarian society. Caused by drought, crop failure, or siege (Ruth 1:1-2; 2 Kgs 25), it was often accompanied by disease or war that brought adversity at many levels of society (Jer 14:12), even for animals (Job 38:41; Joel 1:20). Famines had far-reaching results in price inflation, robbery, social exploitation, agricultural collapse, migration, and even cannibalism (12:10; 26:1; 2 Kgs 6:24-29; Neh 5:1-3; Jer 19:9; Lam 2:20-21; 4:8-10). Therefore, faithfulness to God was a particularly vivid need (Ps 33:18-19; 37:19), and God's blessings on the nation included protection from famine (Ezek 34:29; 36:29-30). God sometimes used famine as divine judgment on the Israelites (Lev 26:14-20; Deut 11:16-17; 28:33; Jer 29:17-18).

Jesus relived Israel's experience in his own wilderness testing and refused to make bread just for himself (Matt 4:3-4; cp. Deut 8:3). His success showed that scarcity and hunger can develop humility and trust in divine providence (Matt 4:2), something that Israel did not learn very well. Jesus fed 5,000 to draw them to himself as the bread of life, God's true manna (John 6:32-35), but the crowds followed Jesus more for the food than for himself (John 6:26-27). Without ignoring physical food, Jesus highlighted spiritual hunger and thirst (Luke 6:21; John 4:34). Eating provides both a context and a metaphor for fellowship (43:34; Luke 22:15-16; Rev 19:9). Heaven will remove the desperation of hunger altogether (Rev 7:16).

father's wishes was God's punishment for their having sold Joseph to the traders. The sense of divine retribution began to awaken feelings of remorse that Joseph's cries for mercy and their father's tears (37:34-35) had failed to arouse.

42:22 you wouldn't listen: Reuben had lost the reins of leadership (see notes on 42:37; 49:3-4).

42:24 Joseph *turned away from them and began to weep* (cp. 43:30; 45:2, 14; 50:1, 17); perhaps he was hearing part of the story that he had never known

(Reuben's attempt to save him, 37:21-22, 29), or his brothers' remorse moved him to forgiveness.

42:25-28 Joseph cared for his brothers' needs; he had forgiven them (see note on 42:24) and was fulfilling his role to provide for them. God used Joseph's care to convict the brothers even more fully of their sin.

42:25 *return each brother's payment:* He was now testing them to awaken their conscience and make them face their past guilt; once again, they were

going home with silver instead of a brother (37:28-35).

42:28 What has God done to us? They knew that God was behind everything that had been happening, so they faced a day of reckoning for their sins.

42:29-34 The brothers' account focused on the accusation that they were spies and on the need to take Benjamin back to Egypt with them. They omitted their growing realization of divine retribution for their crime against Joseph.

one father. One brother is no longer with us, and the youngest is at home with our father in the land of Canaan.'

33"Then the man who is governor of the land told us, 'This is how I will find out if you are honest men. Leave one of your brothers here with me, and take grain for your starving families and go on home. 34But you must bring your youngest brother back to me. Then I will know you are honest men and not spies. Then I will give you back your brother, and you may trade freely in the land.' "

35As they emptied out their sacks, there in each man's sack was the bag of money he had paid for the grain! The brothers and their father were terrified when they saw the bags of money. 36Jacob exclaimed, "You are robbing me of my children! Joseph is gone! Simeon is gone! And now you want to take Benjamin, too. Everything is going against me!"

37Then Reuben said to his father, "You may kill my two sons if I don't bring Benjamin back to you. I'll be responsible for him, and I promise to bring him back."

38But Jacob replied, "My son will not go down with you. His brother Joseph is dead, and he is all I have left. If anything should happen to him on your journey, you would send this grieving, white-haired man to his grave."

The Brothers Return to Egypt
with Benjamin

43 But the famine continued to ravage the land of Canaan. 2When the grain they had brought from Egypt was almost gone, Jacob said to his sons, "Go back and buy us a little more food."

3But Judah said, "The man was serious when he warned us, 'You won't see my face again unless your brother is with you.' 4If you send Benjamin with us, we will go down

and buy more food. 5But if you don't let Benjamin go, we won't go either. Remember, the man said, 'You won't see my face again unless your brother is with you.' "

6"Why were you so cruel to me?" Jacob moaned. "Why did you tell him you had another brother?"

7"The man kept asking us questions about our family," they replied. "He asked, 'Is your father still alive? Do you have another brother?' So we answered his questions. How could we know he would say, 'Bring your brother down here'?"

8Judah said to his father, "Send the boy with me, and we will be on our way. Otherwise we will all die of starvation—and not only we, but you and our little ones. 9I personally guarantee his safety. You may hold me responsible if I don't bring him back to you. Then let me bear the blame forever. 10If we hadn't wasted all this time, we could have gone and returned twice by now."

11So their father, Jacob, finally said to them, "If it can't be avoided, then at least do this. Pack your bags with the best products of this land. Take them down to the man as gifts—balm, honey, gum, aromatic resin, pistachio nuts, and almonds. 12Also take double the money that was put back in your sacks, as it was probably someone's mistake. 13Then take your brother, and go back to the man. 14May God Almighty give you mercy as you go before the man, so that he will release Simeon and let Benjamin return. But if I must lose my children, so be it."

15So the men packed Jacob's gifts and double the money and headed off with Benjamin. They finally arrived in Egypt and presented themselves to Joseph. 16When Joseph saw Benjamin with them, he said to the manager of his household, "These

42:34
Gen 34:10
42:35
Gen 43:12, 15, 18
42:36
Gen 43:14; 44:20-22
42:37
Gen 43:9; 44:32
42:38
Gen 37:35; 44:29, 34
43:1
Gen 41:56-57
43:2
Gen 42:25
43:3
Gen 42:15; 44:23
43:7
Gen 42:13; 43:27
43:8
Gen 42:2
43:9
Gen 42:37
Phlm 1:18-19
43:11
Gen 32:13; 37:25
43:12
Gen 42:25, 35
43:13
Gen 43:3
43:14
Gen 42:24
Ps 106:46
43:16
Gen 44:1

42:36 Filled with grief over two sons lost already, Jacob feared that he would also lose Benjamin if he went to Egypt. • *You are robbing me of my children!* He did not realize the full truth of his words, but they must have stung his sons' guilty consciences.

42:37 *Reuben* tried to take the lead; perhaps he thought he could get back into his father's good favor (see 35:22), first by rescuing Joseph from certain death (37:21-22, 29-30) and now by keeping *Benjamin* safe.

42:38 *Jacob* was resolute in his favoritism toward Rachel's remaining son. Benjamin would not go to Egypt even if it meant that Leah's son Simeon

never returned. Jacob's grief apparently weighed heavily on the brothers' conscience (44:18-34). • *to his grave:* Hebrew *to Sheol.*

43:1-7 As *the famine continued*, Jacob's family needed more grain, but they could not return to Egypt without Benjamin (42:16, 20). Jacob realized that he was in a bind; he needed *more food*, but was loath to lose *Benjamin*.

43:6 *Jacob:* Hebrew *Israel;* also in 43:11. See note on 35:21.

43:8-10 *Judah* broke the deadlock by taking responsibility for Benjamin's well-being, thus succeeding where Reuben failed. His action was fitting, since it had been his idea to sell Joseph to the

Ishmaelites (37:26-27) instead of killing him. Now he would secure Benjamin's safety with his own life (see 44:18-34).

43:11-13 *Jacob* provided everything he could to ensure a favorable reception from the Egyptian governor (*the man;* cp. 32:13-21).

43:13-14 Jacob finally entrusted his family's future to *God Almighty* (Hebrew *El-Shaddai*), the divine title that stresses God's power (see also 17:1; 28:3; 35:11; 48:3; 1 Kgs 19:10, 14; Rev 21:22).

43:16 *When Joseph saw Benjamin with them:* Joseph now knew that Benjamin was well (see note on 42:1–44:34). The feast was both a celebration and a test.

43:18
Gen 42:28, 35

43:21
Gen 42:25, 35; 43:12

43:22
Gen 42:28

43:23
Gen 42:24

43:24
Gen 18:4; 24:32

43:27
Gen 43:7; 45:3

43:28
Exod 18:7

43:29
Num 6:25
Ps 67:1

43:30
Gen 42:24; 45:2, 14-15; 46:29

43:31
Gen 45:1

43:32
Gen 46:34
Exod 8:26

43:33
Gen 44:12

44:1
Gen 42:25; 43:16

44:4
Prov 17:13

men will eat with me this noon. Take them inside the palace. Then go slaughter an animal, and prepare a big feast." 17So the man did as Joseph told him and took them into Joseph's palace.

18The brothers were terrified when they saw that they were being taken into Joseph's house. "It's because of the money someone put in our sacks last time we were here," they said. "He plans to pretend that we stole it. Then he will seize us, make us slaves, and take our donkeys."

A Feast at Joseph's Palace

19The brothers approached the manager of Joseph's household and spoke to him at the entrance to the palace. 20"Sir," they said, "we came to Egypt once before to buy food. 21But as we were returning home, we stopped for the night and opened our sacks. Then we discovered that each man's money—the exact amount paid—was in the top of his sack! Here it is; we have brought it back with us. 22We also have additional money to buy more food. We have no idea who put our money in our sacks."

23"Relax. Don't be afraid," the household manager told them. "Your God, the God of your father, must have put this treasure into your sacks. I know I received your payment." Then he released Simeon and brought him out to them.

24The manager then led the men into Joseph's palace. He gave them water to wash their feet and provided food for their donkeys. 25They were told they would be eating there, so they prepared their gifts for Joseph's arrival at noon.

26When Joseph came home, they gave him the gifts they had brought him, then bowed low to the ground before him. 27After greeting them, he asked, "How is your father, the old man you spoke about? Is he still alive?"

28"Yes," they replied. "Our father, your servant, is alive and well." And they bowed low again.

29Then Joseph looked at his brother Benjamin, the son of his own mother. "Is this your youngest brother, the one you told me about?" Joseph asked. "May God be gracious to you, my son." 30Then Joseph hurried from the room because he was overcome with emotion for his brother. He went into his private room, where he broke down and wept. 31After washing his face, he came back out, keeping himself under control. Then he ordered, "Bring out the food!"

32The waiters served Joseph at his own table, and his brothers were served at a separate table. The Egyptians who ate with Joseph sat at their own table, because Egyptians despise Hebrews and refuse to eat with them. 33Joseph told each of his brothers where to sit, and to their amazement, he seated them according to age, from oldest to youngest. 34And Joseph filled their plates with food from his own table, giving Benjamin five times as much as he gave the others. So they feasted and drank freely with him.

Joseph's Silver Cup in Benjamin's Sack

44 When his brothers were ready to leave, Joseph gave these instructions to his palace manager: "Fill each of their sacks with as much grain as they can carry, and put each man's money back into his sack. 2Then put my personal silver cup at the top of the youngest brother's sack, along with the money for his grain." So the manager did as Joseph instructed him.

3The brothers were up at dawn and were sent on their journey with their loaded donkeys. 4But when they had gone only a short distance and were barely out of the city, Joseph said to his palace manager, "Chase after them and stop them. When you catch up

---

43:18 The brothers were terrified: Cp. 32:6-12. Their guilt would not let them see that something good might happen.

43:19-22 The brothers, completely vulnerable and feeling the weight of God's judgment on their consciences, *approached the manager* in desperation.

43:24 Joseph no longer treated his brothers harshly, but provided kind hospitality.

43:26 For the second time, the brothers *bowed . . . before* Joseph in fulfillment of his first dream (37:7; see 42:6-7; cp. 33:3).

43:29 May God be gracious to you, my son: Joseph's blessing to his full brother fulfilled Jacob's prayer (43:14).

43:30 he was overcome with emotion for his brother: Cp. 42:24. Joseph's tears were of painful memories and years of lost fellowship, as well as of joy and thanksgiving to see his brother again.
• *He went into his private room:* He did not yet plan to reveal his identity.

43:33 to their amazement: This ruler knew more about the brothers than seemed possible (cp. 44:15).

43:34 The brothers were confronted with generous and gracious dealings from God through Joseph, who tested

their tolerance by reenacting the favoritism toward Rachel's son that had galvanized their earlier hostility.

44:1-34 The brothers appeared to have changed; they had shown remorse over what they had done to Joseph, and they showed integrity in returning the money and in bringing Benjamin. Given a chance to get rid of Rachel's other son, Benjamin, would they do it?

44:2 Joseph was giving his brothers the chance to abandon Benjamin if they wanted to. Joseph was testing them to see if they were loyal to the family and faithful to their father.

with them, ask them, 'Why have you repaid my kindness with such evil? ⁵Why have you stolen my master's silver cup, which he uses to predict the future? What a wicked thing you have done!' "

⁶When the palace manager caught up with the men, he spoke to them as he had been instructed.

⁷"What are you talking about?" the brothers responded. "We are your servants and would never do such a thing! ⁸Didn't we return the money we found in our sacks? We brought it back all the way from the land of Canaan. Why would we steal silver or gold from your master's house? ⁹If you find his cup with any one of us, let that man die. And all the rest of us, my lord, will be your slaves."

¹⁰"That's fair," the man replied. "But only the one who stole the cup will be my slave. The rest of you may go free."

¹¹They all quickly took their sacks from the backs of their donkeys and opened them. ¹²The palace manager searched the brothers' sacks, from the oldest to the youngest. And the cup was found in Benjamin's sack! ¹³When the brothers saw this, they tore their clothing in despair. Then they loaded their donkeys again and returned to the city.

¹⁴Joseph was still in his palace when Judah and his brothers arrived, and they fell to the ground before him. ¹⁵"What have you done?" Joseph demanded. "Don't you know that a man like me can predict the future?"

¹⁶Judah answered, "Oh, my lord, what can we say to you? How can we explain this? How can we prove our innocence? God is punishing us for our sins. My lord, we have all returned to be your slaves—all of us, not just our brother who had your cup in his sack."

¹⁷"No," Joseph said. "I would never do such a thing! Only the man who stole the cup will be my slave. The rest of you may go back to your father in peace."

Judah Intercedes for Benjamin

¹⁸Then Judah stepped forward and said, "Please, my lord, let your servant say just one word to you. Please, do not be angry with me, even though you are as powerful as Pharaoh himself.

¹⁹"My lord, previously you asked us, your servants, 'Do you have a father or a brother?' ²⁰And we responded, 'Yes, my lord, we have a father who is an old man, and his youngest son is a child of his old age. His full brother is dead, and he alone is left of his mother's children, and his father loves him very much.'

²¹"And you said to us, 'Bring him here so I can see him with my own eyes.' ²²But we said to you, 'My lord, the boy cannot leave his father, for his father would die.' ²³But you told us, 'Unless your youngest brother comes with you, you will never see my face again.'

²⁴"So we returned to your servant, our father, and told him what you had said. ²⁵Later, when he said, 'Go back again and buy us more food,' ²⁶we replied, 'We can't go unless you let our youngest brother go with us. We'll never get to see the man's face unless our youngest brother is with us.'

²⁷"Then my father said to us, 'As you know, my wife had two sons, ²⁸and one of them went away and never returned. Doubtless he was torn to pieces by some wild animal. I have never seen him since. ²⁹Now if you take his brother away from

44:5
Gen 30:27
Deut 18:10-14

44:8
Gen 43:21

44:9
Gen 31:32

44:12
Gen 44:2

44:13
Gen 37:29, 34

44:15
Gen 44:5

44:16
Gen 42:11; 43:18

44:18
Gen 37:7-8; 41:40-44

44:19
Gen 42:11; 43:7

44:21
Gen 42:11, 15

44:23
Gen 43:3

44:24
Gen 42:29-34

44:25
Gen 42:2

44:26
Gen 43:5

44:27
Gen 46:19

44:28
Gen 37:33

44:29
Gen 42:38

44:5 This description would make the brothers understand that the ruler knew things that others could not. • *silver cup:* As in Greek version; Hebrew lacks this phrase. *Hydromancy* (pouring water into oil) and *oenomancy* (pouring wine into other liquids) were methods of divination used in the ancient Near East that would have required such a cup. Joseph was continuing his ruse (see 42:7; cp. 30:27; see also Lev 19:26; Num 23:23; Deut 18:10-11)—he knew that only God grants revelation (see 37:5-9; 40:8; 41:16).

44:9-10 The punishment that the brothers proposed was harsher than necessary; it was normal in antiquity to stake your life on what you said. The palace manager was agreeable but enforced a punishment that matched Joseph's intentions (44:17).

44:11-12 The *palace manager knew*

where the cup was, but he created more anxiety by beginning with the oldest.

44:13 *they tore their clothing in despair:* They knew what it would do to Jacob to lose Benjamin (42:38).

44:14 This time, the brothers did not bow politely (see 42:6-7; 43:26); they *fell to the ground* in desperation, fulfilling Joseph's first dream for the third time (see 37:10).

44:16 *Judah* again spoke for the group. • *God is punishing us for our sins:* God was completing the work of repentance in their hearts. Judah again proposed that they all be punished. Benjamin was seemingly guilty of this theft, but all of the others were guilty of sin against Joseph. They preferred not returning to Jacob at all versus seeing his grief at the loss of Benjamin (44:34).

44:18-34 *Judah* made good on his

promise to pay for Benjamin's safety (43:8-10). His lengthy plea to be imprisoned in place of the lad (44:33) is one of the most moving acts of intercession in Scripture. It demonstrated Judah's concern for their father and his willingness to give up everything for the sake of his brother. With this kind of integrity (see John 15:13), Judah showed himself to be a true leader, qualified to receive the blessing of the firstborn, through whom the kings of Israel would come (see 49:10). • The brothers had fully repented, as expressed by Judah's intercession. Because of their change, Joseph could make himself known to them (45:1-15) and arrange for the family to join him in Egypt where there was food (45:16; 47:12).

44:29 *to his grave:* Hebrew *to Sheol;* also in 44:31.

44:30
1 Sam 18:1

44:32
Gen 43:9

45:1
Gen 43:31

45:3
Gen 43:7

45:4
Gen 37:28

45:5
Gen 50:20

45:6
Gen 41:30

45:8
Gen 41:41
Judg 17:10

45:9
Acts 7:14

me, and any harm comes to him, you will send this grieving, white-haired man to his grave.'

³⁰"And now, my lord, I cannot go back to my father without the boy. Our father's life is bound up in the boy's life. ³¹If he sees that the boy is not with us, our father will die. We, your servants, will indeed be responsible for sending that grieving, white-haired man to his grave. ³²My lord, I guaranteed to my father that I would take care of the boy. I told him, 'If I don't bring him back to you, I will bear the blame forever.'

³³"So please, my lord, let me stay here as a slave instead of the boy, and let the boy return with his brothers. ³⁴For how can I return to my father if the boy is not with me? I couldn't bear to see the anguish this would cause my father!"

Joseph Reveals His Identity and God's Plan

45 Joseph could stand it no longer. There were many people in the room, and he said to his attendants, "Out, all of you!" So he was alone with his brothers when he told them who he was. ²Then he broke down and wept. He wept so loudly

the Egyptians could hear him, and word of it quickly carried to Pharaoh's palace.

³"I am Joseph!" he said to his brothers. "Is my father still alive?" But his brothers were speechless! They were stunned to realize that Joseph was standing there in front of them. ⁴"Please, come closer," he said to them. So they came closer. And he said again, "I am Joseph, your brother, whom you sold into slavery in Egypt. ⁵But don't be upset, and don't be angry with yourselves for selling me to this place. It was God who sent me here ahead of you to preserve your lives. ⁶This famine that has ravaged the land for two years will last five more years, and there will be neither plowing nor harvesting. ⁷God has sent me ahead of you to keep you and your families alive and to preserve many survivors. ⁸So it was God who sent me here, not you! And he is the one who made me an adviser to Pharaoh—the manager of his entire palace and the governor of all Egypt.

⁹"Now hurry back to my father and tell him, 'This is what your son Joseph says: God has made me master over all the land of Egypt. So come down to me immediately!

JUDAH (44:14-34)

Gen 29:35; 37:26-
27; 38:1-30; 43:1-
10; 46:28; 49:8-12
Ruth 4:12
1 Chr 2:3-4; 5:2
Ps 108:8

Judah is remembered most often as the ancestor of King David and of Jesus Christ. Despite his indiscretions and his birth as a middle child, God chose Judah to carry the line of King David (1 Chr 2:1-16; 3:1-24) and of the Messiah (49:8-12; Matt 1:2-3; Luke 3:33).

Judah was the fourth of Jacob's twelve sons (35:23; 1 Chr 2:1). Leah, overjoyed to have borne her fourth son, named him Judah, meaning "praise" (29:35). Judah fathered five sons: Er, Onan, and Shelah by Bathshua, a woman from Canaan (38:3-5; 1 Chr 2:3); and the twins, Perez and Zerah, by his daughter-in-law Tamar (38:29-30; 1 Chr 2:4). God killed his first two sons, Er and Onan, in Canaan for disobedience (46:12). Judah eventually settled his family in Egypt with his father and brothers (Exod 1:2).

Though reckless in his behavior with Tamar (38:6-30), Judah took personal responsibility for Benjamin's safety in Egypt and interceded with Joseph for his brothers (44:14-18). When Jacob gave his dying blessing, he granted Judah the position of leadership; the future kings of Israel would come through Judah's offspring (see note on 49:10).

44:32-34 Judah was willing to give up his family, his future, and his freedom for others.

45:1-15 In one of the most dramatic scenes of the book, *Joseph* revealed his identity to his brothers, bringing the process of reconciling with them to a climax (see also 50:14-21).

45:2 This is the third of five times in the story that Joseph *wept* over his brothers (see also 42:24; 43:30; 45:14; 50:17; cp. 50:1).

45:3 The brothers were *stunned* at the news, unable to speak from amazement and fear (45:5; cp. 50:15).

45:5-8 *God . . . sent me* is the central message of the account of Jacob's family (37:2). As the Lord had told Abraham, he was leading the Israelites into Egypt (15:13). God had sent Joseph to Egypt to prepare for his family's rescue during the famine. In what has become a classic statement of God's sovereignty, Joseph explained that God had been working through all of the circumstances and human acts to bring about his plan. The certainty of God's will is the basis for forgiveness and reconciliation with those who do wrong, cause hurt, or bring harm. If people do not believe that God is sovereign, then they will blame others and retaliate. Those

who are spiritual will trust that God is at work even through human wickedness (see also Rom 8:28-30).

45:7 *to preserve many survivors:* Or *and to save you with an extraordinary rescue.* The meaning of the Hebrew is uncertain.

45:8 *an adviser:* Literally *a father.*

45:9-13 Joseph instructed his brothers to inform Jacob. The whole family was to move to *Egypt* and live in *Goshen,* a fertile region in the Nile delta (see 47:1-12). If they did not come to Egypt, they would not survive the *five years of famine ahead.*

¹⁰You can live in the region of Goshen, where you can be near me with all your children and grandchildren, your flocks and herds, and everything you own. ¹¹I will take care of you there, for there are still five years of famine ahead of us. Otherwise you, your household, and all your animals will starve.'"

¹²Then Joseph added, "Look! You can see for yourselves, and so can my brother Benjamin, that I really am Joseph! ¹³Go tell my father of my honored position here in Egypt. Describe for him everything you have seen, and then bring my father here quickly." ¹⁴Weeping with joy, he embraced Benjamin, and Benjamin did the same. ¹⁵Then Joseph kissed each of his brothers and wept over them, and after that they began talking freely with him.

Pharaoh Invites Jacob to Egypt

¹⁶The news soon reached Pharaoh's palace: "Joseph's brothers have arrived!" Pharaoh and his officials were all delighted to hear this.

¹⁷Pharaoh said to Joseph, "Tell your brothers, 'This is what you must do: Load your pack animals, and hurry back to the land of Canaan. ¹⁸Then get your father and all of your families, and return here to me. I will give you the very best land in Egypt, and you will eat from the best that the land produces.'"

¹⁹Then Pharaoh said to Joseph, "Tell your brothers, 'Take wagons from the land of Egypt to carry your little children and your wives, and bring your father here. ²⁰Don't worry about your personal belongings, for the best of all the land of Egypt is yours.'"

²¹So the sons of Jacob did as they were told. Joseph provided them with wagons, as Pharaoh had commanded, and he gave them supplies for the journey. ²²And he gave each of them new clothes—but to Benjamin he gave five changes of clothes and 300 pieces of silver. ²³He also sent his father ten male donkeys loaded with the finest products of Egypt, and ten female donkeys loaded with grain and bread and other supplies he would need on his journey.

²⁴So Joseph sent his brothers off, and as they left, he called after them, "Don't quarrel about all this along the way!" ²⁵And they left Egypt and returned to their father, Jacob, in the land of Canaan.

²⁶"Joseph is still alive!" they told him. "And he is governor of all the land of Egypt!" Jacob was stunned at the news—he couldn't ᵉbelieve it. ²⁷But when they repeated to Jacob everything Joseph had told them, and when he saw the wagons Joseph had sent to carry him, their father's ᶠspirits revived.

²⁸Then Jacob exclaimed, "It must be true! My son Joseph is alive! I must go and see him before I die."

Jacob and His Family Move to Egypt

46 So Jacob set out for Egypt with all his possessions. And when he came to Beersheba, he ᵍoffered sacrifices to the

45:10
Gen 46:28, 34
45:11
Gen 47:12
45:13
Acts 7:14
45:14
Gen 45:2
45:16
Acts 7:13
45:17
Gen 42:26
45:18
Gen 27:28
45:19
Gen 45:27; 46:5
45:20
Gen 46:6
45:22
Gen 24:53
2 Kgs 5:5
45:23
Gen 43:11
45:24
Gen 42:21-22
45:26
Gen 37:31-35
ᵉ*'aman* (0539)
▸ Exod 14:31
45:27
Gen 45:19
ᶠ*ruakh* (7307)
▸ Exod 31:3
45:28
Gen 44:28
46:1
Gen 21:14; 26:24;
28:13; 31:42
ᵍ*zabakh* (2076)
▸ Exod 22:20

. . . .

45:10 *The region of Goshen* was in the northeast corner of Egypt, only a few days' walk from Canaan. Jacob's family stayed there because there was food and water for themselves and their flocks; later, they were kept there by Egyptians who put them to slave labor.

45:14-15 Joseph was reunited with his brothers—first with ***Benjamin*** and then with the rest. Their previous hatred and jealousy of Joseph (37:4-11) had come to an end. The brothers experienced forgiveness from God and from Joseph. Far from commanding ***his brothers*** to bow down to him (see 42:6-7), Joseph welcomed them. Joseph held no grudge because he accepted what had happened as God's work and saw the good that had resulted (see 50:14-21). This is how wisdom rules: The wise leader will forgive and restore (see note on 37:2–50:26).

45:16–47:12 This section is transitional, as the family moved from Canaan to Goshen, where they would live for the next four centuries.

45:16-25 Joseph sent his brothers with instructions to bring Jacob and the entire family to Egypt. Out of gratitude for Joseph's having saved all of Egypt (45:18; see 47:20), Pharaoh promised the ***best of all the land of Egypt,*** and Joseph gave them ***the finest products of Egypt.***

45:21 *Jacob:* Hebrew *Israel;* also in 45:28. See note on 35:21.

45:22 *300 pieces:* Hebrew *300 shekels,* about 7.5 pounds or 3.4 kilograms in weight.

45:24 *Don't quarrel about all this along the way!* When they were away from Joseph, they might begin to accuse one another about the past or argue about how to explain what had happened to Jacob. It was now time to put the past behind them and enjoy the reunion.

45:26-28 As might be expected, ***Jacob was stunned*** when he heard that his son ***Joseph*** was ***still alive*** and ruling ***all the land of Egypt.*** As he heard the details of their story and saw all that ***Joseph had sent*** him, he was convinced that it was *true.* He immediately prepared to move to Egypt and reunite with his son Joseph, whom he had not seen for twenty-two years.

45:27 *their father's spirits revived:* This royal invitation to Jacob, an old man near the end of hope, and to the ten brothers burdened with guilty fears, was a turning point in their lives. It was also a fulfillment of God's prediction (15:13-16) that they would go into seclusion in a foreign country and there become a great nation without losing their identity. The joyful news about Joseph changed the lives of everyone in this family for the good.

46:1-4 God reassured Jacob about his move to Egypt.

46:1 *Jacob* (Hebrew *Israel;* also in 46:29, 30; see note on 35:21) ***set out for Egypt:*** A little over 200 years earlier, Abraham had similarly gone down into Egypt during a famine in Canaan (12:10), and God had protected him there. • Jacob's first stop was at ***Beersheba,*** where Abraham had sacrificed to the Lord and worshiped him after settling his land and water rights with the Philistines (21:31-33). This was where Isaac had

46:2
Gen 22:11; 31:11
Num 12:6

46:3
Gen 17:1; 26:2

46:4
Gen 28:13
Exod 3:8

46:5
Gen 45:19

46:6
Num 20:15
Deut 26:5
Acts 7:15

46:8
Gen 29:32; 35:23

46:9
1 Chr 5:3

46:10
1 Chr 4:24

46:11
1 Chr 6:16

46:12
1 Chr 2:3

46:13
1 Chr 7:1

46:14
Gen 30:20

46:15
Gen 30:21

46:16
Gen 30:11
Num 26:15

46:17
Gen 30:13

God of his father, Isaac. ²During the night God spoke to him in a vision. "Jacob! Jacob!" he called.

"Here I am," Jacob replied.

³"I am God, the God of your father," the voice said. "Do not be afraid to go down to Egypt, for there I will make your family into a great nation. ⁴I will go with you down to Egypt, and I will bring you back again. You will die in Egypt, but Joseph will be with you to close your eyes."

⁵So Jacob left Beersheba, and his sons took him to Egypt. They carried him and their little ones and their wives in the wagons Pharaoh had provided for them. ⁶They also took all their livestock and all the personal belongings they had acquired in the land of Canaan. So Jacob and his entire family went to Egypt—⁷sons and grandsons, daughters and granddaughters—all his descendants.

⁸These are the names of the descendants of Israel—the sons of Jacob—who went to Egypt:

Reuben was Jacob's oldest son. ⁹The sons of Reuben were Hanoch, Pallu, Hezron, and Carmi.

¹⁰The sons of Simeon were Jemuel, Jamin, Ohad, Jakin, Zohar, and Shaul. (Shaul's mother was a Canaanite woman.)

¹¹The sons of Levi were Gershon, Kohath, and Merari.

¹²The sons of Judah were Er, Onan, Shelah, Perez, and Zerah (though Er and Onan had died in the land of Canaan). The sons of Perez were Hezron and Hamul.

¹³The sons of Issachar were Tola, Puah, Jashub, and Shimron.

¹⁴The sons of Zebulun were Sered, Elon, and Jahleel.

¹⁵These were the sons of Leah and Jacob who were born in Paddan-aram, in addition to their daughter, Dinah. The number of Jacob's descendants (male and female) through Leah was thirty-three.

¹⁶The sons of Gad were Zephon, Haggi, Shuni, Ezbon, Eri, Arodi, and Areli.

¹⁷The sons of Asher were Imnah, Ishvah, Ishvi, and Beriah. Their sister was Serah. Beriah's sons were Heber and Malkiel.

. . . .

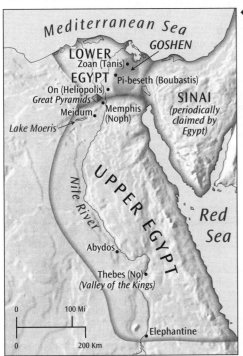

◀ **Egypt, about 1700 BC (39:1–50:26).** Egypt was already a great and ancient civilization when Joseph rose to power (chs 39–41) and Jacob's family traveled there for food (chs 42–46; cp. 12:10-20). As the breadbasket of the region, Egypt was synonymous with abundance. It was protected from enemies by natural barriers: the harborless MEDITERRANEAN SEA to the north, the rugged SINAI peninsula to the east, and a great desert to the west. ON (HELIOPOLIS) was the religious center (see 41:45, 50). Egypt was divided into two regions—LOWER EGYPT (the NILE delta region) and UPPER EGYPT (from the delta to the first cataract of the NILE at ELEPHANTINE). ZOAN and MEMPHIS were administrative centers (see Num 13:22; Ps 78:12, 43; Isa 19:11-13; 30:4; Ezek 30:14). THEBES, the chief city of Upper Egypt, was later conquered by the Assyrians (Nah 3:8-10; cp. Ezek 30:14-16). GOSHEN is also shown, the region where the Israelites settled (45:10; 46:28–47:6, 28-29; see Exod 8:22; 9:26).

46:3 *I am God:* Hebrew *I am El.*

46:4 *you will die:* He would have a peaceful death, surrounded by his family and many blessings from God (49:33).

46:8-27 This genealogy of *the sons of Jacob* shows that all the tribes *of Israel* went together to the land of Egypt; they would all leave together as well (see the book of Exodus).

46:13 *Puah:* As in Syriac version and Samaritan Pentateuch (see also 1 Chr 7:1); Hebrew reads *Puvah.* • *Jashub:* As in some Greek manuscripts and Samaritan Pentateuch (see also Num 26:24; 1 Chr 7:1); Hebrew reads *Iob.*

46:16 *Zephon:* As in Greek version and Samaritan Pentateuch (see also Num 26:15); Hebrew reads *Ziphion.*

lived, and where Jacob had lived before he fled from Esau's anger (28:10). • *all his possessions:* See 46:5-7.

46:2-4 In a night vision, the Lord repeated his promise to go with Jacob and make his family into a great nation in Egypt. The same God who led the family into Egypt promised to bring them out of Egypt to live once again in the land of Canaan.

18These were the sons of Zilpah, the servant given to Leah by her father, Laban. The number of Jacob's descendants through Zilpah was sixteen.

19The sons of Jacob's wife Rachel were Joseph and Benjamin.
20Joseph's sons, born in the land of Egypt, were Manasseh and Ephraim. Their mother was Asenath, daughter of Potiphera, the priest of On.
21Benjamin's sons were Bela, Beker, Ashbel, Gera, Naaman, Ehi, Rosh, Muppim, Huppim, and Ard.
22These were the sons of Rachel and Jacob. The number of Jacob's descendants through Rachel was fourteen.

23The son of Dan was Hushim.
24The sons of Naphtali were Jahzeel, Guni, Jezer, and Shillem.
25These were the sons of Bilhah, the servant given to Rachel by her father, Laban. The number of Jacob's descendants through Bilhah was seven.

26The total number of Jacob's direct descendants who went with him to Egypt, not counting his sons' wives, was sixty-six. 27In addition, Joseph had two sons who were born in Egypt. So altogether, there were seventy members of Jacob's family in the land of Egypt.

Jacob's Family Arrives in Goshen
28As they neared their destination, Jacob sent Judah ahead to meet Joseph and get directions to the region of Goshen. And when they finally arrived there, 29Joseph prepared his chariot and traveled to Goshen to meet his father, Jacob. When Joseph arrived, he embraced his father and wept, holding him for a long time. 30Finally, Jacob said to Joseph,

"Now I am ready to die, since I have seen your face again and know you are still alive."

31And Joseph said to his brothers and to his father's entire family, "I will go to Pharaoh and tell him, 'My brothers and my father's entire family have come to me from the land of Canaan. 32These men are shepherds, and they raise livestock. They have brought with them their flocks and herds and everything they own.' "

33Then he said, "When Pharaoh calls for you and asks you about your occupation, 34you must tell him, 'We, your servants, have raised livestock all our lives, as our ancestors have always done.' When you tell him this, he will let you live here in the region of Goshen, for the Egyptians despise shepherds."

Jacob Blesses Pharaoh and Settles in Goshen
47 Then Joseph went to see Pharaoh and told him, "My father and my brothers have arrived from the land of Canaan. They have come with all their flocks and herds and possessions, and they are now in the region of Goshen."

2Joseph took five of his brothers with him and presented them to Pharaoh. 3And Pharaoh asked the brothers, "What is your occupation?"

They replied, "We, your servants, are shepherds, just like our ancestors. 4We have come to live here in Egypt for a while, for there is no pasture for our flocks in Canaan. The famine is very severe there. So please, we request permission to live in the region of Goshen."

5Then Pharaoh said to Joseph, "Now that your father and brothers have joined you here, 6choose any place in the entire land of Egypt for them to live. Give them the best land of Egypt. Let them live in the region

46:19
Gen 44:27
46:20
Gen 41:45, 50-52
46:21
Num 26:38-41
1 Chr 7:6-12
46:22
Gen 35:24
46:23
Gen 30:6
Num 26:42
46:24
Gen 30:8
46:25
Gen 35:25
46:27
Exod 1:5
Deut 10:22
Acts 7:14
46:28
Gen 43:3; 45:10
46:29
Gen 45:14-15
46:30
Gen 44:28
46:31
Gen 47:1
46:32
Gen 37:2; 47:3
46:33
Gen 47:3
46:34
Gen 13:7; 26:20; 37:2
47:1
Gen 46:31
47:2
Gen 43:15
47:3
Gen 46:32-33
47:4
Gen 46:34
47:6
Gen 45:18
Exod 18:21, 25

. . . .

46:20 *On:* Greek version reads *of Heliopolis* (see note on 41:45).

46:26 *The total number . . . was sixty-six:* This is the number of those who traveled with Jacob to Egypt, excluding *his sons' wives*, the servants, and others attached to the household. It also omits Joseph, Ephraim, Manasseh, and Jacob.

46:27 *two sons:* Greek version reads *nine sons,* probably including Joseph's grandsons through Ephraim and Manasseh (see 1 Chr 7:14-20). • *seventy* (Greek version reads *seventy-five;* see note on Exod 1:5): This number includes Joseph, Ephraim, Manasseh, and Jacob. Seventy is also a symbolic number for perfection or completion (see "Symbolic Numbers" at Rev 4:4, p. 2173). From these seventy (i.e., all Israel) would grow the nation of Israel that would bless the

seventy nations (i.e., all the nations) of the world (see note on 10:2-32; cp. 12:3).

46:28-34 Jacob finally saw his son Joseph again; their reunion was overwhelmingly joyful.

46:29 *Joseph . . . embraced his father and wept:* Joseph was seventeen when he had last seen his father (37:2); now he was thirty-nine.

46:30 *Jacob* was satisfied just to see his beloved son *alive*—the firstborn of his chosen wife Rachel and the designated family leader (see note on 48:5-7; see also 1 Chr 5:1-2). More than just a family reunion, this was confirmation that God's plan was intact.

46:34 In contrast to the syncretistic Canaanites, who would have absorbed the Israelites had they stayed in Canaan,

Egyptians detested Semitic shepherds out of a sense of ethnic superiority and observed a strict ethnic segregation (see 43:32). When Jacob's family settled in Egypt, this separation would allow the people to grow into a great nation without losing their identity.

47:1-6 Pharaoh responded as Joseph hoped by giving Jacob's family the best part of the land; he even gave some of the brothers oversight of his own livestock (47:6).

47:1 *Goshen* (see note on 45:10) is not referred to in ancient Egyptian texts; the name it bore in later Egyptian writings was "the region of Rameses" (47:11; see Exod 1:11). It was fertile and near to Joseph at court, which suggests that it was on the eastern side of the Nile delta.

47:7
Gen 47:10
2 Sam 14:22
1 Kgs 8:66

47:10
Gen 14:19

47:11
Exod 1:11; 12:37

47:12
Gen 45:11; 47:24

47:13
Gen 41:30
Acts 7:11

47:14
Gen 41:56

47:15
Gen 47:18-19

47:17
Exod 14:9

47:19
Neh 5:2
Job 2:4
Lam 1:11

47:22
Deut 14:28-29

47:24
Gen 41:34

47:25
Gen 32:5

47:26
Gen 47:22

47:27
Exod 1:7

47:29
Gen 24:2; 50:24-25

of Goshen. And if any of them have special skills, put them in charge of my livestock, too."

7Then Joseph brought in his father, Jacob, and presented him to Pharaoh. And Jacob blessed Pharaoh.

8"How old are you?" Pharaoh asked him.

9Jacob replied, "I have traveled this earth for 130 hard years. But my life has been short compared to the lives of my ancestors." 10Then Jacob blessed Pharaoh again before leaving his court.

11So Joseph assigned the best land of Egypt—the region of Rameses—to his father and his brothers, and he settled them there, just as Pharaoh had commanded. 12And Joseph provided food for his father and his brothers in amounts appropriate to the number of their dependents, including the smallest children.

Joseph's Leadership in the Famine

13Meanwhile, the famine became so severe that all the food was used up, and people were starving throughout the lands of Egypt and Canaan. 14By selling grain to the people, Joseph eventually collected all the money in Egypt and Canaan, and he put the money in Pharaoh's treasury. 15When the people of Egypt and Canaan ran out of money, all the Egyptians came to Joseph. "Our money is gone!" they cried. "But please give us food, or we will die before your very eyes!"

16Joseph replied, "Since your money is gone, bring me your livestock. I will give you food in exchange for your livestock." 17So they brought their livestock to Joseph in exchange for food. In exchange for their horses, flocks of sheep and goats, herds of cattle, and donkeys, Joseph provided them with food for another year.

18But that year ended, and the next year they came again and said, "We cannot hide the truth from you, my lord. Our money is gone, and all our livestock and cattle are yours. We have nothing left to give but our bodies and our land. 19Why should we die before your very eyes? Buy us and our land in exchange for food; we offer our land and ourselves as slaves for Pharaoh. Just give us grain so we may live and not die, and so the land does not become empty and desolate."

20So Joseph bought all the land of Egypt for Pharaoh. All the Egyptians sold him their fields because the famine was so severe, and soon all the land belonged to Pharaoh. 21As for the people, he made them all slaves, from one end of Egypt to the other. 22The only land he did not buy was the land belonging to the priests. They received an allotment of food directly from Pharaoh, so they didn't need to sell their land.

23Then Joseph said to the people, "Look, today I have bought you and your land for Pharaoh. I will provide you with seed so you can plant the fields. 24Then when you harvest it, one-fifth of your crop will belong to Pharaoh. You may keep the remaining four-fifths as seed for your fields and as food for you, your households, and your little ones."

25"You have saved our lives!" they exclaimed. "May it please you, my lord, to let us be Pharaoh's servants." 26Joseph then issued a decree still in effect in the land of Egypt, that Pharaoh should receive one-fifth of all the crops grown on his land. Only the land belonging to the priests was not given to Pharaoh.

27Meanwhile, the people of Israel settled in the region of Goshen in Egypt. There they acquired property, and they were fruitful, and their population grew rapidly. 28Jacob lived for seventeen years after his arrival in Egypt, so he lived 147 years in all.

Joseph Promises to Bury Jacob in Canaan

29As the time of his death drew near, Jacob called for his son Joseph and said to him,

. . . .

47:7-10 When *Jacob* entered Pharaoh's court and when he left, he *blessed Pharaoh*, an indication of Jacob's position as God's representative (see Heb 7:7). God had promised that he would bless those who blessed Abraham's family (12:2-3), so he now blessed Pharaoh and Egypt.

47:13-26 The Lord blessed Pharaoh because Pharaoh was blessing Abraham's descendants (12:3). Through Joseph's wise administration in Egypt, the Lord saved the people from starvation and prospered Pharaoh. In selling food to the Egyptians during the years of famine, Joseph accepted money, livestock, and finally land as payment, until almost all of Egypt belonged to Pharaoh. Meanwhile, God provided Israel with some of the best land in Egypt where they could live, work, and multiply.

47:21 *he made them all slaves:* As in Greek version and Samaritan Pentateuch; Hebrew reads *he moved them all into the towns*, where the food was. In Hebrew script, the difference is very slight between *slaves* (Hebrew *'abadim*) and *towns* (Hebrew *'arim*). Moving the people into the towns doesn't fit the context very well, so most translations select *slaves* as the reading that makes the most sense (cp. 47:20).

47:27 God blessed his people according to his promise to Abraham that his descendants would be innumerable (15:5; 22:17). They had to wait for the fulfillment of the second promise, that they would own the land of Canaan (17:8).

47:29-31 *bury me with my ancestors:* Cp. 49:29-33. Jacob wanted to be buried with Abraham and Isaac in the cave of Machpelah (see note on 49:29-33; see 23:1-20; 25:7-10; 35:27-29). • *Put your hand under my thigh:* This custom (cp. 24:1-9 and note on 24:2) was a serious oath to carry on the covenant, which had as its main promise innumerable descendants in the Promised Land. • *Jacob:* Hebrew *Israel*; also in 47:31b. See note on 35:21.

"Please do me this favor. Put your hand under my thigh and swear that you will treat me with unfailing love by honoring this last request: Do not bury me in Egypt. 30When I die, please take my body out of Egypt and bury me with my ancestors."

So Joseph promised, "I will do as you ask."

31"Swear that you will do it," Jacob insisted. So Joseph gave his oath, and Jacob bowed humbly at the head of his bed.

Jacob Blesses His Children (48:1–50:26)
Jacob Blesses Manasseh and Ephraim

48 One day not long after this, word came to Joseph, "Your father is failing rapidly." So Joseph went to visit his father, and he took with him his two sons, Manasseh and Ephraim.

2When Joseph arrived, Jacob was told, "Your son Joseph has come to see you." So Jacob gathered his strength and sat up in his bed.

3Jacob said to Joseph, "God hAlmighty appeared to me at Luz in the land of Canaan and blessed me. 4He said to me, 'I will make you fruitful, and I will multiply your descendants. I will make you a multitude of nations. And I will give this land of Canaan to your idescendants after you as an everlasting possession.'

5"Now I am claiming as my own sons these two boys of yours, Ephraim and Manasseh, who were born here in the land of Egypt before I arrived. They will be my sons, just as Reuben and Simeon are. 6But any children born to you in the future will be your own, and they will inherit land within the territories of their brothers Ephraim and Manasseh.

7"Long ago, as I was returning from Paddan-aram, Rachel died in the land of Canaan. We were still on the way, some distance from Ephrath (that is, Bethlehem). So with great sorrow I buried her there beside the road to Ephrath."

8Then Jacob looked over at the two boys. "Are these your sons?" he asked.

9"Yes," Joseph told him, "these are the sons God has given me here in Egypt."

And Jacob said, "Bring them closer to me, so I can bless them."

10Jacob was half blind because of his age and could hardly see. So Joseph brought the boys close to him, and Jacob kissed and embraced them. 11Then Jacob said to Joseph, "I never thought I would see your face again, but now God has let me see your children, too!"

12Joseph moved the boys, who were at their grandfather's knees, and he bowed with his face to the ground. 13Then he positioned the boys in front of Jacob. With his right hand he directed Ephraim toward Jacob's left hand, and with his left hand he put Manasseh at Jacob's right hand. 14But Jacob crossed his arms as he reached out to lay his hands on the boys' heads. He put his right hand on the head of Ephraim, though he was the younger boy, and his left hand on the head of Manasseh, though he was the firstborn. 15Then he blessed Joseph and said,

"May the God before whom my
   grandfather Abraham
and my father, Isaac, walked—
the God who has been my jshepherd
all my life, to this very day,

47:30
Gen 23:17-20; 25:9;
49:29
Acts 7:15-16

47:31
Heb 11:21

48:1
Gen 41:51-52
Heb 11:21

48:3
Gen 28:13-19; 35:9-12
hshadday (7706)
▸ Gen 49:25

48:4
izera' (2233)
▸ Exod 32:13

48:5
Gen 29:32-33

48:7
Gen 35:19

48:9
Gen 33:5

48:10
Gen 27:1

48:11
Gen 44:28

48:12
Gen 33:3; 42:6

48:14
Gen 41:51-52

48:15
Gen 17:1; 49:24
iro'eh (7462)
▸ Gen 49:24

47:31 When the oath was taken, Jacob *bowed humbly* in worship *at the head of his bed:* Greek version reads *and Israel bowed in worship as he leaned on his staff;* cp. Heb 11:21. Jacob thanked the Lord for ensuring that he would be buried with his ancestors in the land of promise (cp. 1 Kgs 1:47).

48:1-22 In blessing Ephraim and Manasseh, Jacob reached out by faith for the promise to be continued, having learned that God's ways are not always the ways of men. Out of Jacob's long life, the writer to the Hebrews selected the blessing of Joseph's sons as his great act of faith (Heb 11:21). As Jacob acted in light of God's will, the primary blessing was again given to the younger instead of the older son, but without scheming and its bitter results.

48:2 *Jacob:* Hebrew *Israel;* also in 48:8, 10, 11, 13, 14, 21. See note on 35:21.

48:3-4 *Jacob* rehearsed how *God Almighty* (Hebrew *El-Shaddai*) had *appeared* to him and had promised him Abraham's blessing—innumerable *descendants* dwelling in the *land . . . as an everlasting possession* (cp. 28:10-22). • *descendants:* Literally *seed;* also in 48:19.

48:5-7 Jacob, prompted by his memory of Rachel (see 35:16-20), blessed Joseph by elevating his two sons as coheirs with his other sons—the tribes of Ephraim and Manasseh would have shares along with the other tribes that came from Jacob (see Josh 16–17). Jacob also gave Ephraim, Joseph's younger son, the birthright (see 1 Chr 5:1-2). As a result of this blessing, Ephraim and Manasseh became large and powerful tribes (see Josh 17:14-18).

48:10 As Isaac his father had done, Jacob now gave the blessing when his

eyesight was failing (cp. 27:1).

48:14 The *right hand* was for the head of the firstborn, and Jacob was deliberately giving that position to the younger son. That pattern was followed for four consecutive generations: Isaac over Ishmael, Jacob over Esau, Joseph over Reuben, and Ephraim over Manasseh. Many years later, Ephraim became the leading tribe in the northern kingdom, superior to the tribe of Manasseh. The entire northern kingdom of Israel was occasionally called Ephraim (see notes on 2 Chr 28:12; Isa 11:13; Ezek 37:16-19; Hos 6:4; Zech 9:10).

48:15-16 In his blessing on Joseph, Jacob used a threefold invocation to describe the God in whom he trusted: (1) *the God* who was in covenant with his fathers *Abraham* and *Isaac* (28:13; 31:5, 42; 32:9; 46:3); (2) *the God* who had been his *shepherd* (cp. 49:24;

48:16
Gen 22:11; 28:13-15;
31:11
*Heb 11:21
ᵏmal'ak (4397)
▸ Exod 3:2

48:19
Gen 28:14; 46:3

48:20
Ruth 4:11

48:21
Gen 28:15; 46:4;
50:24

48:22
Josh 24:32
John 4:5

49:1
Num 24:14

16 the ᵏAngel who has redeemed me from
        all harm—
    may he bless these boys.
May they preserve my name
        and the names of Abraham and Isaac.
And may their descendants multiply
        greatly
        throughout the earth."

17But Joseph was upset when he saw that his father placed his right hand on Ephraim's head. So Joseph lifted it to move it from Ephraim's head to Manasseh's head. 18"No, my father," he said. "This one is the firstborn. Put your right hand on his head."

19But his father refused. "I know, my son; I know," he replied. "Manasseh will also become a great people, but his younger brother will become even greater. And his descendants will become a multitude of nations."

20So Jacob blessed the boys that day with this blessing: "The people of Israel will use your names when they give a blessing. They will say, 'May God make you as prosperous as Ephraim and Manasseh.' " In this way, Jacob put Ephraim ahead of Manasseh.

21Then Jacob said to Joseph, "Look, I am about to die, but God will be with you and will take you back to Canaan, the land of your ancestors. 22And beyond what I have given your brothers, I am giving you an extra portion of the land that I took from the Amorites with my sword and bow."

Jacob Blesses His Sons

49 Then Jacob called together all his sons and said, "Gather around me, and I will tell you what will happen to each of you in the days to come.

. . . .

Blessing (48:8-20)

Gen 1:22, 28;
9:26-27; 12:2-3;
14:19-20; 24:59-60;
27:1-41; 28:1-4;
32:24-30; 49:1-28
Lev 26:3-13
Num 6:22-27
Deut 7:12-15; 10:8;
28:1-14; 33:1-29
1 Sam 2:20-21
Ps 128:1-6
Matt 5:3-12
Luke 6:27-28
Rom 12:14
Gal 3:13-14
Eph 1:3
Heb 7:6-7
1 Pet 3:9

Jacob adopted Joseph's sons and blessed them (48:3-7), just as his father Isaac had blessed him (27:27-29). Blessing enables, enhances, and enriches life, whereas a curse diminishes it (Lev 26:14-39). Blessing is issued publicly by a benefactor and provides power for prosperity and success. Blessing is essential to covenant relationships in that it guides and motivates the parties to obey the covenant's stipulations (Lev 26:3-13; Deut 28:1-14). Obedience leads to blessing, whereas rebellion brings a curse.

The initial realm of blessing is creation, in which God as Creator is the ultimate granter of blessing for animals (1:22) and humans (1:28; see Ps 104; 128:3-4). Humans also serve as channels of divine blessing. Abraham was called to be a blessing to the nations (12:2-3). The institutions of family (27:27-29), government (1 Kgs 8:14, 44, 52, 66), and religion (14:19; Lev 9:22) are nurtured, commissioned, and purified through blessing. Israel's priests mediated God's blessing to Israel (Num 6:24-26; Deut 10:8).

Three basic characteristics can be observed in OT blessings: (1) They are conveyed from a greater party to a lesser one (32:26; Heb 7:6-7); (2) They are signs of favor that result in well-being and productivity (Deut 28:3-7); and (3) They acknowledge that all power and blessing stems from the Creator. All blessings have their source in God's love (Deut 7:7-8, 12-15).

God's blessings in Genesis are in striking contrast with the pagan religions of antiquity. For pagan religions, fortunes and fertility of flock, family, and fields came about through sympathetic magic in cultic observances at their shrines—profane customs that were designed to induce the deities to act on their behalf so that the cycle of life could be maintained. In Genesis, all of life, fertility, and blessing came by God's decree, for he is the only true and living God.

In the NT, the emphasis of blessing shifts from the material to the spiritual, from the nation to the church, and from the temporal to the eternal (Matt 6:25; Eph 1:3; 1 Pet 3:9). In his death, Jesus bore the consequences of sin's curse (Gal 3:13), established God's kingdom (Matt 3:2; 5:3-20; John 3:3-5), and blessed its citizens with forgiveness of sin (Rom 4:6-25). Now believers are called to bless the world (Luke 6:27-28; Rom 12:14; see also Isa 19:24; Zech 8:13).

. . . .

Exod 6:6; Ps 23:1; Isa 59:20); and (3) *the Angel* who rescued him *from all harm.* He prayed the same blessings for Joseph's sons.

48:17-19 *Joseph was upset:* He expected God to act according to convention, but faith recognizes that God's ways are not man's ways, and God's thoughts are not man's thoughts. It took Jacob a lifetime

to learn this lesson, but he did learn it, and here he acted on it.

48:22 *an extra portion of the land:* Or *an extra ridge of land.* The meaning of the Hebrew is uncertain. Joseph was later buried at Shechem (Josh 24:32) as a sign that he possessed this bequeathed portion (Hebrew *shekem*) of land. Jacob had apparently conquered this area though

the occasion is not mentioned elsewhere.

49:1-28 Jacob, by faith and as God's spokesman, looked forward to Israel's settlement in the land, and beyond that to the glorious future. Here at the end of the patriarchal age, he foretold what would happen to each tribe as he evaluated his sons one by one, just as Noah had done at the end of the primeval era

2 "Come and listen, you sons of Jacob;
　　listen to Israel, your father.

3 "Reuben, you are my firstborn, my strength,
　　the child of my vigorous youth.
　　You are first in rank and first in power.
4 But you are as unruly as a flood,
　　and you will be first no longer.
　For you went to bed with my wife;
　　you defiled my marriage couch.

5 "Simeon and Levi are two of a kind;
　　their weapons are instruments of
　　　violence.
6 May I never join in their meetings;
　　may I never be a party to their plans.
　For in their anger they murdered men,
　　and they crippled oxen just for sport.
7 A curse on their anger, for it is fierce;
　　a curse on their wrath, for it is cruel.
　I will scatter them among the descen-
　　dants of Jacob;
　I will disperse them throughout Israel.

8 "Judah, your brothers will praise you.
　　You will grasp your enemies by the
　　　neck.
　All your relatives will bow before you.
9 Judah, my son, is a young lion
　　that has finished eating its prey.
　Like a lion he crouches and lies down;

like a lioness—who dares to rouse
　　him?
10 The scepter will not depart from Judah,
　　nor the ruler's staff from his
　　　descendants,
　until the coming of the one to whom it
　　belongs,
　　the one whom all nations will honor.
11 He ties his foal to a grapevine,
　　the colt of his donkey to a choice vine.
　He washes his clothes in wine,
　　his robes in the ªblood of grapes.
12 His eyes are darker than wine,
　　and his teeth are whiter than milk.

13 "Zebulun will settle by the seashore
　　and will be a harbor for ships;
　　his borders will extend to Sidon.

14 "Issachar is a sturdy donkey,
　　resting between two saddlepacks.
15 When he sees how good the
　　countryside is
　　and how pleasant the land,
　he will bend his shoulder to the load
　　and submit himself to hard labor.

16 "Dan will govern his people,
　　like any other tribe in Israel.
17 Dan will be a snake beside the road,
　　a poisonous viper along the path

49:3
Num 26:5
Deut 21:17
Ps 78:51; 105:36
49:4
Gen 35:22
Deut 27:20
49:5
Gen 29:33-34;
34:25-30
49:6
Gen 34:26
49:7
Josh 19:1, 9; 21:1-42
49:8
1 Chr 5:2
Heb 7:14
49:9
Num 24:9
Mic 5:8
49:10
Num 24:17
Ps 2:6-9; 60:7
49:11
Deut 8:7-8
2 Kgs 18:32
ªdam (1818)
▸Lev 3:17
49:13
Deut 33:18-19
49:15
Josh 19:17-23
49:16
Deut 33:22
Judg 18:26-27
49:19
Deut 33:20
49:20
Deut 33:24-25

. . . .

(cp. 9:25-27). The character and acts of each ancestor affected the lives of his descendants (Exod 20:5-6; 34:6-7; Num 14:18; Jer 32:18).

49:1-2 Jacob's words were deliberately chosen prophetic oracles. The *days to come* refer to the conquest and settlement of the Promised Land, and beyond that to the messianic age. They would all share in the blessing; all the tribes would enter the land with Joshua, but they would not all participate equally.

49:3-4 As firstborn, *Reuben* was entitled to be head of the family, but because he had the ungoverned impulses of boiling or turbulent waters (35:22), Jacob prophesied that Reuben would fail in leadership (see 37:21-22, 29; 42:22, 37-38; cp. Judg 5:15-16; 1 Chr 5:1-2).

49:5-7 *Simeon and Levi* were violent and lawless; instead of serving justice, they indulged their uncontrolled anger and disregarded life (34:24-29). • *I will scatter them:* Simeon's land was largely absorbed into Judah's (Josh 19:1, 9); Levi was given a more honorable future because the Levites became the priestly tribe (see Exod 32:25-29), but they had no region of their own (Josh 21).

49:8-12 The blessing on *Judah* commands the most attention. In this

oracle, Jacob predicted the fierce, *lion*-like dominance of Judah over his enemies and over his brothers, who would *praise* him (cp. 29:35; see, e.g., Ruth 4:11-12; 1 Sam 18:6-7; Pss 2, 45, 72; Isa 11:1-13).

49:10 This verse anticipates the kingship in *Judah* (cp. 17:6, 16; 35:11). Although the birthright blessing went to Joseph, Judah would provide Israel's rulers (see 1 Chr 5:1-2). A long line of kings from Judah would retain *the scepter,* the symbol of rule; the last king would be *the one to whom it belongs,* the promised Messiah (see 2 Sam 7:4-16; Pss 2, 45, 60; Isa 11; Ezek 21:26-27; Zech 9:9; Rev 5:5). • *from his descendants:* Literally *from between his feet,* taking *between his feet* as a poetic euphemism for reproductive organs. • *until the coming of the one to whom it belongs* (Or *until tribute is brought to him and the peoples obey;* traditionally rendered *until Shiloh comes*): These differences arise from ambiguities in the Hebrew text. Rule of Israel *belongs* to Judah's descendant through David's line (2 Sam 7:8-16), and he will eventually rule all nations, as signified by the bringing of *tribute* (see Ps 68:29; 72:8-11; Isa 2:2-4; Eph 4:8-10).

49:11-12 These descriptions envision the abundance of the Messiah's kingdom (see Isa 61:6-7; 65:21-25;

Zech 3:10). When the Messiah comes, there will be paradise-like splendor and abundance on the earth. • *He ties his foal to a grapevine:* Grapevines will be so abundant that they will be used for hitching posts, and *wine* will be as abundant as fresh water (see Amos 9:13-14; Zech 3:10). • The coming one will have *eyes . . . darker than wine* and *teeth . . . whiter than milk:* He will be vigorous and healthy, as will be the era of his rule. Jesus' miracle of changing water into wine (John 2:1-12), his first sign, was an announcement that the Messiah had come; it was a foretaste of even better things to come.

49:13 The oracle said *Zebulun* would dwell by the sea and be a safe harbor, but in the actual settlement they spread inland (see Josh 19:10-16). The oracle did not give specific borders for the tribes.

49:14-15 Like *a sturdy donkey,* the tribe of *Issachar* would be forced to work for others. Issachar was often subjugated by invading armies. • *saddlepacks:* Or *sheepfolds,* or *hearths.* The meaning of the Hebrew is uncertain.

49:16-17 *Dan* was called to provide justice (*Dan* means "judge"), but the tribe would choose treachery, like *a snake beside the road* (see Judg 18).

49:21
Deut 33:23
49:22
Deut 33:13-17
49:23
Gen 37:24
49:24
Ps 132:2, 5
Isa 41:10; 49:26
ᵇro'eh (7462)
 ▸ Exod 3:1
49:25
Gen 28:13
ᶜshadday (7706)
 ▸ Exod 6:3

that bites the horse's hooves
 so its rider is thrown off.
¹⁸ I trust in you for salvation, O LORD!

¹⁹ "Gad will be attacked by marauding bands,
 but he will attack them when they
 retreat.

²⁰ "Asher will dine on rich foods
 and produce food fit for kings.

²¹ "Naphtali is a doe set free
 that bears beautiful fawns.

²² "Joseph is the foal of a wild donkey,
 the foal of a wild donkey at a spring—
 one of the wild donkeys on the ridge.
²³ Archers attacked him savagely;
 they shot at him and harassed him.
²⁴ But his bow remained taut,
 and his arms were strengthened
 by the hands of the Mighty One of
 Jacob,
 by the ᵇShepherd, the Rock of Israel.
²⁵ May the God of your father help you;
 may the ᶜAlmighty bless you

Death (49:29-33)

Gen 2:15-17; 3:19;
6:17; 9:5-6
Exod 21:12-17, 28-
29; 23:7; 31:14-15
Lev 24:16
Deut 32:39
Job 10:18-22;
19:25-27
Ps 90:1-12; 94:17
Prov 14:32
Eccl 12:1-7
Isa 25:6-9; 26:19;
40:6-8
Dan 12:2-3
Mark 12:26-27
Rom 5:12-17
1 Cor 15:20-26,
51-58
Rev 20:4-6, 11-15;
21:3-8

As Jacob lay dying in Egypt, he considered two promises regarding his death: that he would die peacefully (46:4) and that he would join his ancestors (49:29, 33). Humans are mortal, and death is the natural end of earthly life (Ps 90:1-6). Human identity began with the earth's dust being animated by the breath of God (2:7). This passive state returns at death as God withdraws his breath and the human body collapses again into dust (3:19; Job 4:19-21; Isa 40:6-8). Human life depends entirely and continuously on the Creator of life—his breath is a gift that sustains us in life for as long as he grants it (Ps 104:29).

Death entered the human race by sin and brought ruin to it; death comes suddenly, bringing mourning and an apparent end to hopes and dreams. Death is the severest penalty in human justice. In the OT, the death penalty was a punishment for murder (9:6; Exod 21:12) or blasphemy (Lev 24:16; John 10:30-31)—violations that threatened the living community.

In the OT, the opposite of "the land of the living" (Ps 27:13) was *Sheol,* the realm of the dead that was shrouded in darkness and silence (Job 10:21-22; Ps 94:17; Jon 2:6). Yet even in death, believers cannot be separated from God's presence (Ps 17:15; 49:15; Prov 14:32). God is sovereign and rules over death (Deut 32:39).

The OT mentions the fact of resurrection (see Job 19:25-27; Isa 25:6-9; 26:19; Dan 12:2). Eventually, God's redeemed people will triumph over death (1 Cor 15:54-55), the last enemy to be destroyed (1 Cor 15:26). Death results from sin (Rom 5:12), and sinners will be punished in the lake of fire, called the second death (Rev 21:8). Christ's death defeated death, making his resurrection the paradigm for all believers (Col 1:18). He is the Lord of the living and of the dead (Rom 14:9).

In Gen 49:29-33, death is joined with hope by faith. In life, the patriarchs were sojourners; in death, they were heirs of the promise and the occupied land. The patriarchs died without having received the promises (Heb 11:39-40), but that was not the end of the story. God's promises to people are not exhausted in this life, for God makes promises that necessitate a resurrection (see Matt 22:21-32 // Mark 12:26-27). The time of death—when the natural inclination is to mourn—should also be the time of the greatest demonstration of faith, for the recipient of God's promises has a hope beyond the grave.

49:18 At this point, Jacob interjected an expression of hope. He may have been indirectly reminding his sons of their need for dependence on the Lord or expressing his hope in the Messiah's reign, when he and his descendants would be rescued from all trouble, grief, and human treachery.

49:19 Three of the six Hebrew words in this verse are wordplays on the name *Gad* ("attack"). Gad will be *attacked* by *marauding bands* (attackers), but he will *attack*. The tribes that settled east of the Jordan River frequently experienced border raids (see Josh 13; 2 Kgs 10:32-33; 1 Chr 5:18-19).

49:20 *Asher* would be fertile and productive, providing *rich foods*. That tribe settled along the rich northern coast of Canaan.

49:21 *Naphtali,* like *a doe*, would be a *free* mountain people (cp. Judg 5:18). The tribe settled in the hilly region northwest of the Sea of Galilee.

49:22-26 This oracle treats *Joseph* more expansively than any of the others, for here the main blessing lay (see 1 Chr 5:1-2). Jacob lavished promises of victory and prosperity on Joseph's two tribes. Ephraimites recorded as victorious in battle include Joshua (Josh 6, 8, 10, 12) and Deborah (Judg 4). Victorious

descendants of Manasseh include Gideon (Judg 6–8) and Jephthah (Judg 11:1–12:7).

49:22 Or *Joseph is a fruitful tree, / a fruitful tree beside a spring. / His branches reach over the wall.* The meaning of the Hebrew is uncertain.

49:24-26 Five names for God introduce five blessings; God is the giver of all good things.

49:25 The *blessings of the heavens above* meant rain for crops. • The *blessings of the watery depths* were streams and wells of water. • The *blessings of the breasts and womb* were abundant offspring.

with the blessings of the heavens above,
and blessings of the watery depths
below,
and blessings of the breasts and
womb.
26 May the blessings of your father
surpass the blessings of the ancient
mountains,
reaching to the heights of the eternal
hills.
May these blessings rest on the head of
Joseph,
who is a prince among his brothers.

27 "Benjamin is a ravenous wolf,
devouring his enemies in the morning
and dividing his plunder in the evening."

28These are the twelve tribes of Israel, and this is what their father said as he told his sons good-bye. He dblessed each one with an appropriate message.

Jacob's Death and Burial
29Then Jacob instructed them, "Soon I will die and join my ancestors. Bury me with my father and grandfather in the cave in the field of Ephron the Hittite. 30This is the cave in the field of Machpelah, near Mamre in Canaan, that Abraham bought from Ephron the Hittite as a permanent burial site. 31There Abraham and his wife Sarah are buried. There Isaac and his wife, Rebekah, are buried. And there I buried Leah. 32It is the plot of land and the cave that my grandfather Abraham bought from the Hittites."

33When Jacob had finished this charge to his sons, he drew his feet into the bed, breathed his last, and joined his ancestors in death.

50 Joseph threw himself on his father and wept over him and kissed him. 2Then Joseph told the physicians who served him to embalm his father's body; so Jacob was embalmed. 3The embalming process took the usual forty days. And the Egyptians mourned his death for seventy days.

4When the period of mourning was over, Joseph approached Pharaoh's advisers and said, "Please do me this favor and speak to Pharaoh on my behalf. 5Tell him that my father made me swear an oath. He said to me, 'Listen, I am about to die. Take my body back to the land of Canaan, and bury me in the tomb I prepared for myself.' So please allow me to go and bury my father. After his burial, I will return without delay."

6Pharaoh agreed to Joseph's request. "Go and bury your father, as he made you promise," he said. 7So Joseph went up to bury his father. He was accompanied by all of Pharaoh's officials, all the senior members of Pharaoh's household, and all the senior officers of Egypt. 8Joseph also took his entire household and his brothers and their households. But they left their little children and flocks and herds in the land of Goshen. 9A great number of chariots and charioteers accompanied Joseph.

10When they arrived at the threshing floor of Atad, near the Jordan River, they held a very great and solemn memorial service, with a seven-day period of mourning for Joseph's father. 11The local residents, the Canaanites, watched them mourning at the threshing floor of Atad. Then they renamed that place (which is near the Jordan) Abel-mizraim, for they said, "This is a place of deep mourning for these Egyptians."

49:26
Deut 33:15-16
49:27
Deut 33:12
49:28
dbarak (1288)
▸ Num 6:23
49:29
Gen 23:16-20; 25:8-9
49:31
Gen 23:19; 25:9;
35:29
49:33
Gen 25:8
Acts 7:15
50:1
Gen 46:4
50:2
Gen 50:26
50:3
Num 20:29
Deut 34:8
50:5
Gen 47:29-31
50:8
Gen 45:10
50:9
Gen 41:43

. . . .

49:26 *of the ancient mountains:* Or of *my ancestors.* • *Joseph . . . is a prince among his brothers:* A reflection of both his character and his position.

49:27 The oracle about *Benjamin* describes a violent tribe (see Judg 20; 1 Sam 9:1-2; 19:10; 22:17).

49:28 These prophecies are broad in scope, foretelling the future of the different tribes in general terms. Individuals, by faith and obedience, could find great blessing from God regardless of what happened to their clan.

49:29-33 *Bury me with my father:* This grave in the land of Canaan represented hope for the future (cp. 47:29-30). Others buried at the cave of Machpelah near Hebron were Sarah (23:19), Abraham (25:7-9), Isaac (35:27-29), Rebekah, and Leah.

49:33 Jacob died at the age of 147 (47:28), bringing his life of struggle and sorrow to an end. Jacob had always had an unquenchable desire for God's blessing. He had a deep piety that habitually relied on God despite all else. In the end, he died a man of genuine faith. He learned where real blessings come from, and through his faith would be able to hand these on to his sons (Heb 11:21).

50:1-6 As with his father and grandfather, Jacob's death brought the end of an era.

50:2 *Jacob:* Hebrew *Israel;* see note on 35:21. His body was *embalmed* for burial in typical Egyptian fashion.

50:3 *The Egyptians mourned* for Jacob *for seventy days,* just two days short of the mourning period for a pharaoh.

This showed the great respect that the Egyptians had for Joseph.

50:4-6 *Joseph* needed Pharaoh's permission to leave his post temporarily to *bury* his *father* in *Canaan.* Pharaoh readily granted this freedom to the former slave.

50:7-9 This was Joseph's first return to his homeland in thirty-nine years. The trip was temporary. Centuries later, the family of Israel would permanently leave Egypt, taking Joseph's bones with them for burial in the land of promise (see 50:25).

50:10-13 This journey into Canaan was made in sorrow to bury a man; the next journey into the land would be to live there. • *Abel-mizraim* means "mourning of the Egyptians."

50:12
Gen 49:29
50:13
Gen 23:16-18
50:15
Gen 42:21-22
50:16
Gen 49:29
50:17
Gen 45:5, 7
Matt 6:14
Luke 6:27
Rom 12:19
ᵉ*nasa'* (5375)
  ▸ Exod 10:17
ᶠ*pesha'* (6588)
  ▸ Exod 34:7
50:18
Gen 37:7-10
50:19
Gen 30:2
50:20
Gen 37:26-27
50:21
Gen 45:11
50:24
Gen 13:15; 28:13
50:25
Exod 13:19
Josh 24:32
Heb 11:22
50:26
Exod 1:6
ᵍ*aron* (0727)
  ▸ Exod 25:22

¹²So Jacob's sons did as he had commanded them. ¹³They carried his body to the land of Canaan and buried him in the cave in the field of Machpelah, near Mamre. This is the cave that Abraham had bought as a permanent burial site from Ephron the Hittite.

Joseph Reassures His Brothers

¹⁴After burying Jacob, Joseph returned to Egypt with his brothers and all who had accompanied him to his father's burial. ¹⁵But now that their father was dead, Joseph's brothers became fearful. "Now Joseph will show his anger and pay us back for all the wrong we did to him," they said.

¹⁶So they sent this message to Joseph: "Before your father died, he instructed us ¹⁷to say to you: 'Please ᵉforgive your brothers for the great wrong they did to you—for their ᶠsin in treating you so cruelly.' So we, the servants of the God of your father, beg you to ᵉforgive our ᶠsin." When Joseph received the message, he broke down and wept. ¹⁸Then his brothers came and threw themselves down before Joseph. "Look, we are your slaves!" they said.

¹⁹But Joseph replied, "Don't be afraid of me. Am I God, that I can punish you? ²⁰You

intended to harm me, but God intended it all for good. He brought me to this position so I could save the lives of many people. ²¹No, don't be afraid. I will continue to take care of you and your children." So he reassured them by speaking kindly to them.

The Death of Joseph

²²So Joseph and his brothers and their families continued to live in Egypt. Joseph lived to the age of 110. ²³He lived to see three generations of descendants of his son Ephraim, and he lived to see the birth of the children of Manasseh's son Makir, whom he claimed as his own.

²⁴"Soon I will die," Joseph told his brothers, "but God will surely come to help you and lead you out of this land of Egypt. He will bring you back to the land he solemnly promised to give to Abraham, to Isaac, and to Jacob."

²⁵Then Joseph made the sons of Israel swear an oath, and he said, "When God comes to help you and lead you back, you must take my bones with you." ²⁶So Joseph died at the age of 110. The Egyptians embalmed him, and his body was placed in a ᵍcoffin in Egypt.

. . . .

50:15-18 The *brothers* pleaded for Joseph's forgiveness, referring to themselves as Joseph's *slaves* (cp. 37:7; 44:16, 33). The brothers were afraid that Joseph's earlier reconciliation with them had been motivated only by his desire to see his father again. With neither Jacob nor Pharaoh to restrain him, they feared that he might now take revenge on them. But *Joseph . . . wept* because they still feared reprisal.

50:19-21 Joseph reassured his brothers that God planned to fulfill the promised blessing (cp. 45:5, 7-9), and he promised kindness and provision (cp. 45:11).

50:22-23 Joseph lived to see his great-great-grandchildren by Ephraim, and his great-grandchildren by Manasseh—

a sign of God's blessing (see Ps 128:6; Prov 17:6; Isa 53:10).

50:23 *whom he claimed as his own* (literally *who were born on Joseph's knees*): Placing them on his knees at their birth was a symbolic act signifying that they came from him and belonged to him (cp. Job 3:12).

50:24-25 *God will surely come to help you* (literally *visit you*): These words of Joseph, given twice, summarize the hope expressed throughout both the OT and NT. God's visitation in the person of the Messiah, the offspring of Abraham, would bring the curse to an end and establish the long-awaited blessing of God in a new creation. The company of the faithful would wait in expectation

for that to happen. • Like his father before him, Joseph made his brothers promise that his bones would be taken out of Egypt when God would come to take them (*to help you and lead you . . . back*) to Canaan (see Exod 13:19; Josh 24:32; Heb 11:22).

50:26 Joseph's death signified the end of his generation (see notes on 25:7-8; 35:1-29; 35:27-29) and of the patriarchal age. From this point forward, God dealt with Israel as a nation. • Joseph's body was kept in Egypt as a pledge of hope for slaves awaiting the Promised Land (see Exod 13:19; Heb 11:39-40). He was eventually buried in Shechem (see Josh 24:32), where Jacob had originally sent him (37:13).

INTRODUCTION TO THE
NEW LIVING TRANSLATION

Translation Philosophy and Methodology

English Bible translations tend to be governed by one of two general translation theories. The first theory has been called "formal-equivalence," "literal," or "word-for-word" translation. According to this theory, the translator attempts to render each word of the original language into English and seeks to preserve the original syntax and sentence structure as much as possible in translation. The second theory has been called "dynamic-equivalence," "functional-equivalence," or "thought-for-thought" translation. The goal of this translation theory is to produce in English the closest natural equivalent of the message expressed by the original-language text, both in meaning and in style.

Both of these translation theories have their strengths. A formal-equivalence translation preserves aspects of the original text—including ancient idioms, term consistency, and original-language syntax—that are valuable for scholars and professional study. It allows a reader to trace formal elements of the original-language text through the English translation. A dynamic-equivalence translation, on the other hand, focuses on translating the message of the original-language text. It ensures that the meaning of the text is readily apparent to the contemporary reader. This allows the message to come through with immediacy, without requiring the reader to struggle with foreign idioms and awkward syntax. It also facilitates serious study of the text's message and clarity in both devotional and public reading.

The pure application of either of these translation philosophies would create translations at opposite ends of the translation spectrum. But in reality, all translations contain a mixture of these two philosophies. A purely formal-equivalence translation would be unintelligible in English, and a purely dynamic-equivalence translation would risk being unfaithful to the original. That is why translations shaped by dynamic-equivalence theory are usually quite literal when the original text is relatively clear, and the translations shaped by formal-equivalence theory are sometimes quite dynamic when the original text is obscure.

The translators of the New Living Translation set out to render the message of the original texts of Scripture into clear, contemporary English. As they did so, they kept the concerns of both formal-equivalence and dynamic-equivalence in mind. On the one hand, they translated as simply and literally as possible when that approach yielded an accurate, clear, and natural English text. Many words and phrases were rendered literally and consistently into English, preserving essential literary and rhetorical devices, ancient metaphors, and word choices that give structure to the text and provide echoes of meaning from one passage to the next.

On the other hand, the translators rendered the message more dynamically when the literal rendering was hard to understand, was misleading, or yielded archaic or foreign wording. They clarified difficult metaphors and terms to aid in the reader's understanding. The translators first struggled with the meaning of the words and phrases in the ancient context; then they rendered the message into clear, natural English. Their goal was to be both faithful to the ancient texts and eminently readable. The result is a translation that is both exegetically accurate and idiomatically powerful.

Translation Process and Team

To produce an accurate translation of the Bible into contemporary English, the translation team needed the skills necessary to enter into the thought patterns of the ancient authors and then to render their ideas, connotations, and effects into clear, contemporary English. To begin this process, qualified biblical scholars were needed to interpret the meaning of the original text and to check it against our base English translation. In order to guard against personal and theological biases, the scholars needed to represent a diverse group of evangelicals who would employ the best exegetical tools. Then to work alongside the scholars, skilled English stylists were needed to shape the text into clear, contemporary English.

With these concerns in mind, the Bible Translation Committee recruited teams of scholars that represented a broad spectrum of denominations, theological perspectives, and backgrounds within the worldwide evangelical community. (These scholars are listed at the end of this introduction.) Each book of the Bible was assigned to three different scholars with proven expertise in the book or group of books to be reviewed. Each of these scholars made a thorough review of a base translation and submitted suggested revisions to the appropriate Senior Translator. The Senior Translator then reviewed and summarized these suggestions and proposed a first-draft revision of the base text. This draft served as the basis for several additional phases of exegetical and

stylistic committee review. Then the Bible Translation Committee jointly reviewed and approved every verse of the final translation.

Throughout the translation and editing process, the Senior Translators and their scholar teams were given a chance to review the editing done by the team of stylists. This ensured that exegetical errors would not be introduced late in the process and that the entire Bible Translation Committee was happy with the final result. By choosing a team of qualified scholars and skilled stylists and by setting up a process that allowed their interaction throughout the process, the New Living Translation has been refined to preserve the essential formal elements of the original biblical texts, while also creating a clear, understandable English text.

The New Living Translation was first published in 1996. Shortly after its initial publication, the Bible Translation Committee began a process of further committee review and translation refinement. The purpose of this continued revision was to increase the level of precision without sacrificing the text's easy-to-understand quality. This second-edition text was completed in 2004, and an additional update with minor changes was subsequently introduced in 2007. This printing of the New Living Translation reflects the updated 2007 text.

Written to Be Read Aloud
It is evident in Scripture that the biblical documents were written to be read aloud, often in public worship (see Nehemiah 8; Luke 4:16-20; 1 Timothy 4:13; Revelation 1:3). It is still the case today that more people will hear the Bible read aloud in church than are likely to read it for themselves. Therefore, a new translation must communicate with clarity and power when it is read publicly. Clarity was a primary goal for the NLT translators, not only to facilitate private reading and understanding, but also to ensure that it would be excellent for public reading and make an immediate and powerful impact on any listener.

The Texts behind the New Living Translation
The Old Testament translators used the Masoretic Text of the Hebrew Bible as represented in *Biblia Hebraica Stuttgartensia* (1977), with its extensive system of textual notes; this is an update of Rudolf Kittel's *Biblia Hebraica* (Stuttgart, 1937). The translators also further compared the Dead Sea Scrolls, the Septuagint and other Greek manuscripts, the Samaritan Pentateuch, the Syriac Peshitta, the Latin Vulgate, and any other versions or manuscripts that shed light on the meaning of difficult passages.

The New Testament translators used the two standard editions of the Greek New Testament: the *Greek New Testament*, published by the United Bible Societies (UBS, fourth revised edition, 1993), and *Novum Testamentum Graece*, edited by Nestle and Aland (NA, twenty-seventh edition, 1993). These two editions, which have the same text but differ in punctuation and textual notes, represent, for the most part, the best in modern textual scholarship. However, in cases where strong textual or other scholarly evidence supported the decision, the translators sometimes chose to differ from the UBS and NA Greek texts and followed variant readings found in other ancient witnesses. Significant textual variants of this sort are always noted in the textual notes of the New Living Translation.

Translation Issues
The translators have made a conscious effort to provide a text that can be easily understood by the typical reader of modern English. To this end, we sought to use only vocabulary and language structures in common use today. We avoided using language likely to become quickly dated or that reflects only a narrow subdialect of English, with the goal of making the New Living Translation as broadly useful and timeless as possible.

But our concern for readability goes beyond the concerns of vocabulary and sentence structure. We are also concerned about historical and cultural barriers to understanding the Bible, and we have sought to translate terms shrouded in history and culture in ways that can be immediately understood. To this end:

• We have converted ancient weights and measures (for example, "ephah" [a unit of dry volume] or "cubit" [a unit of length]) to modern English (American) equivalents, since the ancient measures are not generally meaningful to today's readers. Then in the textual footnotes we offer the literal Hebrew, Aramaic, or Greek measures, along with modern metric equivalents.

• Instead of translating ancient currency values literally, we have expressed them in common terms that communicate the message. For example, in the Old Testament, "ten shekels of silver" becomes "ten pieces of silver" to convey the intended message. In the New Testament, we have often translated the "denarius" as "the normal daily wage" to facilitate understanding. Then a footnote offers: "Greek *a denarius*, the payment for a full day's wage." In general, we give a clear English rendering and then state the literal Hebrew, Aramaic, or Greek in a textual footnote.

• Since the names of Hebrew months are unknown to most contemporary readers, and since the Hebrew lunar calendar fluctuates from year to year in relation to the solar calendar used today, we have looked for clear ways to communicate the time of year the Hebrew months (such as Abib) refer to. When an expanded or interpretive rendering is given in the text, a textual note gives the literal rendering. Where it is possible to define a specific ancient date in terms of our modern calendar, we use modern dates in the text. A textual footnote then gives the literal Hebrew date and states the rationale for our rendering. For example, Ezra 6:15 pinpoints the date when the postexilic Temple was completed in Jerusalem: "the third day of the month Adar." This was during the sixth year of King Darius's reign (that is, 515 B.C.). We have translated that date as March 12, with a footnote giving the Hebrew and identifying the year as 515 B.C.

• Since ancient references to the time of day differ from our modern methods of denoting time, we have used renderings that are instantly understandable to the

modern reader. Accordingly, we have rendered specific times of day by using approximate equivalents in terms of our common "o'clock" system. On occasion, translations such as "at dawn the next morning" or "as the sun was setting" have been used when the biblical reference is more general.

- When the meaning of a proper name (or a wordplay inherent in a proper name) is relevant to the message of the text, its meaning is often illuminated with a textual footnote. For example, in Exodus 2:10 the text reads: "The princess named him Moses, for she explained, 'I lifted him out of the water.' " The accompanying footnote reads: "*Moses* sounds like a Hebrew term that means 'to lift out.' "

    Sometimes, when the actual meaning of a name is clear, that meaning is included in parentheses within the text itself. For example, the text at Genesis 16:11 reads: "You are to name him Ishmael *(which means 'God hears')*, for the LORD has heard your cry of distress." Since the original hearers and readers would have instantly understood the meaning of the name "Ishmael," we have provided modern readers with the same information so they can experience the text in a similar way.

- Many words and phrases carry a great deal of cultural meaning that was obvious to the original readers but needs explanation in our own culture. For example, the phrase "they beat their breasts" (Luke 23:48) in ancient times meant that people were very upset, often in mourning. In our translation we chose to translate this phrase dynamically for clarity: "They went home *in deep sorrow.*" Then we included a footnote with the literal Greek, which reads: "Greek *went home beating their breasts.*" In other similar cases, however, we have sometimes chosen to illuminate the existing literal expression to make it immediately understandable. For example, here we might have expanded the literal Greek phrase to read: "They went home beating their breasts *in sorrow.*" If we had done this,

we would not have included a textual footnote, since the literal Greek clearly appears in translation.

- Metaphorical language is sometimes difficult for contemporary readers to understand, so at times we have chosen to translate or illuminate the meaning of a metaphor. For example, the ancient poet writes, "Your neck is *like* the tower of David" (Song of Songs 4:4). We have rendered it "Your neck is *as beautiful as* the tower of David" to clarify the intended positive meaning of the simile. Another example comes from Ecclesiastes 12:3, which can be literally rendered: "Remember him . . . when the grinding women cease because they are few, and the women who look through the windows see dimly." We have rendered it: "Remember him before your teeth—your few remaining servants—stop grinding; and before your eyes—the women looking through the windows— see dimly." We clarified such metaphors only when we believed a typical reader might be confused by the literal text.

- When the content of the original language text is poetic in character, we have rendered it in English poetic form. We sought to break lines in ways that clarify and highlight the relationships between phrases of the text. Hebrew poetry often uses parallelism, a literary form where a second phrase (or in some instances a third or fourth) echoes the initial phrase in some way. In Hebrew parallelism, the subsequent parallel phrases continue, while also furthering and sharpening, the thought expressed in the initial line or phrase. Whenever possible, we sought to represent these parallel phrases in natural poetic English.

- The Greek term *hoi Ioudaioi* is literally translated "the Jews" in many English translations. In the Gospel of John, however, this term doesn't always refer to the Jewish people generally. In some contexts, it refers more particularly to the Jewish religious leaders. We have attempted to capture the meaning in these different contexts by using terms such as "the people" (with a

footnote: Greek *the Jewish people*) or "the religious leaders," where appropriate.

- One challenge we faced was how to translate accurately the ancient biblical text that was originally written in a context where male-oriented terms were used to refer to humanity generally. We needed to respect the nature of the ancient context while also trying to make the translation clear to a modern audience that tends to read male-oriented language as applying only to males. Often the original text, though using masculine nouns and pronouns, clearly intends that the message be applied to both men and women. A typical example is found in the New Testament letters, where the believers are called "brothers" (*adelphoi*). Yet it is clear from the content of these letters that they were addressed to all the believers— male and female. Thus, we have usually translated this Greek word as "brothers and sisters" in order to represent the historical situation more accurately.

    We have also been sensitive to passages where the text applies generally to human beings or to the human condition. In some instances we have used plural pronouns (they, them) in place of the masculine singular (he, him). For example, a traditional rendering of Proverbs 22:6 is: "Train up a child in the way he should go, and when he is old he will not turn from it." We have rendered it: "Direct your children onto the right path, and when they are older, they will not leave it." At times, we have also replaced third person pronouns with the second person to ensure clarity. A traditional rendering of Proverbs 26:27 is: "He who digs a pit will fall into it, and he who rolls a stone, it will come back on him." We have rendered it: "If you set a trap for others, you will get caught in it yourself. If you roll a boulder down on others, it will crush you instead."

    We should emphasize, however, that all masculine nouns and pronouns used to represent God (for example, "Father") have been maintained without

exception. All decisions of this kind have been driven by the concern to reflect accurately the intended meaning of the original texts of Scripture.

Lexical Consistency in Terminology
For the sake of clarity, we have translated certain original-language terms consistently, especially within synoptic passages and for commonly repeated rhetorical phrases, and within certain word categories such as divine names and non-theological technical terminology (e.g., liturgical, legal, cultural, zoological, and botanical terms). For theological terms, we have allowed a greater semantic range of acceptable English words or phrases for a single Hebrew or Greek word. We have avoided some theological terms that are not readily understood by many modern readers. For example, we avoided using words such as "justification" and "sanctification," which are carryovers from Latin translations. In place of these words, we have provided renderings such as "made right with God" and "made holy."

The Spelling of Proper Names
Many individuals in the Bible, especially the Old Testament, are known by more than one name (e.g., Uzziah/Azariah). For the sake of clarity, we have tried to use a single spelling for any one individual, footnoting the literal spelling whenever we differ from it. This is especially helpful in delineating the kings of Israel and Judah. King Joash/Jehoash of Israel has been consistently called Jehoash, while King Joash/Jehoash of Judah is called Joash. A similar distinction has been used to distinguish between Joram/Jehoram of Israel and Joram/Jehoram of Judah. All such decisions were made with the goal of clarifying the text for the reader. When the ancient biblical writers clearly had a theological purpose in their choice of a variant name (e.g., Esh-baal/Ishbosheth), the different names have been maintained with an explanatory footnote.

For the names Jacob and Israel, which are used interchangeably for both the individual patriarch and the nation, we generally render it "Israel" when it refers to the nation and "Jacob" when it refers to the individual. When our rendering of the name differs from the underlying Hebrew text, we provide a textual footnote, which includes this explanation: "The names 'Jacob' and 'Israel' are often interchanged throughout the Old Testament, referring sometimes to the individual patriarch and sometimes to the nation."

The Rendering of Divine Names
All appearances of *'el, 'elohim,* or *'eloah* have been translated "God," except where the context demands the translation "god(s)." We have generally rendered the tetragrammaton (*YHWH*) consistently as "the LORD," utilizing a form with small capitals that is common among English translations. This will distinguish it from the name *'adonai,* which we render "Lord." When *'adonai* and *YHWH* appear together, we have rendered it "Sovereign LORD." This also distinguishes *'adonai YHWH* from cases where *YHWH* appears with *'elohim,* which is rendered "LORD God." When *YH* (the short form of *YHWH*) and *YHWH* appear together, we have rendered it "LORD GOD." When *YHWH* appears with the term *tseba'oth,* we have rendered it "LORD of Heaven's Armies" to translate the meaning of the name. In a few cases, we have utilized the transliteration, *Yahweh,* when the personal character of the name is being invoked in contrast to another divine name or the name of some other god (for example, see Exodus 3:15; 6:2-3).

In the New Testament, the Greek word *christos* has been translated as "Messiah" when the context assumes a Jewish audience. When a Gentile audience can be assumed, *christos* has been translated as "Christ." The Greek word *kurios* is consistently translated "Lord," except that it is translated "LORD" wherever the New Testament text explicitly quotes from the Old Testament, and the text there has it in small capitals.

Textual Footnotes
The New Living Translation provides several kinds of textual footnotes, all included within the study notes in this edition:

- When for the sake of clarity the NLT renders a difficult or potentially confusing phrase dynamically, we generally give the literal rendering in a textual footnote. This allows the reader to see the literal source of our dynamic rendering and how our translation relates to other more literal translations. These notes are prefaced with "literally." For example, in Acts 2:42 we translated the literal "breaking of bread" (from the Greek) as "the Lord's Supper" to clarify that this verse refers to the ceremonial practice of the church rather than just an ordinary meal. Then we attached a footnote to "the Lord's Supper," which reads: "Literally *the breaking of bread.*"

- Textual footnotes are also used to show alternative renderings, prefaced with the word "Or." These normally occur for passages where an aspect of the meaning is debated. On occasion, we also provide notes on words or phrases that represent a departure from long-standing tradition. These notes are prefaced with "Traditionally rendered." For example, the footnote to the translation "serious skin disease" at Leviticus 13:2 says: "Traditionally rendered *leprosy.* The Hebrew word used throughout this passage is used to describe various skin diseases."

- When our translators follow a textual variant that differs significantly from our standard Hebrew or Greek texts (listed earlier), we document that difference with a footnote. We also footnote cases when the NLT excludes a passage that is included in the Greek text known as the *Textus Receptus* (and familiar to readers through its translation in the King James Version). In such cases, we offer a translation of the excluded text in a footnote, even though it is generally recognized as a later addition to the Greek text and not part of the original Greek New Testament.

- All Old Testament passages that are quoted in the New Testament are identified by a textual footnote at the New Testament location. When the New Testament clearly quotes from the Greek translation of the Old Testament,

and when it differs significantly in wording from the Hebrew text, we also place a textual footnote at the Old Testament location. This note includes a rendering of the Greek version, along with a cross-reference to the New Testament passage(s) where it is cited (for example, see notes on Proverbs 3:12; Psalms 8:2; 53:3).

- Some textual footnotes provide cultural and historical information on places, things, and people in the Bible that are probably obscure to modern readers. Such notes should aid the reader in understanding the message of the text. For example, in Acts 12:1, "King Herod" is named in this translation as "King Herod Agrippa" and is identified in a footnote as being "the nephew of Herod Antipas and a grandson of Herod the Great."

- When the meaning of a proper name (or a wordplay inherent in a proper name) is relevant to the meaning of the text, it is either illuminated with a textual footnote or included within parentheses in the text itself. For example, the footnote concerning the name "Eve" at Genesis

3:20 reads: "*Eve* sounds like a Hebrew term that means 'to give life.' " This wordplay in the Hebrew illuminates the meaning of the text, which goes on to say that Eve "would be the mother of all who live."

Cross-References
There are a number of different cross-referencing tools that appear in New Living Translation Bibles, and they offer different levels of help in this regard. All straight-text Bibles include the standard set of textual footnotes that include cross-references connecting New Testament texts to their related Old Testament sources. (See more on this above.)

Many NLT Bibles include an additional short cross-reference system that sets key cross-references at the end of paragraphs and then marks the associated verses with a cross symbol. This space-efficient system, while not being obtrusive, offers many important key connections between passages. Larger study editions include a full-column cross-reference system. This system allows space for a more comprehensive listing of cross-references.

AS WE SUBMIT this translation for publication, we recognize that any translation of the Scriptures is subject to limitations and imperfections. Anyone who has attempted to communicate the richness of God's Word into another language will realize it is impossible to make a perfect translation. Recognizing these limitations, we sought God's guidance and wisdom throughout this project. Now we pray that he will accept our efforts and use this translation for the benefit of the church and of all people.

We pray that the New Living Translation will overcome some of the barriers of history, culture, and language that have kept people from reading and understanding God's Word. We hope that readers unfamiliar with the Bible will find the words clear and easy to understand and that readers well versed in the Scriptures will gain a fresh perspective. We pray that readers will gain insight and wisdom for living, but most of all that they will meet the God of the Bible and be forever changed by knowing him.

THE BIBLE TRANSLATION
COMMITTEE, *October 2007*

BIBLE TRANSLATION TEAM
Holy Bible, New Living Translation

PENTATEUCH
Daniel I. Block, Senior Translator
Wheaton College

GENESIS
Allen Ross, *Beeson Divinity School, Samford University*
Gordon Wenham, *Trinity Theological College, Bristol*

EXODUS
Robert Bergen, *Hannibal-LaGrange College*
Daniel I. Block, *Wheaton College*
Eugene Carpenter, *Bethel College, Mishawaka, Indiana*

LEVITICUS
David Baker, *Ashland Theological Seminary*
Victor Hamilton, *Asbury College*

Kenneth Mathews, *Beeson Divinity School, Samford University*

NUMBERS
Dale A. Brueggemann, *Assemblies of God Division of Foreign Missions*
R. K. Harrison (deceased), *Wycliffe College*
Paul R. House, *Wheaton College*
Gerald L. Mattingly, *Johnson Bible College*

DEUTERONOMY
J. Gordon McConville, *University of Gloucester*
Eugene H. Merrill, *Dallas Theological Seminary*
John A. Thompson (deceased), *University of Melbourne*

HISTORICAL BOOKS
Barry J. Beitzel, Senior Translator
Trinity Evangelical Divinity School

JOSHUA, JUDGES
Carl E. Armerding, *Schloss Mittersill Study Centre*
Barry J. Beitzel, *Trinity Evangelical Divinity School*
Lawson Stone, *Asbury Theological Seminary*

1 & 2 SAMUEL
Robert Gordon, *Cambridge University*
V. Philips Long, *Regent College*
J. Robert Vannoy, *Biblical Theological Seminary*

1 & 2 KINGS
Bill T. Arnold, *Asbury Theological Seminary*

William H. Barnes, *North Central University*

Frederic W. Bush, *Fuller Theological Seminary*

1 & 2 CHRONICLES

Raymond B. Dillard (deceased), *Westminster Theological Seminary*

David A. Dorsey, *Evangelical School of Theology*

Terry Eves, *Erskine College*

RUTH, EZRA—ESTHER

William C. Williams, *Vanguard University*

H. G. M. Williamson, *Oxford University*

WISDOM BOOKS

Tremper Longman III, Senior Translator
Westmont College

JOB

August Konkel, *Providence Theological Seminary*

Tremper Longman III, *Westmont College*

Al Wolters, *Redeemer College*

PSALMS 1–75

Mark D. Futato, *Reformed Theological Seminary*

Douglas Green, *Westminster Theological Seminary*

Richard Pratt, *Reformed Theological Seminary*

PSALMS 76–150

David M. Howard Jr., *Bethel Theological Seminary*

Raymond C. Ortlund Jr., *Trinity Evangelical Divinity School*

Willem VanGemeren, *Trinity Evangelical Divinity School*

PROVERBS

Ted Hildebrandt, *Gordon College*

Richard Schultz, *Wheaton College*

Raymond C. Van Leeuwen, *Eastern College*

ECCLESIASTES, SONG OF SONGS

Daniel C. Fredericks, *Belhaven College*

David Hubbard (deceased), *Fuller Theological Seminary*

Tremper Longman III, *Westmont College*

PROPHETS

John N. Oswalt, Senior Translator
Wesley Biblical Seminary

ISAIAH

John N. Oswalt, *Wesley Biblical Seminary*

Gary Smith, *Midwestern Baptist Theological Seminary*

John Walton, *Wheaton College*

JEREMIAH, LAMENTATIONS

G. Herbert Livingston, *Asbury Theological Seminary*

Elmer A. Martens, *Mennonite Brethren Biblical Seminary*

EZEKIEL

Daniel I. Block, *Wheaton College*

David H. Engelhard, *Calvin Theological Seminary*

David Thompson, *Asbury Theological Seminary*

DANIEL, HAGGAI—MALACHI

Joyce Baldwin Caine (deceased), *Trinity College, Bristol*

Douglas Gropp, *Catholic University of America*

Roy Hayden, *Oral Roberts School of Theology*

Andrew Hill, *Wheaton College*

Tremper Longman III, *Westmont College*

HOSEA—ZEPHANIAH

Joseph Coleson, *Nazarene Theological Seminary*

Roy Hayden, *Oral Roberts School of Theology*

Andrew Hill, *Wheaton College*

Richard Patterson, *Liberty University*

GOSPELS AND ACTS

Grant R. Osborne, Senior Translator
Trinity Evangelical Divinity School

MATTHEW

Craig Blomberg, *Denver Seminary*

Donald A. Hagner, *Fuller Theological Seminary*

David Turner, *Grand Rapids Baptist Seminary*

MARK

Robert Guelich (deceased), *Fuller Theological Seminary*

George Guthrie, *Union University*

Grant R. Osborne, *Trinity Evangelical Divinity School*

LUKE

Darrell Bock, *Dallas Theological Seminary*

Scot McKnight, *North Park University*

Robert Stein, *The Southern Baptist Theological Seminary*

JOHN

Gary M. Burge, *Wheaton College*

Philip W. Comfort, *Coastal Carolina University*

Marianne Meye Thompson, *Fuller Theological Seminary*

ACTS

D. A. Carson, *Trinity Evangelical Divinity School*

William J. Larkin, *Columbia International University*

Roger Mohrlang, *Whitworth University*

LETTERS AND REVELATION

Norman R. Ericson, Senior Translator
Wheaton College

ROMANS, GALATIANS

Gerald Borchert, *Northern Baptist Theological Seminary*

Douglas J. Moo, *Wheaton College*

Thomas R. Schreiner, *The Southern Baptist Theological Seminary*

1 & 2 CORINTHIANS

Joseph Alexanian, *Trinity International University*

Linda Belleville, *Bethel College, Mishawaka, Indiana*

Douglas A. Oss, *Central Bible College*

Robert Sloan, *Baylor University*

EPHESIANS—PHILEMON

Harold W. Hoehner, *Dallas Theological Seminary*

Moises Silva, *Gordon-Conwell Theological Seminary*

Klyne Snodgrass, *North Park Theological Seminary*

HEBREWS, JAMES, 1 & 2 PETER, JUDE

Peter Davids, *Schloss Mittersill Study Centre*

Norman R. Ericson, *Wheaton College*

William Lane (deceased), *Seattle Pacific University*

J. Ramsey Michaels, *S. W. Missouri State University*

1–3 JOHN, REVELATION

Greg Beale, *Wheaton College*

Robert Mounce, *Whitworth University*

M. Robert Mulholland Jr., *Asbury Theological Seminary*

SPECIAL REVIEWERS

F. F. Bruce (deceased), *University of Manchester*

Kenneth N. Taylor (deceased), *Translator*, The Living Bible

COORDINATING TEAM

Mark D. Taylor, *Director and Chief Stylist*

Ronald A. Beers, *Executive Director and Stylist*

Mark R. Norton, *Managing Editor and O.T. Coordinating Editor*

Philip W. Comfort, *N.T. Coordinating Editor*

Daniel W. Taylor, *Bethel University, Senior Stylist*

N L T   S T U D Y   B I B L E
CONTRIBUTORS

EDITORS

GENERAL EDITOR
Sean A. Harrison

EXECUTIVE EDITOR
Mark D. Taylor

CONTENT EDITORS
David P. Barrett
G. Patrick LaCosse
Bradley J. Lewis
Henry M. Whitney III
Keith Williams

STYLISTIC EDITOR
Linda Schlafer

COPY EDITORS
Keith Williams, Coordinator
Leanne Roberts, Proofreading
   Coordinator
Paul Adams
Jason Driesbach
Adam Graber
Annette Hayward
Judy Modica
Jonathan Schindler
Caleb Sjogren
Cindy Szponder
Lisa Voth
Matthew Wolf

GENERAL REVIEWERS

GENESIS—DEUTERONOMY
Daniel I. Block

JOSHUA—ESTHER, MAPS
Barry J. Beitzel

JOB—SONG OF SONGS
Tremper Longman III

ISAIAH—MALACHI
John N. Oswalt

MATTHEW—ACTS
Grant R. Osborne

ROMANS—REVELATION
Norman R. Ericson

CONTRIBUTING SCHOLARS

GENESIS
Andrew Schmutzer
Allen P. Ross

EXODUS
John N. Oswalt

LEVITICUS
William C. Williams

NUMBERS
Gerald L. Mattingly

DEUTERONOMY
Eugene H. Merrill

JOSHUA
Joseph Coleson

JUDGES
Carl E. Armerding

RUTH
Joseph Coleson
Sean A. Harrison

1 & 2 SAMUEL
Victor P. Hamilton

1 & 2 KINGS
Richard D. Patterson

1 & 2 CHRONICLES
August Konkel

EZRA, NEHEMIAH, ESTHER
Gary V. Smith

JOB
Dale A. Brueggemann

PSALMS
Willem VanGemeren

PROVERBS
Tremper Longman III

ECCLESIASTES
Sean A. Harrison
Daniel C. Fredericks

SONG OF SONGS
Daniel C. Fredericks
Tremper Longman III

ISAIAH
Willem VanGemeren

JEREMIAH, LAMENTATIONS
G. Herbert Livingston

EZEKIEL
Iain Duguid

DANIEL
Gene Carpenter

HOSEA, JOEL
Owen Dickens

AMOS
William C. Williams

OBADIAH
Carl E. Armerding

JONAH
G. Patrick LaCosse

MICAH
Eugene Carpenter

NAHUM, HABAKKUK, ZEPHANIAH
Richard D. Patterson

HAGGAI, ZECHARIAH, MALACHI
Andrew Hill

MATTHEW
Scot McKnight

MARK
Robert Stein

LUKE
Mark Strauss

JOHN
Gary M. Burge

ACTS
Allison Trites

ROMANS
Douglas J. Moo

1 CORINTHIANS
Roger Mohrlang

2 CORINTHIANS
Ralph P. Martin

GALATIANS
Sean A. Harrison

**EPHESIANS, PHILIPPIANS,
PHILEMON**
Roger Mohrlang

COLOSSIANS
Douglas J. Moo

1 & 2 THESSALONIANS
Gene L. Green

1 & 2 TIMOTHY, TITUS
Jon Laansma

HEBREWS
George Guthrie

JAMES
Norman R. Ericson

B7

1 & 2 PETER, JUDE
Douglas J. Moo

1–3 JOHN
Philip W. Comfort

REVELATION
Gerald Borchert

OLD TESTAMENT PROFILES
Tremper Longman III

NEW TESTAMENT PROFILES
Roger Mohrlang

ARTICLES
Daniel I. Block
Eugene Carpenter
Philip W. Comfort
Iain Duguid
Sean A. Harrison
Tremper Longman III
Douglas J. Moo
Grant R. Osborne

Richard D. Patterson
Daniel H. Williams
William C. Williams

WORD STUDY SYSTEM
James A. Swanson
Keith Williams

SPECIAL REVIEWER
Kenneth N. Taylor (deceased)

BIBLE PUBLISHING TEAM
PUBLISHER
Douglas R. Knox

ASSOCIATE PUBLISHER
Blaine A. Smith

ACQUISITIONS DIRECTOR
Kevin O'Brien

ACQUISITIONS EDITOR
Kim Johnson

OTHER SERVICES
GRAPHIC DESIGNERS
Timothy R. Botts (Interior)
Julie Chen (Cover)

CARTOGRAPHY
David P. Barrett

ILLUSTRATORS
Hugh Claycombe
Luke Daab
Sean A. Harrison

TYPESETTING
Joel Bartlett (The Livingstone
    Corporation)
Gwen Elliott

PROOFREADING
Peachtree Editorial Services

INDEXING
Karen Schmitt
    (Schmitt Indexing)

*Many thanks to all who have had a hand
in the creation of this study Bible,
and most of all to the Lord of heaven and earth,
who gave us his word and Spirit so generously.*

Bridge to understanding
3 questions to ask
what did it mean? (Hist.)

what does it always mean? (Timeless)

what does it mean today? (Today applic.)

what are today's Towers?

"   "   Towers in my life?

what do I need do to tear
em down?